MW01224290

DIGITAL POLITICS IN CANADA

Digital Politics in Canada

Promises and Realities

Edited by TAMARA A. SMALL
and HAROLD J. JANSEN

UNIVERSITY OF TORONTO PRESS
Toronto Buffalo London

Toronto Buffalo London
utorontopress.com
Printed in Canada

ISBN 978-1-4875-8759-8 (cloth)
ISBN 978-1-4875-8758-1 (paper)
ISBN 978-1-4875-8760-4 (EPUB)
ISBN 978-1-4875-8761-1 (PDF)

Library and Archives Canada Cataloguing in Publication

Title: Digital politics in Canada : promises and realities / edited by Tamara A. Small and Harold J. Jansen.
Names: Small, Tamara A. (Tamara Athene), 1975– editor. | Jansen, Harold J., 1966– editor.
Description: Includes bibliographical references and index.
Identifiers: Canadiana (print) 20200279076 | Canadiana (ebook) 20200279300 | ISBN 9781487587598 (hardcover) | ISBN 9781487587581 (softcover) | ISBN 9781487587604 (EPUB) | ISBN 9781487587611 (PDF)
Subjects: LCSH: Canada – Politics and government – Computer network resources. | LCSH: Politics, Practical – Technological innovations – Canada. | LCSH: Political participation – Technological innovations – Canada. | LCSH: Internet in political campaigns – Canada.
Classification: LCC JL86.A8 D54 2020 | DDC 320.9710285467/8 – dc23

We welcome comments and suggestions regarding any aspect of our publications – please feel free to contact us at news@utorontopress.com or visit us at utorontopress.com.

Every effort has been made to contact copyright holders; in the event of an error or omission, please notify the publisher.

University of Toronto Press acknowledges the financial assistance to its publishing program of the Canada Council for the Arts and the Ontario Arts Council, an agency of the Government of Ontario.

Canada Council for the Arts
Conseil des Arts du Canada

ONTARIO ARTS COUNCIL
CONSEIL DES ARTS DE L'ONTARIO
an Ontario government agency
un organisme du gouvernement de l'Ontario

Funded by the Government of Canada
Financé par le gouvernement du Canada
Canada

Contents

Figures and Tables

Figures

Tables

Acknowledgements

We would like to first and above all thank the contributors to this book. You all enthusiastically said "yes" when asked to be a part of this endeavour. It was great to work again with those of you whom we have known for many years as well as to meet some of you for the first time in this project. We appreciate your excellent contributions. And we thank you for putting up with us – this project took a little longer than we had hoped. Special thanks to David Taras for writing the preface. It is an honour to have one of the central figures in Canadian political communication set the foundation for this book. He has been an inspiration to our work and to the work of our contributors.

This collection would not have seen the light of day without the help of numerous people. First, Andrew Mattan and Syvanne Avitzur at the University of Guelph, who provided invaluable research assistance. We would not be surprised to see either as editors of their own books one day, so we hope they found this experience useful. We would also like to thank the team at the University of Toronto Press, especially our editor Marilyn McCormack. Despite inheriting this project, Marilyn was so helpful in completing it. Also thanks to Leah Connor and Irina du Quenoy for helping us through the production phase. Thank you to Mat Buntin, our first editor, for helping to get the project off the ground. Thank you to the reviewers of both the initial proposal and the final manuscript. We appreciate your time and helpful comments, which shaped the direction of the book and the individual chapters.

We thank the Social Science and Humanities Research Council and Fulbright Canada for financial support during this project. Thank you to our colleagues at our respective institutions, the University of Guelph and the University of Lethbridge. We are proud to place this book among your research contributions. Thank you also to our colleagues in the Canadian political science community. We have acknowledged our debts to many of you specifically in the citations in this book, but this can never fully reflect the many conversations we have had with you at conferences and over coffee or other beverages.

We would like to thank our students over the years at Mount Allison University, the University of Guelph, and the University of Lethbridge. We had you in mind when we planned this book. The questions you have been asking us over our teaching careers directly shaped the questions we posed to the contributors to this volume. We hope you will find their answers as interesting and stimulating as we have. Keep asking those hard questions to push us all further.

Lastly, we thank our families. It is because of them that we have the space and the opportunity to be able to do work like this.

TAS & HJJ

PREFACE

The Politics of Disruption

The scholarly world owes a debt of thanks to Tamara A. Small and Harold Jansen for editing this important collection of vital perspectives and ideas about the changing nature of Canadian democracy. The collection brings together reflections from leading scholars on how new digital technologies are changing the landscape of Canadian politics. There is little question that many aspects of Canadian political life have been altered, reinvented, or destroyed by digital technologies. At the very least, we are dealing with the politics of disruption. In their superb introduction, Small and Jansen describe some of the scholarly debates that have been fought over the meaning and effects of the immersive, interconnected, and instant world that has been created over the last twenty years. They highlight the arguments that have divided cyber-optimists from cyber-pessimists and how such realities as polarized echo chambers, surveillance, slacktivism, and patterns of normalization fit into these debates. The key point is that political leaders and parties make choices about how they will navigate the digital world, which tools they adopt, how these are used, and which tools they have chosen not to use. In most cases, the rituals and requirements of the political system impose their own ironclad realities on the uses of technologies.

The premise of this book is that until now there has been little research on how the Canadian political and governmental systems have adapted to the challenges of the new digital world. While there have been excellent pioneering studies, including landmark works by the two co-editors of this volume, the changes that have taken place are continuing and accelerating. To understand the degree to which a new politics has taken hold, we only have to recall a time – say 2004 – when YouTube, Facebook, data collection, selfies, smartphones, memes, and individual targeting of voters had no part in Canadian elections. This book fills in important gaps, maps out this new territory, provides baselines against which future scholarly findings can be measured, and asks critical questions about the future of governance and democracy in Canada. I suspect that *Digital Politics in Canada: Promises and Realities* will be "state of the art" for quite some time to come.

The reason why this volume is so important is that there are so many ways in which the new digital world has made an impact on politics. In my book *Digital Mosaic*, I refer to these changes as "digital shock" (2015). First, it is important to point out that digital technologies have cut a swath of destruction through much of the traditional Canadian media. The growth of online advertising and the dominance of Google and Facebook in particular, which together account for roughly 70 per cent of all online adverting in Canada, deeply wounded the newspaper and conventional broadcasting industries. After Google and Facebook are through eating at the advertising table, the rest of the media are left to feed off the scraps, of which there are not that many to go around. The other killing blow is that Facebook and other social media are now the main providers of news to Canadians, especially the younger generations. Canadians are now used to getting their news free of charge and most of us are unwilling or unable to buy subscriptions or jump over paywalls to pay for news. As a result, there has been a great deal of bloodletting in the traditional media. Thousands of journalists have been let go since 2010; legislative and foreign bureaus have been shuttered or downsized; there are fewer specialist reporters who can report knowledgeably about subject areas such as the courts, foreign policy, or health care; and there is less time and money for investigative pieces. All of these factors have had a decisive impact on politics in Canada. Most importantly, the traditional media, which is the platform on which much of Canadian politics takes place, is unlikely to survive in its current form for much longer.

Second, political life has had to adapt to entirely new media platforms. Ottawa is now obsessed with the power and influence of the so-called FAANGs – Facebook, Amazon, Apple, Netflix, and Google. Canadian politicians and political parties increasingly realize that these megahosts are the principal conveyor belts of political messaging. The media giants are not only the gateways through which the conventional news media must pass in order to reach their publics but are also the portals through which politicians, political parties, and interests groups enter the political bloodstream. What makes the new political game so interesting, convoluted, and complex is that the news is largely decided by processes and algorithms that are secret and hidden from view and that the FAANGs are themselves powerful media organizations that push their own content and compete for the same audiences that journalists and politicians do.

Third, the new media world is a winner-take-all environment. There are a few giant whales, essentially the digital winners, surrounded by tens of millions of minnows that are in effect digital losers. As Matthew Hindman (2018) has explained, giants such as Google, Facebook, eBay, Amazon, Instagram, Tencent, Disney, PayPal, Apple, Netflix, and Comcast dominate the horizon and indeed get the vast majority of online traffic. There is little in the way of a middle class on the web. Small sites exist on the periphery and are quickly killed off or absorbed. Arguably, there has never been so much media power held in so few hands, and it is power that is still largely unregulated – at least in Canada and the United States.

At the same time, never have ordinary citizens been able to exercise so much control. In some ways, "search" is the most powerful tool of the twenty-first century. This is because it projects power in two critical ways. On one hand, it pushes power up by allowing corporations such as Google, Netflix, and Amazon to collect vast amounts of personal data and use it to target users with highly personalized messages; on the other it pushes power down by allowing users to create their own individualized media echo systems. Users not only choose the media they want when they want it but also have the capacity to post, like, spread, comment on, redact, tweet, text, take photographs, and make their own videos. Every person's media world is now different from every other person's media world, with many crosswalks and crossovers between users. In some senses, politics has never been more democratic, as political messages can go viral and explode on the political landscape within minutes or hours. Politics has become bottom up, populist, and grassroots in ways that were unimaginable even a short time ago.

Fourth, what has been produced is a new attention economy where politicians and political parties' chances of being noticed amid the vast cacophony of messages, ads, videos, posts, and texts are less certain than ever. Where Question Period in the Canadian House of Commons was once the great showcase and testing ground of Canadian political life largely because colourful highlights were on the evening news and its great moments relitigated in the press, today it barely penetrates the public consciousness – its voices lost in a sea of billions of media messages. Question Period only matters if at some level the public pays attention. Here, I am reminded of Markus Prior's (2007) groundbreaking work on post-broadcast democracy, in which he demonstrated that with the rise of a large array of entertainment choices, attention to news and politics has faded.

The last point that I will make (among many others that can be made) relates to the debate that surrounds the degree to which the digital world has created echo chambers or ghettos so that we find ourselves receiving information from and interacting with people with whom we largely agree. So-called filter bubbles create news feeds, trending topics, and Google searches that reinforce our pre-existing views. We are rarely exposed to views or scenes that we might find disturbing or not customized to suit our tastes and preferences and those of our friends. Interestingly, legal theorist Cass Sunstein (2018) argues that such cyber-bubbles have taken away our basic freedom, since freedom is predicated on our being exposed to an "appropriately wide and diverse range of options." Without this presentation of options, there can be no real democracy.

Each of the authors in this volume address questions about the state of Canadian democracy in some way. Together this collection is a basic roadmap for how Canadian politics has changed, resisted change, or is about to change. The co-editors deserve great credit for envisioning and then putting together this important volume.

David Taras

REFERENCES

Hindman, Matthew. 2018. *The Internet Trap: How the Digital Economy Builds Monopolies and Undermines Democracy.* New Jersey: Princeton University Press.

Prior, Markus. 2007. *Post-Broadcast Democracy: How Media Choice Increases Inequality in Political Involvement and Polarizes Elections.* New York: Cambridge University Press.

Sunstein, Cass R. 2018. *#Republic: Divided Democracy in the Age of Social Media.* New Jersey: Princeton University Press.

Taras, David. 2015. *Digital Mosaic: Media, Power, and Identity in Canada.* Toronto: University of Toronto Press.

INTRODUCTION

Twenty Years of Digital Politics in Canada

Tamara A. Small and Harold J. Jansen

> There has been a quiet but radical revolution shaking the foundation of our politics.
>
> *Dick Morris*

In his book *Vote.Com*, former Bill Clinton advisor Dick Morris (1999) presented a vision of how the internet would transform American politics. The new technology would bring on nothing short of a revolution. It would reduce the power of the legislature, political parties, lobbyists, courts, and the mass media. At the same time, voters, especially young ones, would be empowered through online direct democracy, which Morris calls vote.com. Through the internet, the American citizenry would triumph over political intermediaries. Indeed, no part of the American political system would remain untouched by the internet.

Two decades later, Morris's optimism regarding the internet's effects on politics might seem a bit naive. However, his perspective was quite common in the 1990s. For many, the internet, like the printing press, was world-changing. In the fifteenth century, the printing press brought about profound socio-political changes. Created by Johannes Gutenberg, it allowed for the mechanical duplication of text, which led to the permanency, standardization, and wide dissemination of the written word. Major changes occurred in literacy and education thanks to democratized publishing. The Protestant Reformation and the Renaissance were aided by the mass production of books (including the Bible) and pamphlets. Yet, from a cursory look at American politics two decades into the new millennium, we can see political intermediaries remain firmly entrenched; online direct democracy has not come to fruition. But is Morris completely wrong? Perhaps not. Hendricks and Schill (2017, 122) suggest that social media "radically upended the traditional campaign norms and practices" in the 2016 US presidential election. Using Twitter, Republican candidate Donald Trump was able to dominate both online and offline political communication. Not only did Trump have significantly more followers on Twitter and Facebook than other presidential candidates but his most incendiary tweets found their way into the reports of the mainstream or legacy media (Wells et al. 2016). Once elected, Trump continued to use Twitter to such an extent that the platform became a defining feature of his presidency. Considerable attention has also been paid to the use of social media by Trump's predecessor, Barack Obama, dubbed the "Internet President" by the media (Harnden 2008). Indeed, his election campaigns in 2008 and 2012 are considered the model for the full potential of digital technologies in elections (Stromer-Galley 2014). While the internet and social media have not caused a complete overhaul of American politics, it is undeniable that they have had a remarkable impact on that country's politics over the past two decades.

It might seem strange to begin a book on digital politics in Canada with a discussion of the United States. However, American digital politics must be the starting point, because it dominates our academic understanding of the topic (Graber et al. 2004). Canadian scholar Shelley Boulianne has conducted a number of important meta-analyses on the relationship between digital technologies and political engagement (2015, 2017, 2018); in the most recent study, she finds that the United States is the focus of 52 per cent of the academic studies included in her sample (2018), while Canada is the subject of four studies. Similarly, Jungherr's (2016) systematic literature review of digital campaigning on Twitter finds most research focuses on American politics. Only three studies included in his sample are Canadian. While scholars outside the US, including those focused on Canada, are exploring issues of digital politics and have been doing so for some time, there continue to be calls for greater academic attention beyond American politics (see Enli and Moe 2013). Italian-British scholar Cristian Vaccari (2013, 5) perhaps puts it best: "if we really want to comprehend how digital politics is developing across Western democracies and what implications might follow, we must abandon the US-centric focus of most public discourse on internet politics." We take up this call with *Digital Politics in Canada*. The objective of this book is to understand what digital politics looks like in Canada.

What do we mean by digital politics? Our general focus is concerned with the political uses of digital technology. These are extensions of political life that existed pre-internet and, typically, would exist without it (Margolis and Resnick 2000). We are less concerned with the governing, or political economy, of digital technologies in Canada, although we recognize that these are important topics. Rather, this collection explores how digital technologies are "treated as an object of citizenship" and the role they play in "restructuring the political possibilities of the Canadian state" (Barney 2005, 22). As Vaccari (2013) puts it, digital politics is concerned with how political actors employ the affordance of digital technologies and the possible uses thereof.

We would be remiss to suggest that important academic contributions to Canadian digital politics are not being made. They certainly are, and by many of the contributors to this book. At the same time, however, Canadian digital politics remains understudied. This, unfortunately, is not a new problem. In the introduction to the 1998 Canadian edited collection *Digital Democracy*, the editors write: "In the 1990s the parameters of our political lives are increasingly circumscribed by the bits and bytes of information and communication technologies (ICT). Individually and collectively, as consumers and citizens, our lives are increasingly computer mediated. While we readily and even enthusiastically embrace these technologies, we know much less about their political and policy impacts" (Alexander and Pal 1998, 2).

This statement, made at a time when less than 50 per cent of Canadians were online, rings true today. To date there are only a few monographs or edited collections that address the broader topic of Canadian digital politics (see Alexander and Pal 1998; Barney 2005; Roy 2006; Borins et al. 2007; Elmer, Langlois, and McKelvey 2012; Clarke 2018). The diversity of disciplinary perspectives within the field means that many of the books that have been published previously only address one aspect of the topic.

Canada is a fruitful site for analyzing digital politics. Digital technology use is ubiquitous here, as Canadians were early adopters of digital technologies. In the mid-1990s, Canada had one of the world's largest online populations (Deschamps 2018). While much of the Western world has caught up, a 2014 survey of Canadians found 87.8 per cent of respondents had used the internet in the previous twelve months (Small et al. 2014). Indeed, internet use is part of daily life for most Canadians. The survey shows that most internet users go online from home, several times a day. Moreover, a variety of devices are used, including desktop computers, smartphones, and tablets. The same survey highlighted the popularity of social media in Canada. Consistent with global user trends, Facebook is the most popular social media among respondents, with Twitter followingly distantly. Smartphone use in Canada continues to grow as well. A survey by Reuters Institute for the Study of Journalism found over half of the respondents engaged with news on smartphones (Brin 2019). This data suggests that there are plenty of opportunities for Canadians to engage in online political activity given how regular and diverse their use of digital technologies is. Moreover, as David Taras points out in the preface to this book, the media world that exists today is vastly different than the one in existence two decades ago. The lives of Canadians are now shaped socially, culturally, economically, and politically by the so-called FAANGs – Facebook, Amazon, Apple, Netflix, and Google. Elsewhere Taras (2015, 5) describes this process as a "media shock" – which can be "both energizing and deflating" for democratic life. Moreover, how Canadians access the internet has changed. Whereas desktop computers were once the primary gateway, smartphones and mobile technologies are considerably more important today.

The objective of *Digital Politics in Canada* is to address a significant lacuna both in the scholarly literature on digital politics and in Canadian political science. It does so through a comprehensive, multidisciplinary, historical, and focused analysis of Canadian digital politics. It is comprehensive in the sense that the book covers the full scope of actors in the Canadian political system. This includes traditional political institutions of the government, elected officials, political parties, and the mass media. Additionally, the digitization of Indigenous people, women, and young people is explored. The key issues of online surveillance and internet voting are also included. It should be noted that the book focuses mainly on politics at the federal level. Future research must consider digital politics at other levels of government. Taken as a whole, the book is also multidisciplinary, drawing on scholars from the many fields that contribute to the study of digital politics, including political science, communication studies, public administration, and journalism. It brings together knowledge, viewpoints, and expertise from senior scholars as well as new voices in research on digital politics. In terms of history, rather than simply looking at the current state of digital politics, we start at the beginning. The result is more of a long view of digital politics in Canada rather than an exploration of current hot topics (e.g., fake news or social media in the 2019 election). The contributors consider how and why digital politics has changed over the past twenty years from their respective vantage points. This is an important contribution.

Finally, this book presents a focused analysis. All the contributing chapters structure their analysis of digital politics in Canada using the same three-pronged framework:

1 *Definitions, history, and context* – Each chapter considers the role that their particular political institution or political actor plays in democratic politics. The chapter reflects on the historical context within Canadian politics and examines how political communication was used prior to the digital revolution.
2 *Digitization* – Each chapter considers both the promises and the perils of digital technologies for their particular political institution or political actor. The chapter then reflects on current practice, asking what those institutions or actors have been doing and/or attempting in relation to digital technologies. The successes, failures, and challenges of digitization are assessed.
3 *Potentials* – Each chapter concludes by looking forward and considering what we can expect in the future of digital politics within the specific realm the chapter examined.

This framework provides a continuity to this collection and encourages contributors to synthesize and take stock of the key literature and analyses in their particular area. What emerges out of this methodology is a consideration of the way contextual and institutional constraints shape the adoption and impact of digitization in Canada. This comprehensive, multidisciplinary, historical, and focused approach allows *Digital Politics in Canada* to take stock of the two decades of digital technologies usage by Canadian political actors and institutions, something that, to our best knowledge, has not been done before.

PROMISES AND PERILS OF DIGITAL POLITICS: PERSPECTIVES AND HYPOTHESES

The objective of the rest of this introductory chapter is to situate the analysis that follows within the broader debates in the digital politics literature and to provide some conceptual clarity. There are few areas of social, economic, or cultural life that have remained untouched by the widespread adoption of digital technologies. Over the past twenty years, the technology in question has changed considerably. In the early 1990s, it was common to hear terms like information superhighway, cyberspace, or World Wide Web in popular and academic discussions. Later, terms such as ICTs (Information and Communication Technology), social media, and digital media came into parlance. For the sake of clarity, we use the term *digital technologies* in this book. Digital technologies refer to the broad range of applications and devices that connect to and through the internet, including websites, email, social media, instant messaging, podcasting, and mobile devices. This definition includes both Web 1.0 and Web 2.0. Web 1.0, such as websites and email, involves the distribution of one-way information. Similar to the relationship between producers and audiences of television or radio, producers create content and users read that content. Users are passive. Web 2.0 changes the nature of participation from passive to active (Sweetser and Lariscy 2008). Users do not receive content but actively contribute to it (Cross et al. 2015). Web 2.0 technologies, such as social media, build participation directly into the architecture of the applications (Jackson and Lilleker 2009). While social media are certainly very important today due to their ability to enable users to create and share content and collaborate and communicate with other users (Marland, Giasson, and Small 2014), Canadian political actors and institutions have used, and continue to use, a wide variety of internet-connected technologies, devices, and services. Overall, we find the term digital technologies more encompassing. Where necessary, contributors to this volume speak to specific technologies in their chapters.

Introducing this chapter with Dick Morris's pronouncement also serves another purpose. It reminds us that people were thinking about the relationship between democracy and digital technologies from the very beginning. Like the printing press before it, there is a profound relationship between these two things. One of the classic questions in this field of research is whether digital technologies serve to support or threaten democratic practice (Oates 2008; Bridgmon and Milewicz 2004). Compared to broadcast technologies (e.g., television, radio, and print media), the internet and related technologies are seen to have "democratic potentials" (Bentivegna 2002, 54; also see Oates 2008). These technologies are interactive, inexpensive, decentralized, hypertextual, have great informational capabilities, and are multimedia (Small 2016). Accordingly, scholars developed several perspectives and hypotheses to help understand these dynamics; these efforts serve as a starting point for understanding digital politics within Canada in this book.

Early speculation saw digital technologies as a force to revitalize and revolutionize democratic politics (for instance, Grossman 1995; Rheingold 2000; Browning 2002). Indeed, the internet and democracy seemed so inherently intertwined that concepts such as "digital democracy," "cyber-democracy," or "electronic democracy" were regularly used in the 1990s. Inherent in these concepts is the idea that the internet and other computer networks had the capacity to change the nature of political communication and democratic politics in positive and powerful ways (Zittel 2004). This perspective came to be known in the literature as *cyber-optimism.* Radical cyber-optimists, such as Morris, saw the internet as a tool for plebiscitary or direct democracy. Citizens would use the internet to initiate, deliberate, and vote on policy options. The result of this would be the erosion or decentralization of the institutions of representative government, such as parties and legislatures. According to Pippa Norris, whose books *Digital Divide* (2001) and *Virtuous Circle* (2000) provided important early work in this field, less radical optimists believed that the internet would contribute to the revitalization of representative democracy by "facilitating communications between citizen and the state, and strengthening support for these institutions"

(Norris 2001, 96). Central to the cyber-optimists' thinking was the interactive nature of the internet. It is interactivity that makes the internet fundamentally different from communication technologies that came before (Bentivegna 2002). Television, radio, and newspapers are unilateral, meaning information flows in one direction, from sender to receiver. The arrival of internet interactivity meant that information now moved in multiple directions – from top to bottom, bottom to top, and side to side. Within politics, this meant that citizens had a tool to directly speak with elites and to speak with one another.

Two key academic hypotheses developed from the cyber-optimist perspective (Table I.1). The *mobilization* hypothesis focuses on the individual level. It holds that digital technology usage will have a positive effect on political behaviour. This is because digital technologies have the capacity to lower the cost, both financially and timewise, of acquiring political information and engaging in political activities. Accordingly, digital technologies may serve to "inform, organize, and engage those who are currently marginalized" from the current political system (Norris 2001, 218). This would include young people, racialized and Indigenous people, and women. With regards to young people or millennials, for example, it is suggested that digital technologies could reconnect them to traditional politics since young people are among the most enthusiastic adopters of digital technologies while also being perceived as extremely apathetic (Brooks and Hodkinson 2008). Overall, the mobilization hypothesis suggests that digital technologies will contribute to a more participatory society (Cantijoch 2012). The *equalization* hypothesis is similar in its positive orientation; the difference is that it focuses on institutions. It holds that all political institutions, regardless of ideology, financial and organizational capacity, or appeal, have the same potential to reach citizens using digital technologies (Small 2008). The relatively low costs, lack of editorial control, and decentralized nature of digital technologies allow political actors at the periphery of the political system, such as minor political parties or smaller interest groups, to bypass the traditional media (Lev-On and Haleva-Amir 2018). Both hypotheses see digital technologies as levelling the playing field by providing those on the margins with a resource that they do not have in the offline world.

Many scholars and commentators have been less convinced by the cyber-optimism perspective. Matthew Hindman (2008, 3) puts it

Table I.1. Digital politics hypotheses by level of change

	Individual level	Institutional level
Cyber-optimists	Mobilization	Equalization
Cyber-sceptics	Reinforcement	Normalization

bluntly: "It may be comforting to believe that the Internet is making ... politics more democratic. In a few important ways, though, beliefs that the Internet is democratizing politics are simply wrong." There are two schools of thought on this: *cyber-scepticism* and *cyber-pessimism.* Cyber-sceptics do not deny that digital technologies change politics, but they do question the scope and the direction of that change. Richard Davis (2005), for instance, wonders how the additional cost, involvement, and time commitment incurred by online politics would make people more politically efficacious. The idiom of this perspective is the phrase "politics as usual" (Margolis and Resnick 2000). That is, politics online will look very similar to politics offline – those institutions and actors that dominate the latter will continue to dominate the former: "Cyberspace has not become the locus of a new politics that spills out of the computer screen and revitalizes citizenship and democracy. If anything, ordinary politics and commercial activity, in all their complexity and vitality, have invaded and captured cyberspace" (Margolis and Resnick 2000, 2).

Countering the notion of mobilization is the *reinforcement* hypothesis. It holds that digital technologies will fail to alter pre-existing patterns of political behaviour (Norris 2001). Rather, digital technologies will be used by those who are already most likely to be politically active, interested, and engaged, thereby reinforcing or strengthening political inequalities (Bimber 2003). Rather than bringing new entrants into politics, digital technologies are "preaching to the converted" (Norris 2003, 24). Similarly, Margolis and Resnick's (2000) *normalization* hypothesis takes on the idea of equalization. They argue that the main beneficiaries of digital technologies will not be minor political institutions but mainstream ones. Because they have access to more offline resources than their non-mainstream competitors, mainstream actors will "outperform contenders on more digital channels, generate more content, attract more traffic, and engage more audiences" (Lev-On and Haleva-Amir 2018, 721).

In the digital politics literature, there is sometimes a conflation between mobilization and equalization and between reinforcement and normalization. To create further confusion, the ideas related to mobilization and equalization are sometimes referred to as the innovation hypothesis (see Schweitzer 2008). For conceptual clarity, Table I.1 makes a distinction at the level of the change. The mobilization-reinforcement dichotomy refers to changes at the individual level – that is, changes in political behaviour (e.g., public opinion, interest, knowledge, and/or engagement). At the same time, changes at the institutional level (governments, political parties, or interest groups) are better captured by the equalization-normalization dichotomy.

Like the cyber-sceptics, cyber-pessimists also question the claims made by optimists. However, they highlight the negative repercussions flowing from increasing digital technologies. For example, the "digital divide" refers to the divide or inequalities between those who have regular and quality access to digital technologies and those who do not. Additionally, the digital divide is concerned with inequalities in technical competence and skill (Chadwick 2006). Given how important digital technologies are to daily life, the fact of not having regular and quality access to them or the skill to use them effectively is problematic. One Canadian survey suggests there are "detrimental" effects for those who struggle with the cost of home internet access in the areas of employment, education, access to information on healthcare, and access to government forms and processes (ACORN Canada 2016). Even if one has a cell phone with a reasonable data package, imagine applying for a job or completing a university level course on it if you do not have access to regular home internet on your larger devices. Since the access to digital technology tends to mirror other socio-economic divides, such as income, race, gender, and education (Haight, Quan-Haase, and Corbett 2014), the digital divide has the potential to exacerbate political divides that already exist. It may in this way create a "democratic divide" between those who use digital technologies to engage, mobilize, and participate in politics and those who cannot (Norris 2001).[1] Internet access

---

1 Scholars such as Norris (2001) and Chadwick (2006) suggest there are three main digital divides: (1) a global divide (divergence of digital technologies access between industrialized and developing countries), (2) a social divide (inequalities between the information rich and poor within a country), and (3) a democratic divide, which is discussed in the text.

has long been an important policy consideration in Canada (Barney 2005). In 2016, the Canadian Radio-Television and Telecommunications Commission (CRTC) declared broadband internet an essential service (Pedwell 2016) in an attempt to address inequities, as rural, Indigenous, and income divides remain in Canada.

"Echo chambers" or polarized communities are a second concern. Developed most thoroughly in the work of Cass Sunstein (2001, 2004, 2018), it is argued that digital technologies allow people to filter in the information and opinions they find congenial and filter out the ones they find offensive or uninteresting. Those on the right of the political spectrum could filter out commentary from those on the left. And those who are not interested in politics could filter it out entirely using the internet for baseball or celebrity news. Algorithms in social media further exacerbate the problem of filtering. Facebook, for instance, targets advertising and other content to users based on its algorithms, meaning that users have very different information experiences. Sunstein argues that in a "well-functioning democracy, people do not live in echo chambers or information cocoons. They see or hear a wide range of topics and ideas. They do so even if they did not, or do not choose to see or hear those topics or those ideas in advance" (2018, ix). The echo chambers created through social media hurt politics as a collective experience.

Cyber-pessimists also ask whether digital technologies make politics too easy, to the point of making it meaningless. Slacktivism is used to describe this phenomenon, pejoratively implying that many online political activities have little real-world impact. For instance, Facebook allows users to put a filter over their profile pictures tied in to important political events, such as a rainbow flag filter for the US Supreme Court decision that legalized same-sex marriage or "Blackout Tuesday" to protest policy brutality in 2020. Many analysts wonder if such symbolic actions have any real meaning (Mulvaney 2015). Digital technologies make politics so easy and quick that its main purpose is increasing "the feel-good factor of the participants" rather than real social or political change (Christensen 2016, para. 3). Online petitions, hashtag activism, joining Facebook groups, and retweeting are the subjects of similar criticism. According to Evgeny Morozov (2009), slacktivism "is the ideal type of activism for a lazy generation: why bother with sit-ins and the risk of arrest, police brutality, or torture if one can be as loud campaigning in the virtual space?" Slacktivism is a democratic problem because these digital tools might in fact distract from the forms of engagement that are needed to achieve significant political change.

Surveillance and data privacy are another concern of cyber-pessimists. While surveillance has been around a long time, it is rapidly evolving in the era of computers and the internet. Every time we use a digital technology, data and metadata are created and collected, including our connectivity, searches, likes, tweets, purchases, and downloads (Deibert 2013). Whereas surveillance was once the purview of the state, it is now an unavoidable feature of everyday life, with organizations of all types engaging in it (Lyon 2005). When this data is used by governments, corporations, and other individuals, digital technologies become technologies of control (Castells 2002). Edward Snowden's revelations of mass government surveillance in 2013 or the 2018 Cambridge Analytica-Facebook data breach are both striking examples of controversy around surveillance and privacy related to user data.[2]

Furthermore, misinformation or fake news is a novel troubling issue that fits within the concerns of cyber-pessimists. Fake news can be defined as "news articles that are intentionally and verifiably false" (Allcott and Gentzkow 2017, 213). The intention of fake news is to confuse and deceive readers. While fake news is not new, it has been exacerbated by digital technologies. Online platforms, especially social media, make it very easy to generate and share fake news (Brummette et al. 2018). Fake news controversies arose in 2016 in the contexts of the American presidential election and the Brexit referendum in the United Kingdom. In the case of the former, mostly pro-Donald Trump fake news stories were spread on Facebook by operatives in Eastern Europe. There is concern that these fake news stories may have influenced the

2 In 2013, newspapers began publishing articles about widespread secret surveillance of the public by government agencies, including the American National Security Agency (NSA), the British Government Communications Headquarters, and the Communications Security Establishment Canada. This information was provided to them by US whistle-blower Edward Snowden. In 2018, it was reported that the firm Cambridge Analytica, a political consulting firm that did work for the Donald Trump campaign, harvested raw data from up to 87 million Facebook profiles, including 600,000 Canadians. Using an app created by a Russian-American researcher, Cambridge Analytica acquired data from not only those who used the app but also the personal information of all the people in those users' Facebook social networks.

outcome of the election (Bakir and McStay 2018). According to Allcott and Gentzkow (2017), there are financial and ideological motivations for fake news production. If a fake news story goes viral it can raise revenue for the producer. Other fake news producers seek to advance candidates or positions they favour. Recently, Facebook, other social media companies, and non-profit organizations have launched programs to combat fake news.

It is within the context of these perspectives and hypotheses that *Digital Politics in Canada* positions itself. As the subtitle of this book suggests, we are concerned with contrasting the current realities of digital politics in Canada with the technological promises and perils. While some scholarly research has moved beyond these dichotomies, they continue to structure a significant amount of current empirical analysis in this field. It is crucial for us to point out that we do not attach any normative significance to these perspectives and hypotheses. It is not an either/or choice in understanding digital politics in Canada. That is, anything less than complete equalization or mobilization in Canada would not be the failure of digital technologies. We do not assume that digital technologies are deterministic (see Coleman and Blumler 2009). Unlike a magician, digital technologies cannot simply transform politics into something new, better, and more democratic. Digital technologies, in and of themselves, change little when it comes to democracy. Rather, digital technologies provide affordances and opportunities for political actors and institutions. Political actors and institutions, for their part, make choices in how to incorporate digital technologies into their activities. Those choices are structured not only by the political objectives of those actors and institutions but also by the political, social, and economic context in which they operate as well as the type of digital technology they choose to use. We also do not assign more importance to digital technologies than other modes of political communication. There is little doubt that digital technologies are very important in the modern age. At the same time, however, they continue to coexist with broadcast, print/paper, and oral communication. The communication environment in Canada, as elsewhere, is fragmented and diverse (Small, Marland, and Giasson 2014). This book then provides an opportunity to explore the affordances provided by the new technologies to different political actors in Canada and how they have been incorporated into political activity over the past twenty years. Throughout the analysis that follows, we will see evidence of all three above perspectives playing out in Canada to various degrees.

PLAN OF THE BOOK

This book is divided into two thematic sections: political institutions and citizens. This is in some ways based on the two main types of digital politics research: supply and demand (Norris 2003). Supply research examines the online political content produced by political actors. Methodologically, it employs some form of content analysis of online political materials, often supplemented by interviews to assess the objectives of online digital content. Demand research, by contrast, focuses on the use of political digital content by citizens, using survey research, focus groups, and/or interviews.

Section I: Political Institution focuses on the digitization of key institutions of Canadian politics. As a whole, the chapters in this section consider the way in which digital technologies have affected these institutions and/or how they have (or have not) incorporated them into daily political activities, as well as the rationales behind both of these considerations. The Government of Canada is explored in several chapters and from several disciplinary perspectives, starting with the legislative and executive wings of the Canadian government and their use of digital technologies (chapter 1). Two chapters focus of the bureaucratic uses of digital technologies in Canada by exploring the development and consolidation of e-government at the federal level (chapter 2) and the developing open government movement in Canada (chapter 3). E-government in Canada is one of the more well-studied areas of digital politics (see Roy 2006; Borins et al. 2007; Canadian Public Administration 2017). Internet voting (chapter 4) and surveillance and privacy infrastructure (chapter 5), both issue-based analyses of digital politics related to the government, are also examined. Political parties and digital campaigning are addressed in chapter 6. The final institution considered is the media (chapter 7). The mass media are not political institutions per se. Generally, the media are considered intermediaries between political institutions and civil society, and their watchdog and educator roles make them essential to the functioning of democratic political systems, both in Canada and elsewhere (Small, Marland, and

Giasson 2014, 14). For this reason, it is important to reflect on the digitization of the media; the issue takes on added urgency because the establishment media and journalists are often described as the "old" and "legacy" media that exist in stark contrast to the "new" media. However, as Andrew Chadwick (2013, 159) points out, there has been increasing "hybridity" in the media system, with "interdependence among older and newer media logics."

As mentioned, the mobilization hypothesis suggests that digital technologies will prove effective in increasing citizens' political participation and efficacy. As such, *Section II: Political Digital Citizenship* shifts the focus to citizens, examining the various ways Canadians use (or do not use) digital technologies to engage and mobilize within politics. Using data from the 2014 Canadian Online Citizenship Survey, chapter 8 explores how Canadians use digital technologies to become informed about, discuss, and/or participate in politics. Young people and millennials have also been a popular topic in the digital politics literature. This is because they are thought to be "digital natives" – that is, these young people are the first generations to have spent their entire lives surrounded by and using digital technologies, computers, and video games (Palfrey and Gasser 2011). Chapter 9 explores this unique relationship in the Canadian context. The broad category of social movements is considered in chapter 10. Like the Black Lives Matter or the #MeToo movements in the United States, social movement politics has gone digital in Canada, exemplified by Quebec's Maple Spring and the Indigenous Idle No More. A more detailed discussion of online Indigenous politics is in chapter 11. Chapter 12 reflects on digital feminism, that is the potential in harnessing the power of digital technologies to discuss, uplift, and activate equality of women and girls in the Canadian context (Martin and Valenti 2013). In the conclusion, we take a holistic look at the contributions in this book; taken together, what do these chapters that explore a wide range of political activity tell us about the nature of digital politics in this country? We conclude by considering the future of digital politics from both the practitioner and academic perspectives.

In order to provide a comprehensive overview of digital politics in Canada it was crucial to engage with more than one scholar. As mentioned, *Digital Politics in Canada* brings together an impressive range of scholars from across the country, many who have been foundational in the development of this field and are producing cutting-edge empirical analysis. They are not only digital politics scholars; their work makes important contributions to political communication, communication studies, public administration, and Canadian political science. *Digital Politics in Canada* thus provides an assessment of the full range of digital politics activities in Canada.

REFERENCES

ACORN Canada. 2016. "Internet for All!" https://acorncanada.org/sites/default/files//Internet%20for%20All%20report_0.pdf.

Alexander, Cynthia Jacqueline, and Leslie Alexander Pal. 1998. *Digital Democracy: Policy and Politics in the Wired World.* Don Mills, ON: Oxford University Press Canada.

Allcott, Hunt, and Matthew Gentzkow. 2017. "Social Media and Fake News in the 2016 Election." *Journal of Economic Perspectives* 31 (2): 211–36. https://doi.org/10.1257/jep.31.2.211.

Bakir, Vian, and Andrew McStay. 2018. "Fake News and the Economy of Emotions: Problems, Causes, Solutions." *Digital Journalism* 6 (2): 154–75. https://doi.org/10.1080/21670811.2017.1345645.

Barney, Darin. 2005. *Communication Technology.* Vancouver: UBC Press.

Bentivegna, Sara. 2002. "Politics and New Media." In *The Handbook of New Media,* ed. Leah A. Lievrouw and Sonia Livingstone, 50–61. London: Sage.

Bimber, Bruce Allen. 2003. *Information and American Democracy: Technology in the Evolution of Political Power.* New York: Cambridge University Press.

Borins, Sandford F., Kenneth Kernaghan, David Brown, Nick Bontis, Perri 6, and Fred Thompson, eds. 2007. *Digital State at the Leading Edge.* Toronto: University of Toronto Press.

Boulianne, Shelley. 2015. "Social Media Use and Participation: A Meta-Analysis of Current Research." *Information, Communication & Society* 18 (5): 524–38. https://doi.org/10.1080/1369118X.2015.1008542.

Boulianne, Shelley. 2017. "Revolution in the Making? Social Media Effects across the Globe." *Information, Communication & Society* 22 (1): 39–54. https://doi.org/10.1080/1369118X.2017.1353641.

Boulianne, Shelley. 2018. "Twenty Years of Digital Media Effects on Civic and Political Participation." *Communication Research* Advanced Online Publication: 1–20. https://doi.org/10.1177/0093650218808186.

Bridgmon, Phillip, and Mark Milewicz. 2004. *E-Politics: Technology in American Government.* Dubuque, IA: Kendall Hunt Publishing Co.

Brin, Colette. 2019. "Digital News Report: Canada." Reuters Institute for the Study of Journalism. http://www.digitalnewsreport.org/survey/2019/canada-2019/.

Brooks, Rachel, and Paul Hodkinson. 2008. "Introduction." *Journal of Youth Studies* 11 (5): 473–9. https://doi.org/10.1080/13676260802282968.

Browning, Graeme. 2002. *Electronic Democracy: Using the Internet to Transform American Politics.* Medford, NJ: Information Today.

Brummette, John, Marcia DiStaso, Michail Vafeiadis, and Marcus Messner. 2018. "Read All about It: The Politicization of 'Fake News' on Twitter." *Journalism & Mass Communication Quarterly* 95 (2): 497–517. https://doi.org/10.1177/1077699018769906.

Canadian Public Administration. 2017. "Special Issue: Understanding Governance in the Digital Era: An Agenda for Public Administration Research in Canada." *Canadian Public Administration* 60 (4): 457–75. https://doi.org/10.1111/capa.12246.

Cantijoch, Marta. 2012. "Digital Media and Offline Participation in Spain." In *Digital Media and Political Engagement Worldwide: A Comparative Study*, ed. Eva Aduiza, Michael James Jensen, and Laia Jorba, 118–59. Cambridge: Cambridge University Press.

Castells, Manuel. 2002. *The Internet Galaxy: Reflections on the Internet, Business, and Society.* Oxford: Oxford University Press.

Chadwick, Andrew. 2006. *Internet Politics: States, Citizens, and New Communication Technologies.* Oxford: Oxford University Press.

Chadwick, Andrew. 2013. *The Hybrid Media System: Politics and Power.* Oxford: Oxford University Press.

Clarke, Amanda. 2018. *Opening the Government of Canada: The Federal Bureaucracy in the Digital Age.* Vancouver: UBC Press.

Coleman, Stephen, and Jay G. Blumler. 2009. *The Internet and Democratic Citizenship: Theory, Practice, and Policy.* New York: Cambridge University Press.

Cross, William, Jonathan Malloy, Tamara A. Small, and Laura Stephenson. 2015. *Fighting for Votes: Parties, the Media, and Voters in the 2011 Ontario Election.* Vancouver: UBC Press.

Davis, Richard. 1998. *The Web of Politics: The Internet's Impact on the American Political System.* New York: Oxford University Press.

Davis, Richard. 2005. *Politics Online: Blogs, Chatrooms, and Discussion Groups in American Democracy.* New York: Routledge.

Deschamps, Ryan. 2018. "Canada's Short-Lived Digital Empire." Paper presented at the Canadian Political Science Association Annual Meeting, Regina, SK. May 30–June 1.

Elmer, Greg, Ganaele Langlois, and Fenwick McKelvey. 2012. *The Permanent Campaign: New Media, New Politics.* New York: Peter Lang.

Enli, Gunn, and Hallvard Moe. 2013. "Social Media and Election Campaigns: Key Tendencies and Ways Forward." *Information, Communication, & Society* 16 (5): 637–45. https://doi.org/10.1080/1369118X.2013.784795.

Graber, Doris A., Bruce Bimber, W. Lance Bennett, Richard Davis, and Pippa Norris. 2004. "The Internet and Politics: Emerging Perspectives." In *Academy and the Internet*, ed. Helen Nissenbaum and Monroe E. Price, 90–119. New York: Peter Lang.

Grossman, Lawrence K. 1995. *The Electronic Republic: Reshaping Democracy in the Information Age.* New York: Viking Penguin.

Haight, Michael, Anabel Quan-Haase, and Bradley A. Corbett. 2014. "Revisiting the Digital Divide in Canada: The Impact of Demographic Factors on Access to the Internet, Level of Online Activity, and Social Networking Site Usage." *Information, Communication, & Society* 17 (4): 503–19. https://doi.org/10.1080/1369118X.2014.891633.

Harnden, Toby. 2008. "Barack Obama Will Be America's First 'Internet President.'" *Telegraph,* November 11. https://www.telegraph.co.uk/news/worldnews/barackobama/3443143/Barack-Obama-will-be-Americas-first-internet-president.html.

Hendricks, John Allen, and Dan Schill. 2017. "The Social Media Election of 2016." In *The Social Media Election of 2016,* ed. Robert E. Denton Jr., 121–50. London: Palgrave Macmillan.

Hindman, Matthew. 2008. *The Myth of Digital Democracy.* New Jersey: Princeton University Press.

Jackson, Nigel A., and Darren G. Lilleker. 2009. "Building an Architecture of Participation? Political Parties and Web 2.0 in Britain." *Journal of Information Technology & Politics* 6 (3–4): 232–50. https://doi.org/10.1080/19331680903028438.

Jungherr, Andreas. 2016. "Twitter Use in Election Campaigns: A Systematic Literature Review." *Journal of Information Technology & Politics* 13 (1): 72–91. https://doi.org/10.1080/19331681.2015.1132401.

Lev-On, Azi, and Sharon Haleva-Amir. 2018. "Normalizing or Equalizing? Characterizing Facebook Campaigning." *New Media & Society* 20 (2): 720–39. https://doi.org/10.1177/1461444816669160.

Lyon, David. 2005. *Surveillance as Social Sorting: Privacy, Risk, and Automated Discrimination.* London: Routledge. https://doi.org/10.4324/9780203994887.

Margolis, Michael, and David Resnick. 2000. *Politics as Usual: The Cyberspace Revolution.* Thousand Oaks, CA: Sage.

Marland, Alex, Thierry Giasson, and Tamara A. Small, eds. 2014. *Political Communication in Canada: Meet the Press and Tweet the Rest.* Vancouver: UBC Press.

Martin, Courtney E., and Vanessa Valenti. 2013. "FemFuture: Online Revolution." New Feminist Solutions, 8. New York: Barnard Center for Research on Women.

Morozov, Evgeny. 2009. "The Brave New World of Slacktivism." *Foreign Policy,* May 19. https://foreignpolicy.com/2009/05/19/the-brave-new-world-of-slacktivism/.

Morris, Dick. 1999. *Vote.Com.* Los Angeles: Renaissance Books.

Mulvaney, James. 2015. "Opinion: Enough with French Flag Facebook Logo." CNN, November 18. https://www.cnn.com/2015/11/17/opinions/mulvaney-facebook-french-flag/index.html.

Norris, Pippa. 2000. *A Virtuous Circle: Political Communications in Postindustrial Societies.* New York: Cambridge University Press.

Norris, Pippa. 2001. *Digital Divide: Civic Engagement, Information Poverty, and the Internet Worldwide.* New York: Cambridge University Press.

Norris, Pippa. 2003. "Preaching to the Converted? Pluralism, Participation, and Party Websites." *Party Politics* 9 (1): 21–45. https://doi.org/10.1177/135406880391003.

Oates, Sarah. 2008. *Introduction to Media and Politics.* London: Sage. http://sk.sagepub.com/books/introduction-to-media-and-politics/.

Palfrey, John Gorham, and Urs Gasser. 2011. *Born Digital: Understanding the First Generation of Digital Natives.* ReadHowYouWant.com.

Pedwell, Terry. 2016. "CRTC Declares Broadband Internet a Basic Service." *Toronto Star,* December 21. https://www.thestar.com/news/canada/2016/12/21/crtc-declares-broadband-internet-a-basic-service-like-telephone.html.

Rheingold, Howard. 2000. *The Virtual Community: Homesteading on the Electronic Frontier.* Boston: MIT Press.

Roy, Jeffrey. 2006. *E-Government in Canada: Transformation for the Digital Age.* Ottawa: University of Ottawa Press.

Schweitzer, Eva Johanna. 2008. "Innovation or Normalization in E-Campaigning? A Longitudinal Content and Structural Analysis of German Party Websites in the 2002 and 2005 National Elections." *European Journal of Communication* 23 (4): 449–70. https://doi.org/10.1177/0267323108096994.

Small, Tamara A. 2008. "Equal Access, Unequal Success: Major and Minor Canadian Parties on the Net." *Party Politics* 14 (1): 51–70. https://doi.org/10.1177/1354068807083823.

Small, Tamara A. 2016. "Two Decades of Digital Party Politics in Canada: An Assessment." In *Canadian Parties in Transition,* 4th ed., ed. A. Brian Tanguay and Alain-G. Gagnon. Toronto: University of Toronto Press.

Small, Tamara A., Harold Jansen, Frédérick Bastien, Thierry Giasson, and Royce Koop. 2014. "Online Political Activity in Canada: The Hype and the Facts." *Canadian Parliamentary Review* 37 (4): 9–16.

Small, Tamara A., Alex Marland, and Thierry Giasson. 2014. "The Triangulation of Canadian Political Communication." In *Political Communication in Canada: Meet the Press and Tweet the Rest,* 3–23. Vancouver: UBC Press.

Stromer-Galley, Jennifer. 2014. *Presidential Campaigning in the Internet Age.* Oxford: Oxford University Press.

Sunstein, Cass R. 2001. *Republic.Com.* New Jersey: Princeton University Press.

Sunstein, Cass R. 2004. "Democracy and Filtering." *Communications of the ACM* 47 (12): 57–9. https://doi.org/10.1145/1035134.1035166.

Sunstein, Cass R. 2018. *#Republic: Divided Democracy in the Age of Social Media.* New Jersey: Princeton University Press.

Sweetser, Kaye D., and Ruthann Weaver Lariscy. 2008. "Candidates Make Good Friends: An Analysis of Candidates' Uses of Facebook." *International Journal of Strategic Communication* 2 (3): 175–98. https://doi.org/10.1080/15531180802178687.

Taras, David. 2015. *Digital Mosaic: Media, Power, and Identity in Canada.* Toronto: University of Toronto Press.

Vaccari, Cristian. 2013. *Digital Politics in Western Democracies: A Comparative Study.* Baltimore: Johns Hopkins University Press.

Wells, Chris, Dhavan V. Shah, Jon C. Pevehouse, JungHwan Yang, Ayellet Pelled, Frederick Boehm, Josephine Lukito, Shreenita Ghosh, and Jessica L. Schmidt. 2016. "How Trump Drove Coverage to the Nomination: Hybrid Media Campaigning." *Political Communication* 33 (4): 669–76. https://doi.org/10.1080/10584609.2016.1224416.

Zittel, Thomas. 2004. "Political Communication and Electronic Democracy." In *Comparing Political Communication: Theories, Cases, and Challenges,* ed. Frank Esser and Barbara Pfetsch, 231–50. Cambridge: Cambridge University Press.

Section I

Political Institutions

CHAPTER ONE

Digital Representation: The Normalization of Social Media in Political Offices

Alex Marland and Stephen Power

CONTEXT

The nature of democracy and representation is often deliberated in political science. How should citizens be governed? What is the best system to select the few to represent the many? Which priorities should elected representatives put first? When do the needs of a constituency triumph over those of a political party? Theories of representation are subject to constant study. Even the word "representation" is examined (see Pitkin 1967).

In Canada discussion about representation tends to turn on the 338 Members of Parliament (MPs) elected to the House of Commons in Ottawa. Each of them represents citizens in a defined geographical area formally known as an electoral district, commonly called a constituency or riding. MPs are almost always affiliated with a political party, which brings expectations of operating as a cohesive group and sticking to the party line. They vote on motions and bills, debate issues of the day, and ultimately support or oppose the ability of the governing party to advance an agenda.

MPs are much more than lawmakers. They are liaisons who communicate information about government to constituents and who relay their constituents' concerns to political decision makers. The House of Commons funds staff on Parliament Hill and in constituency offices to act as the first point of communications contact. Some representatives have broader responsibilities and more personnel, particularly party leaders and cabinet ministers, the latter of whom are supported by a team of political staff and public servants. But most MPs are backbenchers who, along with their staff, busily assist constituents. They communicate on the phone, through letters and newsletters, in person on the doorsteps, at events, and via digital technologies (email, websites, and social media). Texting constituents is an emerging practice.

Beginning in 2013, researchers Royce Koop, Heather Bastedo, and Kelly Blidook job-shadowed MPs in electoral districts across Canada to understand how representation works in Canada. Their resulting book, *Representation in Action: Canadian MPs in the Constituencies*, identifies different representational styles and assesses why various forms of connection develop with constituents. They argue that MPs are motivated to stay in touch out of a desire to build a personal following that will withstand the ebbs and flows of preferences for parties, leaders, and other factors. MPs are described as sentinels who listen and provide feedback to Ottawa but who also attempt to "inform, persuade, and correct" (Koop, Bastedo, and Blidook 2018, 175). They attend local functions to listen and show that they were there; they knock on doors between elections; they make small purchases in community stores as an excuse to say hello to shopkeepers; they try to resolve complaints about mouldy mattresses in public housing; and they avoid making policy commitments on localized issues. To many MPs, representation involves personal communication, much of it requiring a physical presence in their electoral districts as they mingle with constituents. Digital technologies supplement these personal interactions.

Compared with other aspects of Canadian politics, such as federal elections, there is inadequate study of elected officials in Canada. In this chapter, we discuss the use of social media by Members of Parliament and their staff. Specifically, we explore who is responsible for posting content on MPs' Facebook and Twitter accounts. We find that staff management of social media is a normalized function of representatives' office responsibilities, raising questions about the nature of cyber-representation. To our knowledge this type of exploration is the first such study in Canada.

DIGITIZATION

Promises & Perils

The promise of digital technologies is that they can create new two-way dialogues between citizens and representatives, empower individual MPs through their abilities to distribute information, and enable citizens to get information from their MPs or hold them to account. There is a "democratic potential" to supplement traditional one-way avenues of communication – such as press releases for the news media and constituents mailing letters to elected officials – with two-way dialogues (Small 2010, 175). Parliamentarians and electors alike have easier avenues of input into the political process, bypassing the filters of gatekeepers such as news editors or political parties. Citizens can better hold their representatives to account and the latter can correct misinformation. Digital technologies are also hailed for their accessibility. The monetary costs of sending emails or creating and broadcasting video are trivial when compared to their pre-internet analogues. As a result, democracy should be more vibrant and inclusive.

Not everyone is convinced. Political offices require more staff to handle an increased volume of correspondence and manage constituents' expectations of speedy replies. Among politically engaged internet users, there are tendencies to self-segregate into ideology-based echo chambers (Gruzd 2012, 8), and online political activities reinforce inequalities and elite domination of discourse (Gidengil and Bastedo 2014, 258; see also chapter 2). Platforms are used disproportionately by some types of representatives (Evans, Cordova, and Sipole 2014), and some citizens are blocked from reading or commenting on an MP's social posts (Raj 2017). Political parties use technology to project openness and democratic discourse, yet they continue to practice traditional top-down communications (Giasson and Small 2017, 122–3; Koop and Marland 2012, 115).

A particular problem in Canada's party-centric parliamentary system of government is that parliamentarians become cogs in a publicity machine, functioning as brand ambassadors for the party by repeating approved messages (Marland 2020). News about their behaviour spreads rapidly to watchful superiors. The practice of digital politics therefore both challenges and reinforces the doctrine of party supremacy.

Questions abound whether MPs are digital pioneers or whether they simply adapt digital technology to fit their existing activities. For the most part they normalize rather than innovate (Small 2016).

Practice

Interest among Canadian elected officials in new communications technologies has been varied and gradual. Bursts of adoption coincide with election campaigns and party leadership races (Clarkson 2005, 226–7; Francoli and Ward 2008, 24; Giasson et al. 2019). A common observation is that political parties and MPs prioritize one-way electronic information over interactive dialogue and consultation (Kernaghan 2007, 236–7; Small 2014).

The adoption of internet technologies in the parliamentary precinct has coincided with a gradual increase in computer literacy, led by the competencies of young MPs (Kernaghan 2007, 238). Email is a staple for providing information about government services and programs to citizens (Francoli 2007; Kernaghan 2007, 240). A 1999 survey found about one-third of MPs used email, a similar proportion had a website and about 10 per cent were using online bulletin boards (Barbour 1999, 23–4). The survey also found that political parties were authoring the content on some MPs' websites. In 2006 similar patterns of haphazard adoption were observed about MPs' blogging, with initial usage limited to the most independent-minded (Francoli and Ward 2008, 24). Initially, most websites and blogs were repositories for text such as press releases, which matched the dial-up internet access capabilities of the time. Today, a visit to a parliamentarian website is a highly visual experience, and engagement occurs via social media.

The Samara Centre for Democracy, a Toronto-based organization that promotes democratic discussion, maintains a website checklist for MPs (Samara Centre 2012). It recommends that a parliamentarian's website should have a biography, identify office location(s), provide an email address, and list the hours of operation. Site visitors should learn about what the MP does in Parliament and in the riding, the MP's attendance at community events, what services the MP's office provides, and be able to find expenses data. Connectivity is impressed through a link to the MP's party, opportunities to sign up for an electronic newsletter, space to leave an online comment, social media account buttons, a list of petitions, information about how to volunteer, and a privacy policy. If possible, an MP's website should be mobile/tablet friendly, feature a team page with staff profiles, and provide links to counterparts at other levels of government. In 2013 Samara Centre researchers compiled fourteen points of data from all MPs' websites (Figure 1.1). Almost all sites had the MP's biography, office location, and email address. Details about work in Parliament outpaced information about constituency work. Only a small number provided guidelines about how to volunteer. Of interest to us here, at that time, 60 per cent of MPs' websites had a link to a Twitter account and 51 per cent a Facebook button – numbers that are implausibly low by today's standards. As we will demonstrate, many more MPs had such accounts after the 2015 election and even more so after the two main opposition parties held leadership contests in 2017. The use of social media by Canadian politicians is nearly universal.

As with email and websites, MP adoption of social media has been geared toward one-to-many communications. Innovative use has been noticed, such as the pithy interactivity of self-portraits (Ottawa Citizen 2014; Small 2014, 99–100). Others use social media mainly to issue press releases and share party campaign messages. The social media activity of party leaders and ministers is more prolific than that of most backbenchers. This digital divide is a function of different image management resources, such as the Prime Minister's Office employing an official photographer to capture visuals of the prime minister, which are disseminated through the government's digital infrastructure (Chu and Fletcher 2014, 161; Remillard et al. 2019). Moreover, party apparatchiks expect candidates and parliamentarians to spread campaign-style and leader-centric communications through social media. The ability of parties to monitor digital technology influences the content: MPs exercise independence in printed newsletters distributed to household mailboxes and tend to project partisan tendencies on their websites (Koop and Marland 2012). The prevalence of party discipline and message control in Canadian politics is thought to explain why MPs rarely use blogs (Francoli 2009, 220). Controversial posts are quickly scrubbed from the internet and repeat offenders risk being expelled from caucus for disruptive online behaviour (Francoli and Ward 2008, 30–31). Consequently, rather than levelling the playing field, digital technologies enable party leaders to exert more power and influence. Normalization appears to be at play here.

Figure 1.1. Samara Centre's observations about Canadian MPs' websites

Source: Samara Centre (2013). *Reprinted with permission.*

Consistent with the reinforcement hypothesis, politically active social media commentators tend to have formal education and possess other economic advantages (Albaugh and Waddell 2014, 103, 110–11; see introduction). Elite accounts, including those run by elected officials, disproportionately influence political discussion (Albaugh and Waddell 2014, 116; Chu and Fletcher 2014, 161). New types of online political elites are emerging, such as independent agitators who use social media to disrupt traditional parties' operations (McKelvey et al. 2018) and former political staffers who post derisive memes and videos (Yun 2018). Finally, while it is possible for backbenchers to cultivate a significant online presence, sites such as Twitter are forums for discussion centring on and around party leaders instead of acting as digital coffeehouses for parliamentarians to engage in freewheeling political debate (Chu and Fletcher 2014, 159–61).

A less obvious trend is that political parties' interest in database management is spurring the use of technology for democratic engagement (Patten 2017; also see chapter 6). Candidates, elected officials, and their staff are expected to canvass electors and input data into mobile dataset apps on smartphones and tablets. The data are uploaded to a party database so that the party can then customize digital advertising, tailor messages, organize events, fundraise, and prepare to get out the vote. This database marketing makes party representatives more dispensable even as they visit more doorsteps than ever before. Canvassers follow a central script. All MPs' use of data management technology is tracked, though some supplemental software exists that is beyond the control of the party, such as NationBuilder (McKelvey and Piebiak 2018). Those who perform well are praised by the party on social media (Watters 2015). There are sanctions for luddites: the Liberal Party uses its database to track local activism and, in 2019, only acclaimed the party nomination for MPs who participated in "voter contact day of action" events; knocked on thirty-five hundred doors or placed five thousand phone calls; met fundraising targets; and recruited new donors (Bryden 2018). These data inform the party's fundraising pitches through email blasts to supporters that offer "scant information" about contacting MPs (Marland and Mathews 2017, 105). Thus, as representatives and their staff populate the party database, they effectively reinforce "the centralized character of parties" (Patten 2017, 61).

There is more going on here than the digital acumen of elected officials. A central question of the relationship between digital politics and representation is whether MPs are the ones authoring and overseeing online content posted under their name. Since the online representation of MPs who are computer savvy is relatively similar to that of those who are not (Kernaghan 2007, 242), we can deduce that MPs hire skilled staff to manage their digital presence. This evokes a crude but useful test of democratic cyber-optimism. If MPs are the ones authoring posts, this makes them more visible and accountable to constituents than ever before; however, if it is their staff pretending to be MPs, this would have the effect of tricking citizens into thinking their representative is accessible. Accordingly, we are curious about the observation in *Representation in Action* that staff use Twitter to project that an MP is in the riding when she is not (Koop, Bastedo, and Blidook 2018, 117).

Staff involvement in social media management is sometimes explicit. For instance, in 2019 Prime Minister Justin Trudeau's Twitter bio stated, "Account run by the 23rd Prime Minister of Canada and staff" (Trudeau 2019). When politicians are speaking in public forums, a staff member may be assigned to live-tweet from the speaker's account, with the ghostwriting sometimes addressed by including the initials of the staff member at the end of the tweet. Otherwise, is staff involvement implicit? We are only beginning to understand the work of political staff in the digital communications environment (for example, Esselment and Wilson 2017). To that end, in this chapter we shed light on their role with respect to Facebook and Twitter.

We collected two sources of data for the purposes of assessing whether MPs are authoring original content in their social media posts. For concision reasons, we focus on social media usage by MPs in the 42nd Parliament, formed after the 2015 Canadian federal election. In December 2017 we mined the Facebook and Twitter biographies of all MPs to establish the role of staff in managing the accounts (see appendix).[1] At that time, fully 100 per cent of MPs in the 42nd Parliament had a Facebook account and 99 per cent had a Twitter account (Table 1.1). However, unlike the prime minister's bio, very few MPs'

1 Four by-elections were held on December 11, 2017. We added data for these new MPs once they were sworn in, in January 2018.

Table 1.1. MP Facebook and Twitter accounts identifying staff role in content generation

	Liberal (n = 183)	Conservative (n = 97)	NDP (n = 44)	Bloc (n = 10)	Green (n = 1)	Independent (n = 2)
Has Facebook account	183	97	44	10	1	2
Facebook identifies staff role	5	3	0	0	1	0
Has Twitter account	182	95	44	9	1	2
Twitter identifies staff role	3	4	1	0	1	0

Note: Data compiled in December 2017 for 333 MPs and in January 2018 for 4 MPs sworn in after by-elections. One Quebec seat was vacant.

bios specified that staff are involved with content production. Less than 2 per cent did so on Facebook and less than 3 per cent did on Twitter. There was inconsistency between the platforms, meaning that if the role of staff was identified on either Facebook or Twitter, this typically did not also occur with the other platform. Only one commonality was evident: party leaders and ministers were more likely to declare staff involvement than were backbench MPs. Even so, the vast majority did not, leaving us to question who is authoring original content on MPs' social media accounts.

For the second phase of our research we submitted two questions to a purposeful sample of seventy-one MPs' offices (see appendix for further methodology details). The responses from them were informative. We sometimes received autoreplies stating that due to the volume of communication there would be a delay in reviewing the email. Consistent with the Samara Centre's advice, a small number of autoreplies contained the MP's office location and hours of operation, while a couple of backbencher offices stated that they were shut for three weeks for the holidays. Some autoreplies requested a name, full mailing address, and telephone number (Figure 1.2), information used to ascertain whether the sender is a constituent. Autoreplies from ministers' parliamentary offices established that priority is given to matters related to the MP's riding and to event requests. Senders were directed to a department email address in the event of a ministry-related matter or were informed that the message had already been forwarded. A few constituency office staff for ministers wrote personal messages

Figure 1.2. Example of email autoreply from minister's MP parliamentary account

Thank you for contacting the office of MP [name]. This message is to acknowledge that we are in receipt of your email and will be in touch shortly. Please note that our first priority is to respond to inquiries from residents of [electoral district].

To help us address your concerns more quickly, please include within the body of your email your full name, address, telephone number and the best time of day to reach you.

Please note that your message will be forwarded to the Department of [X] if it concerns topics pertaining to the Minister's role regarding [X].

Thank you for your note and your patience as we respond to a large number of messages.

to inform us that they were routing our request to ministerial office staff. Finally, we observed that some NDP MPs' autoreplies included the identical line "that in most cases, anonymous, cc'd, or forwarded items will be read but will not receive a response." All of this supports our impression of partisan coordination and that political staff actively manage electronic communication on behalf of parliamentarians and ministers.

We received replies to our questions from twenty-six respondents, of which twenty were email responses and six were unstructured telephone interviews between fifteen to thirty minutes in duration. Our participants were eleven ministerial staff and staff for six Liberal backbenchers, four Conservatives, three New Democrats, and two Bloc Québécois. Interaction with them included telephone interviews with a Conservative MP, an NDP MP, and four ministerial staff. Since this was primarily a qualitative exercise we see little value in reporting frequency counts other than to remark the following: one Bloc Québécois and one Conservative were the only participants who indicated that the MP exclusively authored content; four Liberals, including three ministers, completely delegated all social media responsibility to staff; and the rest involved a combination of staff and MPs collaborating, ranging from MPs with a prolific online presence drawing support from staff to less engaged MPs retaining editorial approval over staff posts.

It is therefore the norm for staff to assist MPs with social media. More striking is that some ministers do not personally practise social media despite the existence of official accounts that suggest otherwise.

Our question asking who is responsible for most of the original content on MPs' official Facebook and Twitter accounts generated varied responses. For example, one staffer explained that the minister had five such accounts and that management of each one was compartmentalized. In that case, ministerial Facebook and Twitter accounts were managed by departmental staff, whose posts required approval from departmental communications staff. The political oversight of the non-partisan posts was straightforward and mostly involved fixing typos. MP Facebook and Twitter accounts are political and were managed by constituency staff. The minister in this case managed a personal Twitter account, sometimes drawing in unspecified staff to assist "with translations, quick turnarounds, photos, and links." The minister did not personally post on Facebook. Another staffer reported that her minister personally maintained an active control over authoring content for her Twitter account but routinely delegated her Facebook account to staff. By comparison, a special assistant to a third minister relayed that:

> Our social media is run out of the minister's office but is supported by staff in the constituency office. Posts relating to the minister's departmental business are handled by the minister's exempt staff. Local riding issues are composed and sent to the minister's office to be posted. For message consistency, it's easier if the same person looks after posting and responding to inquiries.

Conversely a fourth ministerial staffer reported that he did "almost all the posts" for Facebook and Twitter. That minister used Instagram to highlight personal moments, including during the holiday season when staffers are not around. Finally, a fifth minister maintained a separate Twitter account with a neutral voice so that information about the community is available to all constituents regardless of their partisan or political leanings. This is just an indication of the many variances among ministers whose communication is constrained by the boundaries of cabinet solidarity. In opposition, an MP seeks public attention and is critical of the government, but as a minister that same MP may be less active on social media and the posts become positive in tone (Lewis,

Lalancette, and Raynauld 2019). The complexity of disentangling the role of departmental staff (non-partisan), minister's office staff (partisan), and parliamentary and constituency office staff (partisan) is beyond our present purpose, as is differentiating between online accounts. Suffice it to say that the matter tends to be more straightforward with backbenchers given they have fewer human resources.

These findings indicate that MPs are using social media as part of their routine activities without a profound change in their behaviour. That is, rather than innovating, they are normalizing. One minister's executive assistant explained, "The use of social media allows the minister to connect with constituents and highlight local events as well as initiatives undertaken by our government." Another minister's communications and issues manager added, "Social media is a useful way for Members of Parliament to communicate directly with Canadians, particularly about breaking news and day-to-day activities. However, it is important to recognize that it is only one of the ways politics happens and that it is a medium that favours timeliness over depth." Only a fraction of social media users engages with their elected representatives online, we were told.

Ministers, MPs, and their staff are acutely aware of the value and necessity of social media as communication tools. Representatives want citizens to believe that they are working hard on their behalf. They prize regular online updates with community-oriented information, especially visuals of themselves at local events. Some participate in two-way online engagement forums, such as Facebook chats and virtual town halls. Liberals who continue to knock on doors as part of the national party's aforementioned directive are keen to upload selfies or video of themselves canvassing, often alongside volunteers.

Many MPs and their staff recognize that building an online following requires regular and interesting postings to social media. Whether they do so is another matter. Representatives attempt to connect on a personal level through posts about popular culture, sports, pets, and humour. A minister's communications and parliamentary affairs assistant remarked on the humanizing nature of social media:

> It's important to use social media as a way of humanizing MPs (and politics, for that matter), and giving constituents/followers insight into the political and personal lives and experiences of MPs. Just

> posting a picture of a group of people standing in a row, along with text that starts "Great meeting with ..." or "Great discussion with ..." doesn't achieve that. It's important to find an MP's authentic voice, and then doing what you can to build on that.

Time savings are realized by targeting information to specific audiences. For instance, MPs and their staff can readily circulate an invitation to an upcoming local event. A wealth of information is available online to citizens who otherwise would have to depend on news media, newsletters, in-person meetings, and the like. Ministers and backbenchers monitor each other's social media, as does their party. Some of them encourage their staff to share positive news stories. As well, a constant stream of prepared digital content arrives from the caucus research bureau for sharing on social media (Marland 2020, 204–20).

The democratic promises of digital technology are embodied in the overall number of platforms MPs use to communicate with constituents. This includes established technologies such as MP websites and email, and newer interactive media such as live streaming video. Many of these technologies facilitate two-way discussions, reduce or eliminate the costs of civic participation, and add multiple access points for inquiry, information, or assistance with problems. These are positive developments for a country as geographically large as Canada.

As we hypothesized, a major challenge with MPs' use of digital technologies is the repetition of party messaging. Most of the efforts to get parliamentarians to adopt digital technologies have occurred at the behest of party campaign organizations. Campaign staffers often incorporate new digital technology into party communications strategies in an effort to stay competitive in a changing media environment. Staff relayed that they are cautious about what they post because it is likely seen as a pronouncement by the minister or MP. Political personnel find safety in repeating canned talking points on behalf of the member. A minister's press secretary told us that "when it comes to staffers, most are aware that whatever they put up, even on a private account, can and will be attributed to their work for the member. Because of this, the member may be judged according to their staff's posts. So, you will typically find two types of staff: those who have exceptionally tight social media, or none at all, and those who are very public with their social media." Government backbenchers are likewise risk-averse;

as one staffer put it, "The MP takes great care in determining what is posted on his pages, as he seeks to ensure that what is displayed to his followers is received most effectively." We heard the same thing from the opposition benches. A communications advisor informed us that "The MP is aware of what we post. We don't post unless she asks, or we give her notice and she's good with the idea. She does not approve each post right down to the comma but approves in advance of the content or theme." Occasionally a politician will publicly blame staff for a controversial posting (Nielsen 2017). That the public has no way of knowing who is responsible for online content must be balanced against the gravity of the perceived slight. Consequently, depending on who is preparing the content, the online tone of voice can deviate from how the member actually communicates.

The propensity to circulate information that is favourable to the MP and their party is fodder for driving partisan wedges and breeding negativity. A ministerial communications staffer felt that the negative side of digital politics is a problem: "People are critical of everything that is put out and [it is] probably even more openly critiqued on social media than in traditional media. Because of this, there is a more thoughtful approach put into what is put out. Because of that, many posts are fact and language checked numerous times and take a fair bit longer to post than [they] would actually take to just write up." This negative and polarizing nature of online political discussion might deter individual MPs from actively participating in discussions or from devoting more resources to these spaces.

As indicated, party personnel are becoming increasingly metric-driven and routinely monitor the traffic generated by content on different platforms. Facebook and Twitter provide access to metrics that enable users to hone their messages. Due to the nature of the medium politicos are rewarded by oversimplifying serious content that will otherwise fall flat. Details are becoming scanty as news releases are replaced by social media brevity. For example, we were told by our interlocutors that journalists are more receptive to succinct tweets than to Facebook content, which is better for storytelling. The NDP MP elucidated that each medium has different sensibilities. In his experience, Facebook is more social, lends itself to longer posts, and is politics adverse. Facebook is more time consuming and requires more resources for uploading visuals, such as clips from the House of

Commons. A photograph of a personal celebration with a spouse will circulate on Facebook, however not so for political posts. Conversely, Twitter has sharper political content. As the Twitterati are uninterested in a politician's personal life, an opposition MP uses it instead for harder edged criticism of the government. Yet, metrics can be deceiving. One backbencher's assistant cautioned that social media likes "are not necessarily approval of your position or your politics. Many people live in the filter bubble and this may not represent the real opinion of a crowd."

Time constraints, combined with social media's unrestrained atmosphere, are another barrier against MPs using digital technologies to connect with constituents. The public may not be aware that the spontaneous nature of social media is sometimes an illusion in politics and governance. Posts are routinely planned weeks in advance, with many people involved, especially with respect to ministers' accounts. Some staff hinted that the 24/7 nature of social media takes a toll on their ability to disconnect from the office.

Social media content is posted in real time when a minister, and to a lesser extent a backbencher, travels. We were told that the member might be offline, possibly sleeping in another time zone overseas, while posts continue to appear under that individual's name. Other times posts are obviously by staff, such as remarks their member just made in the House. One news report found that fifty tweets a month by the health minister in English (@CDNMinHealth) and French (@MinSanteCAN) requires 1.5 staff positions, two weeks of planning per tweet, a multiple-step vetting process, and work on weekday evenings and on weekends (Beeby 2018). One minister's constituency communications officer explained the challenges of the new demands and expectations of access to the minister created by social media. The officer noted that leveraging social media to serve the public "while maintaining a healthy work/life balance is still in its very nascent stages." Related to this, MPs are highly cognizant that everything they say or do will potentially end up online. Our Conservative MP participant explained that "you've got to live your life like a video recorder is following you around."

A broader and enduring challenge is the blurring of political lines and what public administration scholars refer to as "promiscuous partisanship" by public servants (Grube 2015). Ministerial aides consistently observed that differentiating between departmental and constituency work is difficult. Ministerial personnel are not supposed to engage in electoral district matters, however that is complicated when one person is responsible for the member's social media profile. They constantly triage potential posts to establish who bears responsibility. One ministerial staffer told us that he prepared constituency posts during his private time on the weekends in order to respect separate budgeted roles. He had to ensure that content on a minister's account is neutral and appears in both official languages, which is not a requirement for party or personal accounts. Deciding where to post photos and video is tricky because a department cannot use ministerial resources for the minister's image, only for announcements. Social media advertising is another minefield with respect to whether the national party, the party's electoral district association, or the member is paying the bill. It takes some time for staff to understand what they are permitted to do given that there is no manual to consult about all circumstances. A minister's digital communications advisor reported that he "created a social media guide and a long-term strategic plan for the staff here who are not very into social media, so I can help them when they are staffing the minister, because I can't be with her all the time." Another political staffer felt that members must invest in training to improve staffers' ability to use the media.

On the surface, then, social media communication is a novel way of engaging with citizens. Certainly, more information is available than ever. But mostly it is a story of politicians and political staff figuring out how to integrate social media use into existing processes, thereby opting for normalization over innovation.

POTENTIALS

Studies of representation in Canada would benefit from paying more attention to the political machinery behind MPs' use of social media. In our view, the mining of social media data for research is seriously constrained without understanding the broader backroom context and the role of staff as content authors.

We offer mixed evidence of Canadian parliamentarians living up to the promises of cyber-optimists. Our sample of MPs' offices suggests that most MPs rely on staff to manage their social media accounts. Consequently, digital technologies provide opportunities for direct interaction with elected officials; however, we must question to what extent the illusion of accessibility is projected by their professionally managed social media presences.

Digital technology instantly connects people to information and each other. Barriers to retrieving basic civic information, contacting elected representatives, or engaging with other representatives are declining. A minister's communications assistant observed that politicians do not need to be convinced of the necessity of regular engagement through social media because "everyone seems to understand Facebook/Twitter/Instagram are important." Willing or reluctantly, most politicians make civic information and themselves available through the internet and social media, typically on multiple platforms. MPs and candidates can be further empowered through digital technology. Distribution lists can be compiled and supporters mobilized without the need for expensive consultants or party machines.

Entrenched party communications operations, as well as time and resource constraints, remain obstacles to greater digital engagement. Individual MPs could partially overcome these obstacles through increased parliamentary resources. Staff in caucus research bureaus offer digital training and content; however, because those staff report to the leader's office, this support tends to centralize operations and supress individualism. Many of the MPs and staff we heard from exhibited a willingness to use digital media to serve people in innovative ways. This kind of active engagement demonstrates a human authenticity that staffers believe constituents respond to. However, given the speed of information cycles on the internet, we can expect MPs to be reserved in their usage of technology and partisan message control to remain. Current patterns in usage are ossifying into political rituals; coordinated amplification of party messaging has joined the press releases and pseudo-events. There are, furthermore, more entrenched obstacles inherent to social media. Staffers note the toxic and polarizing nature of online political discourse. Organized actors can brigade social media to sway discussion, drown out competing ideas, or use "bots" to project the illusion of support for a cause (Dubois and McKelvey 2019). MPs can do very little to solve this issue, in small part because there is no obvious Canadian alternative to Facebook or Twitter.

Politicians and their staff routinely collect data on Canadian citizens, whether on the doorsteps or through petitions. MPs must navigate the liability of keeping data about constituents secure to avoid the risk of leaks or hacks. Bill C-76 (the Election Modernization Act), passed in 2018, amended the Canada Elections Act to require that political parties post on their websites a policy for the protection of personal information. There are no provisions in legislation to monitor the implementation of such party policies.

Our finding that social media management is part of the routine daily operations of political offices is consistent with their integration of earlier communications technology. In an email to us, a political staffer summarized the state of Canadian digital politics thusly:

> Due to new technology we have to adapt and change our ways to connect with as many people as possible. Social media played a key role in the last federal election. It's just a good way to connect with the youth. We are still using traditional channels of communication like mass emails, letters, phone calls, but social media adds a new layer on how to connect with people.

All told, while digital technology is a net positive for democracy, Canadian parliamentarians' adaptation of digital technologies falls short of the idealism espoused by cyber-optimists.

APPENDIX

To locate MPs' Facebook and Twitter accounts we culled social media data from MP profiles listed on the Conservative, Liberal, and NDP websites. We verified each one through a Google search of "[name] mp facebook" or "[name] mp twitter." For reasons of simplicity we conducted only a Google search for Bloc Québécois MPs, Green leader Elizabeth May, and the two independents. Consistent with the theory of electoral events prompting adoption, we found higher rates of participation than the Samara Centre for Democracy found prior to the 2015 federal election, and that all four MPs who recently won a by-election had accounts. We then sent emails to a sample of seventy-one MPs, drawn from the distribution listed in Table 1.1. We contacted the parliamentary offices of all thirty-one ministers and all MPs whose Facebook and/or Twitter accounts identified a staff role. To achieve a minimum of ten contacts per party, including a separate category for Liberal backbenchers, we used a random number generator to select additional MPs. We excluded the Green Party leader and two independents. We sent our questions (see below) to parliamentary office email accounts while Parliament was adjourned in mid-December 2017. We followed up by email in January 2018 with a reminder to anyone who did not respond. We observed no obvious commonalities among the twenty-six offices who participated. Of the forty-five offices in our sample that did not participate, only two offices wrote to decline; the rest did not answer our requests. We do not profess that this exploratory research is a representative sample and we are aware that supplementing emails with other forms of communication would have generated a higher response rate. We also recognize that MPs use other social media, such as Instagram or YouTube. Still, we achieved our objective of collecting sufficient data to write an informed summary about the role of staff in managing MPs' social media presence.

EMAIL MESSAGE SENT TO MPS' PARLIAMENTARY OFFICES

To: MP's @parl.gc.ca address
Subject: Two questions about MP social media use

Dear [MP name],
I am writing a book chapter about Canadian MPs' use of social media. Would you or a staff member kindly respond to the following two questions?

1 Who is responsible for authoring the majority of original content on your official MP Facebook and Twitter accounts?
   a) the MP only?
   b) office staff only?
   c) both the MP and office staff?
   d) someone else? (please explain)

2 Is there anything that students should know about MPs' and/or office staffers' use of Facebook and Twitter?

REFERENCES

Albaugh, Quinn, and Christopher Waddell. 2014. "Social Media and Political Inequality." In *Canadian Democracy from the Ground Up: Perceptions and Performance*, ed. Elisabeth Gidengil and Heather Bastedo, 102–24. Vancouver: UBC Press.

Barbour, Michael. 1999. "Parliament and the Internet: The Present and the Future." *Canadian Parliamentary Review* 22 (3): 23–5.

Beeby, Dean. 2018. "Health Minister's Twitter Account Highlights Cost of Government Tweeting." *CBC News*, January 19. Accessed September 1, 2019. http://www.cbc.ca/news/politics/twitter-health-minister-philpott-petitpas-taylor-account-tweets-1.4493130.

Bryden, Joan. 2018. "Liberals Reverse Nomination Rules." *Montreal Gazette*, January 29, N3.

Chu, Wayne, and Fred Fletcher. 2014. "Social Media and Agenda Setting." In *Canadian Democracy from the Ground Up: Perceptions and Performance*, ed. Elisabeth Gidengil and Heather Bastedo, 148–70. Vancouver: UBC Press.

Clarkson, Stephen. 2005. *The Big Red Machine: How the Liberal Party Dominates Canadian Politics*. Vancouver: UBC Press.

Dawson, R. MacGregor, and W.F. Dawson. 1998. *Democratic Government in Canada*. 5th ed. Toronto: University of Toronto Press.

Dubois, Elizabeth, and Fenwick McKelvey. 2019. "Political Bots: Disrupting Canada's Democracy." *Canadian Journal of Communication* 44: 27–33. https://www.cjc-online.ca/index.php/journal/article/view/3511/3727.

Esselment, Anna, and R. Paul Wilson. 2017. "Campaigning from the Centre: Strategic Communications and Issues Management in the Prime Minister's Office." In *Permanent Campaigning in Canada*, ed. Alex Marland, Anna Esselment, and Thierry Giasson, 222–40. Vancouver: UBC Press.

Evans, Heather K., Victoria Cordova, and Savannah Sipole. 2014. "Twitter Style: An Analysis of How House Candidates Used Twitter in Their 2012 Campaigns." *PS: Political Science and Politics* 47 (2): 454–62. https://doi.org/10.1017/S1049096514000389.

Francoli, Mary. 2007. "E-Participation and Canadian Parliamentarians." In *Encyclopedia of Digital Government*, ed. Ari-Veikko Anttiroiko and Matti Mälkiä, 697–702. Hershey, PA: Idea Group Reference.

Francoli, Mary. 2009. "The Digital MP or How I Learned to Stop Worrying and Love MP." *Journal of Media Practice* 10 (2–3): 215–25. https://doi.org/10.1386/jmpr.10.2-3.215_1.

Francoli, Mary, and Stephen Ward. 2008. "21st Century Soapboxes? MPs and Their Blogs." *Information Polity* 13 (1–2): 21–39. https://doi.org/10.3233/IP-2008-0143.

Giasson, Thierry, and Tamara A. Small. 2017. "Online, All the Time: The Strategic Objectives of Canadian Opposition Parties." In *Permanent*

Campaigning in Canada, ed. Alex Marland, Thierry Giasson, and Anna Esselment, 109–26. Vancouver: UBC Press.

Giasson, Thierry, Gildas Le Bars, and Philippe Dubois. 2019. "Is Social Media Transforming Canadian Electioneering? Hybridity and Online Partisan Strategies in the 2012 Quebec Election." *Canadian Journal of Political Science* 52 (2): 323–41. https://doi.org/10.1017/S0008423918000902.

Gidengil, Elisabeth, and Heather Bastedo. 2014. "Conclusion: Taking Stock of Canadian Democracy from the Ground Up." In *Canadian Democracy from the Ground Up: Perceptions and Performance*, ed. Elisabeth Gidengil and Heather Bastedo, 253–72. Vancouver: UBC Press.

Grube, Dennis. 2015. "Responsibility to Be Enthusiastic? Public Servants and the Public Face of 'Promiscuous Partisanship.'" *Governance* 28 (3): 305–20. https://doi.org/10.1111/gove.12088.

Gruzd, Anatoliy. 2012. "Investigating Political Polarization on Twitter: A Canadian Perspective." In *Internet, Politics, Policy 2: Big Data, Big Challenges?* Oxford, UK: Oxford Internet Institute.

Kernaghan, Kenneth. 2007. "Making Political Connections: IT and Legislative Life." In *Digital State at the Leading Edge*, ed. Sanford Borins, Kenneth Kernaghan, David Brown, Nick Bontis, Perri 6, and Fred Thompson, 224–52. Toronto: University of Toronto Press.

Koop, Royce, and Alex Marland. 2012. "Insiders and Outsiders: Presentation of Self on Canadian Parliamentary Websites and Newsletters." *Policy and Internet* 4 (3–4): 112–35. https://doi.org/10.1002/poi3.13.

Koop, Royce, Heather Bastedo, and Kelly Blidook. 2018. *Representation in Action: Canadian MPs in the Constituencies*. Vancouver: UBC Press.

Lewis, J.P., Mireille Lalancette, and Vincent Raynauld. 2019. "Cabinet Solidarity in an Age of Social Media: A Case Study of Twitter Use by MP Carolyn Bennett." In *What's Trending in Canadian Politics? Understanding Transformations in Power, Media, and the Public Sphere*, ed. Mireille Lalancette, Vincent Raynauld, and Erin Crandall, 170–93. Vancouver: UBC Press.

Marland, Alex. 2020. *Whipped: Party Discipline in Canada*. Vancouver: UBC Press.

Marland, Alex, and Maria Mathews. 2017. "'Friend, Can You Chip in $3?': Canadian Political Parties' Email Communication and Fundraising." In *Permanent Campaigning in Canada*, ed. Alex Marland, Thierry Giasson, and Anna Esselment, 87–108. Vancouver: UBC Press.

McKelvey, Fenwick, and Jill Piebiak. 2018. "Porting the Political Campaign: The NationBuilder Platform and the Global Flows of Political Technology." *New Media and Society* 20 (3): 901–18. https://doi.org/10.1177/1461444816675439.

McKelvey, Fenwick, Marianne Côté, and Vincent Raynauld. 2018. "Scandals and Screenshots: Social Media Elites in Canadian Politics." In *Political Elites* in *Canada: Power and Influence in Instantaneous Times*, ed. Alex Marland, Thierry Giasson, and Andrea Lawlor, 204–22. Vancouver: UBC Press.

Nielsen, Kevin. 2017. "Catherine McKenna Accidentally Praises Syria on Twitter, Blames Staff for Error." *Global News*, November 8. Accessed September 1, 2019. https://globalnews.ca/news/3849606/catherine-mckenna-praises-syria-twitter-blames-staff/.

Ottawa Citizen. 2014. "What in the World Is Going on with Tony Clement and His Selfies?" July 18. Accessed September 1, 2019. http://web.archive.org/web/20150508070222/http://ottawacitizen.com/storyline/what-in-the-world-is-going-on-with-tony-clements-weird-fascination-with-selfies.

Patten, Steve. 2017. "Databases, Microtargeting, and the Permanent Campaign: A Threat to Democracy?" In *Permanent Campaigning in Canada*, ed. Alex Marland, Thierry Giasson, and Anna Esselment, 47–64. Vancouver: UBC Press.

Pitkin, Hanna Fenichel. 1967. *The Concept of Representation*. Berkeley: University of California Press.

Raj, Althia. 2017. "Politicians Accused of Violating Canadians' Rights by Blocking Them Online." *The Huffington Post*, August 2. Accessed September 1, 2019. http://www.huffingtonpost.ca/2017/08/02/politicians-accused-of-violating-canadians-rights-by-blocking-t_a_23062157/.

Remillard, Chaseten, Lindsey M. Bertrand, and Alina Fisher. 2019. "The Visually Viral Prime Minister: Justin Trudeau, Selfies, and Instagram." In *Power Shift? Political Leadership and Social Media*, ed. Richard Davis and David Taras, 63–75. Abingdon, UK: Routledge.

Samara Centre. 2012. "Tips for Elected Leaders' Websites." Accessed September 1, 2019. http://www.samaracanada.com/research/political-leadership/mp-website-analysis/tips-for-elected-leaders-websites.

Samara Centre. 2013. "Members of Parliament Websites Infographic." Accessed January 31, 2020. https://www.samaracanada.com/research/political-leadership/mp-website-analysis/members-of-parliament-websites-infographic.

Small, Tamara A. 2010. "Still Waiting for an Internet Prime Minister: Online Campaigning by Canadian Political Parties." In *Election*, ed. Heather MacIvor, 173–98. Toronto: Emond Montgomery Publications.

Small, Tamara A. 2014. "The Not-So Social Network: The Use of Twitter by Canada's Party Leaders." In *Political Communication in Canada: Meet the Press and Tweet the Rest*, ed. Alex Marland, Thierry Giasson, and Tamara A. Small, 92–108. Vancouver: UBC Press.

Small, Tamara A. 2016. "Two Decades of Digital Party Politics in Canada: An Assessment." In *Canadian Parties in Transition*, 4th ed., ed. Alain-G. Gagnon and A. Brian Tanguay, 338–408. Toronto: University of Toronto Press.

Trudeau, Justin. 2019. Twitter profile. September 1. https://twitter.com/JustinTrudeau.

Watters, Haydn. 2015. "Conservative App Puts Voter Identification in Campaign Workers' Hands." *CBC News*, June 12. Accessed September 1, 2019. http://www.cbc.ca/news/politics/conservative-app-puts-voter-identification-in-campaign-workers-hands-1.3104470.

Yun, Tom. 2018. "The Two Ex-Political Staffers behind the Ontario Elections' Most Digital-Savvy Outside Groups." May 28. Accessed September 1, 2019. https://www.macleans.ca/politics/the-two-ex-political-staffers-behind-the-ontario-elections-most-digital-savvy-outside-groups/.

CHAPTER TWO

Digital Government and Democratic Trust: From Online Service to Outward Engagement

Jeffrey Roy

CONTEXT

The purpose of this chapter is twofold: first, to examine the evolution of digital government and digital democracy in Canada over the past twenty years; and second, to illuminate contested notions of digital democracy within today's shifting political and media landscape. Digital, or electronic, government emerged in the late 1990s as a response to the mainstream emergence of the internet and online connectivity – and the effects more broadly of digital technologies on the public sector. Despite a high degree of definitional fluidity, scholars and practitioners have shared a common and flourishing interest in the digitization of the public sector – including both the administrative and democratic realms. While there is no clear boundary between digital government and digital democracy, the former stems primarily from within the executive branch (i.e., elected officials overseeing government and public servants executing their orders) whereas the latter entails a greater focus and emphasis on the legislative branch (see chapter 1).

While acknowledging such fluidity between democracy and government, this chapter dissects both digital government and digital democracy through a public administration lens, emphasizing managerial and media dynamics. Drawing from country case studies formulated at the Organisation for Economic Cooperation and Development's (OECD) unit examining e-government, one early definition from the late 1990s has proved instructive, namely: "Continuous innovation in the delivery of services, citizen participation, and governance through the transformation of external and internal relationships by the use of information technology, especially the Internet" (Roy 2006, 9). What I found appealing about this broad canvas is the emphasis on changing relationships and shifting governance models both internally within government and externally, across society at large. It bears noting, moreover, that the evolution of citizen participation can and does have ramifications for digital government across both executive and legislative branch processes.

In my own book, *E-Government in Canada,* I dissected this OECD definition into four dimensions of change: service, security, transparency, and trust in the Canadian public service (Roy 2006). A key premise of this approach was that not only did each dimension represent an important set of variables in shaping Canadian e-government progress and impediments but so too did the interdependence of these four dimensions in a myriad of ways. In keeping with the spirit of the aforementioned OECD definition – and in a manner that enjoins my 2006 book and the focus of this chapter – a broad distinction can be made between the administrative architecture of digital government on the one hand (emphasizing service and security and orchestrated mainly by executive branch actors) and the emergence of digital democracy much more intertwined with the inter-related dimensions of transparency and trust.

DIGITIZATION

Promises & Perils

Distinctions in how the public is viewed and characterized by governments matter here, notably the invocation of customer relationships versus citizen relationships. Whereas the former implies a more market-oriented and transactional form of interaction, the latter encompasses more complex and multi-faceted elements covering political and public interest dimensions (Dutil et al. 2010; Roy 2013; Roy 2017). In the early days of digital or e-government, the customer service logic of digitization was more enthusiastically embraced by public sector authorities themselves, operating mainly from within the executive branch. A case in point was the 1999 Government Online strategy launched by the Liberal government and championed by its minister of industry John Manley. At the heart of this strategy were the intertwined dimensions of service and security, the latter central to facilitating online transactions. Both dimensions remain highly relevant today, as witnessed by the 2017 launching of Canadian Digital Service by the Government of Canada.

From the outset, the dimensions of transparency and trust – and questions of citizen engagement and democratic reforms – proved especially complex, much as they remain so today. An early and notably influential example of addressing this complexity in Canada was the "Crossing Boundaries" initiative spearheaded by a Canadian scholar (Don Lenihan) and Member of Parliament (Tony Valeri). The initiative, launched in 2003, called for the refashioning of the public's role in democratic decision-making and new power sharing arrangements between elected officials and the public, changes made possible by the advent of the internet (Valeri and Lenihan 2003). It also called for the creation of a "series of e-democracy pilot projects" to explore key issues and questions that remain relevant today.

Part of the relevance of the questions raised by Lenihan and Valeri is that their call to action has largely gone unanswered in Canada. Rather than embrace transparency and trust as pillars for democratic innovation, successive Liberal and Conservative governments sought mainly to apply them to the realm of online service delivery and corresponding efforts to upgrade the internal infrastructure of the public sector (notably database and service processing systems). In doing so, they ensured that the predominance of the executive branch over the legislative branch with respect to digital investments and actions remains a key consideration, as does the inertia of traditional democratic governance that would seem particularly strong within the Canadian Westminster context (Roy 2013).

Despite these challenges, digital democracy in electronic government has remained an important focus for scholars, activists, and even elected officials as potential and actual reforms have been either explored or undertaken (Reddick and Aikins 2012; Clarke 2013; McNutt 2014). In one recent examination of such reforms across a range of democratic-minded countries, Simon et al. (2017) define digital democracy simply as "the practice of democracy using digital tools and technologies." They go on, however, to distinguish between minimalist and maximalist definitions in the following manner: "The former focuses on giving citizens access to governmental information and enabling them to interact with government through, for example, online consultations and transactional services online. The latter envisages a more participatory role for citizens, enabling them to collaborate with government officials as well as make their own decisions about how they and their local communities are governed" (Simon et al. 2017, 11).

In other words, there is a critical distinction between being informed and listened to on the one hand and being directly engaged in governance mechanisms on the other. Furthermore, the complexities of the inter-relationship between trust and transparency are also germane to if and how digital democracy is formulated and pursued. One aspect is technological: the advent of open-source computing and the Google-dominated emergence of search engines created an important counterweight to traditional proprietary systems for both information management and electronic infrastructure. An important political inflection point occurred in 2008 with the election of US president Barack Obama, whose inaugural Presidential Directive on Openness (2009) enshrined in the public and academic discourse three pillars of openness (transparency, participation, and collaboration) that had long aligned closely with the works of citizen engagement advocates but had yet to be adopted into mainstream democratic governance in such an overt and direct manner (Lee and Kwak 2011; Roy 2013).

Here we see "open government" as something of a transitional prism from earlier digital government efforts emphasizing electronic service delivery and the sort of maximalist approach to digital democracy as defined by Simon et al. above (also see chapter 3). Accordingly, a direct lineage may be drawn from the Obama Directive to scholarly reports calling for "ubiquitous engagement" strategies predicated on new forms of open data and public engagement (Lee and Kwak 2011; Gasco 2014), as well as the emergence of the Open

Government Partnership globally (Francoli and Clarke 2014; Roy 2016). In Canada, such influences gave rise to pioneering open data efforts by municipal governments; these eventually spread to all government levels, with the Conservatives launching a federal Open Government Action Plan in 2012 focused upon three main spheres of activity and reform: information, data, and dialogue. For our purposes in this chapter, tied as it is to the emergence of digital democracy, it is the latter dimension of dialogue that is of the greatest interest, as an important shift in the rhetoric of the government itself in embracing, at least implicitly, new engagement possibilities long called for by public participation advocates but now increasingly feasible (and arguably necessary) as societies become more digitally informed and connected.

Changing Notions of Media

At the time of e-government's emergence in the late 1990s, there was no distinction between traditional media and new media, as the latter did not exist. Since that time, the disruption to the media sector and the emergence of social media especially have become fundamental to understanding both digital democracy's evolution (see preface) and the changing and varying potentials for new forms of public engagement led either by the executive branch or stemming more broadly from both political and non-political actors.

The role of digital technologies is fundamental to this orientation as a basis for better informing the citizenry. This is not only in terms of governments directing information to the public and citizens producing and sharing content themselves, but also as a platform for nurturing political and policy dialogues of the sort envisioned by likeminded perspectives on Gov 2.0 emphasizing openness, engagement and more collaborative and participative forms of governance facilitated by online platforms and tools (Lips 2012; Roy 2013). McNutt describes such capacities as second-generation participation, as "these new technologies present opportunities for government to expand collaboration, enhance public engagement, co-produce programs and services, and innovate through crowdsourcing solutions" (McNutt 2014, 56).

Nonetheless, two broad and inter-related limitations have significantly stunted this potential, one stemming from within government itself, the other from the evolving social media landscape and its ability to provide and nurture information flows and open discourse. With respect to the former, domestic and international research on social media usage by government has clearly demonstrated the influences of traditional public administration structures and cultures in shaping social media usage by governments as primarily about information provision rather than new forms of power sharing and public engagement (Mergel 2012; Roy 2013; Reddick and Chatfield 2017). In terms of social media's evolution more widely, a growing array of interventions by state and non-state actors alike are aimed at "disinformation tactics" to shape democratic discourse and reduce internet freedoms within their jurisdiction (Freedom House 2017).

Accordingly, important questions have emerged in recent years surrounding the influences of new media on democratic discourse and legitimacy, notably those surrounding the appropriate (if at all) filtering and curation of information from a myriad of online sources. At the same time, in many democracies – Canada among them – the traditional media sector has faced tremendous disruption, leading to questions about its ability to play a meaningful role as a contributor to robust and adaptive democratic governance (Public Policy Forum 2017; see also chapter 7). As Simon et al. (2017) further explain, despite much experimentation in this regard, the advent of new media (and internet-based technologies more widely) has raised many fundamental questions about the complexities of democratic capacities and institutional adaptation to technological change, especially as new media dynamics are viewed by many as increasingly fragmenting and polarizing (Simon et al. 2017).

Such challenges and questions are obviously fundamental to notions of public trust. The potential for new and more direct informational networks enjoining elected officials and segments of a citizenry drives a multiplicity of digital democracy scenarios that could well emerge. The distinct political structures and cultures of a given jurisdiction are important factors in determining levels of institutional inertia, innovation, and adaptation for specific types of democratic institutions. How such dynamics are playing out in the Canadian Westminster model is the focal point of the subsequent section of this chapter.

Practice

As noted above, the digital government journey in Canada at the federal level began with an emphasis on electronic service delivery within government, albeit with an outward focus on external delivery channels, whereas a rhetorical interest in digital democracy was mainly relegated to external venues with indirect ties to formal legislative bodies. The political capital invested by then-Liberal governments into flagship service delivery initiatives, notably the creation of Service Canada in 2005 and its online service offerings that sought to transcend departmental boundaries, resulted in some early visibility and recognition for the Government of Canada as being on the vanguard of new digital capacities: as just one example, the global consultancy Accenture bestowed upon the federal government the number one ranking for several consecutive years in its flagship international survey of e-government performance (Roy 2006; Borins et al. 2007).

Despite such fanfare, Service Canada has largely failed to achieve cross-governmental service integration, mainly due to the structural and cultural barriers stemming from the vertical and hierarchical orientation of the Westminster governance system (Roy 2017). The inability of Service Canada to overcome such barriers stems mainly from the informality of its architecture: the entity has never had any formal legislative underpinnings and thus most of its cross-governmental partnering has mainly been limited to providing information and links online to service processes housed by other departments and agencies.

Many provinces have created similar bodies, with some such as New Brunswick having even created their own variant (Service New Brunswick) prior to the formation of its federal cousin. Both government levels have cooperated informally on furthering their efforts and sought to better gauge their respective performances in digital service delivery. Accordingly, the Institute for Citizen-Centred Service (ICCS) was created as a secretariat to facilitate such cooperation on key digital priorities, such as identity management and integrated service offerings online. A flagship initiative of this body has been the deployment of the "Citizen's First" survey methodology, which has sought for more than a decade to quantitatively benchmark public service delivery performance to citizens (and separately to businesses) on an annual basis. At the heart of such an effort has been a philosophical belief, championed mainly by public servants, that a direct and quantifiable link could be made between service and trust, with better service outcomes improving public trust and confidence in their governments (Kernaghan 2013).

Although online service delivery has not been without its successes – both in terms of the uptake of digital transactions in specific areas, notably the filing of tax returns, and in terms of pilot initiatives where jurisdictions share information to bundle different services through more integrative processes, such as new birth registration and child benefits – Canada's overall performance in service delivery over the past decade has been stunted by two main issues. First, there have been a range of internal factors within governments rooted in traditional public administration – namely the vertical silos of departmental and budgetary authority and resourcing – that have largely stunted more integrative and collaborative governance models across government. Second, there has largely been an absence of political impetus, especially at the federal level, in championing service reforms and digital initiatives more widely (Roy 2017). This latter characterization applies mainly to previous Conservative governments. In 2017 the Liberals recognized that Canada had lost ground and embraced a much more expansive view of digital government than their predecessors:

> Digital government extends beyond electronic service delivery and self-service. It touches every facet of how governments manage service delivery, and engage citizens and stakeholders – and leverages digital advances to allow citizens to access services anywhere, anytime. In the long run, digital government can help build stronger engagement and trust between citizens and government, and make public institutions more inclusive, effective, accountable and transparent. (Government of Canada 2017)

That said, the Liberal view is very much in keeping with the initial OECD definition of digital government offered at the outset of this chapter. Yet it bears recalling that prior Conservative governments created inaugural and successive Open Government Action Plans beginning in 2012 (see chapter 3). Influenced by the Obama-inspired discourse, the Conservatives were prepared to embrace openness in limited degrees, particularly in the realm of open data, which was presented primarily as an economic development opportunity. Despite modest financial and political investments into building open data capacities (necessitating the creation of an internal governance architecture to spur data sharing awareness and efforts across government), information and dialogue proved to be generally problematic in yielding tangible reforms. The government was especially criticized by traditional media and stakeholders such as the Privacy Commissioner for a control-minded approach to information dissemination in which social media was deployed mainly as a tool for branding government activity and (in its own presentation) accomplishments (Roy 2016).

With respect to dialogue, then, such internal resistance and traditional orientations toward messaging and control predictably constrained much in the way of meaningful public engagement experimentation, despite repeated commitments in Open Government Action Plans to do so. Within the Canadian context, Longo (2017) concurs with this broad characterization, invoking newer technologies and big data capacities as bases for new engagement techniques as yet unexploited by governments. Instead, specifically with respect to the federal government's experience of recent years, Longo observes that "governments still look to public and stakeholder engagement using prior models of intensive involvement, albeit using new electronic mechanisms, which nonetheless do not respond to shifting citizen expectations" (Longo 2017, 531). Such a cleavage between public expectations and government actions was widened during the first Liberal mandate, resulting in stunted democratic reform efforts themselves intertwined with digitization.

In a manner that in some ways mirrors Obama's invocation of openness in governance, the Trudeau Liberals embraced openness with fervour in 2015 not only in terms of promised administrative reforms but also wider democratic renewal. Yet, despite his electoral pledges, Trudeau mainly reverted to the confines of political traditionalism, emphasizing an approach to representational democracy that is closely aligned with the governance dimensions of traditional public administration, namely centralizing decision-making control within the confines of cabinet and central agencies.

In a modest effort to refute critics, the Liberal government launched in 2017 an online report card tracking progress on their main campaign commitments from 2015, including an acknowledgement of those promises that remained unfulfilled.[1] Not surprisingly, however, the online tool showcases progress on the vast majority of Liberal pledges (as either completed or in progress), offering little more by way of details as to how citizens can further understand the progress to date and the policy processes underway. In other words, lacking detail and independently verifiable information, the online reporting scheme is primarily a communications tool that denotes the sort of effort that arguably heightens cynicism in government and politics today.

Defenders of the Liberal government would presumably invoke at least two arguments to justify the cautionary stance around democratic and digital reforms: firstly, growing concerns about information security and electoral integrity globally; and secondly, the internal state of disrepair of much of the public sector's operational infrastructure, much of which was inherited at least in part from prior Conservative regimes.[2]

The first point has certainly been the predominant focus of the newly appointed, in 2017, minister of democratic institutions, Karina Gould. Linking public trust to process stability and cybersecurity, the minister articulated this emphasis in a speech titled "Democracy in the Digital Age":

> Democracy is based on trust in the process and trust in the outcome. We all know that there are those in this world who would seek to undermine or damage Canadian democracy. I can tell you that the Government of Canada takes this seriously and is determined to do all we can to prevent that from happening. We owe it to Canadians to be proactive. That's why I asked the Communications Security Establishment earlier this year to analyze and make

1 Source: https://www.canada.ca/en/privy-council/campaigns/mandate-tracker-results-canadians.html.

2 Two notable examples here being the struggles of Shared Services Canada (separate from Service Canada), the internal agency responsible for electronic infrastructure such as databases and email systems. Moreover, the Government of Canada has struggled mightily with its Phoenix payroll system, resulting in thousands of public sector employees facing errors in their compensation. It is widely expected that Phoenix will eventually be abandoned altogether, with potentially billions of dollars of additional spending required to both correct past failures and create a new and more functional system. The Phoenix debacle is well summarized and analyzed in a 2018 Senate Committee report available online: https://sencanada.ca/content/sen/committee/421/NFFN/reports/NFFN_Phoenix_Report_32_WEB_e.pdf.

> public an assessment of the current risk of cyber threats and possible hacking of Canada's democratic process. (Minister of Democratic Institutions 2017)

While the government's defensive posture around electoral security and stability is understandable in light of mounting global concerns, there is something more revealing in its failure to meaningfully examine a future pathway toward e-voting (see chapter 4). With financial and even health information now routinely processed and shared digitally – and with millennial-age voters increasingly less inclined to partake in elections – e-voting may not be a panacea for democratic renewal, but it still merits inclusion in any serious roadmap for future endeavours. Acknowledging this point, the 2015 UK Digital Democracy Commission championed by the speaker of the House of Commons calls for secure online voting to be implemented by 2020 (Digital Democracy Commission 2015).

Despite such caution to date, Minister Gould does acknowledge some of the deeper challenges confronting democracies:

> To fully participate, citizens need to have the right democratic vocabulary, and democratic literacy. Active citizenship in our digital age demands this, and we have to come to grips with how we can help Canadians navigate this new landscape. What does it mean to be a citizen in our democracy? What obligations do citizens have to be informed, to be accountable for their ability to hold government to account? (Minister of Democratic Institutions 2017)

In my view, what is especially salient about digital democracy's prospects is the minister's invocation of citizen "obligations" and accountability. While the impact of any single speech is not to be exaggerated, raising such questions does seem to mark a stark turning point from the rhetoric of prior Conservative and Liberal governments that instead emphasized the economic benefits of digitization (especially the benefits of open data in the case of the former Conservative government, which sought to emphasize open data as a driver of commercialization) as well as wider service-oriented pledges of better customer service that have been predominant in the e-government storyline since its inception. Furthermore, the minister goes on to acknowledge the complexities of traditional and new media, challenging social media companies themselves to be more accountable and innovative in consideration of their impacts on democratic conduct.

In what might be viewed as an indirect response to such a challenge, as they have done in several countries, Facebook announced various measures designed to combat misinformation and better patrol electoral processes (as it did for example in deleting several accounts during the Vancouver 2018 municipal elections).[3] Yet, overall, the public pronouncements of a minister and a micro-initiative by the world's leading social media provider notwithstanding, the Liberal government has, as of this writing, largely exchanged its own electoral ambitions premised on themes such as openness and innovation for a much more inward and cautionary approach to governance.

POTENTIALS

An important takeaway from the preceding discussion is the overriding importance of public trust in democratic governance generally and matters of digital innovation within democratic institutions specifically. While all of the four dimensions of digital government, as sketched out in this chapter's outset, remain relevant to many aspects of public sector governance today (service, security, transparency, and trust), it is arguably trust that is the most intertwined with each of the other dimensions.

A fundamental vise on democratic innovation at present is the disconnect between a culture of technological innovation and enthusiasm on the one hand and the cultural undertones of traditional governance within existing democratic systems on the other. While urging digital innovation, Simon et al. (2017) caution that digital technology alone cannot be the answer, taking into consideration both historical traditions and institutional complexity and the inherently contested notion of democracy itself. Quoting one submission to its proceedings, the aforementioned UK Digital Democracy Commission underscores that "technology in itself is not a panacea and it will not effectively correct

3 For details, please see https//www.theglobeandmail.com/canada/british-columbia/article-bc-candidates-targeted-by-anonymous-social-media-posts/.

poor existing practices ... we need to look beyond new digital tools to existing processes that do and do not work, and then critically explore how technology can help us to make democracy work better" (Digital Democracy Commission 2015, 14). Such a perspective is consistent with the normalization hypothesis (see introduction).

As a starting point, then, there is a societal and political requirement to embrace the admittedly contested notions (i) that public trust in democratic governance requires and is predicated upon a foundation of robust citizenship, and (ii) that the elements of a robust and resilient basis for citizenship are shifting in today's still infantile digital era. Greater openness and new forms of engagement are at the core of such a shift, as (some) citizens seek newly fashioned roles in a more participative governance order. At the same time, it must be acknowledged that not all citizens seek such roles, as many are disenfranchised both socially and digitally, while the deepening online culture of consumerism and commercialization accentuates what Nabatchi (2010) has termed as the "democratic deficit" (see also Roy 2013). Empirical evidence in Canada, moreover, suggests only modest levels of interest and engagement among the public in leveraging digital channels for political purposes, albeit with interest and activity higher amongst younger Canadians who have grown up more immersed within digital contexts (Small et al. 2014).

Accordingly, any holistic effort to cultivate an expansion of digital democracy into the formal institutional processes of governance must be predicated upon a guiding commitment to digital literacy and inclusion in a manner that has yet to be undertaken in all but a select few jurisdictions around the world (Jaeger 2012; Heller 2017). Beyond creating an accessible and equitable technological and societal infrastructure for digital citizenship and engagement (itself a daunting task and admittedly not our primary focus in this chapter), the predominant accompanying challenge presenting itself is to cultivate a culture of active democratic engagement predicated upon expectations (including rights and responsibilities), incentives, and rewards for doing so.

The emergence of such a culture can only come about through heightened degrees of experimentation. As Simon et al. put it, "To understand how digital technologies could make our institutions more open, and reshape the interactions between citizens and the state, we need greater experimentation, better evaluation to identify 'what works,' and a greater understanding of how online activities can be used to supplement and support more traditional offline methods of engagement" (2017). Such an appeal harks back to the 2003 calls for e-democracy pilots by the Crossing Boundaries initiative in Canada; in a more recent vein, Longo (2017, 531) underscores that "the emphasis should be on making engagement easier and on providing value back to participants, even considering whether incentives to participate are possible."

Despite a lack of such experimentation in Canada, novel governance approaches leveraging digital capacities are spreading around the world. The 2013 World Democracy Forum held by the Council for Europe, for example, showcased a plethora of innovation from across Europe and elsewhere – as did the 2014 version of this same event that emphasized experimentation predicated upon greater youth involvement in democratic governance. The United Nation's e-participation index, as part of its bi-annual Global E-Government Survey, and the OECD have both catalogued widening experimentation in the realm of online engagement. Moreover, the often-cited Simon et al. (2017) report, published by the UK Nesta group that has close associations with the public sector, includes seven "leading" case studies and several other examples (from different regions of the world) of digitally facilitated processes of public engagement within formal governance architectures of localities or countries. The commonality across these cases lies in governments both informing and empowering citizens (or a group of citizens) with deliberative capacities (in both virtual and in-person formats) and formal authority to shape decision-making.

At the same time, the authors of this British report stress the limits of digital democracy and the importance of aligning new and more direct engagement techniques and traditional models of representational democracy. Such a balance is also sought by the UK Digital Democracy Commission of 2015, which seeks to preserve and enhance the role of Parliament through digital extension and innovation rather than undermine it. Striking such a balance is tenuous, however, since as Longo notes, "Offering true collaboration opportunities for participants in citizen and stakeholder engagement exercises will be a significant challenge for governments, requiring governments to give up control and authority over policy deliberation and allow many more voices to enter the conversation" (Longo 2017, 532).

Only an openness to innovation, more direct engagement, and incremental experimentation – ideally in a manner at least partially shielded from traditional partisanship and inherently adversarial political structures (particularly acute within the Westminster context) – can enable governments to find a workable path forward. Accordingly, matching political rhetoric with such action is essential to cultivating the openness and trust required for creative undertakings that invariably carry new risks; to date, the Liberal experience with democratic reform has been characterized by quite the opposite trends, with abandoned campaign rhetoric fuelling cynicism and distrust.

Yet despite traditionalism largely reigning at the federal level, municipalities have been furthering open government efforts to more directly encompass citizen involvement in decision-making, often leveraging online platforms and tools to facilitate such processes (Reddick and Aikins 2012; Roy 2013). Progress, however, has been uneven. The Province of Ontario's creation of a digital minister (a cabinet minister with responsibilities for government-wide digital planning and execution) under the prior Liberal government may have signalled a higher level of political commitment to digital innovation within the public sector – but the 2018 election of Doug Ford suggests a reversion once again to traditionalism. The implication here is that trust is less about transparent processes and more about decisions and outcomes, an approach in keeping more with representational democracy than more direct and participative forms of democracy often associated with digitization. Indeed, it also bears noting that the Ford-led Conservative campaign manifesto said nothing at all about digital reforms, with the words "digital," "electronic," and "internet" all absent from the minimalist set of promises released in the late stages of the provincial campaign.

In their own examination of "digital" democracy's prospects in the UK, Simon et al. (2017) recognize – even within their predominantly digitally inspired effort – the importance of wider democratic reforms as key elements of public trust going forward. At the very least, in the UK, there has been a wider set of voices both within and outside of the public sector contributing to this discourse (as witnessed by the 2015 creation of a Digital Democracy Commission). For reasons perhaps tied to the prior Conservative government's economic focus (especially in the aftermath of the global financial crisis), what has mainly been lacking in the Canadian context is a willingness and enthusiasm on the part of political leaders to play an enabling role of the sort that has underpinned Estonia's efforts, as that country has seized digitization as a national mantra for socio-economic and democratic development and has sought to export such efforts across the European Union (Heller 2017).

One source of new solutions, then, must be a competition of ideas stemming from political parties rather than governing actors, a point made as well by Simon et al. (2017). In Denmark, for instance, widely regarded as a leading digital jurisdiction, one political party has already experimented with blockchain technologies within its own internal governance for leadership selection voting.[4] Australia's coalition government, moreover, released while in opposition an ambitious strategy for digital government, while the Westminster cousin to Canada already features a range of electoral innovations (including mandatory voting and an elected Senate to name but two) that distinguish it from Canada's parliamentary traditions.

There is an equally important if not more central role for civil society and the citizenry at large to exert pressure for change and to be engaged in mechanisms of formal influence. A counterintuitive example from Edmonton, a leader in many facets of open government and online engagement, is illustrative of the disconnect between citizen involvement of this sort and formalized decision-making. In 2012 a citizen's panel recommended the adoption of e-voting for local elections (after considerable deliberations and a significant investment of resources into the process by local Council), only to have their viewpoint rejected by elected officials. A more recent 2017 example, from a citizen's panel established to advise on snow-ploughing services, is similar, as frustrated panellists leaked their recommendations to local media outlets due to a lack of response on the part of elected officials to this body's outputs.

Across local, provincial, and federal levels – in ways that will undoubtedly vary in terms of both scape and impacts – new mechanisms of co-governance must be forged that tie citizen participation and formalized decision-making. The groundwork for such mechanisms readily

4 For additional details and discussion of blockchain technologies and democratic potential see https://medium.com/boulecoin/blockchain-allows-protecting-the-election-from-fraud-2a0cac9625b7.

exists (Clarke 2013; McNutt 2014; Longo 2017; Simon et al. 2017). Beyond immediate term considerations on specific policy, service, and budgetary matters (and perhaps even electoral structures), a new and more participative democratic ethos also necessitates the formation of a non-partisan body or forum tasked with longer term considerations of digitally enabled reforms to present structures of democratic governance rooted in socio-economic and technological contexts far removed from today's realities.

In addressing particularly complex matters of public engagement and accountability – including new rights and responsibilities of citizens and how such shifting roles are intertwined with a changing media landscape – only a pathway grounded in direct and non-partisan public involvement will have any prospect for yielding the sort of deliberative legitimacy that can transcend short term electoral calculus and create a meaningful and sufficiently powerful impetus for democratic innovation. When power is shared in such a manner, some protection is afforded to current elected officials, who are invariably constrained by more immediate agendas and incentives while often being motivated by self-preservation. The importance of a nonpartisan, citizen's body would be to give rise to some fundamental questions about the future course of democracy, questions that extend far beyond the electoral fortunes of any one government or party.

REFERENCES

Borins, S., K. Kernaghan, D. Brown, Perri 6, and F. Thompson. 2007. *Digital State at the Leading Edge*. Toronto: University of Toronto Press.

Clarke, A. 2013. *Exploiting the Web as a Tool of Democracy: New Ways Forward in the Study and Practice of Digital Democracy*. World Forum for Democracy 2013 Issues Paper. Strasbourg: Council of Europe.

Digital Democracy Commission. 2015. "Open Up! Report of the Speaker's Commission on Digital Democracy." London: House of Commons. http://www.digitaldemocracy.parliament.uk/documents/Open-Up-Digital-Democracy-Report.pdf.

Dutil, P., C. Howard, J. Langford, and J. Roy. 2010. *The Service State – Rhetoric, Reality, and Promise*. Ottawa: University of Ottawa Press.

Francoli, M., and A. Clarke. 2014. "What's in a Name? A Comparison of 'Open Government' Definitions across Seven Open Government Partnership Members." *Journal of Democracy and Open Government* 6 (1): 248–66. https://doi.org/10.29379/jedem.v6i3.227.

Freedom House. 2017. "Manipulating Social Media to Undermine Democracy" (Freedom on the Net 2017). *Freedom House.* https://freedomhouse.org/report/freedom-net/freedom-net-2017.

Gasco, M., ed. 2014. *Open Government: Opportunities and Challenges for Public Governance.* New York: Springer.

Government of Canada. 2017. "Beginning the Conversation ... A Made-in-Canada Approach to Digital Government." https://digital.canada.ca/beginning-the-conversation/full-report/.

Heller, N. 2017. "Estonia: The Digital Republic." *New Yorker* (December). https://www.newyorker.com/magazine/2017/12/18/estonia-the-digital-republic.

Jaeger, B. 2012. *New Frontiers in the Digital Divide: Revisiting Policy for Digital Inclusion.* https://www.scss.tcd.ie/disciplines/information_systems/egpa/docs/2012/Jaeger.pdf.

Kernaghan, K. 2013. "Changing Channels: Managing Channel Integration and Migration in Public Organizations." *Canadian Public Administration* 56 (1): 121–41. https://doi.org/10.1111/capa.12006.

Lee, G., and Y. Kwak. 2011. *An Open Government Implementation Model: Moving to Increased Public Engagement.* Washington, DC: IBM Center for the Business of Government.

Lips, M. 2012. "E-Government Is Dead: Long Live Public Adminstration 2.0." *Information Polity* 17 (3–4): 239–50. https://doi.org/10.3233/IP-120292.

Longo, J. 2017. "The Evolution of Citizen and Stakeholder Engagement in Canada, from Spicer to #Hashtags." *Canadian Public Administration* 60 (4): 517–37. https://doi.org/10.1111/capa.12229.

McNutt, K. 2014. "Public Engagement in the Web 2.0 Era: Social Collaborative Technologies in a Public Sector Context." *Canadian Public Administration* 57 (1): 49–70. https://doi.org/10.1111/capa.12058.

Mergel, I. 2012. "The Social Media Innovation Challenge in the Public Sector." *Information Polity* 17 (3–4): 281–92. https://doi.org/10.3233/IP-2012-000281.

Minister of Democratic Institutions. 2017. *Democracy in the Digital Age (Speech).* Government of Canada: Democratic Institutions. November 9. https://www.canada.ca/en/democratic-institutions/news/2017/11/democracy_in_thedigitalage.html.

Nabatchi, T. 2010. "Addressing the Citizenship and Democratic Deficits: The Potential of Deliberative Democracy for Public Administration." *The American Review of Public Administration* 40 (4): 376–99. https://doi.org/10.1177/0275074009356467.

Public Policy Forum. 2017. *The Shattered Mirror: News, Democracy, and Trust in the Digtial Age.* Ottawa: Public Policy Forum.

Reddick, C.G., and S.K. Aikins, eds. 2012. *Web 2.0 Technologies and Democratic Governance: Political, Policy and Management Implications.* New York: Springer.

Reddick, C.G., and A. Chatfield. 2017. "A Social Media Text Analytics Framework for Double-Loop Learning for Citizen-Centric Public Services: A Case Study of a Local Government Facebook Use." *Government Information Quarterly* 34 (1): 110–25. https://doi.org/10.1016/j.giq.2016.11.001.

Roy, J. 2006. *E-Government in Canada: Transformation for the Digital Age.* Ottawa: University of Ottawa Press.

Roy, J. 2013. *From Machinery to Mobility: Government and Democracy in a Participative Age.* New York: Springer.

Roy, J. 2016. "Data, Dialogue, and Innovation: Opportunities and Challenges for Open Government in Canada." *Journal of Innovation Management* 4 (1): 22–38. https://doi.org/10.24840/2183-0606_004.001_0004.

Roy, J. 2017. "Digital Government and Service Delivery: An Examination of Performance and Prospects." *Canadian Public Administration* 60 (4): 538–61. https://doi.org/10.1111/capa.12231.

Simon, J., T. Bass, V. Boelman, and G. Mulgan. 2017. *Digital Democracy: The Tools Transforming Political Engagement.* London: Nesta Group. https://www.nesta.org.uk/sites/default/files/digital_democracy.pdf.

Small, T., H. Jansen, F. Bastien, T. Giasson, and R. Koop. 2014. "Online Political Activity in Canada: The Hype and the Facts." *Canadian Parliamentary Review* (Winter). http://revparl.ca/37/4/37n4e_14_Small.pdf.

Valeri, T., and D. Lenihan. 2003. *Finding Our Digital Voice: Governing in the Information Age: The Crossing Boundaries Final Report and Recommendations by the Crossing Boundaries Political Advisory Committee.* Ottawa: Centre for Collaborative Government. http://unpan1.un.org/intradoc/groups/public/documents/un/unpan010303.pdf.

CHAPTER THREE

Open Government: Was It Just a Moment?

Justin Longo

INTRODUCTION

Governments do many things on our behalf, using our money. How much should citizens[1] in a representative democracy know about the actions and operations of their governments, and when are government secrets justifiable? In what ways should citizens be involved in government deliberations and decisions, especially when we use democratic elections to decide who will have the power to make decisions?

---

1 In this chapter, perhaps more than any other in this book, the term *citizen* can be ambiguous. In some cases, its use is precise and legal: "a member of a nation or Commonwealth, either native or naturalized" (Barber 2005, np). In others, I use the term to refer to individuals who participate in political or civic action in their communities, noting that much of this participation does not require proof of citizenship or even residency (Fung 2006). When terms like *citizen engagement* are used, they are based on a definition of citizenship that aligns with being an inhabitant of a place, rather than having legal status (Longo 2017). This looser definition coincides with newer terms like *citizen science*, wherein non-scientists participate in science projects, often via the internet (Wald, Longo, and Dobell 2016). However, using the term citizen in this imprecise way is not universally accepted, especially in political contexts where the idea of citizenship that indicates the legal right to reside in a place and to fully engage in economic, social, and political life is highly contested (Mossberger, Wu, and Crawford 2013).

And how much freedom should citizens have to create governance solutions, either with government or independently? Open government in the digital era gives new meaning to these long-standing questions. This chapter assesses the extent to which these issues are still relevant, asking whether advances in technology require of us a fundamental reconsideration of the relationship between governments and citizens, and among citizens. Is there a better way for the politics of public policy to be guided? In the digital era, we now have the tools at our disposal to take a different approach to governance, in which closed representative democracy and institutionalized bureaucracy are replaced by open government – something more closely resembling the original direct democracy of ancient Greece. This chapter discusses the origins of the modern open government movement, the experience to date among governments in Canada, the influence of digital technology on the expansion of open government, constraints and retrenchment due to political concerns, opportunities for the future, and concerns about its sustainability in the face of complex governing challenges.

The promise of open government in the digital era must confront a reality – like most environments facing significant disruption – in which the path between two different equilibria passes through uncertainty. Does open government represent a signpost along the road to "liberal democracy [as] 'the end point of mankind's ideological evolution' and the 'final form of human government'" (Fukuyama 2006, xi), the digital era form of the long continuum of citizens' right to know about, be involved in, and collaborate in their own governance? Or was the recent flourishing of open government a brief but unsustainable phenomenon that coincided with the emergence of Web 2.0 functionality and a reaction to post-9/11 government secrecy overreach, paralleling the challenges currently faced by democracy despite its apparent triumph at the end of the last millennium (Kaplan 1997)?

CONTEXT

Defining open government seems particularly troubling for academics and other observers. Described as "complicated" and "frustrating" (Longo, Rogawski, and Young 2013, np), "fuzzy" (Peixoto 2013, np), "difficult to pin down" with "no specific consensus definition"

(Linders and Wilson 2011, 264), "ambiguous" and "vague" (Yu and Robinson 2011, 181, 182), and in danger of "becoming a shapeshifting buzzword" (Clarke and Francoli 2014, 264), the definitional challenge of open government was ironically clarified when one person[2] at the centre of its current revival lamented the term as "a bad choice" (Noveck 2011, np).

Despite these warnings, a chapter on open government in the digital era cannot gracefully avoid venturing a definition. The latter should build on the earlier origins of the term related to the long history of the freedom of information (FoI) and right to know movements, but also account for the digital era factors[3] that have influenced its current incarnation (each of these are discussed below). Some leading definitions focus on government transparency through open access to government information (Yu and Robinson 2011) and avenues for citizen participation in decision-making arenas (Meijer, Curtin, and Hillebrandt 2012). Others are more ambitious, advocating for the use of new technologies "to connect the public to government and to one another informed by open data" in which government asks the public for help in solving public problems (Noveck 2011, np). Here, the influence of digital collaboration – the creation of new value involving the efforts of often unconnected individuals brought together through online platforms (Benkler 2006) – is added to these basic ideas of transparency and participation (Lathrop and Ruma 2010; McDermott 2010).

Following from these priors, the modern usage of the term open government is taken here as centring on government transparency, opportunities for citizen participation in government deliberation and decision-making, and mechanisms for citizens to work with their

2 Beth Noveck was, as the first deputy chief technology officer for open government, the lead on the Barack Obama administration's Open Government Initiative.

3 Despite the leveraging of digital technology that propelled the open government movement over the past ten years, open government should be understood as being distinct from e-government. With e-government defined as the application of digital technology to the business of government, the emphasis there is on the efficiency and effectiveness of government administration and service delivery (see Roy, in this volume). Open government, on the other hand, is a political posture that aims to improve government legitimacy through transparency and citizen participation and improve government effectiveness through government/citizen collaboration. While e-government is premised on the application of technology to the institution of government, open government can be facilitated by technology but by no means does its achievement require digital technology.

governments and other citizens to collaboratively solve public problems. Thus, open government is defined here as government attitudes, actions, and laws that (1) proactively provide citizens with actionable data and information about the operations of government (transparency), (2) initiate and support ways for citizens to participate in government deliberations and decisions (participation), and (3) promote and accommodate mechanisms for the collaborative creation of governance solutions (collaboration). These attitudes, actions, and laws are today more likely (though not exclusively) communicated, implemented, promoted, and facilitated using digital technologies. And while it can be difficult to ascribe motives to actions or statements in this area, the normative aim of open government is assumed to be the improvement of government effectiveness and the legitimacy of government (Barber 1998; Noveck 2009; Renn et al. 1993; Verba and Nie 1987).

Before illustrating what open government looks like in current practice, and where it might be going in the next decade, I uncover where these ideas of transparency, participation, and collaboration came from. Two sequential histories are discussed next: first, the movement away from the original conceptualization of democracy toward the contemporary form that we are most familiar with; and second, how the concept of open government first emerged before its latest digital incarnation.

History 1. Closing Government: From Direct to Representative Democracy

At the birthplace of democracy, in the ancient Greek *ecclesia* or principal assembly, government *was* the people, with the *demos* (or citizens – limited to adult males) having full knowledge of what government was doing, directly involved in government decisions, and able to create the governance solutions it wanted (Rhodes 2004). Thriving for approximately two hundred years, direct Athenian democracy ultimately became unworkable in part because the increasing population and geographic size of political communities made it unwieldy (Scott 2010).

As political entities grew and city-states gave way to the nation-state as the prevailing political model, and as legislative assemblies could only accommodate reasonable numbers of participants, it was no longer feasible for all citizens to be directly engaged on a regular basis in their governance, other than through occasional voting. Direct democracy thus evolved into representative democracy, becoming the norm for most political jurisdictions (Mezey 2008).

Representative democracy, however, introduced three types of communication challenges: literal distance between representatives and their electors, figurative distance between them, and the problem of how to aggregate the diverse views of many citizens. The geographic size of constituencies and the literal distance from the constituency to the central legislature limits the extent to which citizens can know what their representative or the government is doing or be involved in those decision. Representative government also puts professional legislators (assisted by professional administrators) and the machinations of government behind closed doors, figuratively distant from the occasional voting citizen. But even if the problem of distance – literal and figurative – were addressed, the question of how, precisely, a representative should represent the interests of their constituency and how diverse views can be aggregated remains an unsettled debate (see Koop, Bastedo, and Blidook 2018).

Despite the rise of representative democracy, citizens have continued to generate governance solutions, with their governments or on their own. From the informal (e.g., neighbourhood watch arrangements, or the original "sharing economy" of tool lending and barn raising) to the formal (e.g., civil society organizations like benevolent associations and cooperatives or common property management regimes; Ostrom 2015), these flourished with the implicit blessing of government so long as they did not contradict the objectives of the government. These organizations, however, are affected by the same communication challenges that afflict government: over long distances, or in large numbers, the social capital, authority, and monitoring systems required to sustain their organization diminish, and thus their governance solutions remained localized (Putnam, Leonardi, and Nanetti 1994).

History 2. Pre-Digital Open Government: The Right to Know and Participate

While the movement toward representative democracy and the distancing of the people from their government are prevailing trends over the history of the modern state, some counterforces have emerged to help the citizenry wrest control back from the politically and administratively distant. These forces include collective decision and voting techniques such as referendum, proposition, initiative, and recall legislation; judicial interpretation and constitutional amendment that have devolved authority to subnational units in federations or limited the authority of government; public participation and consultation exercises; citizen's forums, local co-management arrangements, and community councils; and checks on administrative and executive power through the creation of offices such as auditors general and ombudsoffices, and legislation dealing with conflict of interest, freedom of information, and open-meeting requirements. This section describes two prominent mechanisms: access to government information and the ability of citizens to participate in government decision-making.

Freedom of Information

The idea of open government through public access to information has a long history.[4] The right of the people to have access to government records emerged during the Enlightenment and was entrenched as a governing principle in early representative democracies like France and the United States (Foerstel 1999). However, the evolution of the modern state has also seen the continued professionalization of politics and the public service, and this embedding of expertise within our democratic systems has further closed off government to those outside of it (Cook and Morgan 1971). Due to the perception that governing has become even more complex, administrative power has continued to grow.

Nonetheless, the general concept of "the right to know" re-emerged under the specific heading of open government during debates in the United States in the late 1950s with calls to protect citizens' right to know through legislation (Parks 1957). The US Freedom of Information Act (FOIA) was enacted in 1966 in response to the expansion of

4 A Google Ngram of "open government" found in books printed between 1800 and 2008 shows a longer history of the phrase (http://bit.ly/2CrrdCU), with its first use in print in 1808 and peaking in the early 1980s (though discerning the meaning of its use over time would require deeper investigation). A Google Trends graph from 2004 to the present (http://bit.ly/2C2ImXJ) shows the relative interest in the phrase in recent years as indicated by web searches.

the federal government during the previous three decades, and the idea spread in the following years to other countries often against the wishes of political leaders and bureaucrats. Throughout the remainder of the twentieth century, "policy stakeholders used the term 'open government' primarily as a synonym for public access to previously undisclosed government information" (Yu and Robinson 2011, 186).

Freedom of information (FoI) legislation is designed to make government institutions more accountable to the public for the data and information it holds. It is now widely viewed as a basic right in a democracy, facilitating transparency and helping to reduce corruption. Westminster political systems were initially less open to FoI legislation than their republican counterparts (Stubbs 2008). Most democratic countries, however, have been unable to resist the prevailing tide propelling the right to know, and Canada's proximity to the United States made it especially vulnerable to criticisms of government secrecy (Bennett 1991). The Pierre Trudeau government tabled a green paper titled "Public Access to Government Documents" in Parliament in 1977 (Canada 1977), taking a tepid approach to disclosure and rejecting the notion of judicial review of ministerial decisions regarding access to information. The 1978 Throne Speech contained a proposal for FoI legislation, and in March 1979 proposals for an Access to Information Bill were presented by the government, providing for an information commissioner but not for judicial review. A similar bill was introduced by the subsequent Joe Clark government, but the bill died in committee when that government fell. A re-elected Trudeau government introduced Bill C-43 in July 1980, providing for access to information with protections for personal information. The Canadian Access to Information Act (AIA) received Royal Assent in 1982 and came into effect in July 1983. Bennett (1991) describes the Canadian AIA as very similar to the United States FOIA, with the addition in Canada of an Information Commissioner tasked with ensuring fairness and overseeing a generous interpretation of the citizens' right to know, with subsequent review by the Federal Court of Canada available in the event of disputes. Despite the long delay from the adoption of the US FOIA in 1966 to Canada's AIA in 1983, Canada was just the eighth country in the world at the time to have FoI legislation. Within Canada, several provinces and territories soon followed, with all having FoI legislation by 2002, with requirements cascading down to local governments.

Public Participation in Government

Participation by those outside of government in policymaking processes has a long history in our political systems, lying at the heart of the theory and practice of democracy (Verba and Nie 1987). Modern democratic governments usually offer opportunities for citizens and stakeholder groups to participate in public policymaking. Whether required to do so by law or proactively engaging the public, participation opportunities are premised on the belief that they can promote government effectiveness and enhance the perception that government actions are legitimate. While the techniques used, the motives for providing access, and the genuineness of those opportunities differ across governments (Arnstein 1969), engagement offers opportunities for citizens and stakeholders to provide input into public decisions. Though occasionally resisted by policy elites and mitigated by the complexity of policy problems, the twentieth century saw a general movement toward greater opportunities for the participation of ordinary citizens in governance, supported through legislation establishing the right of the public to participate in policymaking. Open-meeting laws, led especially by legislation in the United States like the 1976 Government in the Sunshine Act (Stephenson 1976), ensured that the public and the press could at least access government decision-making processes (Piotrowski and Borry 2010). Canadian jurisprudence and legislation has attempted to offset the legal, political, and administrative power of Canadian governments with legal remedies that serve to make such processes more open, accountable, and fair (Woodford and Preston 2013).

Now often falling under the heading of "citizen and stakeholder engagement," opportunities for the public to participate in its governance cover a broad range of government-initiated efforts to communicate with those outside of government and bring outsiders into policymaking processes. Public participation opportunities involve forums where public policy issues are discussed, interests are represented, and recommendations or preliminary non-binding decisions are made. Citizens have the opportunity to provide input into issues of public policy through testimony, written submissions, or simply attending public meetings to show support for an interest. Public participation in such forums can be undertaken either in person, through membership in a group or organization, or through indirect means (e.g., protest rallies or letters to newspaper editors). Public participation activities can also be defined to include voting, joining political organizations, and working on behalf of candidates and issues, contacting elected officials, and forming groups to work on issues (Verba and Nie 1987).

Civil society organizations, academics, and some governments have experimented with novel public participation techniques, such as deliberative democracy (Dryzek 2000; Elster 1998), deliberative polling (Fishkin and Luskin 2005), participatory budgeting (Gilman 2016; Miori and Russo 2011), citizen assemblies (Landemore 2015; Warren and Pearse 2008), consensus conferences (Andersen and Jæger 1999), citizen juries (Armour 1995), collaborative policymaking (Innes and Booher 2003; Noveck 2009), and crowdsourced policymaking (Dutil 2015; Prpić, Taeihagh, and Melton 2015). The interactive nature of Web 2.0 technologies expands the possibilities of how citizens and stakeholders can be involved in policymaking. These are discussed in the following section.

DIGITIZATION

Promises & Perils

The promise of digital technology for open government emerges from the collapse of the traditional arguments against the participation of citizens: that the distance between the people and their governance bodies was too far and that the number of citizens was too large for everyone to be involved in policymaking. With that promise, however, comes the peril of a cacophony of voices in policy deliberations that are impossible to control and difficult to make sense of.

Prior to the ubiquity of digital technologies, the choke point for citizens' knowledge about, and involvement in, government actions and decisions, and the ability of citizens to independently create governance solutions centred on the limits of communication among large numbers of people over long distance. These limits applied to communication from governments to citizens, from citizens to their governments, and between and among citizens. With politicians representing large constituencies, and with central legislatures often being a long distance away, communication from elected representatives to citizens was often limited to official notices, occasional letters and speeches, news reports, and rare face-to-face conversations. Government communication to the citizenry was subject to similar limitations. The ability of citizens to be involved in their government was even more limited, with few opportunities to communicate directly with their representative or government administrators or to speak at a public forum. Those creating new governance solutions faced a principal challenge of finding and communicating with others interested in joining together to solve a public problem, what Coase (1937) identified as the problem of transaction costs.

The digital era follows from the previous half century development of digital electronic computers first deployed as room-sized corporate installations during the Second World War, but rapidly moving toward progressively smaller, cheaper, and less specialized personal devices. Along with the spread of personal computers as an increasingly standard household information management appliance, the modern internet further changed personal computers into networked communication devices. Starting around 1990, governments also began to connect to the internet, taking advantage of the emergence of the World Wide Web in 1991 and graphical user interface web browsers in 1993, aiming to ease communication between governments and citizens. The expansion of internet communications also raised the possibility of internet-based voting as a way to make voting easier, enhancing opportunities for democratic participation, making referenda less costly, and potentially transferring power away from representative legislatures and toward a digital ecclesia (Alvarez and Nagler 2000; Budge 1996; see chapter 4).

The impact of digital technology on open government is simultaneously profound and uncertain. The initial Bill Clinton-era enthusiasm for using the internet to increase government transparency and enhanced opportunities for citizen participation in government was significantly disrupted by the "dot-com bubble" – a period of investor speculation between 1995 to 2002 that saw the rapid growth in internet-based firms followed by their spectacular decline (Howcroft 2001) – and reductions in government transparency and openness generally in reaction to the September 11, 2001, attack on the United States (Hendler 2009).

Renewed enthusiasm for the social power of the internet began to emerge around 2004 with an approach labelled "Web 2.0." This term connotes a second-generation internet built on the technologies of the first generation web, but focused on user control, simple user-publishing of web content, social media communication, user participation, and peer-to-peer collaboration (O'Reilly 2005; see introduction). This change in the underlying communication framework occurred alongside and facilitated a number of other social and political shifts, from changing what government can expect from citizens in competing for user attention to what citizens and stakeholders expect when engaging with policy discussions, the control of policymaking discourse, and where governance itself is exercised (Longo 2017).

Digital technology overcomes differences in the physical location of participants (Cairncross 2001), dispensing with one of the central reasons for representative government and making a digital recreation of the Athenian ecclesia at least technologically possible (Mpoitsis and Koutsoupias 2013). With the emergence of multidirectional Web 2.0 technology, many-to-many communication among citizens, stakeholders, and governments is facilitated, with each having approximately equitable access to communication platforms (O'Reilly 2005). Public participation in policymaking forums – previously limited to attendance in person, membership in a group or organization, or through indirect means (e.g., protest rallies or letters to newspaper editors) – can now happen through online platforms and social media (Small 2012).

Preceding Web 2.0, the free and open source software (FOSS) movement[5] also influenced digital era open government (Lathrop and Ruma 2010). Open source governance allows citizens direct access to public sector data and the legislative process, with the objective of engaging citizens in the identification of public problems and the crafting of policy solutions. The applicability of FOSS for the open government movement drew on early successes such as Apache, Linux, and Mozilla (Benkler 2002) and became a central pillar of the idea of collaboration in open government (Noveck 2012).

Paradoxically, the openness opportunities offered by the new facility of digital technology have led in some settings to a retrenchment in open government (Longo 2017). The corollary of the benefit of many voices in a discussion is the difficulty of controlling and understanding the conversation, of maintaining focus, extracting value from the variety of contributions, and of evaluating expertise and identifying genuine insight. Some critics of virtual participatory democracy argue that

---

5 The essential feature of FOSS is that anyone can have free access to, and the freedom to modify, the open source code for their own benefit and the benefit of others. FOSS enables and encourages technically skilled users to make changes and improvements to the source code, subject to the distribution licence, and then share these with the user community (Crowston and Howison 2005).

the lack of citizen accountability is increased as participation effort is decreased and that virtual deliberation is more susceptible to manipulation than traditional forms (Parkinson 2003). Using communications technology to recreate a participatory Athenian-style direct democracy faces geographic and population challenges when scaling between ancient city-states and modern nation-states, as well as accounting for the fundamental differences between face-to-face and online deliberation (Baek, Wojcieszak, and Delli Carpini 2011; Grönlund, Strandberg, and Himmelroos 2009).

Practice

The modern open government movement is inextricably linked to the Barack Obama administration in the United States and was largely built on the perceived secrecy of the outgoing George W. Bush administration (Skocpol and Jacobs 2012) and the emergence of new digital technologies. In addition to railing against military misadventure and economic collapse, Obama's campaign highlighted the lack of transparency and closed nature of government over the previous eight years (Burke 2009; Kirk and Schill 2011), promising to "restore the American people's trust in their government by making government more open and transparent" (Obama 2007, np). As much as the renewal and resurgence of FoI legislation in the 1970s in the United States was a reaction to the political scandal of Watergate (Michener 2011) (and served to feed an appetite for similar legislation in Canada; Bennett 1991), the modern open government movement in the United States was energized by the post-9/11 experience under Bush (Birchall 2011) and represented a pendulum swing in American politics toward a demand for greater transparency. At the same time, technology-based advocacy emanating from Silicon Valley culminated in a set of principles for open government data[6] (Open Government Data Working Group

6 Open government data involves government attitudes and policies that promote open government through the proactive publishing of public sector information – freely available to anyone – and encourage its use, reuse, and redistribution (Shadbolt et al. 2012). While government motives for providing open data vary (Longo 2011), its provision can increase transparency, inform citizen participation, and be used by citizens to collaborate with their government. However, a government can be open and not provide open data; alternatively, a government open data portal does not guarantee government openness (Yu and Robinson 2011).

2007) that influenced the translation of the candidate's campaign poetry into governing prose.

On Obama's first full day in office, the new president's Memorandum on Transparency and Open Government (White House 2009), leading directly to the Open Government Directive (Orszag 2009), pledged unprecedented and sustained openness and accountability, and directed the administration "to incorporate the values of transparency, participation, and collaboration into the ongoing work of their agency." This approach to open government was much more ambitious and far reaching than previous versions of the right to know and participate (Dumas et al. 2015).

While the reality of governing did occasionally lead to a lack of transparency on internal government communications and the placing of limits on information disclosure when it potentially harmed operational or policy objectives (Becker 2012; Christy 2013; Coglianese 2009), the rhetoric of open government in the digital era spread rapidly during Obama's tenure. In September 2010, the president addressed the UN General Assembly urging member states "to make government more open and accountable ... to promote transparency; to fight corruption; to energize civic engagement; and to leverage new technologies so that we strengthen the foundation of freedom in our own countries, while living up to ideals that can light the world" (Obama 2010). One year later, the multilateral Open Government Declaration was signed by eight countries, creating the Open Government Partnership (OGP). The goal of the OGP is "to secure concrete commitments from governments to promote transparency, empower citizens, fight corruption, and harness new technologies to strengthen governance" (OGP 2018, np). Membership requires the meeting of a minimum set of government accountability and transparency standards and taking measures to promote citizen participation and engagement (OGP 2017).

Canada joined the OGP soon after its establishment, after a period of internal deliberation about the shape and meaning of open government (Standing Committee on Access to Information, Privacy, and Ethics 2011). In May 2010, the federal minister of industry launched an online consultation on innovations for the emerging digital economy, dubbed Digital Canada 150 (DC150). Out of this consultation, during which an innovative collaborative platform was deployed, the most active discussion centred on a proposal to create an Open Access to Canada's Public Sector Information and Data portal at data.gc.ca, something that the federal government did do in March 2011. This was expanded into the open government portal for the Government of Canada in November 2014, which provides access to open data and information and highlights opportunities for citizens and stakeholders to participate in government consultation exercises. The portal features thematic open data communities, capacity for consultation and engagement, tools to support national open government partners, and single-window access to information provided by federal departments and agencies.

As part of its OGP commitments, the government conducted a public engagement process between December 2011 and March 2012. Led by the president of the Treasury Board, online consultations were conducted using the data.gc.ca website, through the first federal government "Twitter Town Hall" and a live "Google Hangout" in 2013 (Longo 2017). The federal government also issued a Directive on Open Government in 2014, requiring departments and agencies to develop and publish open government plans over five years. Yet after being a world leader in e-government in the 1990s in providing government information and services online (Kumar et al. 2007), Canada's attempts to adapt in the shadow of the rapidly moving Obama administration left it with a mixed record on open government (Clarke 2019). As the Stephen Harper government acquired a growing reputation for secrecy (Jaeger, Paquette, and Simmons 2010), a general malaise in the open government community began to set in around 2015 in Canada and elsewhere (Aitken 2017). While the election of the Justin Trudeau government in 2015 signalled a strong rhetorical change at the federal level, the new government's first major citizen participation initiative, on the issue of electoral reform, failed to achieve a consensus satisfactory to the prime minister, leading to the abandoning of the issue as a campaign pledge (Longo 2017).

Among the provinces and territories, nine (as of this writing) have created open data portals (Alberta, British Columbia, Newfoundland & Labrador, Northwest Territories, Nova Scotia, Ontario, Prince Edward Island, Quebec, and Yukon). Some have supplemental efforts that have expanded on their open data offerings to an explicit open government approach (e.g., Alberta, British Columbia, Newfoundland, Northwest Territories, and Ontario), though largely extending only to standard public consultation mechanisms and the opportunity to provide feedback through closed writing channels like mail and email. While national and provincial level government is where attention is usually focused, Roy (2014) notes that equally important innovations in public sector open data initiatives can be found at the local government level. His survey found more than thirty Canadian municipalities had undertaken open data strategies. More than five years later (as of this writing), the list on the federal government's open government portal shows sixty-two local governments providing open data through their web portals. What this cursory scan points to is the limited literature in assessing subnational and local government open data and open government initiatives in Canada and the need for research in this area (see, e.g., Gill and Corbett 2017).

In the previous ten years of open government, perhaps the least referenced of the troika of transparency, participation, and collaboration is the last of these, largely because true collaboration poses the greatest risk to how governing has come to be conceptualized. In the definition of open government given above, the distinction between government and governance was only alluded to. Yet the distinction is important, and more so in the digital era. Networked open governance today involves non-state stakeholders leading community-driven initiatives making meaningful contributions across diverse policy sectors (Park, Longo, and Johnston 2020). This builds on the emergence in recent decades of the idea of "governance without government" (Rhodes 1997), wherein the traditional state and institutional form of government has been undermined by the increased power of networks, partnerships, markets, and global influences (Peters and Pierre 1998). In this new world, governance can be exercised together by governments and non-state actors through collaborative arrangements, or independently by non-state actors without the involvement of governments and possibly despite their wishes (Bevir 2010). Thus the very nature of governance itself is being changed by this new technology, as functions that were once reserved exclusively in the domain of governments can now be vested in networks joined together by technology (Benkler 2006; Shirky 2008).

In the digital era, governance is dispersed, network-based, and increasingly detached from legal authority. We see this with the emergence of services such as Uber and Airbnb, which are challenging traditional approaches to local governance and presupposing a replacement based on in-app governance (Longo and Pohler 2016). Interactions among citizens, between citizens and governing institutions, and the emergence of new governance configurations continue to be shaped by rapidly changing technology and evolving norms (Chun et al. 2010; Farrell 2012). This new environment has important implications for government efforts to engage citizens and stakeholders using internet channels, as loosely formed groups are able to use those same channels to shape governance (DiMaggio et al. 2001). However, if open governance comes to be defined as the creation of governance arrangements by citizens and groups outside of government, made more plausible at large scale by digital technology where the communication and transaction costs incurred in crafting the agreements necessary to forge significant governance arrangements have been significantly lowered (Benkler 2002), this does not absolve governments of their responsibilities to protect the public interest. Just because an Uber or an Airbnb *can* create a governance solution using the tools of the platform economy does not mean that it will represent *good* governance (Fukuyama 2013; Rothstein and Teorell 2008). The creation of "private" governance solutions has social implications for those bound by that governance, those excluded from it, and those who choose not to participate in it.

POTENTIALS

This chapter asks whether the digital era fundamentally changes the limits of distance and numbers that gave rise to representative democracy and whether that affects the rights and responsibilities of citizens in a democracy. Even if we do not recreate the ecclesia, the digital era reframes our earlier questions: How open should government be? How much should citizens know about the actions and operations of their governments? In what ways should citizens be involved in government decisions? And how much control, and under what constraints, should citizens and other private actors have to create governance solutions either with government, or on their own? These questions about the rights and responsibilities of citizens in a democracy have become much more complex in the digital era.

The title of this chapter – "was open government just a moment?" – is in reference to a provocative article in 1997 by the American academic Robert Kaplan. In asking whether Western liberal democracy had the sustainability that its late-century triumph indicated, Kaplan appeared to predict the rise of Donald Trump and the brand of authoritarianism his election appeared to support, not just in the United States but elsewhere. In the first year of the Trump administration, the enthusiasm for open government as articulated in Obama's 2008 Open Government Directive seemed to have largely dissipated (Fenster 2017). While the Obama-era "We the People" petition site (Dumas et al. 2015) continues to exist and gather signatures, the Trump administration no longer responds to petitions that meet a threshold number of signatures, and the administration has also reversed an Obama-era policy of publishing White House visitor logs, citing security concerns and despite a legal action calling for their reinstatement.

Open government, under a range of names, has a long history. Its most recent iteration appears to have been largely driven by the combination of two factors: the political reaction to perceived government secrecy and a lack of transparency during the 2001–2009 Bush administration and the coincidental emergence of Web 2.0 technologies as a mechanism for sharing data and information and for facilitating platforms that allow internet-based users to participate easily and collaborate on outputs of shared value.

What is the status of those factors today, and what do they predict for the future of open government? Today the value of social media for bringing people together is strained to say the least (Anderson et al. 2014; Bennett 2012; Coe, Kenski, and Rains 2014). Indeed, whether the "person" on the other end of a Twitter conversation might be a bot is not a problem that faced the Athenian ecclesia (Ferrara et al. 2016). As we learn the extent to which a foreign power was able to disrupt the 2016 US presidential election using social media channels, the question for future years is whether the habit of open government has been entrenched deeply enough in the persona of Western liberal democracy as to make it resilient in the face of these short-term setbacks or whether representative governments will reflexively close back up in the name of predictability, control, order, and security.

REFERENCES

Aitken, Kent. 2017. "Progress on Open Government Is Not Guaranteed." *Policy Options*, October. http://policyoptions.irpp.org/magazines/october-2017/progress-on-open-government-is-not-guaranteed/.

Alvarez, R. Michael, and Jonathan Nagler. 2000. "The Likely Consequences of Internet Voting for Political Representation." *Loyola Law Review* 34: 1115–53.

Andersen, Ida-Elisabeth, and Birgit Jæger. 1999. "Scenario Workshops and Consensus Conferences: Towards More Democratic Decision-Making." *Science & Public Policy* 26 (5): 331–40. https://doi.org/10.3152/147154399781782301.

Anderson, Ashley A., Dominique Brossard, Dietram A. Scheufele, Michael A. Xenos, and Peter Ladwig. 2014. "The 'Nasty Effect:' Online Incivility and Risk Perceptions of Emerging Technologies." *Journal of Computer-Mediated Communication* 19 (3): 373–87. https://doi.org/10.1111/jcc4.12009.

Armour, Audrey. 1995. "The Citizens' Jury Model of Public Participation: A Critical Evaluation." In *Fairness and Competence in Citizen Participation*, ed. O. Renn, T. Webler, and P. Wiedemann, 175–85. Dordrecht: Springer.

Arnstein, Sherry R. 1969. "A Ladder of Citizen Participation." *Journal of the American Institute of Planners* 35 (4): 216–24. https://doi.org/10.1080/01944366908977225.

Baek, Young Min, Magdalena Wojcieszak, and Michael X. Delli Carpini. 2011. "Online versus Face-to-Face Deliberation: Who? Why? What? With What Effects?" *New Media & Society* 14 (3): 363–83. https://doi.org/10.1177/1461444811413191.

Barber, Benjamin R. 1998. "Three Scenarios for the Future of Technology and Strong Democracy." *Political Science Quarterly* 113 (4): 573–89. https://doi.org/10.2307/2658245.

Barber, Katherine, ed. 2005. "Citizen." *The Canadian Oxford Dictionary*, 2nd edition. Toronto: Oxford University Press.

Becker, Michael D. 2012. "Piercing Glomar: Using the Freedom of Information Act and the Official Acknowledgment Doctrine to Keep Government Secrecy in Check." *Administrative Law Review* 64 (3): 673–700. https://doi.org/10.2307/23317563.

Benkler, Yochai. 2002. "Coase's Penguin, or, Linux and 'The Nature of the Firm.'" *The Yale Law Journal* 112 (3): 369–446. https://doi.org/10.2307/1562247.

Benkler, Yochai. 2006. *The Wealth of Networks: How Social Production Transforms Markets and Freedom.* New Haven: Yale University Press.

Bennett, Colin J. 1991. "How States Utilize Foreign Evidence." *Journal of Public Policy* 11 (1): 31–54. https://doi.org/10.1017/S0143814X0000492X.

Bennett, W. Lance. 2012. "The Personalization of Politics: Political Identity, Social Media, and Changing Patterns of Participation." *The Annals of the American Academy of Political and Social Science* 644 (1): 20–39. https://doi.org/10.1177/0002716212451428.

Bevir, Mark. 2010. *Democratic Governance.* Princeton: Princeton University Press.

Birchall, Clare. 2011. "'There's Been Too Much Secrecy in This City': The False Choice between Secrecy and Transparency in US Politics." *Cultural Politics* 7 (1): 133–56. https://doi.org/10.2752/175174311X12861940861905.

Budge, Ian. 1996. *The New Challenge of Direct Democracy.* Cambridge, MA: Polity Press.

Burke, John P. 2009. "The Contemporary Presidency: The Obama Presidential Transition: An Early Assessment." *Presidential Studies Quarterly* 39 (3): 574–604. https://doi.org/10.1111/j.1741-5705.2009.03691.x.

Cairncross, Frances. 2001. *The Death of Distance: How the Communications Revolution Is Changing Our Lives.* Boston: Harvard Business School Press.

Canada. 1977. "Legislation on Public Access to Government Documents (Green Paper)." Ottawa: Government of Canada, Department of the Secretary of State.

Christy, A. 2013. "The ACLU's Hollow FOIA Victory over Drone Strikes." *George Mason Law Review* 21(1): 1–16.

Chun, Soon, Stuart Shulman, Rodrigo Sandoval, and Eduard Hovy. 2010. "Government 2.0: Making Connections between Citizens, Data, and Government." *Information Polity* 15 (1–2): 1–9. https://doi.org/10.3233/IP-2010-0205.

Clarke, Amanda. 2019. *Opening the Government of Canada: The Federal Bureaucracy in the Digital Age.* Vancouver: UBC Press.

Clarke, Amanda, and Mary Francoli. 2014. "What's in a Name? A Comparison of 'Open Government' Definitions across Seven Open Government Partnership Members." *JeDEM – eJournal of eDemocracy and Open Government* 6 (3): 248–66. https://doi.org/10.29379/jedem.v6i3.227.

Coase, Ronald H. 1937. "The Nature of the Firm." *Economica* 4 (16): 386–405. https://doi.org/10.1111/j.1468-0335.1937.tb00002.x.

Coe, Kevin, Kate Kenski, and Stephen A. Rains. 2014. "Online and Uncivil? Patterns and Determinants of Incivility in Newspaper Website Comments." *The Journal of Communication* 64 (4): 658–79. https://doi.org/10.1111/jcom.12104.

Coglianese, Cary. 2009. "The Transparency President? The Obama Administration and Open Government." *Governance* 22 (4): 529–44. https://doi.org/10.1111/j.1468-0491.2009.01451.x.

Cook, Terrence E., and Patrick M. Morgan. 1971. *Participatory Democracy.* New York: Canfield Press.

Crowston, Kevin, and James Howison. 2005. "The Social Structure of Free and Open Source Software Development." *First Monday* 10 (2). https://doi.org/10.5210/fm.v10i2.1207.

DiMaggio, Paul, Eszter Hargittai, W. Russell Neuman, and John P. Robinson. 2001. "Social Implications of the Internet." *Annual Review of Sociology* 27 (1): 307–36. https://doi.org/10.1146/annurev.soc.27.1.307.

Dryzek, John S. 2000. *Deliberative Democracy and Beyond: Liberals, Critics, Contestations.* Oxford, UK: Oxford University Press.

Dumas, Catherine L., Daniel LaManna, Teresa M. Harrison, S.S. Ravi, Christopher Kotfila, Norman Gervais, Loni Hagen, and Feng Chen. 2015. "Examining Political Mobilization of Online Communities through E-Petitioning Behavior in We the People." *Big Data & Society* 2 (2): 1–20. https://doi.org/10.1177/2053951715598170.

Dutil, Patrice. 2015. "Crowdsourcing as a New Instrument in the Government's Arsenal: Explorations and Considerations." *Canadian Public Administration/Administration Publique du Canada* 58 (3): 363–83. https://doi.org/10.1111/capa.12134.

Elster, Jon. 1998. *Deliberative Democracy.* Cambridge, UK: Cambridge University Press.

Farrell, Henry. 2012. "The Consequences of the Internet for Politics." *Annual Review of Political Science,* 15: 35–52. https://doi.org/10.1146/annurev-polisci-030810-110815.

Fenster, Mark. 2017. "Transparency in Trump's America: Commentary." *Governance* 30 (2): 173–5. https://doi.org/10.1111/gove.12272.

Ferrara, Emilio, Onur Varol, Clayton Davis, Filippo Menczer, and Alessandro Flammini. 2016. "The Rise of Social Bots." *Communications of the ACM* 59 (7): 96–104. https://doi.org/10.1145/2818717.

Fishkin, James S., and Robert C. Luskin. 2005. "Experimenting with a Democratic Ideal: Deliberative Polling and Public Opinion." *Acta Politica* 40 (3): 284–98. https://doi.org/10.1057/palgrave.ap.5500121.

Foerstel, Herbert N. 1999. *Freedom of Information and the Right to Know: The Origins and Applications of the Freedom of Information Act.* Santa Barbara, CA: Greenwood Publishing Group.

Fukuyama, Francis. 2006. *The End of History and the Last Man.* New York: Simon & Schuster.

Fukuyama, Francis. 2013. "What Is Governance?" *Governance* 26 (3): 347–68. https://doi.org/10.1111/gove.12035.

Fung, Archon. 2006. "Varieties of Participation in Complex Governance." *Public Administration Review* 66 (s1): 66–75. https://doi.org/10.1111/j.1540-6210.2006.00667.x.

Gill, Mark, and Jon Corbett. 2017. "Downscaling: Understanding the Influence of Open Data Initiatives in Smaller and Mid-Sized Cities in British Columbia, Canada." *The Canadian Geographer/Le Géographe Canadien* 61 (3): 346–59. https://doi.org/10.1111/cag.12372.

Gilman, Hollie Russon. 2016. *Participatory Budgeting and Civic Tech: The Revival of Citizen Engagement.* Washington, DC: Georgetown University Press.

Grönlund, Kimmo, Kim Strandberg, and Staffan Himmelroos. 2009. "The Challenge of Deliberative Democracy Online – A Comparison of Face-to-Face and Virtual Experiments in Citizen Deliberation." *Information Polity* 14 (3): 187–201. https://doi.org/10.3233/IP-2009-0182.

Hendler, Clint. 2009. "What We Didn't Know Has Hurt Us." *Columbia Journalism Review* 47 (5): 28–33.

Howcroft, Debra. 2001. "After the Goldrush: Deconstructing the Myths of the Dot.com Market." *Journal of Information Technology Impact* 16 (4): 195–204. https://doi.org/10.1080/02683960110100418.

Innes, Judith E., and David E. Booher. 2003. "Collaborative Policymaking: Governance through Dialogue." In *Deliberative Policy Analysis: Understanding Governance in the Network Society*, ed. Maarten A. Hajer and Hendrik Wagenaar, 33–59. Cambridge, UK: Cambridge University Press.

Jaeger, Paul T., Scott Paquette, and Shannon N. Simmons. 2010. "Information Policy in National Political Campaigns: A Comparison of the 2008 Campaigns for President of the United States and Prime Minister of Canada." *Journal of Information Technology & Politics* 7 (1): 67–82. https://doi.org/10.1080/19331680903316700.

Kaplan, Robert D. 1997. "Was Democracy Just a Moment?" *Atlantic Monthly*, December. https://www.theatlantic.com/magazine/archive/1997/12/was-democracy-just-a-moment/306022/.

Kirk, Rita, and Dan Schill. 2011. "A Digital Agora: Citizen Participation in the 2008 Presidential Debates." *The American Behavioral Scientist* 55 (3): 325–47. https://doi.org/10.1177/0002764210392167.

Koop, Royce, Heather Bastedo, and Kelly Blidook. 2018. *Representation in Action: Canadian MPs in the Constituencies.* Vancouver: UBC Press.

Kumar, Vinod, Bhasker Mukerji, Irfan Butt, and Ajax Persaud. 2007. "Factors for Successful E-Government Adoption: A Conceptual Framework." *Electronic Journal of E-Government* 5 (1).

Landemore, H. 2015. "Inclusive Constitution-Making: The Icelandic Experiment." *The Journal of Political Philosophy* 23 (2): 166–91. https://doi.org/10.1111/jopp.12032.

Lathrop, Daniel, and Laurel Ruma. 2010. *Open Government: Collaboration, Transparency, and Participation in Practice.* Sebastopol, CA: O'Reilly Media.

Linders, Dennis, and Susan Copeland Wilson. 2011. "What Is Open Government? One Year after the Directive." In *Proceedings of the 12th Annual International Digital Government Research Conference: Digital Government Innovation in Challenging Times*, 262–71. New York: ACM. https://dl.acm.org/citation.cfm?id=2037599.

Longo, Justin. 2011. "#OpenData: Digital-Era Governance Thoroughbred or New Public Management Trojan Horse?" *Public Policy and Governance*

Review 2 (2): 38–51. http://ppgr.files.wordpress.com/2011/05/longo-ostry.pdf.

Longo, Justin. 2017. "The Evolution of Citizen and Stakeholder Engagement in Canada, from Spicer to #Hashtags." *Canadian Public Administration/Administration Publique du Canada* 60 (4): 517–37. https://doi.org/10.1111/capa.12229.

Longo, Justin, and Dionne Pohler. 2016. "Governance in the Digital Era: The Über-Example." Paper presented at the 2016 Public Management Research Association Conference, Aarhus University, Denmark, June 23.

Longo, Justin, Christina Rogawski, and Andrew Young. 2013. "Open Government: What's in a Name." *The GovLab Blog.* The GovLab @ NYU. August 5. http://thegovlab.org/open-government-whats-in-a-name/.

McDermott, Patrice. 2010. "Building Open Government." *Government Information Quarterly* 27 (4): 401–13. https://doi.org/10.1016/j.giq.2010.07.002.

Meijer, Albert J., Deirdre Curtin, and Maarten Hillebrandt. 2012. "Open Government: Connecting Vision and Voice." *International Review of Administrative Sciences* 78 (1): 10–29. https://doi.org/10.1177/0020852311429533.

Mezey, Michael L. 2008. *Representative Democracy: Legislators and Their Constituents.* Lanham, MD: Rowman & Littlefield Publishers.

Michener, Greg. 2011. "FOI Laws around the World." *Journal of Democracy* 22 (2): 145–59. https://doi.org/10.1353/jod.2011.0021.

Miori, Vittorio, and Dario Russo. 2011. "Integrating Online and Traditional Involvement in Participatory Budgeting." *Electronic Journal of e-Government* 9 (1): 41–57.

Mossberger, Karen, Yonghong Wu, and Jared Crawford. 2013. "Connecting Citizens and Local Governments? Social Media and Interactivity in Major US Cities." *Government Information Quarterly* 30 (4): 351–58. https://doi.org/10.1016/j.giq.2013.05.016.

Mpoitsis, Ioannis, and Nikos Koutsoupias. 2013. "E-Ekklesia: The Challenge of Direct Democracy and the Ancient Athenian Model." In *E-Democracy, Security, Privacy, and Trust in a Digital World,* ed. Alexander B. Sideridis, Zoe Kardasiadou, Constantine P. Yialouris, and Vasilios Zorkadis, 52–63. Communications in Computer and Information Science. Berlin: Springer.

Noveck, Beth S. 2009. *Wiki Government: How Technology Can Make Government Better, Democracy Stronger, and Citizens More Powerful.* Washington, DC: Brookings Institution Press.

Noveck, Beth S. 2011. "Defining Open Government." *Cairns Blog* (blog). April 14. http://cairns.typepad.com/blog/2011/04/whats-in-a-name-open-gov-we-gov-gov-20-collaborative-government.html.

Noveck, Beth S. 2012. "Demand a More Open-Source Government." Paper presented at TEDGlobal 2012, Edinburgh, Scotland, June. https://www.ted.com/talks/beth_noveck_demand_a_more_open_source_government.

Obama, Barack. 2007. "Restore Trust in Government and Improve Transparency." http://obama.3cdn.net/5102497e9778a249ee_j5y0mv85p.pdf.

Obama, Barack. 2010. "Remarks by the President to the United Nations General Assembly." Presented at the United Nations General Assembly, New York, September 23. https://obamawhitehouse.archives.gov/the-press-office/2010/09/23/remarks-president-united-nations-general-assembly.

OGP. 2017. "Eligibility Criteria." Open Government Partnership. November 1. https://www.opengovpartnership.org/resources/eligibility-criteria.

OGP. 2018. "About OGP." Open Government Partnership. https://www.opengovpartnership.org/about/about-ogp.

Open Government Data Working Group. 2007. "Eight Principles of Open Government Data." https://opengovdata.org/.

O'Reilly, Tim. 2005. "What Is Web 2.0: Design Patterns and Business Models for the Next Generation of Software." *O'Reilly Publishing* (blog). September 30. http://www.oreilly.com/pub/a/web2/archive/what-is-web-20.html.

Orszag, Peter R. 2009. "Open Government Directive." https://obamawhitehouse.archives.gov/open/documents/open-government-directive.

Ostrom, Elinor. 2015. *Governing the Commons*. Cambridge, UK: Cambridge University Press.

Park, C.H., J. Longo, and E. Johnston. 2020. "Exploring Non-State Stakeholder and Community-led Open Governance beyond the Three Pillars of Open Government." *Public Performance & Management Review* 43 (3): 587–612. https://doi.org/10.1080/15309576.2019.1677253.

Parkinson, John. 2003. "Legitimacy Problems in Deliberative Democracy." *Political Studies* 51 (1): 180–96. https://doi.org/10.1111/1467-9248.00419.

Parks, Wallace. 1957. "Open Government Principle: Applying the Right to Know under the Constitution." *The George Washington Law Review* 26 (1): 1–77.

Peixoto, Tiago. 2013. "Open Government, Feedback Loops, and Semantic Extravaganza." Democracy Spot. June 17. http://democracyspot.net/2013/06/17/open-government-feedback-loops-and-semantic-extravaganza/.

Peters, B. Guy, and John Pierre. 1998. "Governance without Government? Rethinking Public Administration." *Journal of Public Administration Research and Theory* 8 (2): 223–43. https://doi.org/10.1093/oxfordjournals.jpart.a024379.

Piotrowski, Suzanne J., and Erin Borry. 2010. "An Analytic Framework for Open Meetings and Transparency." *Public Administration and Management* 15 (1): 138–76.

Prpić, John, Araz Taeihagh, and James Melton. 2015. "The Fundamentals of Policy Crowdsourcing." *Policy & Internet* 7 (3): 340–61. https://doi.org/10.1002/poi3.102.

Putnam, Robert D., Robert Leonardi, and Raffaella Y. Nanetti. 1994. *Making Democracy Work: Civic Traditions in Modern Italy*. Princeton: Princeton University Press.

Renn, Ortwin, Thomas Webler, Horst Rakel, Peter Dienel, and Branden Johnson. 1993. "Public Participation in Decision Making: A Three-Step Procedure." *Policy Sciences* 26 (3): 189–214. https://doi.org/10.1007/BF00999716.

Rhodes, Peter John. 2004. "General Introduction." In *Athenian Democracy*, ed. Peter John Rhodes, 1–12. New York: Oxford University Press.

Rhodes, R.A.W. 1997. *Understanding Governance: Policy Networks, Governance, Reflexivity and Accountability*. Philadelphia: Open University Press.

Rothstein, Bo, and Jan Teorell. 2008. "What Is Quality of Government? A Theory of Impartial Government Institutions." *Governance* 21 (2): 165–90. https://doi.org/10.1111/j.1468-0491.2008.00391.x.

Roy, Jeffrey. 2014. "Open Data and Open Governance in Canada: A Critical Examination of New Opportunities and Old Tensions." *Future Internet* 6 (3): 414–32. https://doi.org/10.3390/fi6030414.

Scott, Michael. 2010. *From Democrats to Kings: The Downfall of Athens to the Epic Rise of Alexander the Great*. London: Icon Books Ltd.

Shadbolt, Nigel, Kieron O'Hara, Tim Berners-Lee, Nicholas Gibbins, Hugh Glaser, Wendy Hall, and M.C. Schraefel. 2012. "Linked Open Government Data: Lessons from Data.gov.uk." *IEEE Intelligent Systems* 27 (3): 16–24. https://doi.org/10.1109/MIS.2012.23.

Shirky, Clay. 2008. *Here Comes Everybody: The Power of Organizing without Organizations*. New York: Penguin.

Skocpol, Theda, and Lawrence R. Jacobs. 2012. "Accomplished and Embattled: Understanding Obama's Presidency." *Political Science Quarterly* 127 (1): 1–24. https://doi.org/10.1002/j.1538-165X.2012.tb00718.x.

Small, Tamara A. 2012. "E-Government in the Age of Social Media: An Analysis of the Canadian Government's Use of Twitter." *Policy & Internet* 4 (3–4): 91–111. https://doi.org/10.1002/poi3.12.

Standing Committee on Access to Information, Privacy and Ethics. 2011. "Evidence: Hearings on Open Government." Parliament of Canada. February 9. http://www.ourcommons.ca/DocumentViewer/en/40-3/ETHI/meeting-43/evidence.

Stephenson, Susan T. 1976. "Government in the Sunshine Act: Opening Federal Agency Meetings." *American University Law Review* 26: 154–96.

Stubbs, Rhys. 2008. "Freedom of Information and Democracy in Australia and Beyond." *Australian Journal of Political Science* 43 (4): 667–84. https://doi.org/10.1080/10361140802429270.

Verba, Sidney, and Norman H. Nie. 1987. *Participation in America: Political Democracy and Social Equality*. Chicago: University of Chicago Press.

Wald, Dara M., Justin Longo, and A.R. Dobell. 2016. "Design Principles for Engaging and Retaining Virtual Citizen Scientists." *Conservation Biology: The*

Journal of the Society for Conservation Biology 30 (3): 562–70. https://doi.org/10.1111/cobi.12627. PMid:26365126.

Warren, Mark E., and Hilary Pearse. 2008. *Designing Deliberative Democracy: The British Columbia Citizens' Assembly*. Cambridge, UK: Cambridge University Press.

White House. 2009. "Memorandum on Transparency and Open Government." http://edocket.access.gpo.gov/2009/pdf/E9-1777.pdf.

Woodford, M.R., and S. Preston. 2013. "Strengthening Citizen Participation in Public Policy-Making: A Canadian Perspective." *Parliamentary Affairs* 66 (2): 345–63. https://doi.org/10.1093/pa/gsr065.

Yu, Harlan, and David G. Robinson. 2011. "The New Ambiguity of Open Government." *UCLA Law Review Discourse* 59: 178–208.

CHAPTER FOUR

Internet Voting: Strengthening Canadian Democracy or Weakening It?

Nicole Goodman and Chelsea Gabel

INTRODUCTION

Elections and voting are widely regarded as the "lifeblood" of democracy (Franklin 1996, 216). Of all the political institutions in a democracy, elections are seen as the "critical democratic instruments" (Powell 2000, 4) and the "defining institutions of modern democracy" (Katz 1997, 1). In the context of representative democracy, the focus on popular participation in government puts voting at the heart of democracy and identifies it as a key indicator of democratic health (Franklin 2004). Giving citizens an opportunity to choose representatives in competitive elections allows people to have a say in government and policymaking. This process helps to ensure that voter interests are represented in public policies, acts as a measure of legitimacy for the election of governments, and provides a regular opportunity to remove governments, serving as an important check on power (Katz 1997; Powell 2000).

Voting is often regarded as one of the simplest means of participating in a democracy, since it requires less effort than other acts. The simplicity of voting and its importance for democracy are primary reasons why academics and policymakers have called attention to the decline of voter turnout in recent decades. Over the past thirty years, there have been declines in voter turnout at all levels of government in Canada (Blais and Rubenson 2013). More recently, rates of participation in many elections have reached all-time lows. In the 2011 Ontario provincial election, for example, 49 per cent of registered voters cast a ballot (Ibbitson 2011). In addition to lower rates of voter participation, a greater proportion of voters have begun casting a ballot during the advance polls instead of on Election Day – an indication that some voters prefer additional convenience when voting.

These developments have prompted questions about the effectiveness of electoral institutions and stirred debate about the potential of institutional reforms to enhance voter engagement. Such discussions have resulted in electoral system assessments municipally (e.g., the allowance of ranked voting in Ontario municipal elections), provincially (in BC, Ontario, and PEI), and as part of an investigation into electoral reform undertaken by the federal government in 2016. Reforming the voting system is a commonly considered change, given that research has demonstrated the possible positive effects of switching our current system, a single member plurality system, to one based on proportional representation (Blais and Carty 1990). Changes to voting rules, such as compulsory voting and online voting, have also been debated. Notably in recent years, digital technologies such as online voting have been regarded as having the power to change the political environment (Bridgmon and Milewicz 2004) and make the franchise more accessible and convenient, presenting a possible countermeasure to low voter participation and thereby improving democratic health (Solvak and Vassil 2018; Goodman et al. 2010).

This chapter examines the extent to which elections in Canada have adopted voting technologies, with a particular focus on online voting and its effects on politics and democracy. The chapter addresses three questions in the context of voting in Canada:

1. How has online voting been used in elections in Canada?
2. To what extent do the current realities of online voting in Canada live up to the technological promises? And what accounts for those differences?
3. Does online voting have a future in elections in Canada?

Though debates about the answers to these questions are longstanding, recent studies and data allow us to evaluate the potential promise and peril of online voting better than was possible in the past. We argue that online voting has the potential to deliver both positive and negative outcomes for elections in Canada. While the technology has the potential to strengthen electoral institutions by improving voter access and participation, it also poses risks to voting equality and the integrity of elections. The outcomes of digital voting depend in large part on government action (or inaction) in terms of policy development, design of the online voting system and features of the approach (e.g., eliminating paper voting), the degree to which governments and election agencies adhere to best practices, and continued research into and development of digital technologies. While the future of elections in Canada is almost certainly digital, the degree to which technology permeates voting will depend on the policies put in place, system design, and technological developments.

CONTEXT

Voting can be digitized in a number of ways commonly referred to under the general term *electronic voting*, which may or may not involve casting a ballot using an internet connection. The International Institute for Democracy and Electoral Assistance defines electronic voting as "systems where the recording, casting or counting of votes in political elections and referendums involves information and communication technologies" (Wolf et al. 2011, 6). In this chapter, we focus primarily on *internet voting*, defined as the casting and counting of a ballot using an internet connection (Goodman and Stokes 2018; Goodman 2017). Internet voting can involve casting a ballot from a device at a polling location, via a public kiosk, or from a remote location such as home or work (Alvarez and Hall 2003). The final type – *remote internet voting* – is regarded as having the most promise to improve voter engagement, given that it affords the greatest access to electors by allowing them to vote from anywhere, reducing voting costs such as the time it takes to travel to a poll location. However, remote online voting is also associated with the greatest potential peril since election officials have the least control over the approach (Goodman et al. 2010). This tension between access and security in large part characterizes the online voting debate (Hall 2015) and is explored more fully in this chapter.

Despite significant debate over the possibility of electoral reform in Canada, little has changed in that arena. Though political institutions are usually slow to change, some institutions and processes have begun to modernize by utilizing digital technology, such as moving the nomination process for Senate online and the adoption of open government and data by government departments and agencies (see chapters 2 and 3 in this volume). Elections, however, have experienced little digitization, especially at the federal level.

Federally, the modernization of elections via the introduction of technology has occurred only twice. In 1997 Canadian voter registration changed from pre-election enumeration[1] to an electronic National Register of Electors (Black 2000). More recently Elections Canada launched an online voting registration service that allows voters to register to vote online. Voters can also verify their registration status and update the address associated with their registration. Otherwise, federal elections remain a largely manual process that has barely evolved since the nineteenth century (Roussel 2018). Election Day tasks such as the administration of oaths, changes to poll books, voter strike-off at the polls, and ballot casting and counting are done manually using paper (Goodman 2017), raising questions about the responsiveness of electoral institutions in an increasingly digitally connected and busy society. Research has shown that perceived responsiveness of political institutions and actors is correlated with voting behaviour (Blais and Rubenson 2013; Clark and Acock 1989). Therefore, being seen as responsive is desirable to the extent that it can improve electors' outlooks of the political system and enhance their willingness to vote.

At the provincial and territorial level, electoral institutions have also been slow to embrace technology but have done so to a greater degree than their federal counterpart. E-poll books and electronic tabulators, for example, are tools provincial election agencies are increasingly trialling. An e-poll book, otherwise known as an electronic poll book, is a digital tool (either hardware, software, or both) that allows election officials to strike voters off voters' lists in real time (Montjoy 2008; Scytl 2018). It can provide a dashboard of the entire election and allow officials to obtain voter analytics almost instantly. British Columbia trialled e-poll books in the advance polls of the 2017 provincial election; Ontario did so in the 2018 provincial election. Electronic

1 Enumeration refers to the registration of people as eligible voters in an election.

tabulation of paper ballots is also growing in popularity. Elections Ontario trialled electronic tabulators in forty-two of seventy polls in a 2016 Whitby-Oshawa by-election (Weiers 2016) and included a full rollout of the machines in the 2018 provincial election (Yun 2018). Likewise, Elections Alberta deployed tabulators in a December 2017 Calgary-Lougheed provincial by-election (Dippel 2017). Elections PEI also used the voting machines in its 2016 plebiscite on electoral reform and trialled online and telephone voting (Pitt 2016). Finally, the 2019 general election in the Northwest Territories offered online ballots as an option for electors that had applied for an absentee ballot. Despite these efforts to digitize provincial elections, they remain mostly manual events that rely on paper.

The real growth in the adoption of voting technologies is happening at the community level in Canada. In 2003, twelve municipalities in Ontario first trialled online voting, which has now been offered in nearly four hundred municipal elections providing millions of unique online voting opportunities. In the 2018 Ontario municipal elections, for example, 2.74 million voters, approximately 29 per cent of the voting population, had the option to vote by internet (Cardillo et al. 2019). In addition, electronic tabulators and poll books are readily used across municipal elections, often as an accepted component of election procedure. Indigenous communities are also increasingly deploying online voting. More than eighty First Nations in the provinces of Ontario, British Columbia, Quebec, Manitoba, Alberta, Newfoundland, and Nova Scotia have adopted online voting to support local voting processes, often to better reach youth and off-reserve members (Gabel et al. 2016). These experiences and the effects of online voting are explored in further detail below.

DIGITIZATION

Promises & Perils

When online voting was first trialled in the early 2000s, scholars and practitioners had high hopes it could be a silver bullet solution to enhance turnout, strengthen the representativeness of elections, improve vote tabulation, and prevent electoral fraud (Norris 2001, 2004; Solvak and Vassil 2017). The best-case scenario of digital voting was to counter declining rates of turnout through improved voter access and convenience to the ballot box. In particular, voting remotely online promised to make voting easier for groups that often face additional barriers to voting, such as citizens living abroad, immobile electors, young people, busy electors, and persons with disabilities (Goodman et al. 2010; Hall 2015). With sip and puff applicators,[2] for example, some persons with disabilities could vote unassisted and cast a secret ballot for the first time. Enhanced efficiency for election administrators was another identified benefit. Online voting could improve the speed of ballot tabulation, reduce counting errors, and eliminate spoiled ballots, improving accuracy and efficiency. Furthermore, the modernization of electoral institutions was seen as a way of keeping pace with societal change. In interviews[3] many federal and provincial election officials in Canada recount that if you had asked them in 2000 what elections would look like in 2018, they would have said everyone would be voting online (Anonymous Interview 2016).

As international pilot projects[4] took place and governments began to carry out research and engage with computer scientists, however, uncertainty about online voting grew. Early international trials revealed mixed effects on voter turnout (Solvak and Vassil 2018) and high financial costs, leading Canadian authorities to conclude that the benefits of modernizing elections were modest at best (Elections BC 2014). Some Canadian election officials argue that the hesitation to digitize elections is not necessarily a sign that government is behind the times but rather stems from concerns about securing the anonymity of the voter (Anonymous Interview 2016). Electoral integrity has long been a

2 There are various assistive devices that can be used to electronically improve access for voters with disabilities. A sip and puff device is ideal for those who already use one, facilitating the casting of a ballot by audio session.

3 As part of another project examining the feasibility of online voting in federal elections in Canada, one of the authors carried out semi-structured interviews and consultations with thirty-two officials with expertise in voting technologies between October and December 2016. Interviewees included a mix of Canadian (sixteen) and international officials (sixteen) from academia, law, government, and the private sector and were asked a variety of questions probing legal, operational, and technical aspects of online voting.

4 Early pilots took place in the United States' primaries (2000), referendums in Geneva, Switzerland (2001), and in local elections in the United Kingdom (2002), Canada (2003), and Estonia (2005) (Goodman et al. 2010).

core principle of elections and possible issues such as family members voting together, coercion, intercepted votes, and vote-buying could compromise that (Goodman and Smith 2017). The worst-case scenario envisioned by officials and scholars working on issues of electronic or online voting is a tampered election or outcome, wherein electoral legitimacy is called into question due to interference such as hacking, viruses, or denial of service attacks.[5] Other identified perils of online voting implementation include the erosion of the social ritual of voting (Goodman et al. 2010) and issues that may occur as a consequence of digital divides. These include lack of access to the internet or a poor quality connection (Alvarez and Hall 2003), as well as voters' insufficient knowledge of, or familiarity with, computers and the internet (Bélanger and Carter 2010). All of these divides can be exacerbated on the basis of socio-economic status, posing additional concerns.

In reality, neither the best nor worst-case scenarios have materialized. In a Canadian context, online voting has not been tested sufficiently at higher levels of government to draw firm conclusions about its potential. In local elections, online voting has shown considerable promise to improve participation, albeit not to the extent of a silver bullet. While there have been some technical issues and lessons learned about best practices, to date no doomsday situations have been realized.

Practice

Federal, Provincial and Territorial: Primarily, federal, provincial, and territorial election agencies have not pursued online voting because of concerns relating to security and electoral integrity. In 2012, for example, Elections BC assembled an Independent Panel on Internet Voting to examine the adoption of the practice in local or provincial elections. The final report, released in 2014, recommended not proceeding with online voting, citing security of voters' devices and reduced transparency and auditability as two of the most significant risks (Elections BC 2014). Similarly, in its examination of online voting the federal 2016 Special Committee on Electoral Reform concluded that "the secrecy and integrity of an online ballot cannot be guaranteed to a sufficient

5 A denial of service attack "occurs when a server is flooded with connection requests from numerous computers or devices" (Goodman 2017).

degree to warrant widespread implementation in federal elections" and recommended against proceeding with the technology at this time (ERRE 2016, 115–16). Though worries about security and possible threats to electoral outcomes have been paramount, cost, voter authentication, ballot secrecy, and a belief that online voting would not improve voter turnout have also discouraged governments from moving forward with online voting.

While some agencies have conducted research and published reports on the topic (e.g., Elections Canada, Elections BC, Elections PEI, and Elections Ontario), as noted above, Elections PEI and Elections NWT are the only agencies to have trialled online voting. In PEI's 2016 plebiscite on electoral reform, electors could cast ballots by paper, telephone, or internet. Online and telephone voting were open from October 29 at 12:00 p.m. to November 7 at 7:00 p.m. and were well received by voters. Positive observations included the diversity of voting opportunities, possible increased voter participation,[6] and quicker election reporting (Anonymous Interview 2016). Officials also commented that online voting was by far the fastest method, averaging a time of two minutes and forty-nine seconds to successfully cast a ballot and lowering voting costs such as time and travel.

At the same time, electoral administrators in PEI identified voters' list inaccuracies and internet connectivity as key barriers to online voting use. Concerns were also raised regarding the security of the authentication process. To vote, electors were required to enter a unique PIN located on their Voter Information Card and their birthdate. Officials explained that this approach was used to ensure voting was easy. For a binding election, however, additional authentication measures would have to be used since spouses or relatives may have access to mail and personal information such as birthdates. Given security concerns and the need for improved authentication, Elections PEI is sceptical of using online voting in the next decade. In the meantime, anticipated changes include the inclusion of live voters' lists that allow for improved mobilization of voters by candidates and eliminate the need for scrutineers (Anonymous Interview 2016).

6 Election officials noted that this observation was anecdotal, based on the turnout of earlier plebiscites.

Elections NWT's use of online voting in the 2019 general election represented the first time a province or territory offered online voting in a binding election in Canada. The agency limited use to persons who had applied for an absentee ballot, which needed to be requested by September 21 in advance of the October 1 Election Day (Bird 2019).

Overall, there has not been much practical evaluation of online voting by federal and provincial and territorial governments in Canada, although extensive research has been carried out by some agencies. Such research is a positive step; however, a key failure of the approach is that officials assess online voting at one point in time and then move on to other projects. As the Canadian polity digitizes, and the lives of electors increasingly move online, the expectation for online services will grow. Research and pilots of online voting have demonstrated that system development takes time to test, refine, and apply to the specific jurisdictional context (Goodman 2017). By not commencing trial programs, election agencies in Canada are missing a decisive opportunity to develop and evaluate digital voting so that it may be used in elections one day. While online voting is presently only used for national votes in Estonia, other countries such as Switzerland are amenable to using it provided the technology meets certain technical requirements outlined by the Swiss Federal Chancellery.

Municipal: The bulk of online voting use has taken place in municipalities. Indeed, municipalities that are modernizing voting are often also digitizing other aspects of elections, such as using electronic tabulators in place of manual counting systems and digital lists or e-poll books instead of paper strike-off lists. Primarily, the adoption of digital voting at the local level has been based on desired improvements in voter access and turnout. In the late 1990s, many municipalities introduced mail voting to better engage electors, particularly seasonal residents (AMO Background Report 2005). Not seeing desired results, however, twelve cities and towns in Ontario turned to telephone and internet ballots in 2003. This number grew to 20 communities in 2006, 44 in 2010, 97 in 2014, and 177 municipalities in 2018 (Cardillo et al. 2019).

Local approaches to online voting in Canada have resembled a patchwork of models (Goodman and Pammett 2014). On one hand, this has allowed for the evaluation of multiple digital voting approaches. On the other, it has meant a lack of consistency in voting procedures and options across communities. For example, some municipalities offer a combination of online and paper ballots, while others opt for a mixture of telephone, online, and paper voting. As a third option, some localities have eliminated paper voting and offer fully electronic elections. In Ontario, 59 municipalities ran electronic elections in 2014 and 131 did so in 2018 (Cardillo et al. 2019; Goodman et al. 2018).[7]

Generally, two approaches have characterized online voting implementation in municipal elections in the first decade of deployment. These have involved policy learning, whereby smaller communities have mimicked the approach taken by the towns that used online voting for the first time in 2003, while larger places have mirrored the model used by Markham, Ontario, the first larger municipality to adopt online voting (Goodman and Smith 2016; Goodman and Spicer 2019). The approach taken by larger municipalities with populations greater than one hundred thousand persons has entailed maintaining paper voting and adopting internet ballots as a complementary voting method in advance polls. Larger places have also typically required a two-step process whereby electors are required to register online before gaining access to an online ballot. By contrast, the approach taken in communities with populations fewer than twenty-five thousand has been to offer internet voting alongside telephone ballots and to make these voting options available for the full election. Telephone voting is usually provided by technology vendors at no additional cost and is used to improve access for rural voters and older residents who may be more familiar with a telephone. Smaller municipalities have also been more likely to eliminate paper voting, often due to budget constraints. Finally, in terms of the online voting process smaller communities have tended to adopt a one-step approach where electors can vote online at any time by providing a unique PIN located on their Voter Information Card and a credential (typically their birthdate) (Goodman and Smith 2016; Goodman and Spicer 2019).

At the same time, a decade of positive effects and growing comfort with online voting is changing the landscape of approaches. Larger

7 When municipalities eliminate paper voting, a majority choose to offer both internet and telephone voting. In 2014, the municipality of Leamington in Ontario was the first community to run a binding municipal election offering only online ballots.

municipalities are beginning to adopt online ballots for the full election, introducing one-step voting, and, in some cases, eliminating paper voting. For example, the City of Greater Sudbury, with a population of 160,000, ran an all-online election in 2018.

Online voting is increasingly seen as a municipal success story. Although telephone voting is regularly offered, its uptake is typically the lowest of available voting methods, whereas online voting is often the most popular.[8] A majority of online voters (95 per cent) report being satisfied with the voting experience, commenting that it was "easy," "simple," "private," and "convenient" (Goodman and Pyman 2016). Initial worries about older electors not voting online have been put aside as evidence has emerged that those aged fifty years and older are the biggest users. At the same time, research in the context of municipal elections has also shown that online voting is not the solution to engage young people (Goodman and Pyman 2016).

Likewise, administrators report being satisfied with online voting. In a 2014 survey of administrators in forty-seven of the ninety-seven Ontario municipalities that used online voting, 96 per cent reported being "very" or "fairly" satisfied with the online voting process and 97 per cent said that internet voting should "definitely" or "probably" be used in the next election. Officials noted improvements in voter convenience, access, and counting efficiency as the greatest benefits. As one participant commented, "I was able to use far less staff to run the election. Instant results. Great feedback from residents" (Goodman and Pyman 2016, 55). By contrast, public education and outreach, negative media coverage, and potential for voter fraud were cited as the greatest administrative challenges. In terms of cost, the effect of online voting on election expenditures was found to depend on the approach to implementation. Typically, administrators introducing online voting have been able to keep budgets in line by reducing the number of voting booths in physical polling locations. Lowering the number of polling locations, by contrast, has been observed to negatively impact voter access.

The positive effects of online voting as observed by voters and election officials also find confirmation in studies of municipal online

8 Of the twenty-three Ontario municipalities that offered internet, paper, and telephone ballots in 2014, 55.6 per cent were cast by internet, 31.6 per cent by paper, and 12.8 per cent by phone (Goodman and Stokes 2018).

voting. On the question of turnout, a study that examines 490 elections in Ontario municipalities from 2000 to 2014 finds online voting can increase voter participation by 3.5 percentage points. Larger increases in turnout (7 percentage points) are observed if voting by mail was not in place beforehand (Goodman and Stokes 2018). These results represent success for online voting, since they show the voting method can have a positive effect on voter participation in the Canadian municipal context. Evidence of larger increases in situations where mail voting was not used already suggests that internet ballots may be a particularly powerful reform given that larger institutional modifications such as changing the electoral system from single member plurality to proportional representation have been associated with smaller turnout increases, of 5 percentage points (Blais and Carty 1990). Online voting has also been documented to improve voter access for persons with disabilities (Goodman and Pyman 2016) and to encourage the participation of non-voters (Couture et al. 2017).

Despite these benefits, online voting implementation has also resulted in failures and challenges. Early research suggests a key failure might be the elimination of in-person paper voting, given the impact of this change on the composition of the voting population. One study that examines voter data from the 2014 Ontario municipal elections suggests that when paper voting is eliminated some electors are disenfranchised on the basis of digital literacy, creating a new digital divide (Goodman et al. 2018). Though more research is needed to evaluate how the composition of the voting population changes when paper voting is removed, these preliminary findings suggest that, ironically, an attempt to increase voter access may be stifling it.

Additional challenges include security issues, fraud, and possible technical malfunctions or delays. Despite the fact that experts have identified many potential security threats (Essex 2016; Goodman 2017), a detected security breach has yet to occur in a municipal election. There has, however, been speculation about possible cases of fraud, where a family member has access to a voter's mail and knows their birthdate. To reduce the likelihood of this occurring, municipalities have passed bylaws to strengthen the penalties for voting fraud and carried out rigorous public education to inform electors of these policies. The municipality of Truro, Nova Scotia, for example, increased the penalty for giving an online voter PIN to someone else, or using someone else's

PIN, to a fine between five and ten thousand dollars or imprisonment for two years less a day.

Technical malfunctions are another challenge, which may or may not be related to the internet voting technology. In the 2018 Ontario municipal elections, for example, the voting websites of forty-three municipalities were affected on the evening of Election Day when an online voting vendor's IT subcontractor placed an unauthorized limitation on server bandwidth causing some sites to slow down or stop working, preventing electors from voting (Cardillo et al. 2019). To ensure electors were not disenfranchised, municipalities extended voting. Eight cities kept polls open an extra hour or two, while thirty-five declared a state of emergency and continued voting the next day (Goodman and Spicer 2019). Likewise in the 2014 elections, results were delayed in a group of municipalities because of an administrative error where an employee of the online voting vendor entered the names of the result files incorrectly. The error was caught promptly, and the results were retallied. The company reduced their fees by 25 per cent as a result (Sacheli 2014). Finally, the accuracy of voters' lists and delays in postal service are other issues that have been raised as presenting challenges to online voting functionality.

Indigenous communities: Indigenous communities in Canada are embracing online voting. In First Nations, for example, the technology is often used for ratification and agreement votes and sometimes for elections. Regulations of the Indian Act and First Nations Elections Act, legislation written by the federal government, do not permit the 223 First Nations whose elections and referendums are governed by these acts to use alternative voting methods (Midzain-Gobin et al. 2017). However, online voting can be employed for votes on matrimonial real property and on framework agreements such as the passage of land codes.[9]

In this context, online voting is most often implemented to improve access and inclusion for off-reserve members, enhance youth engagement, and for reasons of counting efficiency. In cases where First Nations intend to pass their own legislation, online voting has

9 There are 634 First Nations in Canada. First Nations whose elections are not governed by the Indian Act or First Nations Elections Act are free to use the voting methods of their choosing.

sometimes served as a necessary tool to engage off-reserve members and meet participation thresholds that were imposed by the federal government (Gabel et al. 2016).[10] Typically, First Nations use online voting as a complementary voting method, though some northern communities have eliminated paper voting because of low attendance at the polls. Telephone voting is not used often, except in remote communities where internet connectivity is limited.

In terms of successes, First Nations have observed that online voting has improved engagement of off-reserve citizens, those with mobility challenges, busy young parents, and electors who missed postal voting deadlines. It has also permitted communities to extend advance voting, providing additional voting opportunities and enhancing voter access and convenience. The result has been broader community consultation in key matters. Furthermore, by enabling the passage of laws that enhance First Nations autonomy, such as control of their own lands, online voting is supporting and enhancing self-determination (Gabel et al. 2016; Gabel et al. 2017; Midzain-Gobin et al. 2017).

Top challenges for First Nations include obtaining accurate voters' lists and email contact information and internet access and connectivity, particularly in remote and northern communities. While some First Nations have used telephone voting to extend access, others have gone door-to-door with iPads to promote inclusiveness. As noted above, another challenge communities face is not being able to use online voting for elections and referendums. Changing the regulations that govern First Nation elections and referendums would give communities more control over their voting and community engagement. While there has been some opposition to online voting in First Nations based on fears it will erode traditional voting processes, generally it has been well received.

Overall, while fears about security and perceptions of modest benefits have held higher levels of government back from embracing online voting, at the community level it may be considered a success and modernization is progressing rapidly.

---

10 Historically this was problematic for the passage of land codes, which required a 25 per cent threshold of yes votes from eligible electors. The passage of Bill C-86 in December 2018, however, simplified things by allowing First Nations to set their own minimum threshold.

POTENTIALS

What, if any, are the unrealized democratic potentials of digital technology in relation to voting? What benefits can online voting deliver for elections in Canada and for democracy? At the same time, does online voting have potentially negative outcomes and are these avoidable? The short answer is that online voting holds the potential for great democratic promise, yet at the same time could result in considerable peril if critical elements of design and implementation are not accounted for. While certainly not a magic bullet that will restore voter turnout to pre-decline levels (no one institutional change will), online voting can have an important and positive impact on voter access and equality. On the other hand, potential security issues, technological challenges, and the elimination of paper voting pose noteworthy risks to electoral integrity.

In terms of democratic potentials, online voting has the ability to reduce voting barriers, especially for electors who face additional hurdles when accessing the ballot box. These can include citizens overseas, young people away at post-secondary school, older electors, persons with disabilities, Indigenous peoples, young families, and inhabitants of rural or northern communities. In all of these cases barriers such as geography, accessibility or mobility issues, the busyness of life, and weather can act as impediments to voting that can be addressed with voting online. As discussed above, research on Canadian municipalities has documented a positive effect on voter turnout (Goodman and Stokes 2018) and the ability of online voting to engage non-voters (Couture et al. 2017). Results suggest that other, more substantial reforms such as electoral system change (Blais 1990) or compulsory voting (Jackman 1987) may not have much larger effects on turnout. Although compulsory voting is associated with increases in the range of 7–16 per cent (Franklin 2001), making voting mandatory may raise constitutional issues. Online voting could be the simplest change to voting rules with the biggest turnout payoff.

A second potential to enhance democracy is the retention of current voters. Recent changes in voting patterns in Canada and other countries such as the United States (Hall 2015) indicate an increasing number of electors are voting early. Advance turnout in recent federal and provincial elections has seen unprecedented increases, suggesting electors want greater choice and control in their voting options. In addition, a growing number of electors report not voting because of everyday life issues such as being "too busy" (Elections Canada 2016). Making voting easier and more accessible while the pace of life hastens supports the regular participation of voters who might otherwise drop off in certain elections based on their life circumstances. In addition, as enhanced citizen choice and control increasingly become an expectation of government service provision, such changes could be important for improving attitudes toward electoral institutions. While increasing voter engagement is important, maintaining the participation of current voters is crucial for preserving levels of turnout.

Finally, online voting and associated technology has the potential to make elections more transparent. Mechanisms such as individual verification can allow voters to confirm that their ballot was cast as intended and recorded correctly. A further type of verification, universal verifiability, could permit any member of the public to verify that all votes have been recorded and counted correctly, providing additional auditability and transparency (Benaloh et al. 2014). While some jurisdictions such as Estonia and Switzerland are incorporating versions of verifiability into their online voting systems (Goodman 2017), a lack of development and trials in Canada has limited such advancements. Online voting systems have the potential to improve the auditability of elections and perhaps even their legitimacy in contentious races, but getting to that point in development requires an investment in research and testing from governments and election agencies that is not happening currently in Canada.

Despite its potential to improve elections, online voting also has the ability to compromise voter equality and electoral integrity. Implemented a certain way, online voting can improve voter access, but if elements such as internet connectivity, affordability, and digital literacy are not taken into account, it can have the opposite effect. The digital divide, discussed in the introductory chapter, remains a concern. Communities have overcome these obstacles by offering public access points to vote online and providing specially trained election officers or helplines to walk electors through the process. The elimination of paper voting, however, poses a significant risk to voter equality by potentially excluding electors on the basis of digital literacy (Goodman et al. 2018) and other factors. The composition of the voting population is critically important given that those who vote determine who governs. If variables such as income, education, and other resources or skills might limit an electors' ability to vote online, this poses problems for representation and the development of equitable public policies in cases where online ballots are the only voting option. Preliminary research suggests paper voting should not be eliminated at this time. In addition, to counter the potential of any exclusionary effects, governments should focus on promoting access to the internet and digital devices and enhancing residents' technical skill development.

Worries about security, such as the possibility of someone hacking or tampering with an election, is another concern. While online voting systems have been refined to counter potential issues as they have arisen (i.e., Estonia and Switzerland), the fact that technology is always changing means there is no everlasting solution to potential security breaches (Goodman 2017). Consequently, online voting systems must continually evolve and respond to changes in technological advancements. One option to achieve universal verifiability and improve the auditability of elections is to forgo the principle of the secret ballot, a longstanding electoral principle that has not always been practised in Canada. Vote selling and coercion are other potential challenges of online voting since, when it is carried out remotely, there is no direct supervision by election officials.

Policy development can limit the effects of these obstacles. In the case of vote selling and coercion, for example, putting policies in place that increase the penalties for these offences has been effective municipally, but this outcome is not guaranteed. More generally, the development of operational and technical guidelines for online voting is badly needed in Canada. Currently, there are no minimum technical requirements that online voting systems must meet to operate elections and votes. This means that communities are not vetting online voting service providers as comprehensively as possible, posing important risks for electoral integrity. Communities in Canada presently select online voting providers based on locally determined criteria. While large cities are able to hire experts to carry out risk assessments and have bigger IT teams to vet systems, smaller localities have less capacity and resources. The creation of guidelines outlining minimum technical requirements would provide communities with a valuable tool as they evaluate vendors. Such technical resources would enhance local knowledge and result in improved quality assurance for elections. They could also serve as a baseline for when higher levels of government begin to explore the use of online voting more seriously. Such a document could be put together by a group of communities, the province, the federal government, or a combination of the three. Of all the countries where online voting experimentation is occurring, places with far less activity than Canada have much more advanced regulation and governance frameworks.

Ultimately, online voting presents many opportunities to both enhance and hinder democracy. By carefully considering development, carrying out regular research, and refining technology, using online voting as a complementary voting method and leading the development of technical guidelines, Canada is putting itself in a better position to mitigate possible negative outcomes.

Does online voting have a future in elections in Canada? In interviews with thirty-two experts in elections from academic, private, and government sectors in Canada and abroad, nearly all described the future of elections in Canada as being digital (Goodman 2017). Respondents were asked to reflect on the future of elections in Canada in about five to ten years and then in about fifty years. In the near future experts believe that elections in Canada will continue to make headway in terms of modernization, however, they cautioned these developments will largely involve the incremental use of technology such as real time strike-off of voters' lists, candidates' direct access to voters' lists, and the elimination of scrutineers and electronic ballot tabulation. Online voting is viewed by election officials as the component of electoral modernization that offers the greatest potential to enhance voter access but also poses the greatest risk and provides election officials the least control. Reflecting specifically on local elections, experts were more open to consider growth in online voting, predicting that it would likely become a mainstream component of many municipal election programs across the country. Though not commenting on Indigenous elections and votes, one can envision a similar pattern of growth in Indigenous communities given the accessibility benefits of online voting for engaging off-reserve citizens.

Thinking of voting in fifty years, respondents reflected that elections will undergo dramatic transformation as a result of technology and some type of digital voting will be commonplace, perhaps using biometrics or iris scanners. Some speculated that as data are collected and citizens become willing to give up privacy, there may be a shift in the expectation of ballot secrecy, which would make online or other types of digital voting easier. This would not be such a dramatic shift, since before the principle of the secret ballot came into force, electors voted by a show of hands.

It is interesting to think of the past 150 years of elections in Canada and how little change has taken place, yet how much transformation the next 50 years could bring. The future of elections, and the degree to which technology is adopted, will be determined by the extent to which policymakers ensure thorough research, sufficient testing processes, and stay true to the core principles that guide elections in Canada, chief among them accessibility and trust. Online voting has the power to significantly improve voter access and strengthen trust in elections, yet at the same time can inhibit access and weaken trust if not implemented with certain considerations in mind. Like any technology, online voting is a tool. Whether that tool improves voting in elections and enhances democracy in Canada or poses challenges for it depends on the people writing policy, designing voting systems, and running and participating in elections. It is almost certain, however, that the future of elections in Canada is a digital one.

REFERENCES

Alvarez, R. Michael, and Thad E. Hall. 2003. *Point, Click, and Vote: The Future of Internet Voting*. Washington, DC: Brookings Institution Press.

Anonymous Interview. 2016. November 14.

Anonymous Interview. 2016. November 22.

Association of Ontario Municipalities (AMO). 2005. AMO Background Report on Alternative Voting Methods.

Bélanger, F., and L. Carter. 2010. "The Digital Divide and Internet Voting Acceptance." In *Proceedings of the Fourth International Conference on Digital Society, St. Maarten, Netherlands Antilles*, 307–10. IEEE Computer Society. http://ieeexplore.ieee.org/stamp/stamp.jsp?arnumber=5432779.

Benaloh, Josh, Ronald Rivest, Peter Y.A. Ryan, Philip Stark, Vanessa Teague, and Poorvi Vora. 2014. *End-to-End Verifiability*. https://www.microsoft.com/en-us/research/publication/end-end-verifiablity/?from=http%3A%2F%2Fresearch.microsoft.com%2Fen-us%2Fum%2Fpeople%2Fbenaloh%2Fpapers%2Fe2e-primer.pdf.

Bird, Hilary. 2019. "N.W.T. to Be 1st Province or Territory to Use Online Voting in General Election." CBC News, July 4. https://www.cbc.ca/news/canada/north/nwt-election-online-1.5199115.

Black, Jerome. 2003. *From Enumeration to the National Register of Electors: An Account and an Evaluation.* Montreal: Institute for Research on Public Policy.

Blais, André, and R. Kenneth Carty. 1990. "Does Proportional Representation Foster Voter Turnout?" *European Journal of Political Research* 18 (2): 167–81. https://doi.org/10.1111/j.1475-6765.1990.tb00227.x.

Blais, André, and Daniel Rubenson. 2013. "The Source of Turnout Decline: New Values or New Contexts?" *Comparative Political Studies* 46 (1): 95–117. https://doi.org/10.1177/0010414012453032.

Bridgmon, Phillip, and Mark Milewicz. 2004. *E-Politics: Technology in American Government.* Dubuque, IA: Kendall Hunt Publishing Co.

Cambell, Kerry. 2017. "Online Voting Not Ready for Federal, Provincial Election: Officials." CBC News, May 4. http://www.cbc.ca/news/canada/prince-edward-island/online-voting-not-ready-for-federal-provincial-election-officials-1.4100297.

Cardillo, Anthony, Nicholas Akinyokun, and Aleksander Essex. 2019. "Online Voting in Ontario Municipal Elections: A Conflict of Legal Principles and Technology?" *Lecture Notes in Computer Science.* Berlin: Springer.

Clarke, Harold D., and Alan C. Acock. 1989. "National Elections and Political Attitudes: The Case of Political Efficacy." *British Journal of Political Science* 19 (4): 551–62. https://doi.org/10.1017/S0007123400005639.

Couture, Jérôme, Sandra Breux, and Nicole Goodman. 2017. "Le vote par Internet augmente t-il la participation électorale?" In *Cyberespace et science politique de la méthode au terrain, du virtuel au reel,* ed. Hugo Loiseau and Elena Waldispuehl, 123–47. Quebec City: Presses de l'Université du Québec.

Dippel, Scott. 2017. "Elections Alberta to Test New Voting Technologies in Calgary-Lougheed Byelection." CBC News, December 1. http://www.cbc.ca/news/canada/calgary/provincial-byelection-calgary-voting-machines-1.4429652.

Elections BC. 2014. *Independent Panel on Internet Voting British Columbia: Recommendations Report to the Legislative Assembly of British Columbia.* February.

Elections Canada. 2016. *Survey of Electors following the 42nd General Election.* http://www.elections.ca/content.aspx?section=res&dir=rec/eval/pes2015/surv&document=index&lang=e.

Essex, Aleksander. 2016. "Internet Voting in Canada: A Cyber Security Perspective." Online Voting Roundtable, Centre for e-Democracy.

Franklin, Mark N. 1996. "Electoral Participation." In *Comparing Democracies: Elections and Voting in Global Perspective,* ed. Lawrence LeDuc, Richard G. Niemi, and Pippa Norris. Thousand Oaks, CA: Sage.

Franklin, Mark N. 2001. "How Structural Factors Cause Turnout Variations at European Parliament Elections." *European Union Politics* 2 (3): 309–28. https://doi.org/10.1177/1465116501002003003.

Franklin, Mark N. 2004. *Voter Turnout and the Dynamics of Electoral Competition in Established Democracies since 1945*. Cambridge: Cambridge University Press.
Gabel, Chelsea, Karen Bird, Nicole Goodman, and Brian Budd. 2017. "The Impact of Digital Technology on First Nations Participation and Governance." *The Canadian Journal of Native Studies* 36 (2): 107.
Gabel, Chelsea, Nicole Goodman, Karen Bird, and Brian Budd. 2016. "Indigenous Adoption of Internet Voting: A Case Study of Whitefish River First Nation." *International Indigenous Policy Journal* 7 (3): 1–20. https://doi.org/10.18584/iipj.2016.7.3.3.
Goodman, Nicole. 2017. "Online Voting: A Path Forward for Federal Elections in Canada." Ottawa: Privy Council Office.
Goodman, Nicole, Michael McGregor, Jérôme Couture, and Sandra Breux. 2018. "Another Digital Divide? Evidence That Elimination of Paper Voting Could Lead to Digital Disenfranchisement." *Policy & Internet* 10 (2): 164–84. https://doi.org/10.1002/poi3.168.
Goodman, Nicole J., and Jon H. Pammett. 2014. "The Patchwork of Internet Voting in Canada." In *Electronic Voting: Verifying the Vote (EVOTE), 2014 6th International Conference on*. IEEE.
Goodman, Nicole, Jon H. Pammett, and Joan DeBardeleben. 2010. *A Comparative Assessment of Electronic Voting*. Gatineau, QC: Elections Canada.
Goodman, Nicole, and Rodney Smith. 2017. "Internet Voting in Sub-National Elections: Policy Learning in Canada and Australia." *International Joint Conference on Electronic Voting*. London: Springer.
Goodman, Nicole, and Zachary Spicer. 2019. "Administering Elections in a Digital Age: Online Voting in Ontario Municipalities." *Canadian Public Administration* 62 (3): 369–92. https://doi.org/10.1111/capa.12342.
Goodman, Nicole, and Leah C. Stokes. 2018. "Reducing the Cost of Voting: An Empirical Evaluation of Internet Voting's Effect on Local Elections." *British Journal of Political Science* 1–13. https://doi.org/10.1017/S0007123417000849.
Hall, Thad E. 2015. "Internet Voting: The State of the Debate." In *Handbook of Digital Politics*, ed. S. Coleman and D. Freelon, 103–17. Cheltenham, UK: Edward Elgar Publishing.
Ibbitson, John. 2011. "The Alarming Decline in Voter Turnout." *Globe and Mail*, October 14. https://www.theglobeandmail.com/news/politics/the-alarming-decline-in-voter-turnout/article4247507/.
Jackman, Robert W. 1987. "Political Institutions and Voter Turnout in the Industrial Democracies." *American Political Science Review* 81 (2): 405–23. https://doi.org/10.2307/1961959.
Katz, Richard S. 1997. *Democracy and Elections*. New York: Oxford University Press on Demand.
Midzain-Gobin, Liam, Nicole Goodman, Chelsea Gabel, and Karen Bird. 2017. "Reforming the Indian Act to Allow for Online Voting." *Policy Options*, October.

Montjoy, Robert S. 2008. "The Public Administration of Elections." *Public Administration Review* 68 (5): 788–99. https://doi.org/10.1111/j.1540-6210.2008.00919.x.

Norris, Pippa. 2001. *Digital Divide: Civic Engagement, Information Poverty, and the Internet Worldwide.* Cambridge, UK: Cambridge University Press.

Norris, Pippa. 2004. "Will New Technology Boost Turnout? Evaluating Experiments in UK Local Elections." In *Electronic Voting and Democracy: A Comparative Analysis*, ed. Norbert Kersting and Harald Baldersheim, 193–225. London: Palgrave Macmillan UK.

Pitt, Sally. 2016. "Meet 'the Tabulator': Able to Count 300 Paper Ballots a Minute." CBC News, October 26. http://www.cbc.ca/news/canada/prince-edward-island/pei-plebiscite-electoral-reform-computer-voting-1.3813387.

Powell, G. Bingham. 2000. *Elections as Instruments of Democracy: Majoritarian and Proportional Visions.* New Haven: Yale University Press.

Roussel, Michel. 2018. Deputy Chief Electoral Officer, Electoral Events and Innovation, Elections Canada. Email correspondence. February 15.

Sacheli, Sarah. 2014. "Angry Towns Consider Withholding Payment to Internet Voting Company." Canwest News Service, October 28. http://windsorstar.com/news/angry-towns-consider-withholding-payment-to-internet-voting-company.

Scytl. Electronic Poll Book. 2018. https://www.scytl.com/en/electronic-pollbook/.

Solvak, Mihkel, and Kristjan Vassil. 2018. "Could Internet Voting Halt Declining Electoral Turnout? New Evidence That E-Voting Is Habit Forming." *Policy & Internet* 10 (1): 4–21. https://doi.org/10.1002/poi3.160.

Special Committee on Electoral Reform (ERRE). 2016. *Strengthening Democracy in Canada: Principles, Process, and Public Engagement for Electoral Reform: Report of the Standing Committee on Electoral Reform.* https://www.ourcommons.ca/Content/Committee/421/ERRE/Reports/RP8655791/errerp03/errerp03-e.pdf. December.

Weiers, Bob. 2016. "Electronic Voting Comes to Ontario in Whitby-Oshawa Byelection" CBC News, February 10. http://www.cbc.ca/news/canada/toronto/electronic-voting-comes-to-ontario-in-whitby-oshawa-byelection-1.3441127.

Wolf, Peter, Rushdi Nackerdien, and Domenico Tuccinardi. 2011. *Introducing Electronic Voting: Essential Considerations.* Stockholm: International Institute for Democracy and Electoral Assistance.

CHAPTER FIVE

Electronic Surveillance: The Growth of Digitally Enabled Surveillance and the Atrophy of Accountability in Law Enforcement and Security Agencies

Christopher Parsons

INTRODUCTION

Governments have engaged in telecommunications surveillance since the earliest inception of publicly available communications tools. Letter mail, telegraphs, phone calls, text messages, and internet communications have all been subject to surveillance (Chan and Camp 2002; Landau 2010; Beck 1968). Such surveillance, indeed all forms of surveillance, entails "the focused, routine attention to personal details for purposes of influence, management, protection, or direction" and, moreover, "usually involves relations of power in which watchers are privileged" (Lyon 2007, 14–15). In effect, surveillance constitutes practices of collecting information for the purposes of influencing another party's actions, with state surveillance focused on exerting sovereign influence to detect, and respond to, "aberrant" behaviours or practices that either contravene social norms, the rule of law, or both. In the Canadian context, many of the surveillance intrusions into private life and the ability to exercise rights and freedoms constitute "political policing" insofar as opposition political groups, as well as politicians, activists, and civil advocates, have been targeted on the basis of their intellectual positions or non-violent demands rather than being engaged in criminal behaviours (Whitaker et al. 2012). State agencies have used a litany of surveillance tools, with some of the most closely guarded methods entailing the monitoring of communications.

It is in light of the intrusive nature of communications surveillance that, throughout the twentieth century, most Western governments, including Canadian governments, have passed laws to restrict the state's ability to use surveillance practices to intrude into citizens' private lives. Perhaps most notably, following concerns in the 1960s and 1970s about the computerization of information and new ways of conducting electronic surveillance, the Government of Canada passed the Protection of Privacy Act (Beck 1968; Protection of Privacy Act 1974; Koutros and Demers 2013). The Act, as amended in 1977, established safeguards designed to protect Canadians' privacy by, in part, imposing mandatory reporting requirements on government agencies that engage in real-time electronic surveillance (Koutros and Demers 2013). The intent of such laws was and remains to hold government agencies to account before their legislative assemblies and the citizenry more broadly for how such agencies intrude into the private sphere.

Fast-forward to 2018, and state agencies have assumed and developed a wide range of new surveillance capabilities and been endowed with additional lawful powers. Because of digital technologies, vast volumes of information are stored as business records by private companies (Solove 2004), mobile device communications can be intercepted and select pieces of information extracted using a device capable of fitting inside a backpack or being mounted on the underbelly of airplanes (Parsons and Israel 2016), internet communications can be collected en masse for retroactive searching (CSE Undated), and more. Much of this surveillance constitutes "bulk" surveillance, wherein a mass of digital data is collected by state agencies and is subject to analysis afterwards to understand the data's value; much of our awareness of such surveillance comes following whistle-blowers such as Edward Snowden providing documents that explain what state agencies are capable of doing (Landau 2013, 2014). Despite the rise of these new technologies and the creation of lawful powers to collect information for policing and security purposes, there have been few accompanying reporting mechanisms. In effect, as ostensibly lawful state surveillance activities in Canada have expanded, the requirements imposed on governments to account for their behaviour have atrophied (Parsons 2016).

This chapter begins with a discussion of real-time electronic surveillance that has historically been conducted in Canada and the importance of government accountability for how law enforcement and security agencies (LESAs) conduct surveillance. It then proceeds to examine how such surveillance has been transformed in an era of digitization, and how contemporary surveillance simultaneously enables state actors to massively intrude upon Canadians' Charter rights. It specifically notes how the atrophy of accountability regimes raises serious concerns for the democratic legitimacy of government surveillance activities. The chapter concludes by outlining briefly how surveillance accountability regimes might be reformed and what such reformation would mean for rendering government bulk surveillance activities more accountable to legislative assemblies and citizens alike.

CONTEXT

Real-time government surveillance is perhaps most commonly thought of as involving a wiretap, with state agents listening intently to what the targets of the surveillance are saying and with whom the targets are communicating. Western governments tend to understand real-time surveillance more broadly, however, and in Canada it can assume many different forms, including audio and visual recordings, interception of communications, and planting of equipment designed to conduct surveillance in vehicles, homes, or businesses (Parsons and Molnar 2018). These kinds of surveillance tend to be regarded as deeply intrusive of private life because individuals often reveal sensitive aspects of their lives while communicating with other persons, such as information about their sexuality, financial situation, medical issues, religious beliefs, or political leanings. Given these sensitivities, and the fact that there is a historical legal presumption that content is more revelatory than the metadata surrounding content (e.g., phone number dialled or place to which a letter is mailed as opposed to the content of a phone call or letter), criminal codes have tended to restrict government agencies' ability to engage in such intrusive surveillance. As an example, the standards to obtain non-content information such as internet routing information, or metadata associated with communications, tend to be lower as compared to the legal standard government agencies must meet to obtain interception orders or access to the content of communications.[1] In the United States, the National Commission for the Review of Federal and State Laws Relating to Wiretapping and Electronic Surveillance argued in 1976 that "wiretaps and eavesdrops are potentially more penetrating, less discriminating and less visible than ordinary searches" and recommended a stringent process for prior judicial authorization be met before law enforcement or security agencies be allowed to engage in such surveillance (National Commission 1976). This logic was adopted by the Canadian government when it established its own accountability and oversight regimes concerning electronic surveillance in the 1970s (Kourtros and Demers 2013; Law Reform Commission of Canada 1986; Manning 1978), with the passage and amendment of the Protection of Privacy Act during that decade (Beck 1968; Protection of Privacy Act 1974). Regardless of whether the acquired information is content or metadata, or captured in real time or after the fact, government surveillance is conducted with the intent of influencing other parties. In the case of law enforcement agencies, such influence is linked with the prospect of bringing criminal charges and thus influencing an individual's behaviour through the criminal justice system. In the case of security and intelligence agencies, which do not have the power of arrest in Canada, the influence might be less apparent to the affected persons: foreign agents might be expelled from Canada, or have counter-intelligence operations run against them to dissuade or neutralize their activities or provide the agents with false information. Or the efforts might be even more subtle, and involve interfering with communications, banking, or other key components of modern life to hinder a foreign person's activities or even the activities of a Canadian resident who is identified as posing a threat to the national interests of Canada. In all cases, surveillance can be distinguished from merely monitoring another person's actions. Acts of monitoring do not necessarily include a built-in feedback loop – a person can monitor activities and not ever plan or intend to even prospectively influence the activities or party responsible for them – whereas

1 For an American perspective, see John Villasenor, "What You Need to Know about the Third Party Doctrine," *The Atlantic*, December 30, 2013, https://www.theatlantic.com/technology/archive/2013/12/what-you-need-to-know-about-the-third-party-doctrine/282721/.

acts of surveillance presume the possibility of such influence as a rationale for conducting the data collection activity. More broadly, surveillance technologies are inherently technologies of control insofar as they are designed to "plan, predict, and prevent by classifying and assessing profiles and risks" (Lyon 2003, 13). This means that surveillance technologies used by LESAs and corporations alike operate as a way of asserting control over populations and users, often in ways that privileged portions of society desire (e.g., to identify and address socially risky behaviour that threatens the social order preferred by those holding social privilege), but which can also have disproportionate effects across a population writ large or unduly discriminate against those who enjoy less social privilege.

Canadian LESAs must typically obtain a judicially authorized warrant before they can engage in real-time interception activities.[2] Such warrants operate as a control-based means of accountability, insofar as judges are situated to approve, approve with conditions, or deny the authorization request. Judges must be satisfied that the LESA officer in question has reasonable and probable grounds to believe that the real-time surveillance is necessary to advance an investigation, that affected persons have been identified, that all places the interception will take place have been disclosed, and that no other less intrusive mode of surveillance is available (Koutros and Demers 2013; Criminal Code, RSC 1985, s. 184–6). Furthermore, the Protection of Privacy Act also requires Canada's provincial and federal governments to prepare and table annual electronic surveillance reports that detail the frequency, reasons, and efficacy of real-time electronic surveillance.[3] These reports provide accountability in the form of a review that takes place after the surveillance activities have been authorized by a judge and undertaken by the relevant LESA. A range of statistics are included in the reports, including the total number of requests for interceptions, how many

2 The exception to the rule is in the case of an emergency electronic surveillance operation; in such cases, the target(s) must be notified of the surveillance after the fact and a justice may authorize the surveillance for up to thirty-six hours without the LESA officer(s) having to prepare a completed warrant.

3 The Government of Canada's reports are available through the Department of Public Safety's website (see https://www.publicsafety.gc.ca/cnt/rsrcs/pblctns/index-en.aspx). Some provinces have public online repositories with these reports and others include reports in their respective Gazettes. It is relatively common for provinces to fail to reliably issue these reports every year.

such requests are granted, types of investigative methods employed, the regularity at which collected information is introduced as evidence, and the number of times that the information is used in securing a conviction. Also included are the types of crimes for which real-time electronic surveillance warrants are authorized to investigate. The reports are tabled annually in the provincial and federal legislatures. Whereas control-based modes of accountability are concerned with the reasonableness, proportionality, and necessity of electronic surveillance at the time of the request, review-based modes of accountability such as the annual electronic surveillance reports are concerned with how the government more generally is undertaking such intrusive surveillance. The annual reviews do not focus on specific cases but, instead, on the efficacy of the surveillance in advancing investigations and ultimately securing convictions for different kinds of serious crimes.

DIGITIZATION

Promises & Perils

As we have embraced the digital era in our personal and professional lives, LESAs have also developed new techniques and gained additional powers in order to keep pace as our memories have shifted from personal journals and filing cabinets to blogs, social media, and cloud hosting providers. LESAs now subscribe to services designed to monitor social media services for intelligence purposes (McGuire 2015), collect bulk data from telecommunications providers in so-called tower dumps of all the information stored by cellular towers (*R. v. Rogers Communications* 2016; Kari 2017), establish their own fake cellular towers to collect data from all parties proximate to such devices (Parsons and Israel 2016; 2017 FC 1047), use malware to intrude into either personal endpoint devices (e.g., mobile phones or laptops) or networking equipment (e.g., routers) (author interview;[4] Molnar, Parsons, and Zouave 2017), and can even retroactively recreate our daily online activities

4 Author in conversations with members of Canada's federal and provincial governments, 2016–17.

with assistance from Canada's foreign signals intelligence agency.[5] In the past, each of these kinds of activities would have required dozens or hundreds or thousands of government officials to painstakingly follow persons – many of whom might not be specifically suspected of engaging in a criminal activity or activity detrimental to the national security of Canada – and gain lawful entry to their personal safes, install cameras in their homes and offices, access and copy the contents of filing cabinets, and listen in on conversations that would otherwise have been private. As this edited collection shows, so many aspects of our lives have become digital that entirely new investigative opportunities have arisen that were previously restricted to the imaginations of science fiction authors, both because it is easier to access information but also because we generate and leave behind more information about our activities vis-à-vis our digital exhaust than was ever possible in a world dominated by analogue technologies.

Each of the aforementioned kinds of digital surveillance opens novel investigative lines for LESAs, and each technique tends to be justified as needed in order to keep pace with criminal activities that increasingly either include a digital component or can be more "efficiently" investigated using contemporary bulk surveillance capabilities. In the case of monitoring social media, LESAs can track protests to understand who is central to creating or amplifying messages, develop a social networking map of persons who are directly involved (e.g., marching in a protest or participating digitally) as well as those who are affiliated (e.g., sharing or amplifying messages in support of the protest, while not being directly involved in it), and also identify those who respond positively or negatively to the messaging. What once, in an analogue era, would have required placing officers in a crowd and taking photos of participants to subsequently identify them, can be done by paying a third party to harvest the data and deliver it in real time or in after-action reports at a fraction of the cost associated with deploying masses of officers. By

5 This involves a federal LESA obtaining stored content or metadata from the Communications Security Establishment's (CSE) bulk content and metadata stores under the Technical and Operational Assistance part of the CSE's mandate under Bill C-59 (An Act Respecting National Security Matters). For more, see Christopher Parsons et al., "Analysis of the Communications Security Establishment Act and Related Provisions in Bill C-59 (An Act Respecting National Security Matters), First Reading (December 18, 2017)," *Citizen Lab/CIPPIC*, 32–5, https://citizenlab.ca/wp-content/uploads/2017/12/C-59-Analysis-1.0.pdf.

collecting bulk digital data from telecommunications providers' cellular towers, LESAs can identify which mobile devices were proximate to the towers during the times requested. Quite often this data is released on a relatively low standard of reason to suspect, is for data stored by multiple towers, and the relevant court orders LESAs acquire can compel telecommunications companies to disclose data about tens or hundreds of thousands of customers with each request. To engage in a similar kind of retroactive surveillance in the pre-digital era, the government would have had to install cameras or other recording devices throughout every room, public space, and vehicle and subsequently task hundreds or thousands of officers to determine who was in what location, at what time. Using tower dump orders, they can compel telecommunications providers to provide similar kinds of data at a fraction of the cost. And where the government decides to collect mobile device identifiers without the assistance of a mobile telecommunications provider, it can do so using IMSI Catcher devices the relevant government agency either owns itself or borrows from a partner agency. IMSI Catcher devices compel all mobile devices within range to connect to the given IMSI Catcher and, subsequently, provide a series of unique identifiers that the LESA can then bring to telecommunications carriers to identify the persons who have registered the devices. Such surveillance devices are sometimes used in cases where government agents believe that a suspect or suspects are using mobile devices but lack the identifiers associated with them; these devices can also potentially be used to identify all persons at a protest, those proximate to a VIP such as a government dignitary, or even to deliver malware to mobile devices which connect to the IMSI Catcher in order to subsequently access content on their devices. Each of these kinds of activities would be time consuming – and likely quite obvious to those affected – were officers required to manually inspect devices or request the identities of persons proximate to the area of surveillance.

There are also a range of ways in which LESAs can retroactively acquire information about communications, activities, and engagements that are communicated using digital technologies. First, LESAs can obtain a production order and serve it on private companies which are in the business of retaining this information for their own commercial purposes. Sometimes data are retained because such retention is part of why citizens use the service in question: email services, as an example, have made a business of keeping our mail for us. The same is true of cloud storage providers, such as Apple, Amazon, Dropbox, or Google, all of which can provide LESAs with access to their customers' stored records after receiving a lawful request from a LESA. But this is only the most obvious source of retroactive records. Second, Western intelligence agencies such as the National Security Agency and Canada's own Communications Security Establishment (CSE) collect vast quantities of data about foreign persons as well as citizens and residents of their own countries. Such data can potentially be accessed by non-intelligence parties, such as security agencies like the Canadian Security Intelligence Service (CSIS), or law enforcement agencies, such as the Royal Canadian Mounted Police (RCMP), should those parties make formal and lawful requests for some of the bulk data which is collected by the CSE. In Canada, the CSE has capabilities that far exceed those of any other federal agency insofar as it is lawfully authorized to engage in surveillance activities that no other LESA can engage in. Moreover, the CSE can develop systems of surveillance that no other agency is competent, let alone legally permitted, to create. Such systems include, for example, those that monitor the internet writ large for file downloads, monitor metadata associated with our digital movements to populate vast databases that can subsequently be queried to understand every place we have been online and many of the people we have communicated with, or track a vast swathe of the data sent into, and exiting from, all Canadian networks. Once these systems collect data and store them in the CSE's databases, the RCMP or CSIS can obtain a warrant to compel the CSE to disclose data pertaining to certain suspects or activities named in the warrant. Furthermore, depending on the warrant, the CSE can potentially even delve into its partner intelligence agencies' databases in Australia, New Zealand, the United Kingdom, or the United States and query those foreign systems for information which is relevant to the warrant. This is a kind of surveillance that is grossly in excess of what any LESA in Canada could do in the past, let alone today with their own independent surveillance capabilities.

LESAs have a range of legal instruments which provide the requesting agency a right to attempt to obtain the data they want to further their investigation. There are, however, a set of instruments that are more commonly used in the course of agency investigations. Preservation demands can be issued on companies that process information and, upon receipt, compel the companies to store the identified data for twenty-one days for domestic offences and ninety days for international offences. LESAs must subsequently obtain and serve a production order on the company to gain access to whatever has been preserved. Where the data are normally retained in the course of business, such as subscriber data records pertaining to a user of a company's services or the email or other documents the customer stores with the company in question, then a LESA might obtain and serve a production order to obtain all of the historical documents denoted in the court order. The produced data can be deeply revealing given that it may include the content of digital communications and activities, yet the production order can be obtained after meeting a reasonable grounds to suspect standard. Number dialler orders can also be obtained on grounds to suspect that the collected information will assist in the investigation of an offence that is suspected will be, or has been, committed. Such orders are used to collect the numbers dialled from, and to, specified devices and can reveal more than just phone numbers: where a mobile phone is used for banking to input account numbers, enter passwords, enter conference calls or otherwise interact with a phone-based computer system, the number dialler warrant will authorize the collection of such information.

In 2014 the Criminal Code was amended to, in part, establish three different types of lawful tracking. The first type of tracking is used to track objects (e.g., motor vehicles or mobile devices), the second for tracking transmission data (e.g., data which are emitted from devices and which can be used to track the device(s) in question). Either of these types of tracking orders can be obtained on grounds that the LESA suspects that the privacy invasion will assist in the investigation of an offence. The third type of transmission order is used to track individuals and is obtainable on a higher standard, in those cases where the LESA has a belief that the privacy invasion will assist in the investigation of an offence. As noted, previously, interception orders are granted exclusively on reasonable grounds to believe that the overseeing justice has been satisfied that the real-time surveillance is necessary to advance an investigation, that affected persons have been identified, that all places the interception will take place have been disclosed, and that no less-intrusive mode of surveillance would produce evidence needed for the investigation. And finally, there is a broad category to catch many of the most controversial kinds of government surveillance, namely, general warrants, which are distinguished from the tracking warrants described above. General warrants tend to be difficult to obtain, insofar as the LESA officers in question must demonstrate there are reasonable grounds to believe that an offence has been, or will be, committed and that relevant information can be obtained using the methods described in the general warrant application. Surveillance techniques such as IMSI Catchers, malware, and other activities that are not better captured by other powers denoted in the Criminal Code or other act of Parliament have tended to rely on general warrants to authorize LESA activities.

Due to the relatively high standard that must be met before a LESA can obtain an interception order, agencies tend to use alternate surveillance methods to conduct their operations. As an example, in 2014, the federal and provincial governments obtained 250 court orders that authorized their respective agencies to engage in real-time surveillance.[6] By contrast, a subset of telecommunications providers operating exclusively in Canada reported receiving 81,443 court orders or warrants (Parsons 2015, 45–6); this number does not reflect orders issued to cloud service providers, social media companies, hotels, insurance companies, or even all telecommunications providers in Canada. Nevertheless, the juxtaposition does indicate that real-time electronic surveillance accounts for a small fraction of the surveillance activities conducted by government agencies. Only real-time electronic surveillance must be tabulated in annual reviews to legislative assemblies, and federal and provincial agencies have historically been unwilling or unable to independently collate statistics on their use of other warranting methods,[7] even to advance their own arguments for increased surveillance powers.[8]

The Perils of Contemporary Canadian Surveillance Activities

There are significant perils associated with the Government of Canada's contemporary surveillance activities. These include issues related to the very secrecy of the surveillance activities themselves; the refusal of

---

6 Based on the author's collection of Annual Electronic Surveillance Reports tabled by federal and provincial governments. Note that several provincial governments did not issue their statutory reports in 2014, or otherwise did not make the information available to the public, legislators, or the author.

7 Minister of Public Safety and Emergency Preparedness's Responses to MP Charmane Borg's Q-233 Order Paper Questions, March 24, 2014, retrieved January 17, 2015, https://www.christopher-parsons.com/Main/wp-content/uploads/2014/03/8555-412-233.pdf.

8 See Access to Information and Privacy document released by Public Safety Canada, A-2011-00220.

LESAs to admit they are engaged in certain kinds of surveillance; Crown prosecutors' blocking the disclosure of such activities in the courts; the failure of government bureaucrats to adequately account for even traditional forms of electronic surveillance; and the fact that persons are only likely to realize they have been targeted by government surveillance should evidence from such surveillance be presented against them in a court of law. These are all significant problems but potentially pale in comparison to the democratic perils associated with the inability of the public to realize or understand how many of these activities are linked with public legislation. In effect, the greatest peril associated with government surveillance is linked to citizens no longer seeing themselves as democratically authorizing government activities vis-à-vis public law, which has the effect of unhinging government activity from the citizenry's democratic legitimation of government activities.

While the public knows about many of the government's contemporary surveillance techniques and technologies, this knowledge has only followed from persistent, ongoing, and challenging research endeavours undertaken by academics, journalists, members of civil rights organizations, and whistle-blowers. One of the most commonly used techniques by all of the aforementioned groups – save for whistle-blowers – is reliance on freedom of information (FOI) laws to compel government agencies to disclose information pertaining to different surveillance devices and techniques. Unfortunately, many Canadian LESAs have adopted stances that any revelation of techniques that are not widely disclosed to the public would have deleterious impacts on the future use of those techniques and operation of associated devices. This has meant, for example, that knowledge about the operation of IMSI Catcher devices in Canada was stymied for years as government agencies alternatively denied they had any knowledge of the devices (partially on the basis that the agencies referred to the technologies as Mobile Device Identifiers instead of IMSI Catchers)[9] or claimed that any disclosure of whether they did or did not use the devices would hinder investigative practices (Israel and Parsons 2016; Parsons and Israel 2016, 31–49). Indeed, given the challenges in learning about government surveillance capabilities and the regularity with which such capabilities are used, researchers have entered into collaborations with parliamentarians to

9 Author in conversations with Canadian investigative reporters, 2017.

compel agencies to explain their surveillance activities, brought legal challenges against federal and provincial governments of Canada that have led to government agencies producing internal documents in the course of legal discovery processes, encouraged corporations to explain how they are compelled to provide information and assistance to LESAs, incited the public to try and learn about whether and if so how they have been subject to surveillance, and issued complaints to independent officers of parliament so that they will launch investigations and reveal information concerning LESA activities (Parsons 2015b).

One of the reasons that such a varied set of practices must be used to understand the breadth of LESAs' surveillance activities stems from the ability of government prosecutors to invoke sections of the Canada Evidence Act during criminal trials. Such successful invocations limit the defendant, their defence lawyers, and the public from understanding the methods and techniques that were used to collect evidence introduced in a case. Such an invocation follows when the Crown believes that the disclosure of specific information would either be injurious to the public interest (Canada Evidence Act, S. 37.) or to international relations, national defence, or national security (Canada Evidence Act, S. 38.). If defence attorneys do not challenge such invocations, or if they are unsuccessful in their challenge to compel the Crown to disclose information it is attempting to suppress, then no court record of the technique or device(s) being used will be generated. As a result of the government's often aggressive efforts to mask its less-publicized methods of surveillance, the aforementioned parties of academics, journalists, and civil rights advocates must use a range of atypical processes to ascertain what LESAs are doing in the course of exercising their lawful authorities.

Citizens cannot appreciate the extent to which LESAs may be intruding into their private lives if they are unaware of the existence of government surveillance techniques and devices, let alone the regularity of their operation. Annual electronic surveillance reports are designed to ensure that the government minister responsible for agencies conducting such surveillance can be held accountable to legislators and, also, to the citizenry writ large. Accountability exists "when there is a relationship where an individual or institution, and the performance of tasks or functions by that individual or institution, are subject to another's oversight, direction, or request that the individual or institution provide information of justification for its actions" (Pelizzo and Stapenhurst

2013, 2). In effect, this means that when a government agency or minister is compelled to provide information to another body, and that body can sanction the agency or minister based on its provision of information, then an accountability framework exists. This kind of directed accountability conforms to a traditional understanding of the concept, wherein an actor that is accountable to a forum for particular activities or actions and where the forum could discipline the actor if they fall short of expected activities or actions (Mulgan 1997; Anderson 2009). This traditional approach to understanding accountability regimes stands in contrast to the broader literature on accountability, which is focused on understanding how governmental accountability more broadly operates in an era where private actors assume roles and responsibilities that have historically been undertaken by states (Scott 2000). In the case of real-time electronic surveillance, it is ultimately a governmental LESA that obtains the warrant for the activity and, thus, even should there be assistance from a non-government party, that assistance is the direct result of being judicially compelled to cooperate with the government agency in question.

Annual electronic surveillance reports facilitate traditional modes of accountability in at least two ways. First, in preparing the reports the relevant ministers who will table them will become aware of what their agencies have done and, in the process, be better able to direct and control their behaviours (Przeworski and Stokes 1999; Strøm et al. 2003). Receiving this information is essential for Canadian ministers to assume responsibility for their agencies and be able to correct deficient or problematic behaviours. Second, legislative assemblies can ask questions of the minister when the reports are tabled as required each year. Questions might be raised concerning whether the surveillance capabilities are useful in collecting evidence to secure convictions or why there were significant increases or decreases in the numbers of affected persons from one year to the next. Using information in the annual reports, legislators can try and determine "whether the government is judiciously exercising its surveillance powers, whether the exercised powers are effectively addressing social ills, or whether the powers and their associated practices represent a good investment of taxpayer money" (Parsons 2015).

There are significant limitations associated with the accountability reporting concerning real-time electronic surveillance in Canada. Reports are often not tabled on a regular basis, their actual formatting can be so variable as to frustrate comparative analyses (both within and across jurisdictions), statistics can be irregularly updated and call into question the veracity of any information presented to legislative assemblies, and the narrative sections of the reports explaining and contextualizing the reported year's activities are sometimes missing or are simply copies of the same statement year over year (Parsons and Molnar 2018). Moreover, it is not self-evident that legislators, independent members of government, civil society organizations, or academics have comprehensively examined the reports on any kind of regular basis (Parsons and Molnar 2018). Nevertheless, these annual electronic surveillance reports represent the most comprehensive review of government surveillance activities. Despite all their flaws, these rarely read documents constitute the gold standard of government surveillance accountability in Canada.

Furthermore, potentially thousands of persons have their information collected in the course of LESA social media analytics, police requests for tower dump information from cellular providers, IMSI Catchers being operated within a kilometre or two of a person's location, authorities' use of malware to target routing equipment, or the CSE's mass, global surveillance activities capturing Canadian and non-Canadian persons' information alike. All these modes of mass surveillance are conducted without accountability regimes which correspond with that linked to real-time electronic surveillance. The only time when an affected person is likely to realize their information has been collected using one of these contemporary means of surveillance is when they are charged with an offence and subsequently have information entered into evidence. Outside this situation they may never know that their life chances have been affected or are at risk as a result of the government's intrusion into their private lives. Contrasted against existing accountability regimes which were created concerning real-time electronic surveillance, and which include annual reports to legislative assemblies and notifications to persons affected by the surveillance regardless of whether a criminal charge is laid, the lack of equivalent regimes for today's dominant tools of surveillance reveals a significant shift in the treatment of Canadians' Charter-protected rights generally and privacy rights, specifically.

There are real risks associated with these contemporary surveillance technologies and powers without a correspondingly robust accountability regime. Specifically, many of the aforementioned powers, such as the receipt of tower dump information, operation of IMSI Catchers, deployment of malware, or bulk collection of Canadians' digital activities vis-à-vis the CSE, are all highly secretive activities: evidence may be suppressed in court proceedings or, alternately, may be used to secretly influence targets' life chances by a security agency that does not have to disclose to persons it targets how it has received or used the acquired information. Furthermore, the very laws which are used to authorize these investigative techniques are often unclear to lawyers, let alone parliamentarians or the general public: while general warrants, tracking orders, and production orders can be used to exercise the aforementioned powers, it is exceedingly rare that the debates surrounding the passage of those laws include reference to the specific techniques used by LESAs today.[10] In many cases the techniques did not even exist at the time the legislation was debated and subsequently passed into law, and parliamentarians have no mechanism to understand how previously passed legislation is being used to intrude into private life. Without a mechanism to alert them of how old laws are being used in new ways, legislators remain unaware of whether debates are even required about how LESAs are (ab)using the old law in the course of their contemporary investigative efforts, or whether new laws are needed to authorize entirely new kinds of investigative techniques.

A key risk associated with the new techniques of surveillance, then, is associated with the fact that such techniques and corresponding activities rest on laws or interpretations of laws that parliamentarians and the public alike could not have been said to have legitimated. Without understanding the implications of law, citizens cannot be said to have reasonably approved a law through the activities of the political representatives. This is not to say that citizens must *agree* that the legislation in question should have been passed into law but, instead, that they should *understand* how a given law is associated with activities which

---

10 During Committee hearings for Bill C-13 (An Act to amend the Criminal Code, the Canada Evidence Act, the Competition Act and the Mutual Legal Assistance in Criminal Matters Act) parliamentarians reacted with open shock when they learned that aspects of the bill would authorize LESAs to target motor vehicles with malware. This was raised by the Canadian Civil Liberties Association; no member of government who was called to testify alerted committee members to this element of the legislation.

intrude into their private lives. The opacity of secretive digital investigative techniques and their legal justifications effectively "function outside of the scope of citizen-authorization and separate the government's actions from the actions of citizens. Instead of citizens being at the centre of democratic power, they become serfs who are protected by their government" (Parsons 2015, 83). In effect, while the surveillance activities undertaken by government may be said to be lawful – they are justified under the auspice of legislation passed by legislative assemblies – they cannot be said to be legitimate, on the basis that neither the legislative assemblies that passed the legislation nor the citizens who are affected by the law can perceive the link between the law as passed and the activity as undertaken (Habermas 1998). This gap between lawfulness and legitimacy threatens to separate the lawful from the legitimate activities of government and, in the process, promote distrust in governmental activities, the value of legislators and legislative assemblies, and potentially chill Charter rights of speech and association, among others, as citizens avoid engaging in activities that are lawful but fall outside of the norm (Penney 2017; Penney 2016).

POTENTIALS

Potential Ways of Reforming Government Surveillance of Surveillance

The current impoverishment of surveillance accountability as it relates to the Government of Canada's investigative powers in the digital era is the direct result of successive governments introducing legislation that expands the state's capabilities to intrude into private life without the legislation also including corresponding robust accountability regimes. But the current state of affairs is also the result of how members of opposition parties and civil society organizations have sought to limit the government's ability to intrude. In the case of new powers introduced in C-13 (An Act to amend the Criminal Code, the Canada Evidence Act, the Competition Act, and the Mutual Legal Assistance in Criminal Matters Act), civil society organizations fought a decade-long campaign to prevent LESAs from obtaining powers that would authorize certain kinds of warrantless surveillance or compel private companies to develop surveillance-supportive communications infrastructures (Parsons 2015c). More recently, the same classes of parties have tried to delimit the abilities of CSIS to use newly gained powers to violate Canadians' Charter rights (Forcese and Roach 2015) as well as argue against the CSE obtaining powers that could be used to further collect information about Canadians and persons in Canada, among other classes of powers (Parsons et al. 2017; British Columbia Civil Liberties Association 2018; Canadian Civil Liberties Association 2018). Only recently, in the case of Bill C-59 which extended the CSE's capabilities, have there been strong calls for a robust accountability regime to be baked into the CSE's actual use of those powers (Parsons et al. 2017; Parsons and Molnar 2017; Communications Security Establishment Commissioner 2018; Blais and Bowers 2018); this is, in part, based on the fact that the legislation itself included suggestions for accountability reform as well as a more prominent effort to include publicly accessible review-based accountability that parallels those of Canada's closest intelligence allies in the legislation as introduced at first reading (Barker et al. 2017).

Broadly, surveillance accountability can be restored following a study to understand the kinds of annual reporting that are appropriate to the different kinds of activities. Such reporting could subsequently be used to better appreciate the actual activities that are carried out to ensure peace, order, and good government in Canada and, where appropriate, expand or curtail the activities in question by way of legislation. In the case of existing deficiencies with electronic real-time surveillance reporting, which include problems tabling reports annually as required under the law as well as reports not being comparable year over year or across jurisdictions, the reports themselves might be reviewed and updated to clarify how agencies are to compile and present statistics. The legislation setting out what must be in these reports has not been updated since the mid-1970s and it is perhaps appropriate over forty years later to reflect on what is working well, what needs improvement, and whether additional granularity is required in the presented statistics. In the case of surveillance activities which are not currently subject to a dedicated annual review process, legislation might be passed to require LESAs to provide details about the kinds of investigative activities they are involved in and the legislation that authorizes such activities. Such details need not specify particular models of equipment or versions of software being employed to conduct lawful surveillance but should, at a minimum, provide actionable and specific information concerning the activities.

It may sometimes be challenging to establish an appropriate review format. In the case of production orders, for example, which can be used to compel documents from any organization from a hotel to a gas station to an internet company, it may be important to clarify the kinds of businesses or organizations that receive such orders, the volume(s) of records requested, and the kinds of records requested. Each of the aforementioned categories would admittedly be challenging to establish, given the wide breadth of possible records that might be sought by a LESA in the course of its investigation. Such difficulty, however, should not prevent legislators and stakeholders external to government from engaging in the hard work of rebuilding Canada's accountability frameworks pertaining to government surveillance activities.

The Importance and Value of Renewed Surveillance Accountability

It is particularly important that citizens and residents of Canada can clearly understand which laws are used to authorize different kinds and classes of surveillance activities. Such understandings are important for at least two reasons. First, they help to close the gap between the lawfulness of activities and the legislative branch's legitimization of the activities in question: should it become apparent that general warrants are being heavily relied on for a given type of surveillance, the link between law and a specific type of intrusive government practice would be better understood. Second, where the government adopted an interpretation of legislation that varied significantly from that of the parties who drafted the legislation, a political contest could arise surrounding the appropriateness (and, correspondingly, lawfulness) of the interpretation in question. In the United States, a legislative effort to restrict how the National Security Agency could obtain business records in the course of engaging in intelligence activities was ultimately interpreted by government lawyers as *expanding* the numbers of business records the Agency could collect (Sensenbrenner, Jr. 2013). The government's (mis)interpretation of Congress's will only came to light following revelations associated with Edward Snowden's disclosures about intelligence activities undertaken by the National Security Agency and its closest national and international partners. By compelling the government to explain how it is interpreting law, a bridge can be built between lawful activity and legitimate activity, thus better empowering LESAs in Canada to act with the broader consent of the public.

As an added advantage to government, in being more publicly accountable for its agencies' surveillance activities it becomes possible for external parties to evaluate the appropriateness of the exercise of lawful power (in terms of activities conducted) as well as the legal soundness linked with using certain techniques and devices under particular parts of the Criminal Code and other Canadian laws. These evaluations can lead government agencies to realize that there are more appropriate techniques to conduct investigations or legal avenues that would better ground the techniques being used. In the former case, if external parties can identify less intrusive measures to conduct the same kinds of investigations, then LESAs could carry out their activities in even more rights-protective ways and, in the process, better secure citizens' rights by intruding upon them in a more restricted manner. In the latter case, if external parties identify more appropriate laws that should be used to authorize LESA activities, this can have a direct impact on the strength of the investigations and criminal cases emerging from these investigations. In effect, by identifying the best laws to rest different techniques on, LESAs can adopt stronger legal arguments that they are, indeed, authorized to carry out different techniques and thus reduce the likelihood that an investigation is for naught when evidence or information collected is thrown out of court or ordered deleted on the basis that it was collected under an inappropriate legal standard or based on a flawed legal theory.

The reform of surveillance accountability can thus better ground the lawfulness of LESAs' surveillance activities while, at the same time, more firmly establishing the democratic legitimacy of the activities in question. Bridging the gap between lawfulness and legitimization would not necessarily restrict the actual kinds of surveillance that are being undertaken: it may simply reassure legislators and the public of the appropriateness of existing activities and operations. Admittedly, any accountability regime will impose an additional fiscal and operational burden on agencies interested in conducting surveillance operations, especially those with the potential to massively intrude into the private lives of Canadians and persons in Canada. But such accountability requirements were imposed on government agencies in the 1970s when they used what was, at the time, the most intrusive form of activity: real-time electronic surveillance. The principles of the 1970s are as applicable today as they were then. All that is lacking is the political will to apply them in the service of expanding Canada's surveillance accountability regime. Should this political will not manifest, and should LESAs continue to expand the scope of their digital surveillance activities without providing clarity as to how often they exercise their powers, for what reasons, to what effect, and at what economic and Charter-rights cost, then the gap between lawfulness and legitimization will only continue to widen, to the detriment of Canada's democracy.

REFERENCES

Anderson, Jonathan. 2009. "Illusions of Accountability." *Administrative Theory & Praxis* 31 (3): 332–9. https://doi.org/10.2753/atp1084-1806310302.

Barker, Cat, Claire Petrie, Joanna Dawson, Samantha Godec, Holly Porteous, and Pleasance Purser. 2017. "Oversight of Intelligence Agencies: A Comparison of the 'Five Eyes' Nations." Ottawa: Library of Parliament.

Beck, Stanley M. 1968. "Electronic Surveillance and the Administration of Criminal Justice." *The Canadian Bar Review* 46 (4): 643–93.

Blais, Pierre, and Chantelle Bowers (SIRC). 2018. "Speech for Bill C-59: Presented to the Standing Committee on Public Safety and National Security (SECU)." Standing Committee on Public Safety and National Security, February 6.

British Columbia Civil Liberties Association. 2018. "Written Submissions of the British Columbia Civil Liberties Association ('BCCLA') to the Standing Committee on Public Safety and National Security regarding Bill C-59, An Act Respecting National Security Matters." Standing Committee on Public Safety and National Security, January 30.

Canadian Civil Liberties Association. 2018. "Submission to the Standing Committee on Public Safety and National Security regarding Bill C-59, An Act Respecting National Security Matters." Standing Committee on Public Safety and National Security, January.

Chan, Serena, and L. Jean Camp. 2002. "Law Enforcement Surveillance in the Network Society." *IEEE Technology and Society Magazine* 21 (2): 22–30. https://doi.org/10.1109/MTAS.2002.1010054.

Communications Security Establishment (CSE). Undated. "CSEC Cyber Threat Capabilities: SIGINT and ITS: An End-to-End Approach." *Technology, Thoughts, and Trinkets – Canadian SIGINT Summaries*. https://

christopher-parsons.com/writings/cse-summaries/#cse-cyber-threat-capabilities.

Communications Security Establishment Commissioner. 2018. "Substantial Proposals Regarding the Intelligence Commissioner's Role." Standing Committee on Public Safety and National Security, January 30.

Forcese, Craig, and Kent Roach. 2015. *False Security: The Radicalization of Canadian Anti-Terrorism*. Toronto: Irwin Law.

Habermas, Jürgen. 1998. "On the Internal Relation between the Rule of Law and Democracy." In *The Inclusion of the Other: Studies in Political Theory*, ed. C. Cronin and P. De Greiff, 253–64. Cambridge, MA: MIT Press.

Israel, Tamir, and Christopher Parsons (for Open Media). 2016. "Written Inquiry Under Part 5 of the Freedom of Information & Protection of Privacy Act ('FIPPA') of British Columbia: In re: Vancouver Police Department." Office of the Information and Privacy Commissioner of British Columbia, March.

Kari, Shannon. 2017. "The New Surveillance State." *Canadian Lawyer*, October 2. http://www.canadianlawyermag.com/author/shannon-kari/the-new-surveillance-state-13735/.

Koutros, Nicholas, and Julien Demers. 2013. "Big Brother's Shadow: Decline in Reported Use of Electronic Surveillance by Canadian Federal Law Enforcement." *Canadian Journal of Law and Technology* 11 (1): 79–116.

Landau, Susan. 2010. *Surveillance or Security? The Risks Posed by New Wiretapping Technologies*. Cambridge, MA: MIT Press.

Landau, Susan. 2013. "Making Sense from Snowden: What's Significant in the NSA Surveillance Revelations." *IEEE Security & Privacy* 11 (4): 54–63. https://doi.org/10.1109/MSP.2013.90.

Landau, Susan. 2014. "Highlights from Making Sense of Snowden, Part II: What's Significant in the NSA Revelations." *IEEE Security & Privacy* 12 (1): 62–4. https://doi.org/10.1109/MSP.2013.161.

Law Reform Commission of Canada. 1986. "Electronic Surveillance." Department of Justice. http://trove.nla.gov.au/work/18626452?versionId=45109635.

Lyon, David. 2003. "Surveillance as Social Sorting: Computer Codes and Mobile Bodies." In *Surveillance as Social Sorting: Privacy, Risk, and Digital Discrimination*, ed. David Lyon. New York: Routledge.

Lyon, David. 2007. *Surveillance Studies: An Overview*. Cambridge: Polity Press.

Manning, Morris. 1978. *Wiretap Law in Canada: A Supplement to the Protection of Privacy Act, Bill C-176: An Analysis and Commentary*. Toronto: Butterworths.

McGuire, Patrick. 2015. "Toronto Police Chief Bragged about Monitoring Protesters and Anonymous Is Pissed." *Vice*, March 19. https://www.vice.com/en_ca/article/dpk5am/watch-torontos-police-chief-brag-about-spying-on-political-protesters-263.

Molnar, Adam, Christopher Parsons, and Erik Zouave. 2017. "Computer Network Operations and 'Rule-with-Law' in Australia." *Internet Policy Review* 6 (1): 1–15. https://doi.org/10.14763/2017.1.453.

Mulgan, Richard. 1997. "The Processes of Public Accountability." *Australian Journal of Public Accountability* 56 (1): 25–36. https://doi.org/10.1111/j.1467-8500.1997.tb01238.x.

National Commission for the Review of Federal and State Laws Relating to Wiretapping and Electronic Surveillance. 1976. *Commission Studies.* Washington, DC: United States Government.

Parsons, Christopher. 2015a. "The Governance of Telecommunications Surveillance: How Opaque and Unaccountable Practices and Policies Threaten Canadians." *Citizen Lab.* Accessed June 3, 2018. http://www.telecomtransparency.org/wp-content/uploads/2015/05/Governance-of-Telecommunications-Surveillance-Final.pdf.

Parsons, Christopher. 2015b. "Beyond the ATIP: New Methods for Interrogating State Surveillance." In *Access to Information and Social Justice,* ed. Jamie Brownlee and Kevin Walby. Winnipeg: Arbeiter Ring Publishing.

Parsons, Christopher. 2015c. "Stuck on the Agenda: Drawing Lessons from the Stagnation of 'Lawful Access' Legislation in Canada." In *Law, Privacy, and Surveillance in Canada in the Post-Snowden Era,* ed. Michael Geist, 257–83. Ottawa: Ottawa University Press.

Parsons, Christopher. 2016. "Transparency in Surveillance: Role of Various Intermediaries in Facilitating State Surveillance Transparency." *Centre for Law and Democracy.* Accessed June 3, 2018. http://responsible-tech.org/wp-content/uploads/2016/06/Parsons.pdf.

Parsons, Christopher, and Adam Molnar. 2017. "Horizontal Accountability and Signals Intelligence: Lesson Drawing from Annual Electronic Surveillance Reports." *Social Sciences Research Network.* Accessed June 3, 2018. http://dx.doi.org/10.2139/ssrn.3047272.

Parsons, Christopher, and Adam Molnar. 2018. "Government Surveillance Accountability: The Failures of Contemporary Canadian Interception Reports." *Canadian Journal of Law and Technology* 16 (1): 143–69.

Parsons, Christopher, Lex Gill, Tamir Israel, Bill Robinson, and Ron Deibert. 2017. "Analysis of the Communications Security Establishment Act and Related Provisions in Bill C-59 (An Act Respecting National Security Matters), First Reading (December 18, 2017)." *Citizen Lab / CIPPIC.* Accessed June 3, 2018. https://citizenlab.ca/wp-content/uploads/2018/01/C-59-Analysis-1.0.pdf.

Parsons, Christopher, and Tamir Israel. 2016. "Gone Opaque? An Analysis of Hypothetical IMSI Catcher Overuse in Canada." *Citizen Lab / CIPPIC.* Accessed June 3, 2018. https://citizenlab.ca/wp-content/uploads/2016/09/20160818-Report-Gone_Opaque.pdf.

Pelizzo, Riccardo, and Frederick Stapenhurst. 2013. *Government Accountability and Legislative Oversight.* New York: Routledge.

Penney, Jonathon W. 2016. "Chilling Effects: Online Surveillance and Wikipedia Use." *Berkeley Technology Law Journal* 31 (1): 117–82. https://dx.doi.org/10.15779/Z38SS13.

Penney, Jonathon W. 2017. "Internet Surveillance, Regulation, and Chilling Effects Online: A Comparative Case Study." *Internet Policy Review* 6 (2): 1–39. https://doi.org/10.14763/2017.2.692.
Przeworski, Adam, and Susan C. Stokes. 1999. *Democracy, Accountability, and Representation*. Cambridge, UK: Cambridge University Press.
Scott, Colin. 2000. "Accountability in the Regulatory State." *Journal of Law and Society* 27 (1): 38–60. https://doi.org/10.1111/1467-6478.00146.
Sensenbrenner, F. James, Jr. 2013. "Brief Amicus Curiae of Congressman F. James Sensenbrenner, Jr. in Support of Plaintiffs." ECF Case No. 13 Civ. 3994 (WHP). https://www.eff.org/document/aclu-v-clapper-amicus-brief.
Solove, Daniel. 2004. *The Digital Person: Technology and Privacy in the Information Age*. New York: New York University Press.
Strøm, Kaare. 2003. "Parliamentary Democracy and Delegation." In *Delegation and Accountability in Parliamentary Democracies*, ed. Kaare Strøm, Woldgang C. Muller, and Torbjorn Bergman. New York: Oxford University Press.
Whitaker, Reg, Gregory S. Kealey, and Andrew Parnaby. 2012. *Secret Service: Political Policing in Canada from the Fenians to Fortress America*. Toronto: University of Toronto Press.

LEGISLATION

Protection of Privacy Act, 1974.
Canada Evidence Act, R.S.C., 1985.

COURT CASES

R. v. Rogers Communications, 2016, ONSC 70.
2017 FC 1047.

CHAPTER SIX

Political Parties: Political Campaigning in the Digital Age

Tamara A. Small and Thierry Giasson

CONTEXT

Political parties' use of digital technologies during elections has garnered considerable attention from digital politics scholars across the world and, as will be discussed in this chapter, in Canada. Fundamentally, political parties are organizations that contest elections in the hope of attaining or influencing political power within a government and/or legislature. In representative democracies such as Canada, political parties serve as intermediaries between citizens and the state. At their best, they allow for citizens' public opinion to be reflected in public policy and government actions. At the federal level, Canada currently has a multi-party system, wherein five parties (Liberals, Conservatives, NDP, Bloc Québécois, and Greens) have seats in the House of Commons, although only two as of this writing seem to have the ability to form the government (Liberals and Conservatives).

Parties' scholar William Cross notes that "political parties are the central players in Canadian democracy" (2004, 3). Unlike the United States, Canadian parties rather than individual candidates structure legislative processes and election campaigning. In the system of responsible government, the House of Commons and the provincial legislatures are organized around party lines.[1] It is near impossible to be elected to either the federal or provincial legislatures without party backing. Since 1980, only seven independent candidates have been elected to the House of Commons, several of whom were elected after they had left or been kicked out of a party. Parties also play a key role in structuring the vote and elections (Meisel and Mendelsohn 2001; Cross 2004). Not only do parties, through local candidates, make up the options available to citizens at election time, the administrative and organizational components of the electoral campaign are structured by parties. Consider the leaders' tour, in which the leaders of the major political parties cross the country on buses and planes, going from riding to riding attending rallies, giving speeches, and making policy announcements. This tour is considered the focal point of the national campaign (Bélanger, Carty, and Eagles 2003). With media accompanying the party leaders, the campaigns are featured extensively in the daily news coverage of elections. Moreover, restrictive election laws govern how parties operate during elections, including spending limits and rules about advertising.

While scholars generally agree that parties are crucial to democratic politics, Canadians are more critical of their role. Samara (2013) conducted a survey in which Canadians were asked to evaluate roles performed by the country's parties. Respondents awarded parties barely passing (D) or failing (F) grades on all the roles. The survey also found that almost 70 per cent of respondents believe that parties are only interested in their votes, not their opinions. Canadian parties certainly face significant citizen engagement challenges that, perhaps, digital technologies may help alleviate.

Before addressing the promises, perils, and reality of the digitization of party politics and election campaigning in Canada, we first seek to place digital technologies within the broader context of political communication research. Political communication refers to the "role of communication in the political process" (Chaffee 1975, 15). It is important to remember that digital technologies are simply the latest way for parties to communicate with citizens during elections. Consider the oft-cited 1891 election poster for John A. Macdonald's Conservatives

1 Responsible government refers to the need of the governing party to maintain majority support of the elected members of the legislature in order to govern.

called "The Old Flag, The Old Policy, The Old Leader."[2] In the poster, Canada's first prime minister is carried on the shoulders of a farmer and an industrial worker; the image connotes Macdonald's Britishness, his experience, the continuation of the National Policy, and his support by different sectors of society. This example shows that political communication in Canada is at least as old as Confederation.

"The Old Flag, The Old Policy, The Old Leader" case is also useful in highlighting different objectives of political communication. The poster is an example of political advertising, namely, "any controlled message communicated through any channel designed to promote the political interest" of a political actor (Holtz-Bacha and Kaid 2006, 4). This would include posters, billboards, brochures, radio, and television spots as well as internet ad placement. Political advertising is an example of paid media, where political actors communicate with citizens by creating promotional or attack messages and paying to have them distributed. This is opposed to free or earned media, which political actors receive through coverage in the traditional mass media. It is free in the sense that parties and candidates do not have to pay to appear in news stories. However, parties do need to get the attention of reporters, so such attention is earned. Finally, there is also owned media, which relates to "channels the brand controls" (Tuten and Solomon 2014, 25) and includes the websites, blogs, and social media of political actors. Digital technologies have a place in all three of these media types. However, when scholars consider the role of digital technologies in party and electoral politics, it is often within the context of owned media. Such research explores how parties and candidates use their websites, Facebook pages, Twitter feeds, and YouTube channels to communicate with citizens during election campaigns. This is known as the supply side of digital politics research (Norris 2003). As discussed in the introduction, this scholarship examines the online political content produced by political actors. It is within this tradition that this chapter situates itself. Finally, we would be remiss not to note that Canadian parties also use digital technologies as paid media. Parties create and place ads on Google, within social media, or on the websites of the mass media. For

2 A copy of this poster can be seen at http://activehistory.ca/2011/04/canadian-political-leaders-the-campaign-trail-and-the-%E2%80%9Cordinary-joe%E2%80%9D/.

instance, Facebook's Ad Library, a database that includes a copy of any social or political ads running on Facebook products, includes paid ads by the major parties including ones from the 2019 election.

Scholars have divided the history of political communication into different eras or stages (Blumler and Kavanagh 1999; Norris 2000; R. Gibson and Römmele 2001). Direct, face-to-face communication was the focus of the first stage. In addition to public meetings and canvassing, Canadian politicians such as Macdonald and Wilfrid Laurier took part in the "political picnics" and the "whistle-stop tour" to engage with voters. These early leaders also benefited from party newspapers. Unlike the mass media of today, post-Confederation newspapers received financial support from politicians who were, therefore, provided favourable coverage (Taras 1990).

Broadcast media – radio and then television – brought forth a new era of political communication, enlarging the audience for political communication that could be addressed simultaneously. Carty, Cross, and Young (2001) argue that this led to a standardization of political messages across Canada. Canadian political leaders were slower to embrace radio compared to their American counterparts. Alberta premier William "Bible Bill" Aberhart was the first leader to exploit radio for campaigning in 1935. Prior to turning to politics, Aberhart was a successful radio evangelist with the popular program the *Radio Sunday School Mission*, through which he had mastered the technique of bypassing the traditional media by speaking directly to one's constituents (Carty, Cross, and Young 2001). Political advertising on radio was important during this time. One example is the Conservative Party's "Mr. Sage" ads in the 1935 federal election. These were a series of dramatized ads featuring Mr. Sage chatting with his wife or his friend Bill, accusing the Mackenzie King Liberals of engaging in fraud, intimidation, lying, and blackmail (Small, Marland, and Giasson 2014). At first, it was not known that the Conservatives were the sponsors of the messages. Dramatized political advertisements were banned by the King Liberals after the 1935 election and remain so today.

Significant as radio was, the arrival of television profoundly changed political communication. The medium added new dimensions to political communication, including a predisposition toward the visual, the dramatic, and mass appeal (Taras 1990). Being able to perform on television became as important as one's policies. This became abundantly clear in Canada's first televised election, in 1957. Conservative leader John Diefenbaker, an exceptional orator, was far more comfortable on television than Liberal prime minister Louis St. Laurent. Duffy (2002, 203) describes St. Laurent's use of broadcast technologies as "uncomfortable" and "leaden." Diefenbaker's election ended twenty-two years of Liberal rule. No discussion of television in Canadian politics is complete without a mention of Pierre Elliot Trudeau. The charismatic, youthful, fashionable Trudeau capitalized on television, creating his own brand of political celebritization called "Trudeaumania" (Marland 2016). According to Litt, "Pierre Trudeau could always be counted on for a quip or pseudo-profundity, and he provided the visuals that the medium required: an interesting gesture, flips off a diving board, boogying beside a broken campaign bus, a fake fall down a staircase. In the first 'truly made-for-TV campaign,' Trudeau gave good television" (2008, 51).

Even today, broadcasting remains central to Canadian election campaigning. While in decline, television remains the main source of information of Canadians (Nadeau and Bastien 2016). Political advertising on television is one of the main ways that parties communicate their policies, present their leaders, and criticize the opposition. In the 2015 election, $47 million was spent on radio and television advertising by all the parties.[3] At 39 per cent of the entire campaign budget, radio and television together continue to be the single largest expense for Canadian parties.[4] Also, during this second era, the press became less partisan. This resulted in political leaders and parties competing for media attention. As a result of these factors, media management, polling, and professionalization became the innovative tools of the trade for political actors during the era (Carty, Cross, and Young 2001).

3 At seventy-eight days, the 2015 campaign was one of the longest in Canadian history, which meant parties were able to spend more than usual. According to law, if an election period is longer than thirty-seven days, then the maximum spending limit will increase by 1/37 of the initial limit for every day beyond the thirty-seventh. The amount of spending in the 2015 election is therefore atypical. As a comparison, the 2019 federal campaign lasted forty days.

4 Breakdown of Paid Election Expenses by Expense Category and Registered Political Party – 2015 General Election, http://www.elections.ca/content.aspx?section=fin&dir=oth/pol/break&document=brk42ge&lang=e.

The most recent era is characterized by a fragmentation and diversification of the media environment (see chapter 7). Not only is there a multiplicity of channels and an increased number of innovative emergent communication technologies, the information environment exists twenty-four hours a day, seven days a week. While television continues to be important, there are considerably more channels, many of which focus on news and public affairs (e.g., CBC News Network, RDI, CNN, or Fox News). Digital technologies, including the internet, mobile devices, social media, and related applications, have furthered this fragmentation. Political communication today is accelerated and exists in a hybrid environment where old and new media as well as old and new campaign techniques coexist (Chadwick 2013; Giasson, Greffet, and Chacon 2018). From breaking news on TV to live-tweeting, political information can move around faster than ever on a diversity of platforms. This makes political communication both easier and more difficult for parties and political candidates (Small, Marland, and Giasson 2014). On the one hand, parties and political candidates have significantly more venues to communicate with citizens, several of which are unmediated and allow for direct communication. On the other, campaigners need to have content for all these channels and technologies and need to quickly develop proficiency in constantly changing technologies. As such, new campaign techniques such as message personalization, political marketing, data analytics, and microtargeting are now used by parties to get political messages to citizens more effectively. It is within this era of a hybrid media ecosystem driven by instantaneous communication that we focus our analysis of Canadian political parties and election campaigning vis-à-vis digital technologies.

Scholars of the stages/eras of political communication remind us that while technological changes have the capacity to change the former, this process is one of supplementation rather than displacement (Small, Marland, and Giasson 2014). In this hybrid environment, old political communication techniques such as lawn signs and television ads exist alongside newer ones like Instagram stories and Twitter posts. While digital technologies are certainly the latest tools for parties to communicate with citizens, their relative importance compared to other technologies remains up for debate. In what follows, we explore this third era in more detail, specifically as it applies to the Canadian context.

DIGITIZATION

Promises & Perils

Parties all follow the same fundamental objective when engaging in election preparedness: to win the contest, gain power, and form government. However, the political landscape in Canada and in other democratic regimes has changed considerably in recent decades. Citizens are more critical of their elites, their trust in political institutions has eroded significantly, and they vote in fluctuating numbers. Electoral participation and party membership have been in steady decline in Canada, both strong indicators of the growing distrust of citizens in these institutions and their leaders. Political parties have been facing this crisis of legitimacy for decades and turned to digital technologies and the internet, in conjunction with other strategic approaches such as political marketing, as possible tools to correct the negative effects of democratic malaise on their electoral success.

Over the last twenty years, an enormous body of scholarly work has been dedicated to the investigation of digital politics and campaigning. However, academics have failed to arrive at a consensus regarding the capacity of the internet to mitigate the perils of democratic malaise. So far, two competing perspectives have been guiding research (see Table I.1). The first, known as the equalization hypothesis, is characterized by a very optimistic take on the potential role the web could play in bridging the gaps between critical citizens and their political elites. The equalization hypothesis depicts cyberspace as a levelled and egalitarian battlefield where citizens could engage directly with parties and governments, where smaller parties would get visibility and a better chance to reach voters, and where partisan political communication should be an interactive two-way dialogic process (Tkach-Kawasaki 2003; Gibson and McAllister 2015). The internet is seen here as an affordable open public space facilitating political debate, protecting free speech, and therefore stimulating political engagement and democratic vitality.

Some of these expected outcomes have in fact been observed, especially since the advent of social media platforms. Citizens now have more channels to address their elites directly, to share political content, and express their points of views on issues and politics. From political blog entries of 2004 to Instagram stories in 2020, millions of internet users have used social media to engage in political debates online. Nevertheless, empirical work also indicates that most of the positives expected under the equalization theory have failed to manifest, and that online politicking has reproduced values and practices observed offline for many years. Rather, a normalization process, in which political communication and campaigning online merely reflect more of the same, has seemed to emerge as the dominant theoretical conclusion in scholarly work from the last fifteen years (Margolis and Resnick 2000; Gibson et al. 2003; Gibson and McAllister 2015; Small 2016).

Practice

International research indicates that the egalitarian ideal that was associated with digital campaigning has failed to manifest on three important fronts. First, past scholarship revealed that smaller parties do not benefit at the polls from their digital campaigning (Small 2008). Having more resources for digital campaigns usually means getting more visibility online and offline, which is the case for large traditional parties. The web is still not a fair battleground. Some research does indicate that social-democratic, fringe, or challenger parties from the opposition usually engage in more innovative digital campaigns than large traditional, conservative, or incumbent governing parties (Gibson, Nixon, and Ward 2003; Copsey 2003; Lilleker and Vedel 2013; Vaccari 2013; Giasson, Greffet, and Chacon 2018). For instance, Chadwick and Stromer-Galley (2016, 283) argue that digital technologies create organizational experimentation that allows newer and smaller parties that "reject norms of hierarchical discipline and habitual partisan loyalty" to have electoral success.[5] But innovation is not always synonymous with electoral success.

Second, most political parties are terrified of losing control over their communications online and therefore do not actively engage

5 We have not seen too much evidence of this at the federal level in Canada. The mainstream political parties continue to dominate. One possible exception may be the People's Party of Canada (PPC), which some have likened to a party-movement (Budd 2018). In the 2019 election, the PPC received less than 2 per cent of the vote, and party leader Bernier lost the seat he held since 2006. The success and permanence of the People's Party remains to be seen, as does its relationship with digital technology.

in dialogic two-way communication with citizens during elections. Instead, they still practice very coherent messaging strategies and develop mobilization platforms used to channel and manage internet users in digital campaigning. The logic behind this tactic is that if you provide online sympathizers with the right script to follow, you better manage the risk of losing control of your party message online. In this normalizing approach to online political communication, the internet and social media are considered as additional spaces where partisan messages are broadcasted to targeted publics.

Finally, and probably most concerning in terms of democratic malaise, in their efforts to design and implement more effective campaigns, parties are collecting massive amounts of personal data on citizens. The 2018 scandal involving the British online political consulting firm Cambridge Analytica exposed unethical practices of covert harvesting and misuse of Facebook data for American and British political campaigns (Rosenberg, Confessore, and Cadwalladr 2018; Zimonjic 2018). Faced with a disaffected electorate, a fractured media environment, fragmented audiences, restrictive campaign legislations, and diminished public financing, parties use data management tools to segment and profile electors and draft messages that will reach them more precisely. These data are collected online (largely without their proprietors' awareness or consent), combined in databases, and analyzed with algorithms to help election strategists target voters or predict voting patterns. This electoral data marketing has been facilitated in recent years by analytics that parties access online through their social media presences. Known as a citizen "data shadow" (Howard 2006, 199), this readily available online information may help parties develop platforms and campaigns with limited direct contact with voters. This is a far cry from the idealized open public space advocated in the equalization thesis. Rather, parties have adapted their campaigning practices to the particularities of digital technologies. As Margolis and Resnick (2000), two of the first scholars to bring forth the normalization thesis, stated in 1997, online political communication is just "politics as usual" from a political party perspective.

Canadian investigations into digital campaigning by parties largely confirm this conclusion. Over the last twenty years, scholars of online politics in Canada have been depicting how political parties – with very few exceptions – have adapted their election preparedness in similar ways to the technological transformations brought forth by the digitization of communication. Past research has approached the field from three related angles: the depth of adoption/adaptation by parties to different online technologies, the level of interaction of partisan formations with voters in digital campaigning, and the guiding strategic objectives and philosophies in parties' internet electioneering efforts.

The first type of scholarly contributions has studied how Canadian parties have been integrating technologies in their electoral communication arsenals. Most of this research has focused on federal organizations and indicates that, without being trendsetters, Canadian parties are often early adopters of novel digital communication platforms. From blogs to Facebook, Twitter, and voter information databases, Canadian politicians and their parties quickly invest in emergent technologies for campaigning purposes. The earliest instance of internet adoption in a campaign to have been studied in Canada was the 1995 Quebec referendum, during which both the YES and NO camps created and maintained campaign websites (Launaz 1996). At the federal level, the 2000 election is often presented as the first internet campaign in Canada and the 2011 election as the first real social media campaign (Small 2016). More recent work on technological adoption investigates online data collection and analysis in Canadian parties (Patten 2017, 2016; Giasson and Small 2017; Giasson 2017; also see chapter 1). These contributions indicate that all federal organizations collect and analyze large datasets of voter information to help them target audiences and predict voting patterns in different segments of the electorate. The processes are ongoing between electoral cycles, bringing Canadian federal parties to a permanent state of election readiness.

At the same time, as a significant body of international work indicates, the fact that parties are online does not mean they engage in interactive communication during their campaign. This conclusion is largely shared by most researchers investigating this question in Canada. As social media became a staple of Canadians' daily life, more attention has been directed at how parties negotiate the inherent interactive and reactive principles embedded in these digital platforms. Scholars have found that limiting, guiding, or controlling interaction with electors seems to be the norm in online Canadian political communication. Content analyses of parties' online message postings by

Small (2011, 2014), Giasson et al. (2013), and Chen and Smith (2010a) all show that they use online platforms first and foremost to broadcast content in a top-down approach. Canadians parties do not frequently initiate online interaction and dialogue with voters. Rare instances of interaction are usually reactive to voters' initiatives and are carried out in relatively safe and controlled settings, such as chat sessions or Facebook responses to commentaries. Current research also seems to support Karpf's (2012) opposition innovation hypothesis indicating that challenger parties with less chance to form government do engage in much more active dialogic and interactive communication and campaigning than incumbent governing parties (Small 2011; Giasson et al. 2013; Giasson and Small 2017; Giasson, Greffet, and Chacon 2018). Parties do not really engage in real "2.0" social media campaigning. Rather, they follow a safe, controlled "1.5 to 1.75" way of communicating with voters. Message cohesion remains key.

Finally, Canadian research also investigates the strategies guiding parties' digital campaigning. Following years of inferred hypotheses developed from content analyses of online strategic objectives, scholars have more recently engaged in expert interviews with party strategists to get a better sense of the motivations that drive digital campaigning. As Table 6.1 indicates, interviews with digital advisers to federal and provincial campaigns suggest that parties go online first and foremost to spread their messages and reach targeted audiences. Communication objectives remain the top priority in parties' digital campaigning initiatives. Online strategic objectives are also platform specific. Some strategists also evoke marketing goals (including voter data collection) and the importance of mobilizing online supporters to help protect the party brand and message on the internet. These "brand ambassadors" are brought into the campaigns and used by strategists as social media spin doctors, invested with the mission to share content, reply to attacks, or reframe opponent interpretations and media coverage items, therefore expanding a party's online reach. Most parties build and manage their own communities of online supporters because they are considered to be central components of their peer-to-peer, viral persuasion campaigns in digital platforms. Finally, having had to adjust to radical transformations in financing following legislative reforms in the last decade, Canadian parties have all turned to digital tools to generate resources (Marland and Matthews 2017). Concerted campaigns

Table 6.1. Strategic objectives related to specific digital platforms in Canada

Facebook	Objectives • Broadcast targeted messages • Broadcast partisan or campaign activities (Facebook Live) • Personalization of the party leader (mostly using photos) • Manage teams of online party "ambassadors" or "supermilitants" (via private groups)
Twitter	Objectives • Broadcast message of the day • Spin or reframe message interpretations • Reach influencers (political reporters, militants, citizen opinion leaders) • Personalization of the party leader (using tweets and photos)
YouTube	Objectives • Broadcast the party's message (television ads) • Broadcast partisans or campaign activities (live feeds or not)
Emails	Objectives • Generate resources (financial contributions) • Broadcast issue position to targeted voters (according to issues) • Mobilize participation with "calls to action," online and offline
Party website and online mobilization platforms	Objectives • Broadcast the party's message (ideological position and electoral platform, pledges) • Guide online users' contributions and mobilization • Mobilize participation with "calls to action," online and offline

Source: Adapted from Giasson and Small (2017) and Giasson et al. (2018).

using emails to targeted publics, A/B testing procedures,[6] SMS, robo-calls, online petitions, memes, Twitter hashtags, and social media info graphs on "issues of the day" are the daily online communication tactics mobilized by parties to attract the attention of Canadians, collect additional data on them, and convince them to donate contributions. As Giasson and Small's account of Canadian opposition parties' online

6 A/B testing is an online marketing process used to measure and strengthen the efficiency of messages through stimulating specific behaviours in targeted audiences. It entails emailing two slightly modified versions (A and B) of the same message to two identical samples of target receptors to evaluate which content elicits the highest levels of desired reaction from the target. The most reactive content is then selected and forwarded to the entire targeted segment of the population.

strategic objectives for permanent campaigning reveals, online financing now accounts for a third of those parties' annual contributions, most of them being small donations.

As diverse and coherent as it stands, this body of Canadian work on digital campaigning by parties still reveals important gaps. Some of these limits are theoretical and others seem more empirical in nature. One glaring omission in current scholarship concerns the knowledge and perception of voters about parties' efforts in digital campaigning. What do Canadians really know about digital campaigning and what do they think about these online electoral initiatives? Are parties providing them with content and information they find useful to make their electoral decisions? Do Canadian have sufficient digital skills to engage properly in digital campaigning initiatives? How is this impacting their perception of the role of political parties in Canadian democracy? Is digital campaigning contributing to alleviating democratic malaise in Canada, or does it heighten it? So far, scholars have failed to address these questions in research.

Second, with a few rare exceptions, most of Canadian scholarship on digital campaigning has been dedicated to the main federal parties (see Montigny et al. 2019; Jansen 2004; Chen and Smith 2010b; Bastien and Greffet 2009; Giasson et al. 2013; Verville 2013; Cross et al. 2015; Giasson, Greffet, and Chacon 2018). Provincial parties and elections are rarely investigated, and comparative analyses of digital campaign initiatives are virtually non-existent. Federal parties have so far attracted the bulk of scientific attention because they possess more resources than their provincial counterparts and have been depicted as innovators in digital campaigning, especially in terms of voter data collection and management. However, as the *enpolitique.com* project revealed in its investigation of parties' digital campaigns during the Quebec 2012 provincial election, innovation in digital campaigning techniques also occurs during provincial contests. When comparing the Twitter campaigns of parties and leaders in the 2011 federal election and the Quebec provincial election of 2012, Giasson and his collaborators (2013) demonstrated how much more active and dialogic the official feeds of parties were during the Quebec campaign. Held only sixteen months apart, these two Twitter campaigns could not have been more dissimilar in their approach to content distribution and openness to interaction with voters. Provincial distinctiveness can also manifest itself in digital campaigning. Giasson and Small (2014) compared the use of the microblogging platform by parties in the 2011 Ontario and the 2012 Quebec provincial elections. Their findings reveal that Quebec parties were three times more likely to engage in interactions with users on Twitter than their Ontario counterparts. Quebec parties were also much more active on the platform, with an average thirty-five tweets a day compared to nine a day during the campaign in Ontario. The authors point to incumbency, ideological congruence, and resources to explain the similarity and differences in campaign tactics observed in the two studied cases. Finally, municipal elections are also understudied (see Raynauld and Greenberg 2014). This is despite claims that Naheed Nenshi won the 2010 Calgary mayoral race because of his innovative social media use (Davy 2010). In an analysis of that campaign, Dumitrica (2014) explores Nenshi's authenticity on social media, a rare example of scholarship on municipalities in this area. The country's strong regional and cultural identities of its provinces may explain why scholars have yet to fully engage in a concerted pan-Canadian research initiative on digital campaigning, where online electoral strategies and efforts would be studied with similar methodological instruments. It may be time to remedy this unfortunate trend, which limits knowledge production and a more comprehensive understanding of digital campaigning strategies and practices in Canada.

Also contributing to the lack of comparative perspectives – and this may be less obviously addressed by Canadian scholars – large international comparative studies rarely integrate Canada into their research designs. With the exception of Chen and Smith's (2010a) work comparing digital campaigning in Canada, Australia, and New Zealand, Canadian digital campaign strategies have been overlooked in comparative projects. Other British parliamentary regimes such as the UK and Australia are more commonly featured in comparative studies, leaving Canada isolated and somewhat understudied. Canadian scholars may need to take a stronger lead in developing comparative projects with their international counterparts to help bring the Canadian experience and particularities into perspective.

Third, although research has been dedicated over the years to Canadian parties' different digital contents, platforms, electoral strategies and practices, a significant part of these contributions has focused in recent years on Twitter. Three reasons explain this. First, Twitter offers academics one of the easiest datasets to collect in social media. Numerous low-cost harvesting services available online help scholars collect tweets directly from the network's application programming interface (API) (Jungherr 2016). Second, its very concise and mostly text format facilitates content analysis of large datasets of messages. Third, Twitter remains to this day an influential social media platform where elites, political reporters, influencers, and decision makers share opinions and information instantaneously. It is a polarized space of political debate and conflict from which many news items are carried over to mainstream media to reach society. It therefore remains an important platform to study.

However, in Canada, Twitter's actual reach is limited. In this country, political conversations carried over the platform are somewhat of a niche affair and have yet to generate significant effects on the course of election campaigns. Other social media platforms, such as Facebook or Instagram, generate larger membership and should attract more attention from Canadian academics. Access to, collection, and analysis of data from these digital platforms may complicate scholarly work, but the sheer numbers of Canadian users and the very high and diverse levels of campaigning carried on them by national parties should warrant more scientific attention. In recent years, Canadian scholars such as Lalancette and Raynauld (2019) have started to broaden the research agenda by focusing on different digital social media platforms and applications.

POTENTIALS

What lies ahead for Canadian digital campaigns? Toward what trends should Canadian scholars of digital campaigning direct their attention in the coming years? The context within which strategists map out electoral communication has recently undergone profound transformations. For instance, as in other political contexts, Canadian parties find themselves challenged by the disinformation. One example is the 2019 viral video that appeared to show Prime Minister Justin Trudeau being snubbed by the Brazilian president at the G20 Summit (Sciarpelletti 2019). After it was shared on both social and legacy media, it was learned that the video's creators had edited out the part where the Brazilian president turned back to Trudeau and embraced him a moment later. Political actors need to be concerned both with cyber-protection of their own digital footprints and combatting false messages about themselves. Regardless of this transformation or others (e.g., years of hybridity in practices, diversity of communication outlets, instantaneity in communication and reaction, individualization of campaigns, permanent campaigning), the main objectives of parties remain the same: get voters to the poll to win the election. Getting every needed ballot in the box is what matters and the campaign, whether online or offline, should be entirely dedicated to achieving this most basic of electoral objectives.

The future of digital parties and campaigning in Canada and elsewhere may also take us beyond the equalization-normalization dichotomy, as novel practices of online electioneering may compromise the quality of democracy and citizenship. As other scholars have noted (Savigny 2011; Giasson, Lees-Marshment, and Marland 2012; Howard 2006), political parties are increasingly reliant on political marketing techniques and voter data management, which both carry the potential to restrict interest representation, impact the common good, and limit public debate. For instance, the campaigns of Barack Obama in 2008 and 2012 and of Donald Trump in 2016 were extremely successful in using social media data to glean insights into what mattered to voters and target specific demographic groups (Hendricks and Schill 2017). The exercise of voting is more and more determined by algorithms analyzing citizens' data shadows and by electoral promises designed to answer individualized needs and wants. While the media has shown increased interest in the issue of voter data collection and analysis in its coverage of party campaigning (Delacourt 2016; McGregor 2014; Pare 2017), the vast majority of Canadians lack knowledge on the depth and impact of these practices on their lives and our democracy.

Each Canadian's exposure to political issues and debates and campaign and partisan messages is determined by algorithms and therefore individualized and practically unique. Their experience of a campaign may not resemble that of their co-worker or of their next-door neighbour. These tactics remain largely hidden; party strategists rarely reveal them and those who do speak anonymously. Further, as Howard (2006) reminds us in his ethnography of the American community of digital strategists, technologies carry in their codes the values of their developers and of the communities of professionals who design and implement them. These values celebrate efficiency, political gain, and precision in targeting at the expense of transparency and privacy (Howard 2006, 170–1). This digital electoral science has the potential to isolate citizens from one another and to redefine the public sphere into a multiplicity of micro-publics, separated partisan bubbles or echo chambers in which the political conversation remains ideologically undifferentiated. In doing so, the pervading use of electoral data marketing and digital microtargeting may be announcing the end of political debate and confrontation of ideas. And it will happen without Canadians knowing about it, as the secretive process is practically undetectable. Future political science and digital politics scholarship in Canada will be crucial in assessing the practice and effects of big data and political marketing on citizenship.

In some ways, Canada may not be the first place to look for the future of digital campaigning. Rather, our neighbour to the south is a far better place to begin. American presidential campaigns and scholarship about them dominate our understandings of digital politics (Graber et al. 2004). From the earliest uses of digital technologies, candidates and political parties worldwide, including in Canada, have attempted to emulate what has occurred in the previous American election (Radwaski 2014). This is not necessarily a new practice; the "Americanization" literature suggests that American political actors are often the first to use and master political campaigning techniques and that other countries tend to follow their lead (Norris 2000). It remains to be seen if and how Donald Trump's unique use of social media, including his use of Twitter to both bypass and dominate the traditional media, translates into campaigns in Canada or elsewhere. However, it is important to recognize that the United States may serve as inspiration for political actors, but it does not seem to provide a "reliable empirical guide to the actual development and outcomes" in other digital campaigns (Vaccari 2013, 4). This is because other national political systems vary considerably from the American presidential arrangement. Moreover, digital technologies are a "moving target" (Ward et al. 2008) for political communication. The "it" technology changes from year to year. In the late 1990s, having a political or campaign website was a sign of technological sophistication. Then came email, followed by blogs, and now social media. Each technology has its own unique set of practices, rules, and opportunities. Canadian parties watch future American digital campaigns closely, but how the use of digital technology plays out in Canada will likely differ from the experience of their southern neighours.

REFERENCES

Bastien, Frédérick, and Fabienne Greffet. 2009. "Les campagnes électorales sur Internet: Une comparaison entre France et Québec." *Hermès* 54: 211–19. https://doi.org/10.4267/2042/31762.

Bélanger, Paul, R. Kenneth Carty, and Munroe Eagles. 2003. "The Geography of Canadian Parties' Electoral Campaigns: Leaders' Tours and Constituency Election Results." *Political Geography* 22 (4): 439–55. https://doi.org/10.1016/S0962-6298(02)00113-0.

Blumler, Jay G., and Dennis Kavanagh. 1999. "The Third Age of Political Communication: Influences and Features." *Political Communication* 16 (3): 209–30. https://doi.org/10.1080/105846099198596.

Budd, Brian. 2018. "What I Learned at a People's Party of Canada Rally." The Conversation, November 19. http://theconversation.com/what-i-learned-at-a-peoples-party-of-canada-rally-107051.

Carty, R. Kenneth, William Cross, and Lisa Young. 2001. *Rebuilding Canadian Party Politics*. Vancouver: UBC Press.

Chadwick, Andrew. 2013. *The Hybrid Media System: Politics and Power*. Oxford, UK: Oxford University Press.

Chadwick, Andrew, and Jennifer Stromer-Galley. 2016. "Digital Media, Power, and Democracy in Parties and Election Campaigns: Party Decline or Party Renewal?" *The International Journal of Press/Politics* 21 (3): 283–93. https://doi.org/10.1177/1940161216646731.

Chaffee, Steven H. 1975. *Political Communication: Issues and Strategies for Research*. Vol. 4. Beverly Hills: Sage.

Chen, Peter John, and Peter Jay Smith. 2010a. "Adoption and Use of Digital Media in Election Campaigns: Australia, Canada, and New Zealand Compared." *Public Communication Review* 1 (1): 3–26. https://doi.org/10.5130/pcr.v1i1.1249.

Chen, Peter John, and Peter Jay Smith. 2010b. "Campaigning and Digital Media in Alberta: Emerging Practices and Democratic Outcomes?" *Canadian Political Science Review* 4 (2–3): 36–55. https://ojs.unbc.ca/index.php/cpsr/article/view/185/299.

Copsey, Nigel. 2003. "Extremism on the Net: The Extreme Right and the Value of the Internet." In *Political Parties and the Internet: Net Gain*, ed. Rachel K. Gibson, Paul G. Nixon, and Stephen J. Ward, 232–47. London: Routledge.

Cross, William. 2004. *Political Parties*. Vancouver: UBC Press.

Cross, William, Jonathan Malloy, Tamara A. Small, and Laura Stephenson. 2015. *Fighting for Votes: Parties, the Media, and Voters in the 2011 Ontario Election*. Vancouver: UBC Press.

Davy, Steven. 2010. "How Calgary's Mayor Used Social Media to Get Elected." MediaShift, December 8. http://mediashift.org/2010/12/how-calgarys-mayor-used-social-media-to-get-elected342/.

Delacourt, Susan. 2016. *Shopping for Votes: How Politicians Choose Us and We Choose Them*. Madeira Park, BC: Douglas & McIntyre Publishers.

Duffy, John. 2002. *Fights of Our Lives: Elections, Leadership, and the Making of Canada*. Toronto: HarperCollins Canada.

Dumitrica, Delia. 2014. "Politics as 'Customer Relations:' Social Media and Political Authenticity in the 2010 Municipal Elections in Calgary, Canada." *Javnost – The Public* 21 (1): 53–69. https://doi.org/10.1080/13183222.2014.11009139.

Giasson, Thierry. 2017. "Du marketing à la science électorale." In *Le Parlementarisme Canadien*, ed. Réjean Pelletier and Manon Tremblay, 153–72. Quebec City: Presses de l'Université Laval.

Giasson, Thierry, Fabienne Greffet, and Geneviève Chacon. 2018. "Relever le défi de l'hybridité: Les objectifs des stratégies de campagnes numériques lors des élections française et québécoise de 2012." *Politique et Sociétés* 37 (2): 19–46. https://doi.org/10.7202/1048875ar.

Giasson, Thierry, Gildas Le Bars, Frédérick Bastien, and Mélanie Verville. 2013. "Qc2012: L'utilisation de Twitter Par Les Partis." In *Les québécois aux urnes: Les partis, les médias et les citoyens en campagne*, ed. by Éric Bélanger, Frédérick Bastien, and François Gélineau, 133–46. Montreal: Les Presses de l'Université de Montréal.

Giasson, Thierry, Jennifer Lees-Marshment, and Alex Marland. 2012. "Challenges to Democracy." In *Political Marketing in Canada*, ed. Alex Marland, Thierry Giasson, and Jennifer Lees-Marshment, 241–55. Vancouver: UBC Press.

Giasson, Thierry, and Tamara A. Small. 2014. "#elections: The Use of Twitter by Provincial Political Parties in Canada." Paper Presented at the British Association of Canadian Studies, London, UK, April 2014. Unpublished.

Giasson, Thierry, and Tamara A. Small. 2017. "Online, All the Time: The Permanent Campaign on Web Platforms." In *Permanent Campaigning in Canada*, ed. Alex Marland, Thierry Giasson, and Anna Lennox Esselment, 109–26. Vancouver: UBC Press.

Gibson, Rachel K., Michael Margolis, David Resnick, and Stephen J. Ward. 2003. "Election Campaigning on the WWW in the USA and UK: A Comparative Analysis." *Party Politics* 9 (1): 47–75. https://doi.org/10.1177/135406880391004.

Gibson, Rachel K., and Ian McAllister. 2015. "Normalising or Equalising Party Competition? Assessing the Impact of the Web on Election Campaigning." *Political Studies* 63 (3): 529–47. https://doi.org/10.1111/1467-9248.12107.

Gibson, Rachel K., Paul G. Nixon, and Stephen J. Ward, eds. 2003. *Political Parties and the Internet: Net Gain?* London: Routledge.

Gibson, Rachel, and Andrea Römmele. 2001. "Changing Campaign Communications: A Party-Centered Theory of Professionalized Campaigning." *Harvard International Journal of Press/Politics* 6 (4): 31–43. https://doi.org/10.1177/108118001129172323.

Graber, Doris A., Bruce Bimber, W. Lance Bennett, Richard Davis, and Pippa Norris. 2004. "The Internet and Politics: Emerging Perspectives." In *Academy and the Internet*, ed. Helen Nissenbaum and Monroe E. Price, 90–119. New York: Peter Lang.

Hendricks, John Allen, and Dan Schill. 2017. "The Social Media Election of 2016." In *The Social Media Election of 2016*, ed. Robert E. Denton Jr., 121–50. London: Palgrave Macmillan.

Holtz-Bacha, Christina, and Lynda Lee Kaid. 2006. "Political Advertising in International Comparison." In *The Sage Handbook of Political Advertising*, ed. Lynda Lee Kaid and Christina Holtz-Bacha, 3–14. Thousand Oaks, CA: Sage.

Howard, Philip N. 2006. *New Media Campaigns and the Managed Citizen.* Cambridge, UK: Cambridge University Press.

Jansen, Harold. 2004. "Is the Internet Politics as Usual or Democracy's Future? Candidate Campaign Web Sites in the 2001 Alberta and British Columbia Provincial Elections." *The Public Sector Innovation Journal* 9 (2): 1–20.

Jungherr, Andreas. 2016. "Twitter Use in Election Campaigns: A Systematic Literature Review." *Journal of Information Technology & Politics* 13 (1): 72–91. https://doi.org/10.1080/19331681.2015.1132401.

Karpf, David. 2012. *The MoveOn Effect: The Unexpected Transformation of American Political Advocacy.* Oxford: Oxford University Press.

Lalancette, Mireille, and Vincent Raynauld. 2019. "The Power of Political Image: Justin Trudeau, Instagram, and Celebrity Politics." *American Behavioral Scientist* 63 (7): 888–924. https://doi.org/10.1177/0002764217744838.

Launaz, Philippe. 1996. "La campagne référendaire sur Internet." In *La bataille du Québec: Troisième épisode*, ed. Denis Monière and Jean H. Guay, 119–30. Montreal: Fides.

Lilleker, Darren, and Thierry Vedel. 2013. "The Internet in Campaigns and Elections." In *The Oxford Handbook of Internet Studies*, ed. William H. Dutton, 401–20. Oxford: Oxford University Press.

Litt, Paul. 2008. "Trudeaumania: Participatory Democracy in the Mass-Mediated Nation." *Canadian Historical Review* 89 (1): 27–53. https://doi.org/10.3138/chr.89.1.27.

Margolis, Michael, and David Resnick. 2000. *Politics as Usual: The Cyberspace Revolution.* Thousand Oaks, CA: Sage.

Marland, Alex. 2016. *Brand Command: Canadian Politics and Democracy in the Age of Message Control.* Vancouver: UBC Press.

Marland, Alex, and Maria Matthews. 2017. "'Friend, Can You Chip in $3?' Canadian Political Parties' Email Communication and Fundraising Emails." In *Permanent Campaigning in Canada*, ed. Alex Marland, Thierry Giasson, and Anna Lennox Esselment, 87–108. Vancouver: UBC Press.

McGregor, Glen. 2014. "If the 2011 Vote Was the 'Twitter Election,' Then 2015 Will Be the 'Big Data Election.'" *National Post*, October 17. http://nationalpost.com/news/if-the-2011-vote-was-the-twitter-election-then-2015-will-be-the-big-data-election.

Meisel, John, and Matthew Mendelsohn. 2001. "Meteor? Phoenix? Chameleon? The Decline and Transformation of Party in Canada." In *Party Politics in Canada*, 8th edition, ed. Hugh G. Thorburn and Alan Whitehorn, 163–78. Toronto: Prentice Hall.

Montigny, Eric, Philippe Dubois, and Thierry Giasson. 2019. "On the Edge of Glory (...or Catastrophe): Regulation, Transparency and Party Democracy in Data-Driven Campaigning in Québec." *Internet Policy Review* 8 (4). https://doi.org/10.14763/2019.4.1441.

Nadeau, Richard, and Frédérick Bastien. 2016. "Political Campaigning." In *Canadian Parties in Transition: Recent Trends and New Paths for Research*, 4th ed., ed. Alain-G. Gagnon and A. Brian Tanguay, 364–87. Toronto: University of Toronto Press.

Norris, Pippa. 2000. *A Virtuous Circle: Political Communications in Postindustrial Societies.* New York: Cambridge University Press.

Norris, Pippa. 2003. "Preaching to the Converted? Pluralism, Participation, and Party Websites." *Party Politics* 9 (1): 21–45. https://doi.org/10.1177/135406880391003.

Pare, Isabelle. 2017. "Les algorithmes, ces nouveaux acteurs dans l'arène politique." *Le Devoir*, February 18. https://www.ledevoir.com/societe/science/492017/les-algorithmes-nouveaux-joueurs-sur-l-echiquier-politique.

Patten, Steve. 2016. "The Evolution of the Canadian Party System: From Brokerage to Marketing-Oriented Politics." In *Canadian Parties in Transition: Recent Trends and New Paths for Research*, 4th ed., ed. Alain-G. Gagnon and A. Brian Tanguay, 3–27. Toronto: University of Toronto Press.

Patten, Steve. 2017. "Databases, Microtargeting, and the Permanent Campaign: A Threat to Democracy?" In *Permanent Campaigning in Canada*, ed. Alex Marland, Thierry Giasson, and Anna Lennox Esselment, 47–64. Vancouver: UBC Press.

Radwaski, Adam. 2014. "Former Obama Aides Advising NDP, Liberals on Campaign Strategy." December 27. https://www.theglobeandmail.com/news/politics/ndp-liberals-using-grassroots-mobilization-tactics-from-obama-campaigns/article22216447/.

Raynauld, Vincent, and Josh Greenberg. 2014. "Tweet, Click, Vote: Twitter and the 2010 Ottawa Municipal Election." *Journal of Information Technology & Politics* 11 (4): 412–34. http://dx.doi.org/10.1080/19331681.2014.935840.

Rosenberg, Matthew, Nicholas Confessore, and Carole Cadwalladr. 2018. "How Trump Consultants Exploited the Facebook Data of Millions." *New York Times*, March 17. https://www.nytimes.com/2018/03/17/us/politics/cambridge-analytica-trump-campaign.html.

Samara. 2013. "By Invitation Only: Canadians' Perceptions of Political Parties." Samara. http://www.samaracanada.com/docs/default-source/default-document-library/samara_byinvitationonly.pdf?sfvrsn=fc083c2f_4.

Savigny, Heather. 2011. *The Problem of Political Marketing*. London: Continuum.

Sciarpelletti, Laura. 2019. "How Memes Could Be the New Political Attack Ads." CBC, July 5. https://www.cbc.ca/news/canada/british-columbia/memes-politics-ads-justin-trudeau-1.5198271.

Small, Tamara A. 2008. "Equal Access, Unequal Success: Major and Minor Canadian Parties on the Net." *Party Politics* 14 (1): 51–70. https://doi.org/10.1177/1354068807083823.

Small, Tamara A. 2011. "What the Hashtag? A Content Analysis of Canadian Politics on Twitter." *Information, Communication, & Society* 14 (6): 872–95. https://doi.org/10.1080/1369118X.2011.554572.

Small, Tamara A. 2014. "The Not-So Social Network: The Use of Twitter by Canada's Party Leaders." In *Political Communication in Canada: Meet the Press and Tweet the Rest*, ed. Alex Marland, Thierry Giasson, and Tamara A. Small, 92–110. Vancouver: UBC Press.

Small, Tamara A. 2016. "Two Decades of Digital Party Politics in Canada: An Assessment." In *Canadian Parties in Transition*, 4th ed., ed. A. Brian Tanguay and Alain-G. Gagnon, 388–408. Toronto: University of Toronto Press.

Small, Tamara A., Alex Marland, and Thierry Giasson. 2014. "The Triangulation of Canadian Political Communication." In *Political Communication in Canada: Meet the Press and Tweet the Rest*, 3–23. Vancouver: UBC Press.

Taras, David. 1990. *The Newsmakers: The Media's Influence on Canadian Politics*. Scarborough: Nelson Canada.

Tkach-Kawasaki, Leslie M. 2003. "Politics@Japan: Party Competition on the Internet in Japan." *Party Politics* 9 (1): 105–23. https://doi.org/10.1177/135406880391006.

Tuten, Tracy L., and Michael R. Solomon. 2014. *Social Media Marketing*. 2nd ed. London: Sage.

Vaccari, Cristian. 2013. *Digital Politics in Western Democracies: A Comparative Study*. Baltimore: Johns Hopkins University Press.

Verville, Mélanie. 2013. "Usages politiques des médias sociaux et du Web 2.0. Le cas des partis politiques provinciaux québécois." Master's thesis, Quebec City: Université Laval.

Ward, Stephen, Diana Owen, Richard Davis, and David Taras. 2008. *Making a Difference: A Comparative View of the Role of the Internet in Election Politics.* Lanham, MD: Lexington Books.

Zimonjic, Peter. 2018. "Canada's Privacy Watchdog Launches Investigation into Facebook after Allegations of Data Leak." CBC News, March 20. http://www.cbc.ca/news/politics/canada-privacy-watchdog-facebook-investigation-1.4585210.

CHAPTER SEVEN

Digital Journalism: The Canadian Media's Struggle for Relevance

Christopher Waddell

CONTEXT

Monday, November 14, 1977, was an interesting news day on the front page of the *Globe and Mail* newspaper. The day's headlines included: The royal commission investigating Royal Canadian Mounted Police domestic intelligence activities indicated it may include Canada's military in its inquiry, while another story noted the RCMP had, in the early 1970s, leaked information obtained from confidential medical files to try to disrupt radical groups. Finance minister Jean Chrétien blamed separatist uncertainty for Quebec's poor economic performance. The death of a Red Army Faction terrorist group member in a German prison was ruled a suicide and someone threw eggs at the Queen's Rolls Royce on Saturday as she arrived at Royal Albert Hall for a memorial event for those killed in the two world wars.

At the time no one knew that November 14, 1977, would witness the launch of the digital era in Canadian journalism – the first day the full text of the *Globe* was indexed and made retrievable by computers over phone lines. Initially only *Globe* reporters could search and print stories from this new database, using dedicated InfoGlobe terminals. Before long the paper began marketing the service to governments, businesses, libraries, media, and anyone who would pay for a terminal and the content it could spit out. It was not cheap, but for a few, the almost instant access to any story published after November 14 in the national newspaper-of-record quickly became an essential part of life.

More than forty years later almost everything has changed. The internet and the instant access it provides to global media are now essential for many and the concept of a national newspaper-of-record is a memory. In every subject, what journalists cover and how they cover it is dramatically different. Politics and public policy are no exception. Those changes came in response to revolutions in technology that made it possible to produce print, video, or audio, whether singly or merged into one piece of journalism, delivered to audiences on a website. It can now be done simpler, easier, and faster than ever before, both for the journalists reporting and producing the news and audiences reading, watching, and listening to it. This chapter explores the digitization of the traditional media and political journalism. It highlights both what drove those changes and the implications from that radical reorientation of all aspects of journalism for the future of news organizations, the work of journalists, and most important for audiences. It highlights how digital technologies have changed, and not for the better, the reporting of politics and public policy.

Daily deadlines disappeared as all news organizations became news wire services feeding insatiable digital technologies where the deadline was always now, with demands for updates as soon a story appeared online. News organizations disappeared as well, as advertising left print and broadcast media to go online, giving news media only fractions of the revenue advertisers used to pay for newspaper and television commercials (Pope 2018). The newspapers that survived would love to ditch their print versions with the related costs of paper and ink, printing and distribution, but their aging audiences are still largely print subscribers. There is no guarantee that if they shut down their print operations they could replace print audiences with online viewers who would pay for news through subscriptions to replace continually shrinking advertising revenue. Traditional broadcasters such as CTV and Global, who relied even more heavily than newspapers on advertising to fund their operations, have been caught in the same squeeze. So have journalists. News organizations have dramatically cut reporters, editors, producers, and bureaus (Zeng 2016). What had started a decade earlier as a slow, steady decline had by 2018 accelerated and now threatens even the short-term future of news.

The high point for political journalism in Canada was likely the 1988 free-trade election. That was also one year before CBC Newsworld, Canada's first all-news channel, appeared on cable systems. In 1988 CBC television news had fourteen reporters in its Ottawa bureau filing stories just to a national noon newscast, local supper-hour news programs across the country, and *The National* at night. In fact, two reporters had as their jobs finding stories just for noon and 6 p.m. newscasts for stations in Ontario and east and two others for those in western Canada. Reporters were assigned to specific subject areas and political parties were closely followed. CBC radio news was similarly a separate, fully staffed, operation. By contrast today there are at most half a dozen reporters in CBC's parliamentary bureau for television, but they also file for radio, online, and News Network, the renamed Newsworld. Canadian Press has seen similar shrinkage, going from about thirty-six reporters in Ottawa in 1988 to perhaps a third of that today. The change began in the recession of the early 1990s, when national unemployment hit almost 13 per cent and advertisers sharply cut their spending. News organizations responded by closing or cutting their bureaus in Ottawa. The *Hamilton Spectator, London Free Press, Windsor Star,* BCTV, CFTO-TV in Toronto, and CJOH-TV in Ottawa, among others, all eliminated their own reporters and bureaus in Ottawa (Waddell 2012; Paré and Delacourt 2014). At the time, the *Montreal Gazette* had two reporters and a columnist and other Southam papers – the *Calgary Herald, Edmonton Journal, Vancouver Sun,* etc. – each had their own dedicated reporters in the parliamentary press gallery.

By the early 2000s, most news organizations from individual communities had shut down operations in Ottawa. By the mid-point of the first decade of the twenty-first century, they had almost all gone. The English-language parliamentary press gallery had become the repository of national news organizations, namely, CBC, CTV, Canwest Global, *Globe and Mail,* Canadian Press, and the *National Post* (followed after Canwest's bankruptcy in 2009 by Postmedia). The only local media left were the *Winnipeg Free Press* and the *Halifax Chronicle-Herald,* as the *Toronto Star* saw much of southern Ontario as its market.

Parenthetically, the same abandoning of press galleries was happening in provincial legislatures across the country (see Small 2017), but there were no national news organizations to fill in the gaps. There was just less news. Slowly but surely, the loss of that local connection changed the nature and quality of political reporting in ways no one really noticed at the time. The losses became much more obvious when added to the changes that technology brought to how reporters did their jobs.

Prior to these changes, journalists in Ottawa from individual local news organizations had a very different function than those working for national media. They reported on how the activities of the federal government and their local Members of Parliament (MPs) affected their communities, often ignoring the "big" national stories. They would pitch their ideas to their editors back home, who might tell them no one cares about that in their community but here is what they are really interested in. They would then take that feedback and question Members of Parliament or attend committees and track the responses of their local MPs. Their stories demonstrated the links between what happened in Ottawa and local issues, developments, people, and institutions in those communities.

By contrast national news organizations did none of that. Their stories needed to be understood by audiences living both in Corner Brook, Newfoundland, and Kitimat, British Columbia. Those journalists could not put in local references and did not highlight or care what individual MPs were doing. The result was a gradual homogenization of political coverage around fewer issues and a steadily growing focus on Question Period. Fewer reporters on Parliament Hill meant a narrower range of issues were being covered. News organizations still wanted stories on staged events, such as news conferences, the release of reports, photo opportunities, etc. But with smaller newsrooms there were fewer reporters left to break away from "pack" coverage for distinctive reporting.

Equally important was the collapse of the feedback loop. With only national reporters covering politics, there was no way for local issues to make it onto the news agenda. Reporters were no longer talking to editors back home to inject their story ideas into the daily confrontations between MPs and the media in the House of Commons foyer. Most of the national media is based in Toronto so that perspective has become even more dominant in the political news available to Canadians across the country.

Political journalism was not supposed to end up like this. In the late 1980s, the federal government changed the rules that had prevented an organization from owning radio and television stations and a newspaper in the same community (Bartley 1988). There would no longer be a problem of concentration of ownership, it was thought, as digital technologies would lead to more media competition. It would also make existing news organizations even richer. With a radio or TV station, a newspaper, and website in a community, the same news could be spread across multiple outlets. Even better, news owners assumed, one reporter could file a story on an event for all the outlets. Output could be tripled with no increase in labour costs. Revenue would grow exponentially as advertising could be sold across all the different platforms. Underlying that assumption was the belief that advertisers would pay as much or more to advertise online as they did for radio, television, and newspaper ads. Confident in that assessment and backed by lenders, media owners led by BCE, Canwest, Quebecor, and Torstar began a wave of convergence, bringing together different formerly independently owned media – television and radio stations, newspapers and websites – all now bought and consolidated under a parent company with the purchases financed by debt. The revenue that would flow to the new owner from advertising across all these media platforms would more than cover interest payments, they believed, allowing the consolidated enterprises to maintain their historic rates of return in excess of 20 per cent.

Just to be sure, though, convergence came with newsroom cutbacks. As an example, why would Canwest Global, with papers in a dozen major urban centres in the country, need a movie reviewer for each paper? The same was true for political reporting. Why have separate stories or columnists for each publication when one could write for all? Why does each paper or television station need its own advertising sales department? Why should each outlet have its own specifically designed website to suit its own community? If the design was the same for all the websites across a chain, then advertisers could be guaranteed the same spot on the screen on all the organization sites.

Convergence catalysed the deterioration of the breadth and quality of political coverage. It still might have worked as a business strategy had it not been crippled by three developments. Newspapers had not anticipated how easily and quickly online advertisers such as Craigslist and Kijiji could dominate classified advertising, as they were used by anyone selling almost anything from a used car or a household appliance to puppies. From a high of $875 million in 2005, classified advertising revenue at Canadian newspapers fell to $119 million by 2015 (Public

Policy Forum 2017, 17). Second was the global economic meltdown of 2008–9. Real estate, financial services, the automobile industry, and consumer retailing were all hard hit as the economy contracted, people lost their jobs, and companies cut spending and advertising. The industries hardest hit were precisely the advertising backbone of mainstream media. Finally, there was the internet itself. It provided space for advertising on everything from search engines to individual websites, including the rapidly expanding influence of social media led by Facebook. No longer were newspapers, television, radio, and their websites the only games in town for anyone wanting to place an ad. As a result, daily and community newspaper advertising revenue fell to $2.3 billion by 2015 from $3.85 billion in 2006 (Public Policy Forum 2017, 18). The media sold almost none of that internet advertising. It was dominated by Google, the leading search engine, and Facebook, the pre-eminent global social media site. By 2015, annual digital advertising sales in Canada hit $4.6 billion but only $433 million of that was digital sales at the online sites of newspapers and television stations (Public Policy Forum 2017, 19). Google and Facebook had the analytics that could tell advertisers who was clicking on their ads, where they lived, and almost everything else about them. Using IP addresses, they could target ads to show up on the computers of individuals in narrow geographic or demographic communities. Advertisers paid a fraction of what they had paid to the media and learned a lot more about their potential customers. Some news organizations even turned their advertising sales over to Google.

By 2011–12, the media owners' dream of a future driven by online advertising revenue had collapsed and it only got worse thereafter. Existing advertising sales continued to fall dramatically and revenue from online ads came nowhere close to replacing it. The pace of newsroom layoffs and media closures accelerated. By then, Canwest Global had gone bankrupt and convergence was dead, costing billions of dollars and thousands of jobs. In its place was "vertical integration," as newspapers set out on their own while the cable and satellite television/internet service/wireless giants Rogers, Bell, and Shaw took over the broadcasters. Quebecor already owned TVA, the private television network in Quebec. The distributors of content would own the content producers with the hope that conglomeration would produce the revenue that convergence did not. It did in part, but there was no interest in or regulatory requirement for a conglomerate to use its profits from wireless services to boost revenue at its increasingly unprofitable television operations. That forced media organizations back to their traditional tactics to offset declining revenue, namely, layoffs, consolidations, and closures of newspapers and television stations that inevitably meant fewer reporters in newsrooms covering a narrow range of issues less substantially. That was true across the country in large and small communities, helping to shrink political journalism even further.

DIGITIZATION

Promises & Perils

The advances of digital technologies designed to maximize their benefits have changed everything about journalism: how news is gathered, how it is distributed, the role and engagement of the audience, and who is a journalist. It has broken down the gatekeeper role the media once held (Chadwick 2013). Anyone – politicians, political parties, governments, lobbyists, policy interest groups and advocates, partisans and activists – can now distribute a message to whichever broad or targeted audience they want to reach. They do not need to go through the media anymore.

Neither do those who want to spread misinformation or disinformation, whether it be governments, organized interest groups, or individuals, all anxious to push a point of view, to discredit others and their views, or to spread lies to undermine the social fabric of communities, pitting groups against each other. They do it through social media posts, online advertising, and direct targeting of messages to specific communities based on data collected from individual internet users.

Amid all that, the mediated and edited news still provided by radio, television, print, and online news organizations is now but one stream in a flood of opinion, commentary, rantings and ravings, personal attacks, and misogyny in which it has become increasingly difficult to separate fact from fiction and news from comment and opinion. It is now up to each citizen to be his or her own editor, deciding what to listen to, watch, and read, what to believe, and whether to comment on it.

The perceived threat reached such a level in the lead up to the 2019 federal election that the Government of Canada established a "digital citizen initiative" designed both to educate the public in identifying disinformation and funding research on the subject (Canada 2019). That has been supplemented by media and many other groups engaged in media literacy projects targeted at everyone from high school to retirement. The federal government's spy agencies, the Canadian Security Intelligence Service and the Communications Security Establishment, have also spent considerable time investigating and publicizing attempts at disinformation and foreign hacking attempts against Canadian organizations and institutions (Elections Canada 2019).

Technology has made all this disruption possible and for journalists, technology has changed everything. Cameras, audio recorders, mobile and satellite phones, video and audio editing systems are lighter to transport, simpler and easier to use, and produce better quality material than ever before. Reporting live can be done from anywhere: the middle of a desert or in the midst of a demonstration, riot, or war. The journalist's main tool is either a laptop computer or a smartphone, as everything can be done on either: gathering information and writing; shooting and editing photos, video, and audio; presenting data and transmitting all of it in finished form either to a news organization or directly to audiences without any editorial oversight. Those audiences are no longer local but global, allowing anyone to feel part of any story, whether it is reported by journalists or just by people on the scene.

The simplicity of technology has also complicated the work of professional journalists (see Small 2017). In the interests of cutting costs, their employers have loaded work that used to be done by those with dedicated technical training – video and audio editing, shooting video and photos, laying out stories and pages – onto the backs of the editorial staff. All that takes time that could otherwise be spent doing another interview or the additional research needed to provide background and context to stories, at a time when such research has never been easier to do. Reports, news stories, releases, speeches, and chronologies – globally everything is online and available at any time of day or night. That should enhance reporting by giving it depth, history, and breadth, helping audiences place any event in context while separating fact from fiction. People are much more available as well – by mobile phone, email, text messages – any time of day or night. Journalists do not have to wait for an office or a library to open in the morning to reach people or dig up the background to build the data and graphics that are now an important part of many stories.

For many journalists, conquering technology is a sufficient challenge in itself, but it has been complicated by the fact that digital technologies have eliminated deadlines (Swasy 2016). News organizations no longer hold an exclusive story until the next day's paper hits the streets or the next newscast is on the air. Journalists file as soon as they have enough information to make a coherent story and then update that story as often as necessary by adding more details as they emerge. That plays to the goals of news organizations to keep audiences coming back to their online sites looking for the latest news and hopefully seeing advertisements as well. Long feature stories are released online during the week, no longer scheduled for the weekend when audiences are assumed to have more time to view them leisurely.

Another layer of work and complexity comes from the growth and influence of social media (Swasy 2016). It can be an early warning system, alerting journalists to events and developments, as well as a way to find witnesses to an event or experts on an issue (Hermida 2012; Chadwick 2016). It is also a simple way for politicians to distribute comments or reaction to events while avoiding questioning and scrutiny from journalists. Moreover, it can cut out the communications department intermediaries, allowing journalists and politicians to communicate directly, almost as if they were talking on the phone or face-to-face. But all the power in those exchanges has shifted to the politician, who can terminate any conversation when he or she wishes simply by not responding, without the negative images associated with walking away from a microphone or fleeing down a flight of stairs from cameras. What is most surprising is that journalists let it all happen, having simply surrendered the requirement that they had to talk to someone before they would quote them in a story. It has become acceptable to pose questions by email rather than in person and even more perniciously, to accept and report the emailed answers, no matter how irrelevant they may be to the questions being posed. From that it was a small step to start reporting Twitter comments as an acceptable substitute for comments in an interview, scrum, or news conference where lines of questioning could be pursued. All of this flowed from the media's self-imposed dictate that stories online had to be updated constantly, with little regard to the value of the additional information in advancing the audience's understanding of a story or issue. Once journalists started accepting handouts as the equivalent of interviews, they surrendered much of the pretext that they were holding public officials to account for their actions. The role of the mass media as a watchdog has been and is continually being diminished as a result (Taras 2015).

Thanks to social media, the workload for journalists has also increased, as they are expected to contribute regularly to platforms such as Facebook, Twitter, Instagram, and Snapchat, often even as they are gathering information themselves. It is all part of "engaging with audiences," a tactic news organizations believe will encourage those audiences to visit the organization's online site more frequently or, even better, subscribe online to the news source (Chadwick 2013). Tweeting speeches and events live adds immediacy and makes the audience feel part of the action, but it also cuts into the time journalists need to frame their stories, understand the details of complex issues, assess what an audience really needs to know, and identify new developments worth reporting in long-running stories. While employers are quick to demand journalists embrace all these new platforms, it is usually done without an analysis that pits the benefits of the incremental gains in audience that may come from adding content on another social media platform against the costs in time and quality lost in reporting and crafting stories.

At the same time, social media does have a positive side for journalism. It has allowed journalists to communicate directly with their audiences, getting reaction to stories, engaging in debates, and hearing from those who might have additional details to add to a story (Fenton 2012). This is particularly true as a story develops after the initial version is filed and the journalist is looking for material for updates.

This is all occurring against the backdrop of cutbacks and layoffs, now into their second decade and sweeping through both mainstream and digital start-up newsrooms such as *Vice* and *Buzzfeed*, both of which closed their Ottawa newsrooms in 2016 within two years of opening them. Not only is national politics now overwhelmingly covered by national news organizations, virtually all the latter have fewer reporters in Ottawa than in the past. The press gallery is the smallest it has been in the past two decades (Britneff 2016). The result is a toxic mix: fewer people asked to do more while trying to understand complex and complicated issues in an era when declining numbers mean fewer beat or specialist reporters. Those given designated subjects to cover in depth over time are a thing of the past in political reporting. Most political journalists are now either general assignment reporters covering a women's rally one day, military procurement the next, and carbon tax policy the day after that or they are commentators and columnists, not writing news but commenting on it. The result has left facts far too often drowning in a sea of opinion.

Practice

In almost every respect, the reality of political journalism over the past quarter century has fallen short of the perhaps idealistic promise and opportunities held out by digital technologies. In the duel between the *mobilization* and *reinforcement* hypotheses purporting to explain the impact of digital technologies, the narrowing of the practices of political journalism and of journalists generally gives plenty of ammunition to those who argue the case for reinforcement. Some of this is a function of the collapse of the mainstream media as it lost advertising revenue. That decline has yet to be offset significantly by online newcomers, although they are trying. Yet, the biggest challenge for political journalists is the counterproductive combination of their decline in numbers and the increase in the range of tasks they are asked to perform on a daily basis. Fewer reporters with less expertise asked to cover a wider variety of issues and subjects across a range of changing media without technical support is a prescription for declining breadth and quality of both what is covered and how it is covered. Not surprisingly that is exactly what has happened. Audiences have responded in an entirely predictable way, by leaving. Radio news, except for the CBC, is virtually dead, replaced by phone-in talk shows dominated by opinion, often in the absence of facts.

The lack of journalists generates another damaging by-product. There is no time to spend days doing background research. Journalists need to file every day to fill up newscasts and shrinking news pages, making them vulnerable to the legions of government, political, corporate, and interest-group communications people anxious to push their agendas through stories in the media. They can provide journalists with everything – the story line, video and audio clips, and "real" people or experts who can talk about the subject in question, as well as news conferences. It is all handed to frazzled reporters on a plate. It is simple, quick, and easy to do for the journalists but does not automatically make it newsworthy and often it is not, even though stories are done and posted online. Governments hand reporters stories the morning an announcement is to be made and the story goes online, often without the context, other interviews, and critique that help audiences understand its significance. Only sometimes do those elements get added later and with audiences relying increasingly on social media for news, it is not clear whether they come back to read the more complete later story. The same tactic is used by politicians and political parties. A late 2017 Canadian Press story about NDP leader Jagmeet Singh supposedly launching a Scarborough, Ontario, by-election in the wrong riding is a perfect example. The story was a plant from the Liberals that embarrassingly Canadian Press had to withdraw after distributing it to its wire service customers (LeRoy 2017).

Digital technologies provide political reporters in Ottawa with the opportunity to read, watch, and listen online every day to the stories making news in communities across the country. But they do not do it. They do not have the time and they know that working for national news organizations they will never do local stories, so they do not care. Communication is easier than ever but those daily phone conversations between reporters in Ottawa and editors in communities across the country are long gone. That makes it easy for reporters to turn inward, thinking that whatever they cover and whatever is being talked about on Twitter must be important to people across the country in direct proportion to the amount of social media activity they see. Too often to their regular surprise, it simply is not.

Rather than deepening engagement and the relationships between journalists and the public, social media has heightened the degree to which political journalism is out of touch with its audience. Twitter has come to dominate much of national political discussion as journalists and political operatives trade insider gossip, react to stories and rumours, and compete to show each other how clever, insightful, dismissive, condescending, or simply angry they are. In many ways political Twitter has become like a meeting of postage stamp collectors, insiders trading their knowledge of the obscure and persuading each other of its importance and the degree to which a politician or party's future may hinge on that issue (Waddell 2010). Again, too often that simply is not true. The demographics of Twitter users bear no relationship to the voting population and as the 2016 US presidential election demonstrated, the platform can be relatively easily captured by vested interests and bots (Bessi and Ferrara 2016).

Technology has also made it all far too easy for journalists to never leave their desks. Their reporting is done from video feeds and social media, not from going somewhere, seeing something, assessing a situation for themselves, and meeting the public, people they would not ordinarily speak to and whom they did not know they were going to meet. Journalists always learn something when they leave their offices, yet an organization such as the CBC, in its push to become all digital, now has a class of journalists whose job description includes "reporting" without ever leaving their desks.

Additionally, the communications promise of email has turned out to be at best a mixed blessing. It is now possible to reach anyone any time of the day but that does not mean a journalist will get a response to a question. Email has given governments, corporations, and institutions the excuse to not answer telephones. Initial contact by journalists is made through an email and is most frequently met with a request to pose questions by email, allowing the person being "interviewed" to answer the same way. Journalists then use those "answers" in their stories, usually noting it was an email response. It is a perfect solution for governments and politicians as it creates the illusion of openness and availability without the risks of a real back-and-forth interview with follow-up questions that is a prerequisite for actual accountability.

At the same time, email is a form of communication that serves the interests of journalists facing constant time pressures. It lets them report a comment from a participant in a story, thereby satisfying a journalistic shibboleth. They did get a comment. It also lets the individual or organization being questioned off the hook, responding in whatever way it chooses, secure in the knowledge it will not be challenged by a follow-up question. Journalists and politicians both get what they want and can move on. The real loser in the exchange is the audience, which usually receives no substantive response to whatever question is posed.

Digital technologies have produced other challenges for online journalists: the never-ending parade of new software tools, social media platforms, and mobile applications. News organizations want to be on all of them, anxious to scoop up as large an audience as possible, knowing that demographics are fracturing such that certain age groups favour certain communication tools. Providing material to all of them takes journalistic time that might better be devoted to other tasks. Despite the degree to which digital technologies now dominate every aspect of news and journalism, news organizations have no systematic way to assess the value to their businesses of the tools they use. What are the costs and benefits of adopting a new technology and when should one be abandoned? For example, is an audience for a Facebook Live event large enough to justify the time and effort spent setting it up and broadcasting it or would time be better spent providing something else for the organization's primary audience on its own online site?

Despite the promise of a new relationship between citizens and the media, news organizations have barely embraced the promise of two-way interactivity and engagement with audiences that the internet offers. One interesting example is the CBC-Vote Compass partnership. Vote Compass is an online application that surveys users about their political views and, based on their responses, calculates the individual alignment of each user with the parties or candidates running in a given election contest.[1] CBC has made Vote Compass available during several federal and provincial elections (CBC 2018). The site stated it had more than 475,00 participants in May and June 2018 for the Ontario election and seems a valuable use of digital technologies to engage and educate audiences about the link between party policies and vote preferences. Along the same lines, in January 2018, the *Globe and Mail* asked its readers to help it monitor political advertising on Facebook, using a web browser extension designed by *ProPublica* in the United States. According to the *Globe and Mail*, "The extension is designed to collect only the text, links, images, and metadata within a political ad on Facebook. The political ad data that ProPublica collects will be contributed to a public database, viewable through the extension itself, that will allow the public to see them all ... Aside from assisting *The Globe* in reporting on the evolving use of Facebook political advertisements within Canada, ProPublica's extension will use its database to show you Facebook political ads that were not specifically targeted at you and that you would otherwise never see" (2018). But those experiments are the exception, not the rule. While news organizations talked about using Facebook in innovative ways in the 2015 federal election

1 http://votecompass.com/.

campaign to enliven discussion and understanding of the issues, their contributions never moved beyond simply posting material on their Facebook pages that had been initially printed, broadcast, or posted to their own news sites. Generally speaking, social media for news organizations are simply another way to distribute material prepared primarily for their own online sites. There seems little interest in taking advantage of any distinctive, innovative, or controversial opportunities social media could provide (Francoli, Greenberg, and Waddell 2016).

This is true more broadly as well. Digital technologies have the potential for journalists to bring media formats together to tell stories in new ways using text, photographs, video, audio, data, and interactive elements – whatever media best suits each part of the story. The results can be displayed in different formats depending on the screen the viewer is using, whether it be a smartphone, tablet, laptop, or desktop computer. It is a whole new dimension that can add depth and context to political and public policy journalism, but its introduction has been limited by two factors. Doing it well requires a range of skills that many mid-career journalists just do not possess, and shrinking newsrooms are often not able to hire young journalists who, if they graduated from post-secondary journalism programs over the past decade, are now steeped in multimedia storytelling theory, skills, and practice. They possess both the needed skills and the unconventional presentation ideas and concepts worth trying, based on their own experiences in finding, reading, watching, and listening to information online. Inevitably such presentations are neither simple nor quick to produce. They almost always require a team to put together, consuming dedicated resources that many newsrooms simply do not have. Good online journalism is time-consuming and costly, which, perhaps ironically in the digital technology age, means it usually does not happen.

POTENTIALS

In January 2018, Justin Trudeau's now annual town hall tour offered interesting insights into the ongoing shortcomings of political journalism in Canada. It came after more than a year of media handwringing and head scratching over how journalists missed the Donald Trump phenomenon in the 2016 US presidential election (Mazzoleni 2016).

Canada has had its own minor version of media inability to gauge the public's political sentiment in a series of provincial elections in British Columbia, Alberta, Ontario, and Quebec between 2013 and 2018, the results of most catching political journalists by surprise. Despite the interactive potential that digital technologies offer between the media and its audiences, journalists seem no closer to changing how they approach political journalism. Reporting on the Trudeau town halls followed time-honoured traditions, focusing on the prime minister's answers (always empathetic and usually anodyne) and those who yelled, shouted, and ultimately were dragged out of the events attended by hundreds from the general public. What received little coverage was the nature of the questions asked by those who had lined up to attend in large numbers everywhere Mr. Trudeau went. Stories did not include a tally of the subjects raised by the audience, nor any qualitative assessment of the questions asked. Such an analysis might provide clues about what issues interested the public and, more specifically, what aspects of those issues concerned them and how their questions reflected their knowledge of the former. It was a classic demonstration of how little the thinking had changed from the pre-digital era about how to report and what to report, even given all the potential that digital technologies contain to engage audiences and make them an important part of stories. Did the public care about the issues the parliamentary press gallery had been covering and assumed would be crucial in determining Mr. Trudeau's re-election prospects? If not, what did they care about, and what does that say about what journalists should be looking for in their stories?

In short, the lesson from recent elections in Canada and the United States is that the focus of political stories needs to be much less about the politicians, campaign strategy, insider trivia, and gossip and rumours, and much more about the public who are voters. That is a worthwhile description of how digital technologies could change political journalism but have not. It remains about the politicians, not the voters; the legislative process, not the impact of legislation on communities, groups, and individuals; events in Ottawa, not how they are perceived from across the country or how they play out on the ground in communities from coast to coast to coast. Digital technologies have changed how public opinion polling is done, replacing telephone calls with online panels of respondents, but it has not altered the addiction of political journalists to polls and polling results as indicators of the future, even though they are not.

The potential provided by digital technologies for a new form of political journalism remains obvious but largely unfulfilled. It allows journalists to report live from anywhere and lets audiences read, watch, and listen to their reporting anywhere at any time. A quarter century after the first appearance of digital technologies much more can and should be done than simply taking a text story and accompanying photos from a newspaper and slapping it on a screen or making a story from a television newscast available online in a menu of stand-alone stories. A single story can be told using a variety of media – video, audio, photos, sound, interactive data and graphics – selecting the media for each part of the story best suited to ensuring that part of the story has an impact on audiences, yet it usually is not.

Audiences engage with stories differently on smartphones than on tablets than on computer screens than on mainstream media's traditional distribution platforms (Tewksbury and Rittenberg 2012). One size does *not* fit all, and stories need to be designed and produced for the medium on which the audience will view them. That is particularly true as mobile devices are now as popular in Canada as computers for obtaining news and information (Reuters 2018, 118).

Political journalism must understand how to engage and build new audiences across generational, ethnic, and demographic divides. In a world flooded with information, it can no longer assume audiences will find quality political journalism. For example, almost half of Canadians identify social media as a source for news, compared to 76 per cent who say they get their news online, 67 per cent from television, and 31 per cent from print (Reuters 2018, 118).

The promise of two-way engagement between audiences and journalists remains largely unfulfilled as well. Twitter communities are not demographically representative of the general public in any way (Small et al. 2014). Comments sections on news sites have been captured by trolls, partisans, and those spewing abuse to the point where many news organizations have eliminated them as more trouble than they are worth.

Engagement may most easily come through new online media formats that have a narrow and defined editorial focus. Mainstream general interest media, whether in print, broadcast, or online that include political coverage as well as sports, arts, business, and lifestyle, seem headed for extinction. Advertising is disappearing and overwhelmingly Canadians will not pay for online news from one source that they think they can find for free elsewhere. That reflects the public's almost complete lack of understanding about how news is produced, how to differentiate quality from quantity, and how much news costs to gather, edit, and distribute, even in the internet age. Journalists and news organizations never bothered to educate the public on these issues and no one thought it needed to be done. As long as there were advertisers, it did not.

But specific audiences will pay for specialized publications online that offer better information on a specific topic or subject than can be found anywhere else – more details, more background, more analysis, and greater subject expertise than today's political journalists possess as assignments bounce them from subject to subject. That is demonstrated by publications such as *Politico* and *Axios* in the United States and *iPolitics* in Canada. Part of that model also includes revenue from providing political intelligence to audiences that have dealings with governments.

With more specialized subjects and audiences paying for the privilege of getting information comes a greater likelihood of fulfilling the promise of two-way engagement that leads to informed public policy, political discussion, and debate. Will cranks want to pay for the privilege of spouting off? Will bots programmed by special interests flood sites with messages if they have to pay to get access to those sites? It is a bet worth taking that they will not.

Perhaps the most encouraging news for political journalism is the continuing overwhelmingly positive attitude Canadians have toward the country's media, unlike in the United States. In a January 2018 global study of public attitudes to the news media in thirty-eight counties, the Pew Research Center found between three-quarters and four-fifths of Canadians thought Canadian media were doing very or somewhat well at covering different positions on political issues fairly, reporting news accurately, reporting news about government leaders and officials, and reporting most important news events (Pew Research Center 2018). In each of those categories, public perception of the media's performance in Canada was twenty percentage points higher than the views of Americans on the same set of questions. That means data, anecdotes, commentary, and analysis from the United States, based on US examples, are simply not relevant to Canada and should not be used as evidence of any problem or a prescription for a solution in this country.

Indeed, the media systems are very different in the two nations. Since the days of Richard Nixon's vice president Spiro Agnew, the Republican Party has vilified the media for partisan advantage, politicizing everything it does. This has not happened in Canada, despite the efforts of a few on the right wing of the political spectrum. Canada also has nothing to match the distortions and mendaciousness of Fox News and the Rupert Murdoch media empire. Sun TV, an attempt to replicate elements of the Murdoch approach in Canada, was a dismal failure. No one was interested in watching a network featuring hours of non-stop partisan babble. Additionally, despite all those who complain about the CBC, the public broadcaster sets a standard with its political coverage that the private broadcasters emulate if not surpass. In this case competition works in raising everyone's performance.

Public satisfaction with media performance in Canada is an important building block in trying to realize the potential of digital technologies to transform political journalism for the benefit of audiences. Across the country, 74 per cent of those aged eighteen to twenty-nine say they get news online at least once a day versus 69 per cent of those thirty to forty-nine and 45 per cent of those over fifty years of age. That is not much different than in the United States (Pew Research Center 2018). Interestingly 92 per cent of supporters of the governing party in Canada are satisfied with the news media while even 70 per cent of those who are not supporters of the Liberals express general satisfaction with media performance. By contrast, in the United States, the comparable satisfaction numbers are 58 per cent and 24 per cent (Pew Research Center 2018). There is also widespread interest in Canada in all types of news, as 88 per cent follow national news very or somewhat closely, 83 per cent have the same attitude about local news, and 69 per cent follow news about other countries very or somewhat closely. The latter number is likely a reflection of the multicultural nature of the country and the diverse origins of its citizens and residents. The major role played by the United States in Canada is also reflected in the fact that 78 per cent of respondents say they follow US news. But older Canadians are somewhat more interested in local news, with 88 per cent of those over fifty saying they follow news about their city or town closely, falling to 81 per cent for those between thirty and forty-nine, and 72 per cent for eighteen to twenty-nine-year-olds (Pew Research Center 2018). At the same time, studies in the United States have found that older readers are much more likely to spread misinformation online through sharing social media posts than are those eighteen to twenty-nine (*The Verge* January 9, 2019), making them much more susceptible to online disinformation campaigns.

There is an audience for political journalism, but it will need to pay for it, which suggests political journalism in the future will be more of an online niche. It will be more like the audience *The Athletic* is building for sports journalism and less like the general interest publications and broadcasters that have dominated the political world for decades. That suggests it would be wise to start considering how the replacement of mainstream media by niche media for political journalism will alter public knowledge and perceptions of politics, politicians, public policy, and participation in the political process across the country as changes in one will drive change in the other.

REFERENCES

Bartley, Allan. 1988. "The Regulation of Cross-Media Ownership: The Life and Short Times of PCO 2294." *Canadian Journal of Communications* 13 (2): 45–59. https://www.cjc-online.ca/index.php/journal/article/view/449/355.

Bessi, Alessandro, and Emilio Ferrara. 2016. "Social Bots Distort the 2016 US Presidential Election Online Discussion." *First Monday* 21 (11). https://doi.org/10.5210/fm.v21i11.7090.

Britneff, Beatrice. 2016. "Parliamentary Press Gallery Now the Smallest It's Been in 22 years." *iPolitics,* December 8. https://ipolitics.ca/2016/12/08/parliamentary-press-gallery-now-the-smallest-its-been-in-22-years/

Canada.ca. n.d. "Online disinformation." Accessed September 21, 2019. https://www.canada.ca/en/canadian-heritage/services/online-disinformation.html.

CBC (Canadian Broadcasting Corporation). 2018. *Vote Compass.* Accessed September 21, 2019. https://votecompass.cbc.ca/ontario/

Chadwick, Andrew. 2013. *The Hybrid Media System: Politics and Power.* Oxford: Oxford University Press.

Elections Canada. n.d. "Election Security." Accessed September 21, 2019. https://www.elections.ca/content.aspx?section=vot&dir=bkg/sec&document=index&lang=e.

Fenton, Natalie. 2012. "De-Democratizing the News? New Media and the Structural Practices of Journalism." In *The Handbook of Global Online Journalism,* ed. Andreas Veglis and Eugenia Siapera, 119–34. Oxford: Wiley-Blackwell.

Francoli, Mary, Joshua Greenberg, and Christopher Waddell. 2016. "Share, Like, Vote." In *The Canadian Federal Election of 2015*, ed. Christopher Dornan and Jon Pammett. Toronto: Dundurn Press.

Globe and Mail. 2018. "Help the Globe Monitor Political Ads on Facebook." January 31. https://www.theglobeandmail.com/news/national/help-the-globe-monitor-political-ads-on-facebook/article37801040/.

Hermida, Alfred. 2012. "Social Journalism: Exploring How Social Media Is Shaping Journalism." In *The Handbook of Global Online Journalism*, ed. Andreas Veglis and Eugenia Siapera, 309–28. Oxford: Wiley-Blackwell.

LeRoy, Will. 2017. "Singh Launched NDP By-Election Campaign in Wrong Scarborough Riding." *Canadian Press*, December 13. https://www.nationalnewswatch.com/2017/12/13/singh-launched-ndp-byelection-campaign-in-wrong-scarborough-riding-4/#.WzJj2C0ZMq8.

Mazzoleni, Gianpietro. 2016. "Did the Media Create Trump?" In *US Election Analysis 2016*, ed. Darren Lilleker, Daniel Jackson, Einar Thorsen, and Anastasia Venti, 21. Poole, UK: The Centre for the Study of Journalism, Culture, and Community (Bournemouth University).

Newton, Casey, 2019. "People Older than 65 Share the Most Fake News, a New Study Finds." *The Verge*, January 9. https://www.theverge.com/2019/1/9/18174631/old-people-fake-news-facebook-share-nyu-princeton.

Paré, Daniel J., and Susan Delacourt. 2014. "The Canadian Parliamentary Press Gallery." In *Political Communication in Canada: Meet the Press and Tweet the Rest*, ed. Alex Marland, Thierry Giasson, and Tamara A. Small, 111–26. Vancouver: UBC Press.

Pew Research Center. 2018. "Publics Globally Want Unbiased News Media Coverage but Are Divided on Whether Their News Media Deliver." January 11. http://www.pewglobal.org/2018/01/11/publics-globally-want-unbiased-news-coverage-but-are-divided-on-whether-their-news-media-deliver/.

Pope, Amanda. 2018. "New Survey Investigates State of Smaller-Market Newspapers in Canada." Local News Research Project, February 2. http://localnewsresearchproject.ca/2018/04/06/new-survey-investigates-state-of-smaller-market-newspapers-in-canada/.

Public Policy Forum. 2017. *The Shattered Mirror: News, Democracy, and Trust in the Digital Age*. Ottawa, January.

Small, Tamara A. 2017. "Media and Ontario Politics: The Press Gallery in the 21st Century." In *The Politics of Ontario*, ed. Jonathan Malloy and Cheryl N. Collier. Toronto: University of Toronto Press.

Small, Tamara A., Harold Jansen, Frédérick Bastien, Thierry Giasson, and Royce Koop. 2014. "Online Political Activity in Canada: The Hype and the Facts." *Canadian Parliamentary Review* 37 (4): 9–16.

Swasy, Alecia. 2016. *How Journalists Use Twitter: The Changing Landscape of US Newsrooms*. Lanham, MD: Lexington Books.

Taras, David. 2015. *Digital Mosaic: Media, Power, and Identity in Canada*. Toronto: University of Toronto Press.

Tewksbury, David, and Jason Rittenberg. 2012. *News on the Internet: Information and Citizenship in the 21st Century*. Oxford Studies in Digital Politics. New York: Oxford University Press.

Waddell, Christopher. 2012. "Berry'd Alive: The Media, Technology, and the Death of Political Coverage." In *How Canadians Communicate IV – Media and Politics*, ed. David Taras and Christopher Waddell. Edmonton, AB: Athabaska University Press.

Zeng, Anda. 2016. "Shrinking Press Galleries Leave Little Time for Journalists to Dig Deep." J-Source, July 8. http://j-source.ca/article/shrinking-press-galleries-leave-little-time-for-journalists-to-dig-deep/.

Section II

Political Digital Citizenship

CHAPTER EIGHT

Democratic Citizenship: How Do Canadians Engage with Politics Online?

Harold J. Jansen, Royce Koop, Tamara A. Small, Frédérick Bastien, and Thierry Giasson

CONTEXT

When we think about the potential impact of digital technology on Canadian politics, there are few areas with greater expectation than the practice of democratic citizenship. Digital technology would seem to offer individual Canadians an expansive toolbox that would allow them to learn more about the political process, talk with others about it, communicate and interact directly with decision makers, and network with others in order to achieve political goals. This chapter examines the extent to which citizens have taken advantage of these unparalleled opportunities to enhance their participation in the Canadian political system.

Before specifically examining the impact of digital technology on democratic citizenship, it is important to understand the context of democratic citizenship in Canada. In order to function, democracy requires the input and participation of citizens. As Elisabeth Gidengil and Heather Bastedo (2014, 4) put it: "There can be no democracy without the *demos* [people]." Democratic citizenship can be understood

The authors gratefully acknowledge the support of the Social Sciences and Humanities Research Council for this research.

as the range of practices through which Canadians engage with and participate in their political system. This obviously includes the formal role for citizens in voting for their elected officials and its associated activities such as joining or donating to political parties and campaigning, but it also includes so-called informal activities such as petitions, boycotts, and protests. Informal activities also comprise gathering information about politics through news consumption and "discursive participation" (Delli Carpini, Cook, and Jacobs 2004) and the act of talking about politics with other people, particularly in trying to change their political views.

Understanding the extent to which Canadians are involved in and engaged with the political system has been a central preoccupation of scholars of Canadian political behaviour (Gidengil et al. 2012; Clarke et al. 2019). The accumulated research of the last few decades has not painted a particularly optimistic picture of the state of democratic citizenship in Canada. One key indicator is the relatively low rate of participation in elections. Although voter turnout in the federal election of 2015 rebounded from the record lows of the previous decade to 68 per cent, it declined slightly to 66 per cent in 2019. This followed almost two decades of decline from the historical norm of between 70 and 75 per cent (Elections Canada 2018). Provincial voter turnout has experienced similar tendencies (Siaroff and Wesley 2015). Similarly low rates of political participation have long been seen in other forms of political activity, such as volunteering for election campaigns (Gidengil et al. 2004) or joining and participating in the activities of political parties (Cross and Young 2004). If we switch attention away from the formal electoral arena to informal politics, we also note relatively low patterns of participation. Although Canadians sign petitions in relatively large numbers, few engage in more time-intensive political activities like protests or demonstrations (Gidengil et al. 2004). It does not seem to be the case that these informal political activities are replacing electoral participation; it seems that the people who engage in electoral politics are also those who participate in unconventional political activity. In this sense, unconventional politics may be understood as adding to the "repertoire" of the politically active (Painter-Main 2014).

Although Canadians do not seem to participate much in politics, they nevertheless are reasonably interested in it. Based on their analysis of the 2000 Canadian Election Study, Gidengil et al. (2004)

described Canadians' interest in politics as "middling." Analysis of the 2008 Canadian Election Study largely confirmed this, although there was an increase in the proportion of Canadians with very low interest in politics (Gidengil 2012). Analysis of subsequent Canadian Election Studies shows that general interest in politics has increased somewhat since 2008.[1] However, it is hard to know whether this reflects an actual increase or is due to the specifics of the particular elections or to the increasing difficulty of getting representative telephone samples.[2] Comparatively, Canadians' level of interest in politics is similar to that found in other countries (Gidengil 2012, 50).

Existing interest in politics does not seem to translate into a particularly well-informed citizenry. Studies of the levels of political information in Canada have tended to find that Canadians are discouragingly poorly informed (Gidengil 2012, 42–3). Gidengil et al. (2004, 69) identify "deep pockets of political ignorance and political illiteracy" in the country and point to important differences in levels of knowledge on the basis of age, income, and gender, although it should be noted that many of the differences between men and women dissipate if different measures of political knowledge are used (Stolle and Gidengil 2010). Even so, differences in levels of political information between the rich and poor and the old and young remain relevant. Similarly, few Canadians engage frequently in political discussion and those who do tend to be those who are already heavily engaged in the political process (Gidengil et al. 2004, 35–8). Analysis of the 2019 Canadian Election Study shows similar patterns. Only 18.9 per cent of Canadians say they discuss politics often with their close friends or family; 9.3 per cent do so with their co-workers (Stephenson et al. 2020).

This broader context must be kept in mind when assessing the impact of digital technology on the practice of democratic citizenship in Canada. Most Canadians are not – nor have they ever been – deeply engaged in the political process. There is a small group of citizens

---

1 Our analysis of the 2011 and 2015 Canadian Election Studies found that political interest was 6.3 and 6.7, respectively.

2 It has become difficult for telephone surveys to establish representative samples using landlines given that Canadians are increasingly abandoning these for their cellphones and smartphones.

who are highly engaged in politics: they may be involved in formal or informal politics, they have high levels of interest, are well informed, and may discuss politics with others. But they are the exceptions, not the norm. Does digital technology make a difference to citizenship? Do Canadians gather information about politics from online sources? Do Canadians engage directly with politicians using digital technology? How frequently do Canadians talk about politics online? Do Canadians engage with formal politics online? We take up these questions in this chapter. However, when assessing the impact of digital politics on democratic citizenship, it is important to bear in mind that we are starting from a relatively minimal level of engagement.

DIGITIZATION

Promises & Perils

As discussed in the introduction of this book, one of the central perspectives on the impact of digital politics has been the mobilization hypothesis, which predicts that digital technology will reinvigorate democratic citizenship by mobilizing citizens who have been unable, unwilling, or have never been asked to become politically engaged (Norris 2001; Bridgmon and Milewicz 2004). This promise of digital technology featured prominently in early discussions of the latter's impact on the political process. It is easy to see why this might be the case. Digital technology provides greater access to information for a wider variety of people, reducing both the monetary and temporal costs of acquiring political information. Digital technology can also facilitate mobilization by reducing communication costs and by making it easier to find and connect with like-minded citizens. In addition, social media, like Facebook and Twitter, might also result in "accidental exposure" to political content, which might increase political interest and engagement (Valeriani and Vaccari 2016). The combination of these factors means that digital technology might very well reinvigorate democratic citizenship by engaging a wider cross-section of Canadians.

The reinforcement hypothesis challenges this optimistic prediction and suggests that digital technology will serve to merely reinforce existing patterns of inequality in participation and engagement. Digital technology would seem to provide a new set of tools to people who are already inclined to be politically active, enabling them to be even better informed and to communicate more quickly, cheaply, and effectively (Bimber 2003). In that sense, digital political participation would seem to be "repertoire building," in that it adds to the repertoire of politically engaged citizens (Painter-Main 2014, 63). Furthermore, as Markus Prior (2007) argues, increased media choice may reinforce inequality of information because citizens can avoid accidental exposure to political content by choosing their own media sources. In other words, digital technology would do little to motivate those with little political interest to become more engaged but would serve primarily to engage those already politically involved even more deeply. It can still be argued that reinforcement is a positive effect of digitization, even if it falls well short of the tantalizing predictions of the mobilization hypothesis. If already politically engaged citizens can be even better informed and more easily participate in the political process, this is still a positive development from the perspective of democratic citizenship.

PRACTICES

Scholarship that explores how citizens' use of digital technology or undertake political action online is considered the *demand* side of digital politics (Vaccari 2013; also see introduction); it is understudied in Canadian politics. Boulianne's (2018) meta-analysis of twenty years of digital media effects found only four of more than three hundred academic studies focused on Canada. Thus, unlike several of the other chapters in this book, which provide a detailed and historical examination of their respective topics, our understanding of digital citizenship in Canada and how it has changed over time is limited (but see Bastien 2004 and Small et al. 2014). (Though as noted in chapter 9, there are some promising analyses of young Canadians and digital politics).

In what follows, we assess the extent to which digital technology has shaped the practices of democratic citizenship in Canada by relying on data from a survey of three thousand Canadians in fall 2014.[3] To our

3 We have weighted the results to correct for age and gender imbalances in our sample.

best knowledge, this survey is one of the first large datasets focused solely on digital citizenship.[4] We asked our respondents questions about political attitudes and engagement both online and offline. Here we present our survey findings in four different categories: gathering information about politics, discussing politics with others, engagement with the formal politics of elections and elected representatives, and informal political participation through things like protests and petitions.

Our first category of political behaviour is *information gathering*. To what extent do Canadians gather information about politics from offline versus online sources? The proliferation of online sources of news and information has raised the prospect of traditional media outlets in formats such as television, radio, and newsprint becoming obsolete (see chapter 7). To explore this possibility, we asked respondents about their use of a variety of offline and online sources of political information. Respondents reported how often they sought "news and information about Canadian politics" from offline sources (television, radio, and print newspapers) and online sources (the websites of news organizations, social media, the electronic versions of newspapers, and blogs). Figure 8.1 reports the percentage of respondents who sought information from these sources at least once a day.

The most noticeable aspect of our findings is the clear distinction between offline and online sources of information: Canadians are much more likely to consult offline than online sources of news and information, being most likely to get news and information from television. Half of Canadians seek news from television at least once a day. This was followed by radio (32.2 per cent) and print newspapers (24.2 per cent). Only a quarter of respondents consulted the most popular online source (news websites) daily. Clearly the traditional media still matter. And even when Canadians do go online for online news, they are typically going to the websites of traditional media organizations like CBC and the *Globe and Mail.*

Of course, citizens can and do access both online and offline sources of information. Table 8.1 reports the overall percentage of respondents who get their political information in different ways, broken down by

4 This survey was conducted by *Online Citizenship/Citoyenneté en ligne* and is a SSHRC funded project exploring online political activity and democratic citizenship in Canada. For more information about the project, visit www.oc-cel.ca.

Figure 8.1. Proportion of respondents (%) accessing political information source at least daily

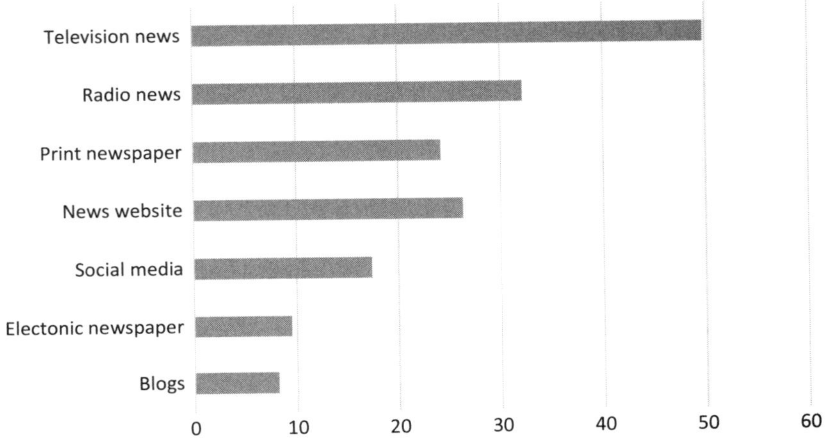

age categories. Looking first at the overall totals, the smallest proportion of people access their news solely from online sources; most people who access online news do so in a way that supplements their offline information gathering. When considering the age breakdowns, however, a few things become clear: older people are more likely to access their political information solely from offline sources, while younger people are more likely to do so solely from online sources. The largest age-based trend is the proportion of people who do not gather political information daily, with younger voters considerably less likely to do so. Not surprisingly, information gathering is closely connected to levels of political interest. Those who do not gather political information daily report an average political interest of 4.77 on our 1 to 10 political interest scale. By contrast, those who gather political information from both sources have a score of 6.99 on the political interest scale. Our respondents who gathered information from offline or online sources only had identical average interest scores of 6.15. The most interested citizens are the ones who gather information from both online and offline sources.

One of the most intriguing aspects of the increasing prevalence of digital technology is the opportunity it provides for citizens to access relevant political information from political actors directly rather than having to rely on the media. Some politicians – most notably US president Donald Trump – relish the opportunity to communicate directly

Table 8.1. Proportion of respondents accessing news daily, by age group

	18–29	30–39	40–49	50–59	60–69	70+	Total
No daily news	47.8%	32.2%	29.8%	21.5%	13.8%	6.5%	26.6%
Daily offline news only	13.7%	21.1%	32.0%	43.8%	54.5%	53.8%	35.3%
Daily online news only	15.5%	17.0%	10.4%	7.6%	3.7%	6.5%	10.4%
Both offline and online news	23.0%	29.6%	27.8%	27.1%	27.9%	33.3%	27.7%

with the public through social media. Even politicians less obviously concerned with seeking publicity maintain social media accounts and websites, as was seen in chapters 2 and 6. To what extent do Canadians take advantage of this opportunity to hear directly from their politicians? We asked respondents whether they had visited a Canadian political party website or the website of a Canadian politician in the last three months. 14.3 per cent said they had done so. Only 5.3 per cent of Canadians follow a politician on Twitter and 9.6 per cent belong to a politician or party Facebook group. While parties and politicians may be eager to publish information online, it appears that there is little appetite among voters for this information. Of course, Canadians may still be exposed to it via "accidental exposure": indirectly through media reports about political content on social media or by it being shared on the social media pages of those they follow. However, in total, it appears that the crucial intermediary role played by Canadian media — particularly news outlets on television and radio — has not been supplanted by parties' efforts to use social media and other online technology to speak directly to voters.

The second category of political engagement we examined is *political discussion.* We are particularly interested in what Delli Carpini et al. (2004) describe as discursive participation. Although discussing politics is not focused on affecting or changing governmental actions directly, attempts to persuade people to change their political views may be understood as indirectly trying to affect governmental action. Online discursive participation may occur across a range of forums, which shift over time. For example, whereas Canadians previously discussed politics on message boards and within blogroll communities (see, for example, Jansen and Koop [2006] and Koop and Jansen [2009]), these have largely been supplanted by social media as sources for political discussion.

We asked respondents about how they communicate with one another about politics across a range of offline and online settings. We began by asking how often they discussed politics and elections with the people in their lives. 14 per cent of respondents said they discussed politics very often, whereas 46 per cent said they did so sometimes, and 33 per cent said they rarely did so. Only 7 per cent of respondents said they never did so. Our survey thus demonstrates that most people engage in some discussion of politics. Given both that Canadians engage in political talk and the substantial number of opportunities digital technology provides for political conversation, how frequently and in what ways do Canadians talk about politics online? Figure 8.2 reports on whether internet users engaged in a range of ways of communicating about politics online and if so, to what extent.

The most striking thing about Figure 8.2 is how few Canadians engage in online discursive activities. The most common activities are liking, recommending, and sharing political content from news websites, something fewer than one in five Canadians report having done in a three-month period. In part, this reflects the fact that Facebook is not universally used by Canadians, and even fewer are active on Twitter. In addition, people who are politically active on Twitter or Facebook often do a variety of political things on those platforms. If we add up all the different ways to be politically active on Facebook, for example, we find that 20.1 per cent of our respondents performed at least one political activity on Facebook; this represents almost 29 per cent of people with Facebook accounts. 8.2 per cent of Canadians engaged in a political activity on Twitter, but this represents 41.3 per cent of all people who are active on Twitter. This shows that although Twitter users are not particularly numerous, they are relatively more politically active than Facebook users. This may reflect in part differences between the two platforms. As Mellon and Prosser (2017, 3) note in explaining their finding that Twitter users are more politically attentive than Facebook users, "These differences reflect the uses of the two platforms. Facebook is regarded as a primarily social platform ... whereas Twitter is seen as a place to follow current events."

Generally, those people who discuss politics online are those who discuss politics more frequently overall. Those who discuss politics less frequently are more likely to have those discussions in person. Among those who discuss politics very often, 48 per cent say they have those conversations exclusively or partially online. That is true of only 29 per cent

Figure 8.2. Proportion of Canadians (%) engaging in online discursive activities in previous three months

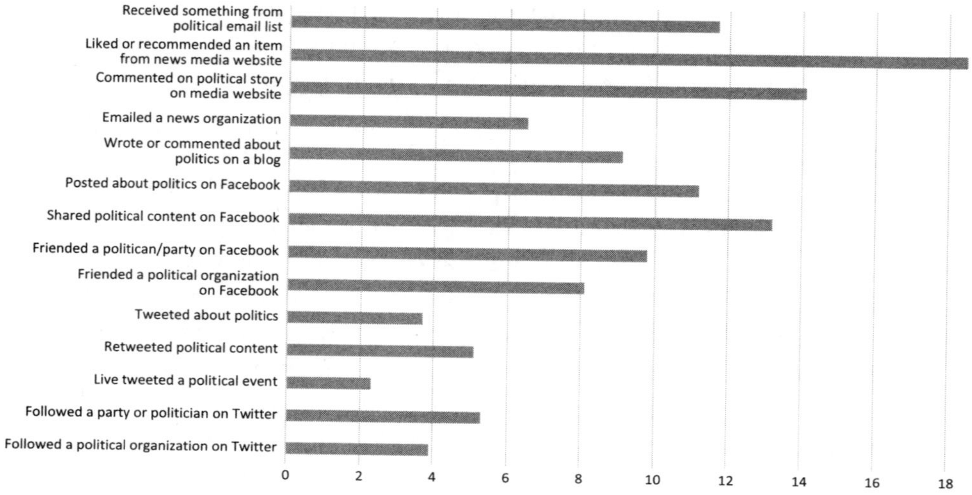

of those who say they sometimes discuss politics and 16 per cent of those who rarely discuss politics. The online arena for political discussion tends to be dominated by those who like to talk about politics a lot, providing some support for the reinforcement hypothesis.

Another way to address the extent to which Canadians engage in discursive politics offline and online is to ask them about the setting in which they try to persuade others to accept their views. Just over 60 per cent of Canadians at least occasionally try to persuade others politically, but only about 4 per cent of respondents to our survey said they did so often. Among those who engaged in political persuasion, two-thirds (66.2 per cent) did so in face-to-face (offline) settings only, 8.1 per cent did so online only, and 17.1 per cent engaged in political persuasion in both online and offline settings. Only a quarter of the 60 per cent of Canadians who are political persuaders did their persuading online. In terms of the democratic practice of attempting to persuade others to come around to our views, Canadians do so in decidedly old-fashioned settings.

One final thing to note about the pattern of discursive politics in Canada is that, as we found in the case of information gathering, there is a clear age pattern to discursive political participation. Table 8.2

Table 8.2. Discursive political participation, by age group

	18–29	30–39	40–49	50–59	60–69	70+	TOTAL
Discuss politics							
Never	10.5%	9.2%	9.6%	5.4%	4.4%	5.2%	7.5%
Online only	13.2%	12.8%	5.5%	3.1%	1.3%	0.5%	6.4%
Offline only	49.6%	55.9%	66.3%	75.7%	78.1%	78.4%	66.8%
Both	26.7%	22.2%	18.7%	15.7%	16.3%	16.0%	19.2%
Persuade others							
Never	38.0%	39.3%	44.7%	46.7%	45.0%	37.8%	42.7%
Online only	8.7%	11.3%	4.6%	2.3%	1.0%	0.5%	5.1%
Offline only	37.0%	36.0%	40.3%	43.8%	46.0%	51.3%	41.5%
Both	16.4%	13.5%	10.4%	7.2%	7.9%	10.4%	10.7%

NOTE: Columns may not add up to 100.0% due to rounding.

breaks down discursive political activities by age group. It shows that younger Canadians are more likely to discuss politics and persuade others online, while older Canadians are more likely to do so offline. Although it is possible that this is a life cycle effect and that people may change their behaviour as they age, it is more likely that this represents a shift in behaviour over time, that an increasing amount of political discussion and persuasion takes place online. We should note, however, that even among the youngest Canadians, those most likely to discuss politics online, offline political conversation is still predominant.

The third type of political behaviour we analyze is *formal political engagement*. This type of political engagement refers to engagement with the formal representational structures of government; for example, this may include contacting a Member of Parliament, being a member of a political party, donating to a party or candidate, or volunteering for a campaign or a party on an ongoing basis. To what extent do Canadians engage with formal politics, both offline and online?

Canadians' formal involvement with political parties is generally recognized to be quite low, especially in comparison to other types of political behaviour. In a 2017 survey, for example, the pro-democracy think tank Samara found rates of formal political engagement to be modest (2017, 20). Our survey produced similar results: just under 8 per cent had donated to a political party, a similar proportion were party members, and only 7 per cent volunteered for or participated in party activities. About one in six Canadians had contacted an elected official.

Even though the overall numbers are not large, more and more people are engaging in these kinds of activities online. We asked those who have contacted an elected official the method of communication they used. Table 8.3 shows the ways in which this contact was made. Email is overwhelmingly the most popular way of contacting elected officials.[5] It is difficult to tell whether more people are contacting elected officials, but the widespread adoption of digital technology has transformed the way in which people are communicating. We can see a similar trend in donations to political parties. Our phone survey found that about 40 per cent of our respondents made their financial contributions to a political party online. Our online survey a year later found that just over 50 per cent did so.[6] It is difficult, however, to determine whether this increase is due to the increasing popularity of internet contributions or due to the different method of survey administration. It is clear, though, that internet-based fundraising can be efficient for political parties (Flanagan and Jansen 2008, 203) and we can expect to see online contributions become more popular over time.

If we shift our attention away from the formal, electoral arena and look at *informal politics*, we again find relatively modest levels of political participation. Figure 8.3 shows how many Canadians engaged in five types of political activities in the preceding three months. Consistent with previous research (Gidengil et al. 2004), we find that signing petitions is a particularly popular activity among Canadians. In fact, it was the most popular participatory activity we found, with boycotts and protests being less popular. Although we might expect that decreased involvement with formal institutions like political parties might correspond to an increase in participation in social movements, interest groups, or unions, our survey did not find large numbers participating in those organizations, either.

Most of these activities require offline participation to carry out; a citizen cannot participate in a march or protest on their phone or

5 Although it could be argued that our online survey administration biased these results toward online forms of communication, an almost identical share (48.6 per cent) indicated they contacted elected officials through email on a telephone survey we conducted in early 2014.

6 Results reported here are from the first wave of a three-wave online survey of Canadians. Results reported here are from the first wave, which interviewed three thousand people in fall 2014.

Table 8.3. Method of contacting elected officials

In person	25.7%
By mail	15.3%
By telephone	22.0%
By email	49.8%
By other internet (including social media)	10.4%

Note: Table does not add up to 100% because multiple answers were allowed.

Figure 8.3. Proportion of Canadians engaging in informal political activities, last three months

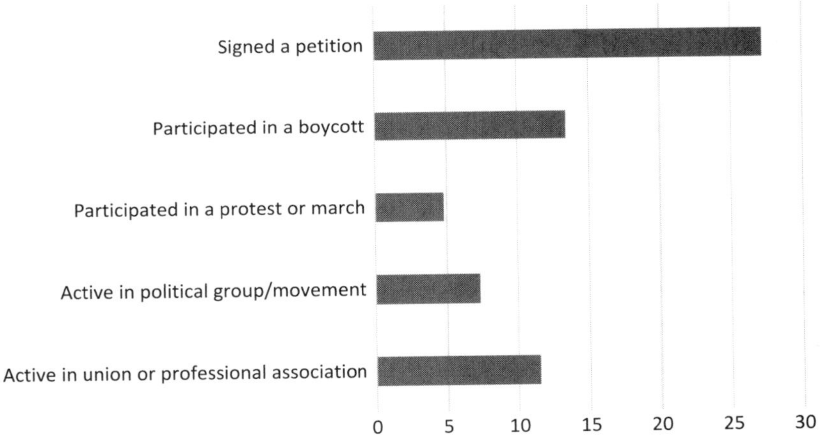

computer. The one exception to this is petitions, which can be done online or offline. Petitions are thus a convenient way to assess the impact of digital technology on the political process (Van Laer and Van Aelst 2010). Change.org is a popular e-petition website, which has featured petitions on issues such as electoral reform and environmental concerns. Moreover, the Canadian House of Commons operates its own e-petition website, where if a petition receives five hundred signatures it is tabled in the House of Commons and will receive a response from the government.[7] Our survey data show that advances in digital technology have transformed the way in which people sign petitions.

7 https://petitions.ourcommons.ca.

Our telephone survey found that almost two-thirds of those who signed petitions did so online, either exclusively or in combination with offline petitions. Our surveys were conducted over a relatively short period of time, so it is difficult to be sure whether there are changes in how frequently people are signing petitions over time, but it is clear – as was the case with contacting elected officials – that digital technology is changing the way this activity happens.

To what extent do our data support the mobilization or the reinforcement hypotheses? Has digital technology reinvigorated citizenship in Canada as promised by cyber-optimists? Or are the cyber-sceptics right that instead of mobilizing citizens, digital technology reinforces existing inequalities and limits to democratic participation? Our survey research into the democratic citizenship practices of Canadians shows that the reality of citizenship in the online age falls well short of the promise of a reinvigorated citizenship facilitated by digital technology. Simply put, there has not been a noticeable surge in political participation and engagement in the digital age, despite the fact that the barriers to information have never been lower and connecting with citizens who share similar concerns has never been easier. In this respect, our findings seem to contradict the mobilization hypothesis and provide support for the reinforcement hypothesis.

We find, for example, that traditional media sources, especially television, are still the most common source of political information for Canadians. When it comes to gathering information about politics, Canadians are still much more likely to consult offline than online sources of information. This suggests that, for a significant number of Canadians, the development of new information technology has had no effect on how they gather information about politics. And, despite hype about how new information technology is providing opportunities for politicians to bypass the media by speaking directly to the people, we find evidence that the latter are not particularly receptive to this: very few Canadians visit party websites, follow politicians on Twitter, or belong to a partisan Facebook group. On the other hand, a significant proportion of people are turning to websites and social media to access information. We found that a quarter of respondents to our survey consult news websites for political information at least once daily. This shows that the internet has opened up new avenues for Canadians to learn about politics and many Canadians are taking advantage of them.

We now turn to whether new communication technology is changing how Canadians converse about politics. Given the availability of social media and news organizations with opportunities to comment, the mobilization hypothesis would lead us to expect that Canadians who would not normally discuss politics would use these new online opportunities to do so. As we saw only small proportions of respondents regularly use online methods to engage in such discussion. Canadians are most likely to "like" or provide comments on political stories, but the proportions that do so are small. Some forms of political discursive activity online occurred remarkably rarely. For example, despite the fact that journalists and politicians seem to be very preoccupied with Twitter, less than 4 per cent of our respondents reported tweeting about politics. A higher proportion (11 per cent) had shared political content on Facebook, but the number of Canadians who post about politics on social media is nevertheless very low. Communication technology provides new opportunities for Canadians to discuss politics, and some are doing so. But, overall, the use of this technology by Canadians provides support for the reinforcement hypothesis. We find that people who discuss politics more often overall are also more likely to do so online.

Finally, we explored the extent to which Canadians were using new communication technology to engage with and participate in politics. The internet provides new opportunities for people to participate in the political process, both the formal political process as well as other informal means of political engagement. The mobilization hypothesis posits that new opportunities created by new communication technology would lead to more Canadians becoming involved in formal politics for the first time. Canadians' engagement with formal politics, especially through political parties, is generally low. While the availability of new technology to participate appears to be having a small impact on how Canadians do so, Canadians who contact elected officials are increasingly embracing the convenience of doing so online. While the internet has not ushered in radical changes in how Canadians engage with political parties and elected officials, it has created new opportunities that Canadians have embraced to some extent. Further, there is some evidence that this use of online technology is increasing over time. There is also some evidence that the availability of petitions online has led to the practice becoming an important new type of political participation for Canadians.

The finding that the increased use of digital technology has not led to a surge in democratic engagement and participation is not the same as saying that digital technology has not made a difference. In fact, we found that digital technology has transformed the way some of these existing activities are carried out. In other words, although digital technology may not change the number of people participating politically, *it has changed the way they engage politically.*

POTENTIALS

In many ways, our analysis is a sobering one. We found little evidence to support the optimistic mobilization hypothesis. We provide evidence that Canadians are not using new information technology to substantially increase their citizenship activities. Either this technology is not as liberating as proponents of the mobilization hypothesis thought it would be, or Canadians are simply not inclined to grab hold of the new opportunities presented to them. That said, the reinforcement thesis is not entirely substantiated, either. We did see some areas where Canadians seem to be shifting their behaviour in response to the opportunities presented by new communication technology. We view this process as one of adaptation. Digital technology is removing some barriers to democratic participation and we find some evidence that Canadians are responding to this trend. The absence of a massive increase in such activities does not mean that new technology is not having some impact. Further, we find some evidence that this process of adaptation will continue over time, and that Canadians will increasingly embrace this technology as a means to more fully participate in Canadian politics as citizens.

A particularly notable example relates to differences in how Canadians learn about politics between age groups. On the one hand, older Canadians are much more likely than younger Canadians to gather their news from offline sources like television. Over half of our respondents over the age of sixty gathered news exclusively from offline sources, whereas only 14 per cent of those aged 18 to 29 did so. In contrast, younger Canadians are much more likely to gather political information exclusively online. This suggests that as young cohorts of Canadians age, they will continue to access information online, leading to continual growth in the use of online technologies to gather information about politics. The next chapter will explore the issue of young Canadians and digital technology more deeply. While the internet has not ushered in a revolution in how Canadians learn about politics, it is certainly changing how they do so and will continue to do so into the future.

The mobilization hypothesis is a lofty standard to hold new communication technology to. The promise of the mobilization hypothesis – that new communication technology would help to overcome previous inequalities in democratic citizenship – has not yet come to pass. In some cases, the reinforcement hypothesis appears to more closely anticipate the results of our research into Canadians' use of new digital technology for citizenship purposes. But this technology *has* led to changes in how Canadians behave as citizens, although in subtler and more nuanced ways than the mobilization hypothesis anticipated. In some ways – such as petitions – Canadians are taking advantage of this technology. In other cases, Canadians are slowly adapting their engagement to a new environment where online technology makes some citizenship activities easier.

As mentioned, there is little demand research of this kind in Canada. Therefore, it is impossible to know whether the numbers we present represent a change in how Canadians have used digital technology politically. The Pew Research Center in the United States has been exploring the relationship between digital technology and American citizenship for more than a decade (for instance, Smith et al. 2009; Smith and Duggan 2016). This sustained longitudinal approach allows for greater nuance than is currently available in Canadian political science. It goes without saying that more demand research on digital citizenship in Canada is required.

REFERENCES

Bastien, Frédérick. 2004. "Branchés, informés, et engagés? Les Canadiens, l'Internet, et l'élection fédérale de 2000." *Politique et Sociétés* 23 (1): 171–91. https://doi.org/10.7202/009511ar.

Bimber, Bruce Allen. 2003. *Information and American Democracy: Technology in the Evolution of Political Power.* New York: Cambridge University Press.

Bridgmon, Phillip, and Mark Milewicz. 2004. *E-Politics: Technology in American Government.* Dubuque, IA: Kendall Hunt Publishing Co.

Boulianne, Shelley. 2018. “Twenty Years of Digital Media Effects on Civic and Political Participation.” *Communication Research*: 1–20. https://doi.org/10.1177/0093650218808186.

Clarke, Harold D., Jane Jenson, Lawrence LeDuc, and Jon H. Pammett. 2019. *Absent Mandate: Interpreting Change in Canadian Politics*. Toronto: University of Toronto Press.

Cross, William, and Lisa Young. 2004. “The Contours of Political Party Membership in Canada.” *Party Politics* 10 (4): 427–44. http://doi.org/10.1177/1354068804043907.

Delli Carpini, Michael X., Fay Lomax Cook, and Lawrence R. Jacobs. 2004. “Public Deliberation, Discurisve Participation, and Citizen Engagement: A Review of the Empirical Literature.” *Annual Review of Political Science* 7 (1): 315–44. http://doi.org/10.1146/annurev.polisci.7.121003.091630.

Elections Canada. 2018. “Voter Turnout at Federal Elections and Referendums.” http://elections.ca/content.aspx?section=ele&dir=turn&document=index&lang=e.

Flanagan, Tim, and Harold J. Jansen. 2009. “Election Campaigns Under Canada’s Party Finance Laws.” In *The Canadian Federal Election of 2008*, ed. Jon H. Pammett and Christopher Dornan, 194–216. Toronto: Dundurn.

Gidengil, Elisabeth. 2012. “The Diversity of the Canadian Political Marketplace.” In *Political Marketing in Canada*, ed. Alex Marland, Thierry Giasson, and Jennifer Lees-Marshment, 39–56. Vancouver: UBC Press.

Gidengil, Elisabeth, and Heather Bastedo. 2014. “Introduction.” In *Canadian Democracy from the Ground Up: Perceptions and Perforamce*, ed. Elisabeth Gidengil and Heather Bastedo, 3–21. Vancouver: UBC Press.

Gidengil, Elisabeth, André Blais, Neil Nevitte, and Richard Nadeau. 2004. *Citizens*. Vancouver: UBC Press.

Gidengil, Elisabeth, Neil Nevitte, André Blais, Joanna Everitt, and Patrick Fournier. 2012. *Dominance and Decline: Making Sense of Recent Canadian Elections*. Toronto: University of Toronto Press.

Jansen, Harold J., and Royce Koop. 2006. “Pundits, Ideologues, and the Ranters: The British Columbia Election Online.” *Canadian Journal of Communication* 30 (4): 613–32. https://doi.org/10.22230/cjc.2005v30n4a1483.

Koop, Royce, and Harold J. Jansen. 2009. “Partisan Blogs and Blogrolls in Canada: Forums for Democratic Deliberation?” *Social Science Computer Review* 27 (2): 155–73. https://doi.org/10.1177/0894439308326297.

Mellon, Jonathan, and Christopher Prosser. 2017. “Twitter and Facebook Are Not Representative of the General Population: Political Attitudes and Demographics of British Social Media Users.” *Research and Politics* July–September: 1–9. https://doi.org/10.1177/2053168017720008.

Norris, Pippa. 2001. *Digital Divide: Civic Engagement, Information Poverty, and the Internet Worldwide*. New York: Cambridge University Press.

Painter-Main, Michael A. 2014. "Repertoire-Building or Elite-Challenging? Understanding Political Engagement in Canada." In *Canadian Democracy from the Ground Up*, ed. Elisabeth Gidengil and Heather Bastedo, 62–82. Vancouver: UBC Press.

Prior, Markus. 2007. *Post-Broadcast Democracy: How Media Choice Increases Inequality in Political Involvement and Polarizes Elections.* Cambridge: Cambridge University Press.

Siaroff, Alan, and Jared J. Wesley. 2015. "Comparative Voter Turnout in the Canadian Provinces since 1965: The Importance of Context." *Canadian Political Science Review* 9 (1): 147–63.

Small, Tamara A., Harold Jansen, Frédérick Bastien, Thierry Giasson, and Royce Koop. 2014. "Online Political Activity in Canada: The Hype and the Facts." *Canadian Parliamentary Review* 37 (4): 9–16.

Smith, Aaron, and Maeve Duggan. 2016. "The Political Environment on Social Media." Pew Research Center. https://www.pewinternet.org/2016/10/25/the-political-environment-on-social-media/.

Smith, Aaron Whitman, Kay Lehman Schlozman, Sidney Verba, and Henry Brady. 2009. "The Internet and Civic Engagement." Washington, DC: Pew Internet & American Life Project. http://www.pewinternet.org/files/old-media/Files/Reports/2009/The%20Internet%20and%20Civic%20Engagement.pdf.

Stephenson, Laura B., Allison Harell, Daniel Rubenson, and Peter John Loewen. 2020. "2019 Canadian Election Study – Online Survey." https://doi.org/10.7910/DVN/DUS88V.

Stolle, Dietlind, and Elisabeth Gidengil. 2010. "What Do Women Really Know? A Gendered Analysis of Varieties of Political Knowledge." *Perspectives on Politics* 8 (1). http://doi.org/10.1017/s1537592709992684.

Vaccari, Cristian. 2013. *Digital Politics in Western Democracies: A Comparative Study.* Baltimore: Johns Hopkins University Press.

Valeriani, Augusto, and Cristian Vaccari. 2016. "Accidental Exposure to Politics on Social Media as Online Participation Equalizer in Germany, Italy, and the United Kingdom." *New Media & Society* 18 (9): 1857–74. http://doi.org/10.1177/1461444815616223.

Van Laer, Jeroen, and Peter Van Aelst. 2010. "Internet and Social Movement Action Repertoires: Opportunities and Limitations." *Information, Communication, & Society* 13 (8): 1146–71. https://doi.org/10.1080/13691181003628307.

CHAPTER NINE

Young People: Politics and Digital Technologies

Allison Harell, Dietlind Stolle, Philippe Duguay, and Valérie-Anne Mahéo

INTRODUCTION

Digital technologies are increasingly important tools for communicating and gathering information in Canadian society; this is particularly true of Canadian youth. Online platforms and wireless communication technologies have become increasingly omnipresent in the lives of Canadians. According to the WorldFact book, almost 90 per cent of Canadians had internet access in 2016. Indeed, Canadians spend more time online compared to the rest of the world, spending on average about forty-five hours connected to the internet per month (CIRA Factbook 2013), with young people being the most connected. One survey as far back as 2013 showed that 99 per cent of young people in grades four to eleven had internet access outside of their school (Steeves 2014).

Digital technologies have the potential to be a source of political information, discussion, and mobilization. Yet, we know that people vary in the ways and extent that they use the internet for political purposes. For example, a study in 2012 showed that among individuals who have used the internet at home in the past twelve months, 58 per cent have searched for government-related information online and only 12 per cent had communicated with a government department or elected official online. These numbers have steadily increased since 2007 but have still not reached an overwhelming majority (Statistics Canada 2013). How people access the internet also affects the types of activities they carry out: desktop users lead in playing games, while using social media is the most popular activity on laptops, tablets, and mobile phones (CIRA 2014).

In this chapter, we examine how the most connected group of the population – Canadian youth – uses the internet for political purposes and whether there are major utilization gaps among groups of young people. Drawing on debates in the literature about the promises and perils of digital technologies for political activism, we ask whether internet use mobilizes young people to be politically active. Do traditional digital divides still characterize how people – especially young people – use digital technologies for political purposes and have these divides changed over time? We draw on existing literature as well as the Canadian Youth Study, a unique two-wave panel survey conducted by the authors in 2005–6 and 2014–15 among young people in Quebec and Ontario (n = 967) (Stolle et al. 2015).

CONTEXT

While the youngest cohorts have always been amongst the least participative in the electoral process both in Canada and other representative democracies, studies have shown that for the more recent generations of Canadians, political participation and, more particularly, voting has declined significantly (Blais and Loewen 2009; Gélineau 2013). Accordingly, since the late nineties, scholars in both political science and communication studies have been increasingly concerned with the potential of the internet to offer a new realm for practising politics and citizenship. Because of their digital skills and socialization, millennials especially have received much scholarly attention. A Pew Research report on the online activities of American adolescents found that 95 per cent of teens have access to a smartphone, with 45 per cent going online "almost constantly." The median young adult (aged eighteen to twenty-nine) uses on average four social networking sites, with Facebook being the most used site followed by other sites such as Snapchat, Instagram, and Twitter (Anderson and Jiang 2018). Meanwhile, among adolescents, 51 per cent use Facebook, far behind YouTube, which is used by 85 per cent of US teens, as well as Instagram (72 per cent) and Snapchat (69 per cent) (Anderson and Jiang 2018). While boys are more likely to own video game consoles and play games, girls are more present on social media platforms (see also Abiala and Hernwall 2013). The omnipresence of these platforms in young people's lives has led to important debates about millennials' internet use. When does it go beyond social interactions and become political? And for whom?

DIGITIZATION

Promises & Perils

As seen throughout this volume, there is an optimistic and a pessimistic view of the potential of digital technologies for young people in politics. While some believe that digital technologies lower the costs of participation and politically mobilizes new groups of citizens (Delli Carpini 2000; Krueger 2002; Ward, Gibson, and Lusoli 2003; Weber, Loumakis, and Bergman 2003), others are more sceptical and believe that digital technologies merely offer non-political uses and entertainment-related participation (Gladwell 2010; Papacharissi 2002; Tyler 2002; Vissers and Stolle 2014) that do not translate into engagement with wider societal issues.

The optimistic view, and the attendant mobilization hypothesis, is centred in part around the idea that digital technologies open up opportunities for a completely new type of engagement that is not practised in the same way offline – e.g., the widespread use of humour in political postings; symbolic, instantaneously visible support for social/political organizations, candidates, and specific social/political goals; mobilization campaigns that reach many people at the same time; or politically motivated hacking (Chadwick 2006; Raine and Smith 2008; Schlozman et al. 2010; Vitak et al. 2011). New types of online participation have developed on social media (Holt et al. 2013; Towner et al. 2013; Vissers and Stolle 2013; Theocharis and Quintelier 2014). Oser, Hooghe, and Marien (2013) find that online participation is a distinct form of political participation, especially for people aged eighteen to thirty-five.

From this point of view, then, online participation opens new avenues for participation. If that is the case, these may require a new and different conceptual and definitional frame than offline participation (Bimber 2003; Chadwick 2006). Several dimensions matter here. For one, the internet allows for activities that are very time consuming or costly offline (e.g., creating and disseminating content or news, online specific forms of communication, as well as online hacktivism). Digital technologies also allow users to customize content to their needs and interests, further reducing information costs. Online participation also means immediate and broad social interaction and exchange, and significantly decreased costs to share information and opinions, and to mobilize one's broader social network (Chadwick 2006; Haynes and Pitts 2009; Ward and Vedel 2006). Indeed, several studies find a spillover from time spent on social media to individual political engagement, both online and offline (Vromen, Xenos, and Loader 2014; see also Vissers and Stolle 2014).

The less optimistic view is that, for young people, online political participation is not any different from its offline counterpart. Some see online engagement as the mirror image of political participation offline, despite any specificity in form. Thus, as more opportunities arise to be active online, people – and importantly, the same politically active people – will simply extend or shift their activities to the online realm. Some evidence indicates that this might be the case. For example, people increasingly donate politically online and less offline (Oser, Hooghe, and Marien 2013; Smith and Duggan 2012).

From this perspective, digital technologies are no more than new tools for politically active segments of society. Thus, digital technologies create new ways to participate, but not new access to politics. This so-called reinforcement hypothesis holds the assumption that the internet, as a new medium, will neither change individuals' political motivation and interest nor be able to lure new people into politics, as already privileged groups simply acquire access to more means of communication to get their voices heard in politics (Allbrecht 2006; di Gennaro and Dutton 2006; Willis and Tranter 2006). As a result, the gap between active and inactive citizens, as well as between heard and unheard voices, will be maintained or even increase (Margolis and Resnick 2000; Norris 2001; Norris 2003), and therefore current participatory inequalities will persist (Bimber 2003; Norris 2003). Indeed, internet use may even accelerate social inequality (van Deursen and van Dijk 2013).

The most important moderator of internet use is socio-economic status, or, more specifically, education, which is related to all types of internet use but also various skills such as the ability to take part in forums, download files, browse the internet, and use email. Such skills reinforce "digital political participation" (De Marco, Robles, and Antino 2014). Consistent with the reinforcement hypothesis, people from a more privileged background generally use the internet for activities that are "capital enhancing," or more personally beneficial (Hargittai 2010), while individuals with lower levels of education engage more in social interaction and gaming online (van Deursen and van Dijk 2014). Importantly, the latter activities are often found to have no or a negative effect on political mobilization.

In addition, gender divides also seem to be reinforced online. Some studies find that men are more likely to participate online (Cicognani et al. 2012; however, see Oser Hooghe and Marien 2012) and tend to seek out more news-related information online than women (van Deursen, Dijk, and Klooster 2015; van Deursen and van Dijk 2014). Women and those with less education are more likely to use social networking sites (Haight, Quan-Haase, and Corbett 2014). Along with gender, there is some evidence of differences across ethnic and immigration backgrounds (e.g. Haight, Quan-Haase, and Corbett 2014; Ono and Zavodny 2008). One study finds that immigrants are less likely than natives to have access to and use computers. However much of this gap could be attributed to English language ability (Ono and Zavodny 2008). In another study, Canadian-born and long-established immigrants were found to be more likely to access the internet, compared to recent immigrants. More recent immigrants who had gone online in the past 12 months were found to complete more online activities than Canadian-born and earlier immigrants (Haight, Quan-Haase, and Corbett 2014). Gaps based on education, socio-economic status, gender, and immigration status may be lessening. However, as online forms of communication and the omnipresence of new information technologies blur the lines between the online and offline worlds, such gaps are likely to be maintained, to a certain extent. These divides also point to the (increasing) importance of looking at various usages of the internet and how they might differ across salient groups.

The most common exception to the reinforcement hypothesis can be found regarding age (see chapter 8). While young people tend to be more politically apathetic, they are much more likely to be active online (Gibson et al. 2005; however, see also Schlozman et al. 2010), with higher rates of internet access (White and Selwyn 2011; Oser, Hooghe, and Marien 2012) and online skills (de Marco, Robles, and Antino 2014; Hargittai and Shafer 2006). Their increased rates of online involvement could moderate one of the offline participation gaps, specifically the one between younger and older citizens. Yet, to fully understand whether this gap is narrowing, scholars argue that we need to disaggregate various uses of the internet to isolate mobilizing and demobilizing spaces. Research thus needs to focus on what young people actually do when they are online. For example, Ekström, Olsson, and Shehata (2014) show that adolescents active in news spaces have higher political interest and a greater propensity to talk about politics. Meanwhile, their results also show that social spaces, such as Facebook or Twitter, have the opposite effect. For example, in their study, Facebook use is not related to online and offline participation in politics (Theocharis and Quintelier 2014). However, this result is clearly contested in the literature. Canadian research on this topic is scant (see chapter 8). Work on a Canadian sample of students indicates that there are spillover effects from Facebook use to several forms of political participation (Vissers and Stolle 2014). Using Facebook for political posting has been shown to improve self-reported turnout in the US, especially in battleground states (Settle et al. 2016). More significant than individual use, however, is social pressure: experiments confirm that targeted social pressures exerted through Facebook can have a substantial positive influence on turnout, much more than traditional get-out-the-vote methods (Haenschen 2016; Teresi and Michelson 2015). Furthermore, political exposure through social media and political sharing on Facebook have also been said to exert a positive influence, directly or indirectly, on forms of offline political participation other than voting (Leyva 2017; Wolfsfeld et al. 2016; Halpern et al. 2017). The platform itself seems to matter: Halpern and his colleagues (2017) demonstrate that Twitter and Facebook respectively boost internal and collective efficacy among individuals, and that the latter has a larger indirect effect on participation. Our analysis picks up on these themes and focuses on how youth have used the internet over time in Canada and its impact on online political communication. We ask: How are young people engaging politically online? What gaps exist in online political engagement? And how have these changed over time?

Practice

To examine the extent to which digitization influences young people's politics, we rely on data from the Canadian Youth Study (CANYS), which provides a wealth of information about the changing engagement of the next generation. The CANYS is a two-wave panel study conducted among tenth- and eleventh-grade classrooms in seven cities in Quebec and Ontario during the 2005–6 school year (n = 3,334); the individuals were re-contacted for a second wave in 2014–15 to complete an online survey (n = 967).[1] This period of life, from sixteen to twenty-four, is a critical period for youth's development of online communication skills, and it is, furthermore, a key period of political socialization.

At the same time, capturing online usage – both in its political and non-political variations – poses a variety of challenges, especially over time. The ways in which people use the internet today did not exist – or were marginal – in 2005, which means the online batteries measuring online behaviour are not perfectly parallel. Something as simple as measuring time spent online in 2005 was measured in terms of a few hours, whereas in 2014 the smartphone means that many people are continuously connected. Capturing political participation online is not self-evident either. There are various definitions and markers of political participation and expression online. Some researchers include action-based items such as contacting a politician or organization online, raising money for an organization, and signing a petition (De Marco et al. 2014; Vissers and Stolle 2014). Others include expression items such as writing comments on a blog or forum with political content or discussing political issues on the internet (De Marco et al. 2014; Jugert et al. 2013; Cicognani et al. 2012; Hsieh and Li 2013). For

1 Details on the wave 1 sample design are available in the technical report (Harell et al. 2008). The wave 2 response rate was 22 per cent. While ideally we would be able to re-contact more respondents, several challenges presented themselves. First, there were eight years between the initial survey and the second wave, meaning that for many people, the contact information that we have is no longer valid. Of the original 3,334 respondents, we had or were able to acquire valid contact information for 1,779, leaving our re-contact rate for those for whom we have contact information at 42 per cent. Obviously, for those for whom we do not have valid re-contact information, recruitment for the second wave was nearly impossible (although extensive efforts were made to find valid contact information through third parties).

some, online participation can include information-seeking behaviour (Cicognani et al. 2012), yet offline news consumption is often a predictor, and not a form of, political participation.

Jensen (2013) provides a useful distinction between "information-based" forms of activity and "participation-based" forms, with information-based activity including searching for information on parties and candidates and watching videos, while participation-based activities include asking questions on blogs, participating in online debates and polls, and friending politicians or joining their groups on social networking sites such as YouTube and Facebook. Participation and engagement on social media is sometimes a category on its own (Holt et al. 2013) or included with other general measures of online participation (Towner 2013; Vissers and Stolle 2013; Oser, Hooghe, and Marien 2013). Social media participation can include following a politician or party on Facebook, Twitter, or YouTube (Holt et al. 2013), posting a comment on a social network or blog (Towner et al. 2013), joining a Facebook group to attain a political goal (Vissers and Stolle 2013), and using the "share button" to publicize a political link online to one's network (Theocharis and Quintelier 2014). Theocharis and Quintelier make a clear distinction between Facebook engagement and online political engagement (2014). Our focus here is on the communicational aspects of online participation. One of the ways in which online environments are distinct from the offline environment is that they provide spaces to find, share, and discuss political information. While this can certainly occur offline, the internet drastically lowers the costs associated with these activities, making it a particularly interesting avenue to explore. Our online political communication battery of questions includes the consumption and creation of online political content. Respondents reported, on an average day, how frequently they (1) discussed public issues and politics online, (2) created or shared social or political content online (e.g., blog posts, video content, etc.), and (3) searched for political and social information online.[2] These three items make up our online political communication index that ranges from 0–9 (alpha = .62).

---

2 Response categories were on a four-point scale from never to three or more times a day.

So how have online practices changed over time? Clearly, there has been concern that the online euphoria would take time away from young people's engagement in the wider society. In other words, does the development of online behaviours hinder young people's connection to society and larger public issues? One of the simplest measures of the changing impact of digital technologies on young people is simply to look at the time spent online. In 2005–6, the modal response for time spent online was one to two hours on an average day, with just 22 per cent reporting spending five or more hours online. About eight years later, 56 per cent of young people reported spending five or more hours a day online. Indeed, we asked respondents in wave two the number of hours, up to twenty-four, to reflect the increasing omnipresence of online spaces in our everyday lives. Over 10 per cent reported being online constantly during every waking hour (e.g., sixteen or more hours a day).

Table 9.1 presents information about who is most likely to spend time online. In the first step of the analysis, we examine who among our respondents are online, who spends more time online in 2006 versus in 2014, and whether there has been any aggregate change overtime. Overall, young people in this sample increased the time spent on the internet in the eight years of our study, documenting a change from an average of one to two hours to an average of three to four hours. This increase is visible in all socio-demographic categories, but particularly among those with low education (i.e., this group experienced a significant increase from wave 1 to wave 2). In fact, while young people who later attended a vocational school spent the most hours online while in high school, they switched to be the least online from all education groups eight years later.

Differences exist with regard to certain socio-demographic backgrounds in both waves (e.g., young men, visible minorities, and those from Ontario spend more time online compared to young women, whites, and people from Quebec, respectively). Francophones are significantly less present online than Anglophones or allophones. Overall, in terms of sheer hours spent online, without making any differentiation as to the activity online, we do see a moderate digital divide that is quite persistent over time but reverses with regard to education levels.

In a final step, we model the impact of these socio-demographic cleavages as well as drawing on the panel design of our survey to model

Table 9.1. Mean time spent online overtime

	Hours on internet (Wave 1)	Hours on internet (Wave 2)	Change
	Mean (0–3)	Mean (0–3)	W2-W1
Gender			
Women	1.36**	2.32**	0.96
Men	1.54	2.48	0.84
Language			
French	1.34**	2.28**	0.91
English	1.42	2.45	0.97
Other	1.56**	2.45	0.86
Visible Minority			
No	1.38**	2.33*	0.94
Yes	1.54	2.48	0.85
SES			
Low	1.46	2.42	0.90
Mid	1.44	2.30	0.84
High	1.40	2.43	1.02
Education			
High School or less	1.29*	2.41*	1.10**
College, Vocational	1.62	2.25	0.63
University Degree	1.43	2.42	0.99
Income			
less than $20k	1.47	2.45	0.98
$20k–$40k	1.43	2.32	0.89
more than $40k	1.52	2.30	0.78
Canadian born			
No	1.58	2.45	0.87
Yes	1.45	2.37	0.91
Province			
Quebec	1.43	2.32**	0.89
Ontario	1.45	2.49	0.95
Total	1.46	2.38	0.91

Note: ** p<.05, * p<.10. Original scale in wave 1 includes 0 = Less than an hour; 1 = 1–2 hours; 2 = 3–4 hours; 3 = 5 or more hours. Wave 2 included a broader range and was recoded to match. Note that significance is within group differences. All overtime increases are significant.

how time spent online and early use of the internet influences later online political communication. Importantly, we control for the mediating role of political interest.

So, to what extent are young people using the internet to engage in the creation and consumption of political content? Table 9.2 provides an overview of the political communication index and compares their levels to other online (social communication) and offline communication activities. In addition, it compares these levels across salient socio-demographic categories.

Table 9.2 indicates that searching for political information is the most common online political communication activity. On the 0–3 scale, it receives 1.29 compared to just .57 and .52 for creation and discussion. This translates into 75 per cent of young people in our survey reporting searching for political information online at least daily. This is of interest, because many young people's primary sources – or at least one of their primary sources – of political news are online sources. The CANYS included a question asking respondents to indicate up to three sources (out of nine) they use most often to obtain social and political news (e.g., TV news broadcast, print newspapers, news aggregator websites, and social media). In 2014–15, over a quarter of young people (27.6 per cent) said they only selected online news sources, with another 56 per cent saying they use both online and offline news sources. This is a drastic transformation from 2005–6, when just 7 per cent of the young people reported getting most of their news from the internet.

In contrast, fewer people report discussing public issues and politics online, with only 39 per cent doing it at least once a day. When asked where such discussions were taking place, the vast majority of young people said through social networks such as Facebook or Twitter (83 per cent), compared to just 11 to 12 per cent reporting discussion on social news websites like Reddit or in the comments of traditional news websites. Clearly, political discussion, when it occurs, can be found on established social network sites.

A very similar number of young people (41 per cent) report creating social and political content at least daily. The fact that discussion and creation are less frequent makes intuitive sense, given these are more intense, resource-intensive activities. The fact that two out of five young people report doing these activities *daily*, though, suggests

Table 9.2. Young people's online and offline political communication

	Discuss	Create/ Share	Search	Online Political Comm	Offline Political Comm
	Mean (0–3)	Mean (0–3)	Mean (0–3)	Mean (0–1)	Mean (0–1)
Total	0.52	0.57	1.29	0.26	0.20
Gender					
Women	0.48	0.58	1.23*	0.25	0.19
Men	0.58	0.55	1.42	0.28	0.21
Language					
French	0.47	0.58	1.19*	0.25	0.19
English	0.53	0.54	1.37	0.27	0.21
Other	0.58	0.62	1.38	0.28	0.19
Visible Minority					
No	0.49	0.54	1.27	0.26	0.20
Yes	0.57	0.62	1.35	0.28	0.19
SES					
Low	0.44	0.60	1.12**	0.24	0.16
Mid	0.49	0.51	1.23	0.25	0.19
High	0.57	0.58	1.50	0.29**	0.23**
Education					
High School or less	0.53*	0.57	1.24	0.26	0.17
College, Vocational	0.42	0.59	1.01	0.22	0.17
University Degree	0.55	0.56	1.40**	0.28**	0.21**
Income					
less than $20k	0.57	0.56	1.40*	0.28	0.21
$20k–$40k	0.50	0.59	1.19	0.25	0.19
more than $40k	0.45	0.57	1.31	0.26	0.19
Canadian born					
No	0.75**	0.57	1.36	0.31	0.22
Yes	0.48	0.57	1.28	0.26*	0.20
Province					
Quebec	0.48	0.56	1.24*	0.25	0.18
Ontario	0.58	0.58	1.42	0.29	0.23**

Note: ** p<.05, * p<.10

a surprisingly high engagement with at least communicational aspects of political content online. Yet, clearly this is not the primary activity that young people engage in when connected online. When asked a similar question about the frequency with which they stay in touch with family and friends online, over 90 per cent reported doing this at least once a day, of which over half reported doing it three or more times a day. The internet, then, is being used heavily for interpersonal communication, and, when politics is discussed, it tends to be in the same spaces.

Table 9.2 also provides evidence of important digital divides among young people, particularly when it comes to searching for information, the most common activity.[3] Fewer young women, Francophones, people with low socio-economic status (SES), and Quebeckers search for online information compared to young men, Anglophones, and allophones, people with high SES, and Ontarians, respectively. However, there is one exception with regard to income—young people with low income search information more frequently than young people with higher income levels. Thus, not all socio-demographic factors work how we expect them to from the political participation literature. Another example is that, while youth with college or vocational training discuss public issues less often than young people at university, they also discuss public issues less than young people with high school degrees. Canadian-born respondents are less engaged in online discussions about public issues compared to their foreign-born counterparts, indicating perhaps how international embeddedness fosters the political use of the internet. The overall political communication scale shows moderate differences for SES, education, and birthplace.

In line with the reinforcement hypothesis, these differences mirror gaps observed for our offline political communication scale (see last column Table 9.2). The offline political communication measure does not perfectly mirror the online measure but provides a useful point of comparison. The items include wearing a patch or other item with a

3 We include: born in Canada (1 = native born), gender (1 = female), visible minority (1 = visible minority), primary language (French is the reference category) and province (1 = Ontario), current highest level of education attained (1 = university degree or more) and current income (20K or less, 20K to 40K, or 40K plus). We also include in some analyses a derived socio-economic status variable from wave 1 (See Harell et al. 2008). For simplicity, terciles are reported in descriptive tables.

Table 9.3. Predicting wave 2 online political communication

	Coefficient	(s.e.)
Gender	0.13	(.13)
Language (ref = French)		
English	0.00	(.17)
Other Languages	0.12	(.20)
Visible Minority	0.08	(.16)
W1 Family SES	−0.01	(.02)
W2 Working Full Time	−0.12	(.16)
W2 University Degree	−0.09	(.15)
Income (ref = <$20k)		
$20K–$40k	−0.08	(.16)
$40k+	−0.18	(.20)
Canadian Citizen	−0.17	(.20)
Ontario	0.04	(.16)
W1# of internet Usage	0.18	(.10)*
W1 Time Spent Online	1.27	(.30)***
Change in Time Spent Online	1.06	(.21)***
W1 Political Interest	0.96	(.11)***
Change in Interest	0.87	(.09)***
W1 Political Discussion	0.56	(.14)***
Change in Political Discussion	0.62	(.11)***
Constant	−1.86	(.52)***
N	751	
Adjusted R Squared		0.31

Note: *** p<.01, ** p<.05, * p<.10

political message, contacting a politician, and discussing politics with one's friends (alpha = .51).

In sum, the internet has become (increasingly) important for news seeking and searching for political and social information, though gaps remain in the extent of use by groups that have historically been less likely to participate in politics, with some exceptions.

As Table 9.3 makes clear, the bivariate differences observed in Table 9.2 disappear in the multivariate model. In other words, the digital divides in online communication disappear once we control for over-time changes in internet usage, as well as young people's changing psychological engagement with politics. It should be noted that two of these socio-demographic divides (gender and higher income) disappear only when political interest and discussion are included in the model. This suggests that the digital divides on these two factors are largely driven by differences in psychological engagement with politics.

Of more interest are the variables associated with internet use over time. The number of internet uses in wave 1 is a score that varies from 0 to 3, where young people were asked to name the three things they did the most online, from emailing to chatting with friends to buying stuff online. In wave 1, about 70 per cent of the sample selected three acts, with the most common activities being chatting with friends (84 per cent), looking at websites (56 per cent), downloading music or movies (46 per cent), and emailing (45 per cent). Those who reported doing more of these activities were more likely to participate in online political communication in wave 2. The effects are even stronger for time spent online. Those who spent more time online during high school are more politically active online in their twenties. Furthermore, those who increase their time online over time are also more active. These effects hold even after controlling for both political interest and political discussion in wave 1 and their changing levels across panels. It seems that those who participate online in their twenties are not only those who are interested and engaged in discussing politics offline (which is logical), but also those who spend more of their time online – both today and years ago when in high school.

POTENTIALS

Overall, online political communication has increased over the eight years of the Canadian Youth Study. Young Canadians use the internet more frequently, and increasingly for seeking political information. Political communication on the internet is relatively widespread as well; however, bivariate and multivariate preliminary analyses indicate that several gaps with regard to gender and socio-economic status continue to exist, though they appear to be largely driven by differences in the level of political interest. Moreover, we also find that early use of the internet and increased general use enhances political communication, further suggesting that using the internet for all kinds of purposes seems to enable engagement in various communication activities related to politics over time. Our study thus demonstrates the potential of digital technologies to provide space for political activities, though they do not appear to erase existing inequalities in engagement with politics.

Importantly, we do not find that millennials are increasingly apolitical. As they moved from their teens to their twenties, they reported surprisingly high levels of information searching, discussion, and creation of social and political topics. This may be partly due to attrition between wave 1 and wave 2 of our study, but the increasingly omnipresent nature of digital technologies in young people's lives suggest that when they are political, there is a high likelihood that this engagement will be informed by or occur through online platforms. The digital environment in which these young people have grown up has and continues to change drastically. Future research needs to explore the multiple and emerging ways in which an interconnected world offers opportunities for engagement with politics. It also must address not only the forms of this engagement but the content and its effects on how we talk about politics, with whom, and the levels of exposure we have to the full range of political opinions in our society. We also must contend with the ways in which such spaces are controlled and manipulated by third party actors. Such questions speak directly not just to the potential of digital technologies to mobilize but to their larger impact on the quality of democratic debate in Canada.

REFERENCES

Abiala, Kristina, and Patrik Hernwall. 2013. "Tweens Negotiating Identity Online – Swedish Girls' and Boys' Reflections on Online Experiences." *Journal of Youth Studies* 16 (8): 951–69. https://doi.org/10.1080/13676261.2013.780124.

Anderson, Monica, and Jingjing Jiang. 2018. "Teens, Social Media, & Technology 2018." Washington, DC: Pew Internet & American Life Project. Retrieved June 3 (2018). https://www.pewresearch.org/internet/2018/05/31/teens-social-media-technology-2018/.

Bimber, Bruce A. 2003. *Information and American Democracy: Technology in the Evolution of Political Power.* Cambridge, UK: Cambridge University Press.

Blais, André, and Peter Loewen. 2009. *Youth Electoral Engagement in Canada.* Ottawa: Elections Canada, April. https://www.elections.ca/content.aspx?section=res&dir=rec/part/youeng&document=index&lang=e.

Canadian Internet Registration Authority. 2013. *CIRA Fact Book 2013.* http://www.cira.ca/factbook/2013.index.html.

Canadian Internet Registration Authority (CIRA). 2014. *FACTBOOK 2014 – The Canadian Internet.* http://cira.ca/factbook/2014/the-canadian-internet.html.

Cicognani, Elvira, Bruna Zani, Bernard Fournier, Claire Gavray, and Michel Born. 2012. "Gender Differences in Youths' Political Engagement and Participation. The Role of Parents and of Adolescents' Social and Civic Participation." *Journal of Adolescence* 35 (3): 561–76. https://doi.org/10.1016/j.adolescence.2011.10.002. Medline: 22032976.

Delli Carpini, Michael X. 2000. "Gen. Com: Youth, Civic Engagement and the New Information Environment." *Political Communication* 17 (4): 341–9. https://doi.org/10.1080/10584600050178942.

De Marco, Stefano, Jose Manuel Robles, and Mirko Antino. 2014. "Digital Skills as a Conditioning Factor for Digital Political Participation." *Communications: The European Journal of Communication Research* 39 (1): 43–65. https://doi.org/10.1515/commun-2014-0004.

Di Gennaro, Corinna, and William Dutton. 2006. "The Internet and the Public: Online and Offline Political Participation in the United Kingdom." *Parliamentary Affairs* 59 (2): 299–313. https://doi.org/10.1093/pa/gsl004.

Ekström, Mats, Tobias Olsson, and Adam Shehata. 2014. "Spaces for Public Orientation? Longitudinal Effects of Internet Use in Adolescence." *Information, Communication, & Society* 17 (2): 168–83. https://doi.org/10.1080/1369118X.2013.862288.

Gélineau, François. 2013. "Who Participates? A Closer Look at the Results of the National Youth Survey." Elections Canada, June 23.

Gibson, Rachel K., Wainer Lusoli, and Stephen Ward. 2005. "Online Participation in the UK: Testing a 'Contextualised' Model of Internet Effects." *The British Journal of Politics & International Relations* 7 (4): 561–83. https://doi.org/10.1111/j.1467-856x.2005.00209.x.

Gladwell, Malcolm. 2010. "Small Change: Why the Revolution Will Not Be Tweeted: Twitter, Facebook, and Social Activism." *New Yorker*, October 4.

Haenschen, Katherine. 2016. "Social Pressure on Social Media: Using Facebook Status Updates to Increase Voter Turnout," *Journal of Communication* 66 (4): 542–63. https://doi.org/10.1111/jcom.12236.

Haight, Michael, Anabel Quan-Haase, and Bradley A. Corbett. 2014. "Revisiting the Digital Divide in Canada: The Impact of Demographic Factors on Access to the Internet, Level of Online Activity and Social

Networking Site Usage." *Information, Communication, & Society* 17 (4): 503–19. https://doi.org/10.1080/1369118X.2014.891633.

Halpern, D., S. Valenzuela, and J.E. Katz. 2017. "We Face, I Tweet: How Different Social Media Influence Political Participation through Collective and Internal Efficacy." *Journal of Computer-Mediated Communication* 22 (6): 320–36. https://doi.org/10.1111/jcc4.12198.

Harell, Allison, Valérie-Anne Mahéo, and Dietlind Stolle. 2008. *Canadian Youth Study, Wave One: Technical Report and Codebook.* Montreal: McGill University.

Hargittai, Eszter. 2010. "Digital Na(t)ives? Variation in Internet Skills and Uses among Members of the 'Net Generation.'" *Sociological Inquiry* 80 (1): 92–113. https://doi.org/10.1111/j.1475-682X.2009.00317.x.

Hargittai, Eszter, and Steven Shafer. 2006. "Differences in Actual and Perceived Online Skills: The Role of Gender." *Social Science Quarterly* 87 (2): 432–48. https://doi.org/10.1111/j.1540-6237.2006.00389.x.

Haynes, Audrey A., and Brian Pitts. 2009. "Making an Impression: New Media in the 2008 Presidential Nomination Campaigns." *PS: Political Science & Politics* 42 (1): 53–8. https://doi.org/10.1017/S1049096509090052.

Holt, Kristoffer, Adam Shehata, Jesper Strömbäck, and Elisabet Ljungberg. 2013. "Age and the Effects of News Media Attention and Social Media Use on Political Interest and Participation: Do Social Media Function as Leveller?" *European Journal of Communication* 28 (1): 19–34. https://doi.org/10.1177/0267323112465369.

Hsieh, Yuli Patrick, and Meng-Hao Li. 2013. "Online Political Participation, Civic Talk, and Media Multiplexity: How Taiwanese Citizens Express Political Opinions on the Web." *Information, Communication & Society* 17 (1): 26–44. https://doi.org/10.1080/1369118X.2013.833278.

"Internet Use by Canadians Highest in World, ComScore Says." 2015. *Huffington Post*, March 27. http://www.huffingtonpost.ca/2015/03/27/internet-use-by-canadians_n_6958156.html.

Jensen, Jakob Linaa. 2013. "Political Participation Online: The Replacement and the Mobilisation Hypotheses Revisited." *Scandinavian Political Studies* 36 (4): 347–64. https://doi.org/10.1111/1467-9477.12008.

Jugert, Philipp, Katharina Eckstein, Peter Noack, Alexandra Kuhn, and Alison Benbow. 2013. "Offline and Online Civic Engagement among Adolescents and Young Adults from Three Ethnic Groups." *Journal of Youth and Adolescence* 42 (1): 123–35. https://doi.org/10.1007/s10964-012-9805-4. Medline: 22903193.

Krueger, Brian S. 2002. "Assessing the Potential of Internet Political Participation in the United States: A Resource Approach." *American Politics Research* 30 (5): 476–98. https://doi.org/10.1177/1532673X02030005002.

Leyva, R. 2017. "Exploring UK Millennials' Social Media Consumption Patterns and Participation in Elections, Activism, and 'Slacktivism.'" *Social Science Computer Review* 35 (4): 462–79. https://doi.org/10.1177/0894439316655738.

Margolis, Michael, and David Resnick. 2000. *Politics as Usual: The Cyberspace "Revolution."* Thousand Oaks, CA: Sage.

Norris, Pippa. 2001. *Digital Divide: Civic Engagement, Information Poverty and the Internet Worldwide.* New York: Cambridge University Press.

Norris, Pippa. 2003. "Preaching to the Converted? Pluralism, Participation, and Party Websites." *Party Politics* 9 (1): 21–45. https://doi.org/10.1177/135406880391003.

Ono, Hiroshi, and Madeline Zavodny. 2008. "Immigrants, English Ability, and the Digital Divide." *Social Forces* 86 (4): 1455–79. https://doi.org/10.1353/sof.0.0052.

Oser, Jennifer, Marc Hooghe, and Sofie Marien. 2013. "Is Online Participation Distinct from Offline Participation? A Latent Class Analysis of Participation Types and Their Stratification." *Political Research Quarterly* 66 (1): 91–101. https://doi.org/10.1177/1065912912436695.

Oser, Jennifer, Jan E. Leighley, and Kenneth M. Winneg. 2014. "Participation, Online and Otherwise: What's the Difference for Policy Preferences?" *Social Science Quarterly* 95 (5): 1259–77. https://doi.org/10.1111/ssqu.12100.

Papacharissi, Zizi. 2002. "The Virtual Sphere: The Internet as a Public Sphere." *New Media & Society* 4 (1): 9–27. https://doi.org/10.1177/14614440222226244.

Pew Research Center. 2012. "2012 Teens and Privacy Management Survey." http://www.pewinternet.org/data-trend/teens/internet-user-demographics/.

Raine, Lee, and Aaron Smith. 2008. *The Internet and the 2008 Election.* Washington, DC: Pew Internet and American Life Project.

Schlozman, Kay Lehman, Sidney Verba, and Henry E. Brady. 2010. "Weapon of the Strong? Participatory Inequality and the Internet." *Perspectives on Politics* 8 (2): 487–509. https://doi.org/10.1017/S1537592710001210.

Settle, J.E., R.M. Bond, L. Coviello, C.J. Fariss, J.H. Fowler, and J.J. Jones. 2016. "From Posting to Voting: The Effects of Political Competition on Online Political Engagement." *Political Science Research and Methods* 4 (2): 361–78. https://doi.org/10.1017/psrm.2015.1.

Smith, A., and M. Duggan. 2012. "Presidential Campaign Donations in the Digital Age." Pew Research Center Internet and American Life Project.

Statistics Canada. 2013. The Daily: Canadian Internet Use Survey 2012. Ottawa, November 26, 2013. http://www.statcan.gc.ca/daily-quotidien/131126/dq131126d-eng.htm.

Steeves, Valerie. 2014. *Young Canadians in a Wired World, Phase III: Life Online.* Ottawa: MediaSmarts.

Teresi, H., and M.R. Michelson. 2015. "Wired to Mobilize: The Effect of Social Networking Messages on Voter Turnout." *The Social Science Journal* 52 (2): 195–204. https://doi.org/10.1016/j.soscij.2014.09.004.

Theocharis, Yannis, and Ellen Quintelier. 2014. "Stimulating Citizenship or Expanding Entertainment? The Effect of Facebook on Adolescent Participation." *New Media & Society* 18 (5): 817–36. https://doi.org/10.1177/1461444814549006.

Towner, Terri L. 2013. "All Political Participation Is Socially Networked? New Media and the 2012 Election." *Social Science Computer Review* 31 (5): 527–41. https://doi.org/10.1177/0894439313489656.

Tyler, Tom R. 2002. "Is the Internet Changing Social Life? It Seems the More Things Change, the More They Stay the Same." *Journal of Social Issues* 58 (1): 195–205. https://doi.org/10.1111/1540-4560.00256.

Van Deursen, Alexander, and Jan van Dijk. 2011. "Internet Skills and the Digital Divide." *New Media & Society* 13 (6): 893–911. https://doi.org/10.1177/1461444810386774.

Van Deursen, Alexander J.A.M., and Jan A.G.M van Dijk. 2014. "The Digital Divide Shifts to Differences in Usage." *New Media & Society* 16 (3): 507–26. https://doi.org/10.1177/1461444813487959.

Van Deursen, Alexander J.A.M., Jan A.G.M. van Dijk, and Peter M. ten Klooster. 2015. "Increasing Inequalities in What We Do Online: A Longitudinal Cross-Sectional Analysis of Internet Activities among the Dutch Population (2010 to 2013) over Gender, Age, Education, and Income." *Telematics and Informatics* 32 (2): 259–72. https://doi.org/10.1016/j.tele.2014.09.003.

Vissers, Sara, and Dietlind Stolle. 2013. "The Internet and New Modes of Political Participation: Online versus Offline Participation." *Information, Communication, & Society* 17 (8): 937–55. https://doi.org/10.1080/1369118X.2013.867356.

Vissers, Sara, and Dietlind Stolle. 2014. "Spill-Over Effects between Facebook and On/Offline Political Participation? Evidence from a Two-Wave Panel Study." *Journal of Information Technology & Politics* 11 (3): 259–75. https://doi.org/10.1080/19331681.2014.888383.

Vromen, Ariadne, Michael A. Xenos, and Brian Loader. 2014. "Young People, Social Media, and Connective Action: From Organisational Maintenance to Everyday Political Talk." *Journal of Youth Studies* 18 (1): 80–100. https://doi.org/10.1080/13676261.2014.933198.

Ward, Stephen, Rachel Gibson, and Wainer Lusoli. 2003. "Online Participation and Mobilisation in Britain: Hype, Hope, and Reality." *Parliamentary Affairs* 56 (4): 652–68. https://doi.org/10.1093/pa/gsg108.

Ward, Stephen, and Thierry Vedel. 2006. "Introduction: The Potential of the Internet Revisited." *Parliamentary Affairs* 59 (2): 210–25. https://doi.org/10.1093/pa/gsl014.

Weber, Lori M., Alysha Loumakis, and James Bergman. 2003. "Who Participates and Why? An Analysis of Citizens on the Internet and the Mass Public." *Social Science Computer Review* 21 (1): 26–42. https://doi.org/10.1177/0894439302238969.

Willis, Suzanne, and Bruce Tranter. 2006. "Beyond the 'Digital Divide': Internet Diffusion and Inequality in Australia." *Journal of Sociology* 42 (1): 43–59. https://doi.org/10.1177/1440783306061352.

Wolfsfeld, G., M. Yarchi, and T. Samuel-Azran. 2016. "Political Information Repertoires and Political Participation. *New Media & Society* 18 (9): 2096–115. https://doi.org/10.1177/1461444815580413.

CHAPTER TEN

Online Mobilization: Tweeting Truth to Power in an Era of Revised Patterns of Mobilization in Canada

Mireille Lalancette and Vincent Raynauld

CONTEXT

Over the last decade, there has been a progressive redefinition of the roles, manifestations, and effects of mobilization in political and democratic life in Canada and other national contexts. The emergence and rapid growth of largely decentralized and highly fragmented political and social protest initiatives with a strong digital component – such as the US-based Tea Party (Rohlinger and Bunnage 2015, 2017), the transnational Occupy (Kavada 2015), the Spain-based Indignados (15M) (Barbas and Postill 2017), the Hong Kong Umbrella (Lee and Chan 2016), the Indigenous-led Idle No More (Raynauld et al. 2018) movements and the 2012 Quebec student strike in Canada (Raynauld et al. 2016, 2019) – illustrate this trend. These protest movements are similar in structure but different in tone, scope, and membership. Moreover, they collectively represent the materialization of a revised blueprint of, or renewed trend in, grassroots-intensive political and civic action, referred to as "new protest movements" (Poell and Van Dijck 2018). This chapter takes an under-the-hood look at this model of political and civic action from a Canadian perspective. It identifies, characterizes, and unpacks the key political, social, and technological factors behind its rise and intensification. More broadly, this chapter explores how the reshaping of grassroots protest movements could lead scholars to rethink and, if warranted, retool existing definitions of more conventional norms and practices of political mobilization in light of digitization, especially with the popularization of social media.

Building on older debates led by democratic theorists like Joseph Schumpeter (1967) and Carole Pateman (1970), political and civic mobilization must be understood through the consideration of two explanatory frameworks. On one hand, elite-led "electoral democracy," also known as "democratic method" (Mackie 2009), can be viewed as an institutionalized system where "competitive, free, fair, and regular elections" lead to the selection of individuals who represent the will of the people and that take part in collaborative decision-making processes[1] (Welzel and Inglehart 2008, 126). On the other hand, and more importantly for this chapter, liberal democracy can be viewed as a system emphasizing "mass voice in self-governance" (Welzel and Inglehart 2008, 126). It depends on "social preconditions such as the wide distribution of participatory resources and a trusting, tolerant public that prizes free choice" (Welzel and Inglehart 2008, 126–7). This conception of democracy rests heavily on citizens' active political and civic engagement influencing decision-making outside the realm of more institutionalized or elite-led power structures. While different, these conceptions of democracy rely on the same core principle: citizen empowerment and engagement through different mechanisms.

Through the lens of the digitization of politics – especially with the popularization of social media over the last decade – this chapter explores the revised blueprint for grassroots-intensive political and civic engagement outside the realm of established political structures in Canada. It also takes an interest in how this blueprint is affecting different facets of Canadian democracy. While some scholars have examined these dynamics in other national contexts (e.g., Xenos, Vromen, and Loader 2014; Vromen 2017; Mercea 2016), research in Canada is still fairly limited and compartmentalized. Existing scholarship consists mainly of case studies providing in-depth analyses of specific mobilization phenomena with a strong digital component. For example, many authors

1 Several scholars point out that electoral democracy is the source of the legitimacy of a political regime (Rothstein 2009).

have examined how supporters of the Idle No More movement (INM) turned to social media to express themselves and build awareness of and mobilize support for their cause (e.g., Callison and Hermida 2015; Raynauld et al. 2018; Wood 2015). Much work has also been conducted on social media's role during the G20 protests in Toronto (Poell 2014; Poell and Borra 2012) and the 2012 student strike against the rise of university tuition fees in the province of Quebec (Gismondi and Osteen 2017; Raynauld et al. 2016). More recently, McCurdy and Groshek (2019) studied social media-based advocacy in the context of the TransCanada's proposed #EnergyEastPipeline.[2]

While providing valuable insights, the narrow focus of these academic works has prevented them from highlighting broader trends in grassroots-intensive mobilization and engagement in Canada. Furthermore, few comparative studies have been conducted in this realm of research. This chapter zeroes in on and fills part of these gaps in the academic literature. It does so by first providing an overview of the digitization of politics, with a particular focus on social media and its effects on the dynamics of grassroots-intensive political mobilization and engagement. Building on recent research on the 2012 student strike in Quebec and the Indigenous-led, pan-Canadian INM, this chapter then offers a comprehensive analysis of how the digitization of politics has led to transformations in political engagement norms and practices in Canada. It concludes with a detailed discussion of the democratic implications, challenges, and opportunities of the growing uses of social media for grassroots-intensive political mobilization and engagement in the country.

DIGITIZATION

Promises & Perils

As seen throughout this book, uses of digital technologies by established political elites – governmental agencies, parties, and candidates during elections – for communication, mobilization, and organizing

2 The representation of social media-based political mobilization and engagement in the mainstream press and the way in which it is perceived by the public in Canada has been the object of several recent studies (Dumitrica and Bakardjieva 2017; Moscato 2016).

in and out of elections have received the lion's share of academic attention over the last ten years in Canada. Much less has been done on how individuals and organizations situated on the peripheries of the formal political arena are leveraging these tools for self-expression, outreach, networking, mobilization, and action. In fact, recent years have been marked by an unmistakable uptick in uses of social media for political organizing and engagement by minorities and marginalized individuals and communities with ideas, causes, or objectives often challenging the elites and/or status quo (e.g., Bennett and Segerberg 2012; Nemer 2016; Raynauld et al. 2018). They have turned to these tools to make their voices heard, build and maintain public support for their mission and, in some cases, alter public opinion and influence decision-making. As Xenos et al. (2014, 154) observe, "social media possess the same quintessential mobilizing features of the internet as a whole, but take them all 'one step further' by overcoming key limitations of the Web 1.0" (see also Poell 2014; introduction). Indeed, Web 2.0 users have more opportunities to create and mass disseminate mixed-media digital political content through "technological aids" as well as the ability to launch, join, observe, or be actively involved in niche social groups tailored to their often-narrow political preferences, interests, and objectives (Cormode and Krishnamurthy 2008).

Recent waves of social media-intensive, people-powered political and social protests across the globe have provided evidence that social media have become go-to platforms for political engagement. This dynamic has generated a lot of academic interest in recent years. Specifically, scholars have focused on "a possible turn in collective action that relies on digitally networked communication to stage and coordinate protests, a capacity previously concentrated in social movement organizations" (Mercea 2014, 386). At first, the digitization of politics in Canada and internationally was met with high levels of enthusiasm by scholars adhering to the mobilization hypothesis,[3] also known as cyber-optimists (Norris 2001, 218; introduction). Some argued that it could lead to increased levels of political knowledge, mobilization, and engagement among some slices of

3 According to Norris (2001, 218), "the mobilization hypothesis holds that the internet may inform, organize, and engage those who are currently marginalized from the existing political system – such as the younger generation, those living in isolated peripheral communities, or fringe political communities disaffected by the traditional system – so that these group will gradually become drawn into public life and civic communities."

the public (Dimitrova et al. 2014). Others opined that it has the potential to "enable stronger participatory democracy through the emergence of online Agoras and Habermasian forums" and, by extension, strengthen democratic governance (Loader and Mercea 2011, 757). In other words, the digitization of politics could help citizens make their voice heard as well as take part in and influence different facets of the formal political process, which can be seen as one of the cornerstones of participatory democracy. This concept can be defined as a democratic environment wherein citizens share "a sense of collective responsibility" and have opportunities to be aware of and participate in decision-making with the support of political institutions (Zittel 2012, 9). However, cyber-sceptics and proponents of the reinforcement hypothesis adopt a more circumspect view of the digitization of politics (Norris 2001). They point out that it has the potential to reinforce existing patterns of offline politicking. In other words, it could reaffirm and, in some cases, expand the power and influence of established, offline-based political elites as well as further disenfranchise those more on the edges of the formal political arena. Furthermore, it could be the source of a "decline in public political efficacy, knowledge, and participation" among some segments of the public (Kenski and Stroud 2006, 176).

Our work favours an approach that eschews the cyber-optimism/scepticism dichotomy. It identifies, characterizes, and unpacks the political mobilization and engagement mechanisms that are at play in the context of grassroots-intensive protest activity on social media. In order to do so, we turn to the concept of "political action repertoires" (Tilly and Tarrow 2015), which offers a helpful explanatory framework for studying these dynamics. Political action repertoires can be defined as diverse sets of actions taken by members of civil society to be active politically and influence elite-controlled patterns of decision-making, whether through institutionalized or more informal – and in some cases illegal – mechanisms of political or civic expression, organizing, and engagement (Dalton 2008; see also Raynauld et al. 2016, 2019). They have expanded and diversified significantly since the end of the Second World War. The nature of political activities – including voting, demonstrating, volunteering, boycotting, blogging, and flash mobs – has also evolved as they have become more personalized, synchronous, informal, "creative, expressive, individualized, and digitally-enabled" (Theocharis and van Deth 2018, 139–40; see also van Deth 2016).

Building on studies on political action repertoires, scholars have proposed the term digital protest repertoire in order to grasp the complexity of uses of social media for political and civic protest. It can be defined as "a diverse collection of digital political and civic engagement practices outside more institutionalized – or traditional – paths of political action seeking to question, contest or, conversely, support established media, governmental, and political entities' decisions or actions" (Raynauld et al. 2018, 628). Based on the work of Theocharis et al. (2015) and others (e.g., Poell and van Dijck 2018), we isolate three interrelated areas of interest related to the revised blueprint of grassroots-intensive political and civic action: (1) patterns of political mobilization and engagement (mobilization); (2) flows of protest information and social interactions (communication); and (3) transformations in the structure of protest organizations, more specifically patterns of leadership and coordination (organization).

First, several authors have explored the first aspect of the revised blueprint, namely the ways in which supporters of protest movements in local, regional, national, and transnational contexts leverage social media in order to initiate, be informed about, coordinate, and engage in wide-ranging formal and informal political activities on their own terms (e.g., Theocharis et al. 2015). On the one hand, these tools offer activists a low-cost, flexible, and relatively easy-to-use platform for timely political activism outside institutionalized politics. Specifically, social media enables individuals and organizations typically on the edges of the formal political arena to participate in and, in some cases, have some influence on the political process. On the other hand, they provide opportunities to individuals and organizations preferring more individualized, entrepreneurial forms of political engagement tailored to their preferences, interests, and goals to be active politically (Earl, Copeland, and Bimber 2017; Albaugh and Waddell 2014). In other words, social media are adapted to dynamics of "unconventional political participation" rooted in "postmaterialist"[4] or lifestyle politics

4 Postmaterialist values have gained traction among Western societies over the last three decades, with the decline in importance of "survival values," which are generally rooted in material considerations such as "physical survival and safety" and the growing prominence of values related to "nonmaterial needs such as those for self-expression and aesthetic satisfaction" (Inglehart 2017, 5). This shift is intimately linked to the rise of new generations of citizens (Inglehart 2017, 5).

values that are often elite-challenging in nature (Scherman et al. 2015). Given that most social media channels are identity-centric in nature, they have also contributed to the blurring, and in some cases meshing, of public and private life in practices of political and civic engagement (Bennett and Segerberg 2012).

Van Laer and Van Aelst (2010) propose a characterization of digitized protest repertoire rooted on two axes. The first establishes a distinction between "internet-supported" and "internet-based" protest action. The former refers to more conventional, offline-inspired modes of protest that are supported and facilitated by digital technologies, such as attending rallies, signing a petition, or engaging in different political consumerism activities. They define the latter as "the traditional tools of social movements that have become easier to organize and coordinate thanks to" digital communication tools (Van Laer and Van Aelst 2010, 1148). They argue that digital technologies are fostering the development and reinforcement of patterns of political and civic engagement likely to affect how activists view and are involved in political processes and how they can affect their social, cultural, political, and economic environment. The second axis identifies a hierarchy of protest action in the digital environment. While some forms of protest activities "entail more risk and higher commitment" (e.g., time, financial and human resources, technical expertise, and consequences), others require less effort and are less risky (Van Laer and Van Aelst 2010, 1150).

The second aspect of the revised blueprint is related to social media's contribution to the decentralization and fragmentation of the structure, composition, and tone of protest-related information flows, social interactions, and political action, whether within networks of protest or for reaching out to outsiders. As indicated previously, social media have enabled a larger field of political players with a large number of often narrow interests to be active politically, make their voice heard in a timely manner, and rally public support to their cause. This is especially the case with the inclusion of minorities and marginalized individuals and communities who often hold elite or status quo-challenging ideas, causes or objectives (e.g. Nemer 2016, Bennett and Segerberg 2012; Raynauld et al. 2018). On the one hand, social media allow them to engage in one-to-one, one-to-many, or many-to-many horizontal conversational practices (Theocharis et al. 2015, 205) more or less on their own terms and share digital content with like-minded users. For example, they can leverage content or social interactive mechanisms, such as hashtags or @mentions in the case of digital platforms like Facebook, Twitter, or Instagram, to express themselves, reach out to and connect with specific segments of the public, and take part in different protest activities.[5]

On the other hand, there has also been an ongoing fragmentation and, to some degree, compartmentalization of protest-related information dispersion, social networking, and, from a broader perspective, political action. Expanding on Bimber (2008) and others (e.g., Bennett 2015; Webster and Ksiazek 2015), it can be argued that social media's flexible structural and functional properties have fostered the further breakdown of political cohesion within society. They have done so by enabling users to independently seek out specialized streams of information and opinion as well as join narrow protest initiatives driven by specific interests and objectives that can be ideological, political, social, or geographical in nature. Critical to this phenomenon are the growing levels of public distrust of and discontent with more institutionalized modes of political engagement that lack flexibility and are not adapted to activists' personal needs and expectations.[6] Recent research confirms these patterns, which are especially prevalent during politically turbulent or unstable times, including periods of protest. For example, Zhu, Skorik, and Shen (2017, 125) show quantitatively that "active use of social media for protest-related matters is associated with greater likelihood of people shielding themselves from attitude-challenging views" (also see Boulianne 2016). Critics raise the possibility that these patterns of online action can turn into "slacktivism." This concept, which has a generally negative connotation, refers to online political engagement activities with limited to no effects outside the internet as they are designed to increase feel-good sentiments among actors engaging in them (Christensen 2011).[7]

Finally, the third aspect of the revised blueprint is linked to social media favouring a shift from collective action to connective action as

5 For instance, there are studies on hashtag activism from various perspectives and in different national contexts (see Bonilla and Rosa 2015; Drüeke and Zobl 2016).

6 Of interest is Cappella and Jamieson's work (1997) on the "spiral of cynicism."

7 Nevertheless, some studies show it is not necessarily the case. For example, meme creators in Canada are highly knowledgeable about politics and generally offer commentary with pointed critiques of political actors or processes (Lalancette, Small, and Pronovost 2019; Lalancette and Small 2019).

well as the redefinition of leadership. Collective action can be viewed as a form of protest action characterized by a fixed and somewhat rigid hierarchical structure; "high levels of organizational resources" (Bennett and Segerberg 2012, 739); broadly recognized, understood, and accepted mission and leadership, all leading to "common action frames" and "persistent collective identities" (Poell and van Dijck 2018). Comparatively, connective action relies on a much less formalized organizational framework, personalized and frequently short-term action frames adapted to individual-based preferences and goals, as well as loose, decentralized, and constantly evolving patterns of leadership (Bennett and Segerberg 2012; Poell and van Dijck 2018). According to Vromen et al. (2015), social media constitute one of the core underpinnings of connective action. They are "reshaping organisational networks into personalised forms of digitally enabled engagement" that can be spontaneous, can be constantly adjusted based on their immediate context, and require limited formal resources (Vromen et al. 2015, 93). Earl, Copeland, and Bimber (2017) concur with this assessment, suggesting that social media facilitate activism outside the realm of more bureaucratized and rigid structures. In sum, social media may be seen as a stand-alone organizational structure.

Practice

In order to unpack the roles, manifestations, and effects of the revised blueprint of – or renewed trends in – grassroots-intensive political and civic mobilization and action in the Canadian context, this chapter considers streams of academic literature focusing on two major protest phenomena in Canada: (1) the Indigenous-led, pan-Canadian Idle No More movement and (2) the student-led strike against higher university tuition in the province of Quebec. While different in terms of their scope, priorities, tone, and membership, these movements represent the materialization of redefined norms and practices when it comes to protest in Canada. They have gained momentum over the last decade, particularly with social media gaining traction among the public, and require further academic research.

Idle No More (INM) is an Indigenous-led grassroots protest phenomenon that emerged and rose to prominence following the introduction of Bill C-38 and omnibus Bill C-45 by Stephen Harper's Conservative government in 2012 (also see chapter 11). These bills proposed important changes to policy areas relating to Indigenous affairs and treaty rights (e.g., environment, governance, natural resources), with little to no consultation with Indigenous stakeholders and their allies. They were ultimately passed on June 29, 2012, and December 14, 2012, respectively. While INM began with four women discussing the effects of the aforementioned legislation through emails in November 2012, it grew rapidly in scope, size, and intensity over the following months as Indigenous activists and their allies engaged in wide-ranging activities on- and offline to generate public awareness, attract media coverage, and mobilize supporters (Raynauld et al. 2018; Wood 2015; Callison and Hermida 2015). Crucially for our analysis here, INM employed social media as a cornerstone tool to achieve their goals.

The student-led strike against university tuition hikes in Quebec – also known as "Maple Spring" – began in a much more conventional fashion. Following an announcement by Jean Charest's Liberal government that university tuition fees would be raised by 75 per cent over five years, CEGEP[8] and university student unions began mobilizing their members as well as taking part in protest efforts intended to pressure the government into reconsidering its decision. Facing a government unwilling to change its course, the student strike was declared on February 12, 2012. Within a few weeks, members of student unions from across the province had joined the movement. Over the following months, students and their supporters turned to social media – particularly Twitter – for political communication, mobilization, and organizing independently of student unions and other formal groups (Latzko-Toth, Pastinelli, and Gallant 2017; Gismondi and Osteen 2017; Raynauld et al. 2016, 2019).

Points of comparison between these protest movements and their supporters' patterns of protest are many and diverse. We zero in on and unpack three tightly interwoven dimensions as they relate directly to the previously discussed revised blueprint of political and civic engagement. It should be noted that the academic research in this chapter focuses on Twitter which, at the time of study, allowed posts of up to 140 characters.

Communication: Twitter was used primarily for one-way mass communication by those who shared tweets discussing matters related to both

8 The acronym CEGEP stands for "Collèges d'Enseignement Général et Professionnel."

movements studied here. Following a content analysis of 1,650 tweets with at least one #IdleNoMore hashtag that appeared on Twitter's public timeline between July 3, 2013, and August 2, 2013, Raynauld et al. (2018) show that slightly more than half of them (51.6 per cent) – including regular tweets, retweets, and modified retweets – served to broadcast political information to a potentially mass and diverse audience. Comparatively, 20.8 per cent served a mobilization function, 15.8 per cent featured opinions (self-expression) and 9.5 per cent provided elements of criticism; tweets playing other roles accounted for only 2.4 per cent of the corpus (Raynauld et al. 2018). Their study also determined that only 4.9 per cent of #IdleNoMore tweets were social interactions.

A similar tendency was detected in the student protests in Quebec. Raynauld et al. (2016) conducted a content analysis of 1,500 tweets with at least one #ggi hashtag[9] that were shared on Twitter's public timeline between April 22, 2012, and July 31, 2012, and found that 59 per cent of them were used for information broadcasting, while 28 per cent served self-expression functions, 10 per cent featured attacks, and 3 per cent were used for mobilization. Much like in the case of the INM study, there were very "few interactions between two or more #ggi tweeters" (Raynauld et al. 2016, 22). The findings of both studies show that Twitter was used for sharing protest-related information and for self-expression to mass audiences. These findings echo those of studies conducted on protest movements of similar structure in Canada and internationally (e.g., Lindgren and Cocq 2017; Latzko-Toth et al. 2017; Macafee and De Simone 2012). In other words, these dynamics of protest tend to revolve around users' ability and willingness to broadcast content shaped by lifestyle politics-oriented concerns and less around interacting with other users or fulfilling a broadly shared protest mission. Hsiao's research (2018) reinforces this point; it shows that the ease with which individuals and organizations can utilize social media to share content and express themselves to mass audiences can push them to learn about and be involved in social movements in a highly personalized way. Without social media, "users are less likely to express grievances; feel more socially isolated; feel emotionally detached to protest groups; and, most importantly, think that they cannot do anything to redress

9 The hashtag #ggi is based on the acronym GGI, which stands for "Grève Générale Illimitée" (translation: "Unlimited General Strike").

their concerns" (Hsiao 2018, 18). In other words, it may be understood as activism for "self-validation" more than for achieving larger-than-self public good (Poell and Van Dijck 2018, 2).

Mobilization: As discussed previously, supporters of both movements used social media for political action in ways suiting their personal interests and goals, outside more institutionalized, or rigid, paths of political and civic engagement. While the Maple Spring focused initially on the government of Quebec's announcement regarding university tuition hikes, the movement quickly compartmentalized on the Twitterverse. Indeed, #ggi tweeters discussed wide-ranging and often hyper-narrow issues or events not necessarily in line with the core concerns of the student protest movement (Raynauld et al. 2016, 2019). These tangential topics included free breakfasts for malnourished youth, affordable housing, international politics, as well as laws regarding demonstrators' rights in the city of Montreal. Therefore, it can be argued that the #ggi hashtag, which allowed horizontal content sharing and "conversational practices" (Theocharis et al. 2015, 205), mobilized large numbers of formal and informal political actors not necessarily adhering to a common protest agenda or objectives. Lalancette et al. (2019) point out that contributors to the #ggi tweeting dynamic included legacy media organizations, interest groups, political and media figures, action networks, and ordinary citizens. It should be noted that #ggi tweets were also frequently posted in reaction to news media reports, editorials, and interviews. Specifically, #ggi tweeters tended to share web links pointing to articles favourable to the student strike and its demands in order to generate, sharpen, and reinforce collectively a more positive public narrative of the strike. Conversely, they were also more likely to criticize, delegitimize and, in some cases, attack headlines and other news media content critical of the student strike and its supporters (Theocharis et al. 2015, 205).

While different in scope, the INM case highlights similar trends. It shows that #IdleNoMore tweeters engaged in protest operations that were highly personal in nature. Raynauld et al. (2018, 626) explore how "references to aspects of Indigenous identities and culture shaped INM-related tweeting and, by extension, activism." Their analysis found that an overwhelming majority of #IdleNoMore tweets (85 per cent) comprised at least one reference to Indigenous cultural markers, with "land, group membership, and epistemologies [being] the most common, followed by cultural production, resistance, and language" (Raynauld et al. 2018, 634). They also determined that references to Indigenous cultural markers were more likely to be embedded in tweets serving a broadcast politics-oriented function, whether it be information dispersion or mobilization.

The findings of both studies show that patterns of Twitter-based political and civic engagement were highly personal in nature. In addition, they demonstrate quantitatively how online protest was highly fragmented, as activists supported these movements but in ways aligned with their personal interests and objectives and not necessarily helpful to the movement as a whole. To some degree, it can be argued that these forms of political and civic engagement illustrate growing levels of intertwining of public and private lives when it comes to political and civic engagement. This can be seen as positive when it comes to personal political and civic action; however, it may have potentially detrimental effects on the cohesion and effectiveness of broader protest phenomena with goals transcending individual activists' interests and goals. These conclusions fall in line with recent work by Poell and Van Dijck (2018). They define this dynamic as "'chaotic pluralism,' which constitutes an individualization of collective action, and 'injects turbulence into every area of politics, acting as an unruly, unpredictable influence on political life'" (Poell and Van Dijck 2018, 2–3; see also Margetts, John, and Yasseri 2016). By being increasingly individualized and personalized, patterns of protest, which are already destabilizing politically for formal political systems, become even more destabilizing as they inject increased levels of political uncertainty into the latter.

Moreover, a large volume of tweets served mass information dissemination and opinion sharing functions that were not necessarily of interest to broad publics as they frequently focused on very specific topics or concerns. Still they could have unintended mobilizational effects on specific members of the public as some of them could appeal to narrow aspects of their identity, which could in turn energize them and push them to contribute in different ways to social movements' activities. For example, the previously discussed repackaging of the public narrative concerning the Quebec student strike or the narrow appeals to Indigenous culture and, to some degree, identity in #IdleNoMore tweets may have had unintended micro-mobilizing appeals for numerous very small slices of the public, who could have been incentivized to step away from the political sidelines and contribute to the protest movements, a phenomenon also known as "participatory surplus" (Blaser, Weinberger, and Trippi 2009). In other words, they could have been generating patterns of mobilizing through informing. Generally speaking, more research is required as interviews with supporters of protest movements with a strong digital component could provide valuable insights.

Organizing: Finally, the findings of studies on INM and Maple Spring demonstrate that these protest movements, at least in the Twitterverse, were not centred around dominant formal or informal political players. They were, for the most part, highly decentralized, as they mobilized a large number of individuals and organizations who did not assume any type of traditional form of leadership. For example, in the case of INM, most tweeters were the source of one or two entries, while only three #IdleNoMore tweeters were the source of 35 posts or more, for a combined total of 277 tweets, which represented 16 per cent of the dataset (Raynauld et al. 2018). In their study of 743,365 #IdleNoMore tweets posted between December 2012 and January 2013, Callison and Hermida (2015) determined that #IdleNoMore tweets were posted by many individuals and organizations, including bloggers, mass media organizations, non-affiliated activists, and members of the public. Their analysis shows "a significant presence of non-elite actors in both the top 500 most influential voices and the top 500 most retweeted sources on Twitter" (Callison and Hermida 2015, 697). In the case of the Maple Spring, the #ggi tweeting dynamic was not driven by a small group of more vocal tweeters. Much like the INM movement, it featured a large number of users who self-identified as "news media organizations, reporters, self-declared students, ordinary citizens (excluding self-declared students), expert and professional communicators, public personalities, activists, or union leaders" (Raynauld et al. 2016, 632).

In the case of the INM and #ggi protest movements, social media played a prominent role in the deployment of new patterns of political engagement and leadership. As Poell and van Dijck (2018, 2) note, the "communication process [through uses of social media] provides key organizational resources, allowing large crowds to act together with little need for prominent leaders, formal social movement organizations, and collective action frames, which require individuals to share common identities and political claims." While beneficial to short-term patterns of decentralized mobilization and political engagement, it is possible to question the efficiency of this model in getting all players to buy into a shared agenda and seek common objectives. In other words, it may not lead to more traditional political dividends, like influencing formal decision-making. However, these patterns may be of interest to individual activists who, as mentioned previously, seek short-term self-validation and a sense of belonging to a political community or political project. While little traditional leadership is identified in the INM and Maple Spring cases, the authors studying them highlight several examples of connective leadership wherein information or opinions shared by individuals have short-term structuring effects on dynamics of engagement (e.g., retweets) (Lalancette et al. 2019; Raynauld et al. 2016, 2018, 2019).

POTENTIALS

While gaining traction in Canada and internationally, the revised blueprint of grassroots-intensive political and civic action is still evolving. This is caused by several contextual social, political, and technological factors, including the "perpetual beta" nature of existing social media channels, the introduction and development of new Web 2.0 tools, as well as constantly shifting interests and expectations among users (Carpenter 2010, 218). Despite it all, this blueprint has experienced varying levels of success. From generating public awareness for the cause of minorities, marginalized individuals, or communities to mobilizing support and, in some cases, affecting government's decision-making, it has played a role in shaping how protest has affected different facets of the political landscape in different national contexts.

While research is still required to further characterize and understand this political and civic engagement blueprint's manifestations and implications, several conclusions can be drawn. First, social media, which are central to the deployment of this blueprint, have fostered a more inclusive and diverse political and civic engagement. Whereas more traditional paths of political engagement are bureaucratized, rigid, and can be geared toward excluding some segments of civil society from the political process, social media have enabled minority and marginalized individuals and communities to be active politically on their own terms. In doing so, they have contributed to the progressive flattening of the political environment, which has given opportunities to more disenfranchised segments of the society to be heard and, to some degree, disrupt mainstream – or business as usual – politics. The Idle No More movement may be viewed as a clear example of this phenomenon.

Also, this blueprint has been the source of the rise of loosely organized counter-discourses unaligned with more mainstream forces within the traditional political arena. In many cases, it has infused some levels of uncertainty and, in some cases, instability, in the political environment. As mentioned previously, supporters of the Maple Spring and Idle No More movement have disrupted in varying ways political dynamics in the province of Quebec and throughout Canada generally. While these movements have led to political and policy changes, more research is needed in order to quantify these transformations. Indeed, few authors have looked at the traditional political dividends coming out of the actions of these two protest movements.

As indicated previously, more work remains to better unpack the roles, manifestations, and effects of this revised blueprint for political and civic engagement. Several questions remain: How does the level of media literacy of individuals and organizations participating in these movements impact their level of protest efficacy? How is the revised blueprint of political and civic engagement impacting more traditional political players whose expectations of engagement with members of the public are far different? How are social media impacting how political engagement is viewed and understood by growing segments of the public in different countries?

The revised blueprint for political and civic engagement is likely to gain traction in Canada and internationally over the next decade. While it might be helping to engage, or re-engage, some segments of the public in the political process, it is also possible to question how it is impacting how formal political actors – including electoral candidates, elected officials, government agencies, and civil servants – use social media to reach out to and engage with members of the public in and out of elections. Consequently, while much research has been done on these matters, questions relating to formal political actors' interactions with the revised blueprint of political and civic engagement could lead to the development of new streams of research that could provide valuable insights. Indeed, recent examples have shown that many governments internationally have struggled with dealing with these patterns of protest, but they are here to stay.

REFERENCES

Albaugh, Quinn, and Christopher Waddell. 2014. "Social Media and Political Inequality." In *Canadian Democracy from the Ground Up: Perceptions and Performance*, ed. Elisabeth Gidengil and Heather Bastedo, 102–24. Vancouver: UBC Press.

Barbas, Angel, and John Postill. 2017. "Communication Activism as a School of Politics: Lessons from Spain's Indignados Movement." *Journal of Communication* 67 (5): 646–64. https://doi.org/10.1111/jcom.12321.

Bennett, W. Lance. 2015. "Changing Societies, Changing Media Systems: Challenges for Communication Theory, Research, and Education." In *Can the Media Serve Democracy? Essays in Honour of Jay G. Blumler*, ed. Stephen Coleman, Giles Moss, and Katy Parry, 151–63. New York: Palgrave Macmillan.

Bennett, W. Lance, and Alexandra Segerberg. 2012. "The Logic of Connective Action: Digital Media and the Personalization of Contentious Politics." *Information, Communication & Society* 15 (5): 739–68. https://doi.org/10.1080/1369118X.2012.670661.

Bimber, Bruce. 2008. "The Internet and Political Fragmentation." In *Domestic Perspectives on Contemporary Democracy*, ed. Peter F. Nardulli, 155–70. Chicago: University of Illinois Press.

Blaser, Britt, David Weinberger, and Joe Trippi. 2009. "Digital Government through Social Networks: How Citizens Can Aggregate Their Money and Votes to Define Digital Government." In *Proceedings of the 10th Annual International Conference on Digital Government Research: Social Networks: Making Connections between Citizens, Data and Government*, 19–24. Digital Government Society of North America.

Bonilla, Yarimar, and Jonathan Rosa. 2015. "#Ferguson: Digital Protest, Hashtag Ethnography, and the Racial Politics of Social Media in the United States." *American Ethnologist* 42 (1): 4–17. https://doi.org/10.1111/amet.12112.

Boulianne, Shelley. 2016. "Campaigns and Conflict on Social Media: A Literature Snapshot." *Online Information Review* 40 (5): 566–79. https://doi.org/10.1108/OIR-03-2016-0086.

Callison, Candis, and Alfred Hermida. 2015. "Dissent and Resonance: #Idlenomore as an Emergent Middle Ground." *Canadian Journal of Communication* 40 (4): 695–716. https://doi.org/10.22230/cjc.2015v40n4a2958.

Cappella, Joseph N., and Kathleen Hall Jamieson. 1997. *Spiral of Cynicism: The Press and the Public Good*. Oxford: Oxford University Press.

Carpenter, Cheris A. 2010. "The Obamachine: Technopolitics 2.0." *Journal of Information Technology & Politics* 7 (2–3): 216–25. https://doi.org/10.1080/19331681003765887.

Christensen, Henrik Serup. 2011. "Political Activities on the Internet: Slacktivism or Political Participation by Other Means?" *First Monday* 16 (2). https://doi.org/10.5210/fm.v16i2.3336.

Cormode, Graham, and Balachander Krishnamurthy. 2008. "Key Differences between Web and Web 2.0." *First Monday* 13 (6). https://doi.org/10.5210/fm.v13i6.2125.

Dalton, Russell J. 2008. "Citizenship Norms and the Expansion of Political Participation." *Political Studies* 56 (1): 76–98. https://doi.org/10.1111/j.1467-9248.2007.00718.x.

Dimitrova, Daniela V., Adam Shehata, Jesper Strömbäck, and Lars W. Nord. 2014. "The Effects of Digital Media on Political Knowledge and Participation in Election Campaigns: Evidence from Panel Data." *Communication Research* 41 (1): 95–118. https://doi.org/10.1177/0093650211426004.

Drüeke, Ricarda, and Elke Zobl. 2016. "Online Feminist Protest against Sexism: The German-Language Hashtag #aufschrei." *Feminist Media Studies* 16 (1): 35–54. https://doi.org/10.1080/14680777.2015.1093071.

Dumitrica, Delia, and Maria Bakardjieva. 2017. "The Personalization of Engagement: The Symbolic Construction of Social Media and Grassroots Mobilization in Canadian Newspapers." *Media, Culture, & Society* 40 (6): 817–37. https://doi.org/10.1177/0163443717734406. Medline: 30111898.

Earl, Jennifer, Lauren Copeland, and Bruce Bimber. 2017. "Routing around Organizations: Self-Directed Political Consumption." *Mobilization: An International Quarterly* 22 (2): 131–53. https://doi.org/10.17813/1086-671X-22-2-131.

Gismondi, Adam, and Laura Osteen. 2017. "Student Activism in the Technology Age." *New Directions for Student Leadership* 153: 63–74.

Hsiao, Yuan. 2018. "Understanding Digital Natives in Contentious Politics: Explaining the Effect of Social Media on Protest Participation through Psychological Incentives." *New Media & Society* 20 (9): 3457–78. https://doi.org/10.1177/1461444817749519.

Inglehart, Ronald. 2017. *Changing Values in the Islamic World and the West.* In *Values and Political Action in the Middle East,* ed. Mansoor Moaddel and Michele Gelfand, 2–24. New York: Oxford University Press.

Kavada, Anastasia. 2015. "Creating the Collective: Social Media, the Occupy Movement and Its Constitution as a Collective Actor." *Information, Communication, & Society* 18 (8): 872–86. https://doi.org/10.1080/1369118X.2015.1043318.

Kenski, Kate, and Natalie Jomini Stroud. 2006. "Connections between Internet Use and Political Efficacy, Knowledge, and Participation." *Journal of Broadcasting & Electronic Media* 50 (2): 173–92. https://doi.org/10.1207/s15506878jobem5002_1.

Lalancette, Mireille, and Vincent Raynauld. 2019. "An Under-the-Hood Look at Social Media-Fueled Protest: Defining Interactions between News Media Organizations, Activists, and Citizens on Twitter during the 2012 Quebec Student Strike." *Communication and Culture Review* (Online first).

Lalancette, Mireille, and Tamara Small (2020). "'Justin Trudeau – I Don't Know Her': An Analysis of Leadership Memes of Justin Trudeau." *Canadian Journal of Communication.*

Lalancette, Mireille, Tamara Small, and Maxime Pronovost. 2019. "Trolling Stephen Harper: Internet Memes as Online Activism." In *What's #Trending in Canadian Politics? Understanding Transformations in Power, Media, and the Public Sphere,* ed. Mireille Lalancette, Vincent Raynauld, and Erin Crandal, 106–26. Vancouver: UBC Press.

Latzko-Toth, Guillaume, Madeleine Pastinelli, and Nicole Gallant. 2017. "Usages des médias sociaux et pratiques informationnelles des jeunes Québécois: Le cas de Facebook pendant la grève étudiante de 2012." *Recherches sociographiques* 58 (1): 43–64. https://doi.org/10.7202/1039930ar.

Lee, Francis L.F., and Joseph Man Chan. 2016. "Digital Media Activities and Mode of Participation in a Protest Campaign: A Study of the Umbrella Movement." *Information, Communication, & Society* 19 (1): 4–22. https://doi.org/10.1080/1369118X.2015.1093530.

Lindgren, Simon, and Coppélie Cocq. 2017. "Turning the Inside Out: Social Media and the Broadcasting of Indigenous Discourse." *European Journal of Communication* 32 (2): 131–50. https://doi.org/10.1177/0267323116674112.

Loader, Brian D., and Dan Mercea. 2011. "Networking Democracy? Social Media Innovations and Participatory Politics." *Information, Communication, & Society* 14, (6): 757–69. https://doi.org/10.1080/1369118X.2011.592648.

Macafee, Timothy, and J.J. De Simone. 2012. "Killing the Bill Online? Pathways to Young People's Protest Engagement via Social Media." *Cyberpsychology, Behavior, and Social Networking* 15 (11): 579–84. https://doi.org/10.1089/cyber.2012.0153. Medline: 23002983.

Mackie, Gerry. 2009. "Schumpeter's Leadership Democracy." *Political Theory* 37 (1): 128–53. https://doi.org/10.1177/0090591708326642.

Margetts, Helen, Peter John, Scott Hale, and Taha Yasseri. 2016. *Political Turbulence: How Social Media Shape Collective Action.* Princeton, NJ: Princeton University Press.

McCurdy, Patrick, and Jacob Groshek. 2019. "Bytes and Bitumen: A Case Study of Mediated Discourse and Digital Advocacy around TransCanada's Proposed #EnergyEast Pipeline." In *What's Trending in Canadian Politics? Understanding Transformations in Power, Media, and the Public Square,* ed. Mireille Lalancette, Vincent Raynauld, and Erin Crandall, 63–85. Vancouver: UBC Press.

Mercea, Dan. 2014. "Towards a Conceptualization of Casual Protest Participation: Parsing a Case from the Save Roşia Montană Campaign."

East European Politics and Societies 28 (2): 386–410. https://doi.org/10.1177/0888325413519672.

Mercea, Dan. 2016. *Civic Participation in Contentious Politics.* London: Palgrave Macmillan.

Moscato, Derek. 2016. "Media Portrayals of Hashtag Activism: A Framing Analysis of Canada's #Idlenomore Movement." *Media and Communication* 4 (2): 3–12. https://doi.org/10.17645/mac.v4i2.416.

Nemer, David. 2016. "Rethinking Social Change: The Promises of Web 2.0 for the Marginalized." *First Monday* 21 (6). https://doi.org/10.5210/fm.v21i6.6786.

Norris, Pippa. 2001. *Digital Divide: Civic Engagement, Information Poverty, and the Internet Worldwide.* Cambridge: Cambridge University Press.

Pateman, Carole. 1970. *Participation and Democratic Theory.* Cambridge: Cambridge University Press.

Poell, Thomas. 2014. "Social Media and the Transformation of Activist Communication: Exploring the Social Media Ecology of the 2010 Toronto G20 Protests." *Information, Communication, & Society* 17 (6): 716–31. https://doi.org/10.1080/1369118X.2013.812674.

Poell, Thomas, and Erik Borra. 2012. "Twitter, YouTube, and Flickr as Platforms of Alternative Journalism: The Social Media Account of the 2010 Toronto G20 Protests." *Journalism* 13 (6): 695–713. https://doi.org/10.1177/1464884911431533.

Poell, Thomas, and José van Dijck. 2018. "Social Media and New Protest Movements." In *The SAGE Handbook of Social Media*, ed. Jean Burgess, Alice Marwick, and Thomas Poell, 546–61. London: Sage.

Raynauld, Vincent, Mireille Lalancette, and Sofia Tourigny-Koné. 2016. "Political Protest 2.0: Social Media and the 2012 Student Strike in the Province of Quebec, Canada." *French Politics* 14 (1): 1–29. https://doi.org/10.1057/fp.2015.22.

Raynauld, Vincent, Mireille Lalancette, and Sofia Tourigny-Koné. 2019. "Rethinking Digital Activism as It Unfolds: Ambient Political Engagement on Twitter during the 2012 Quebec Student Strike." In *What's #Trending in Canadian Politics? Understanding Transformations in Power, Media, and the Public Sphere*, ed. Mireille Lalancette, Vincent Raynauld, and Erin Crandall, 44–62. Vancouver: UBC Press.

Raynauld, Vincent, Emmanuelle Richez, and Katie Boudreau Morris. 2018. "Canada Is #IdleNoMore: Exploring Dynamics of Indigenous Political and Civic Protest in the Twitterverse." *Information, Communication, & Society* 21 (4): 626–42. https://doi.org/10.1080/1369118X.2017.1301522.

Rohlinger, Deana A., and Leslie A. Bunnage. 2015. "Connecting People to Politics over Time? Internet Communication Technology and Retention in Moveon.org and the Florida Tea Party Movement." *Information, Communication, & Society* 18 (5): 539–52. https://doi.org/10.1080/1369118X.2015.1008541.

Rohlinger, Deana A., and Leslie Bunnage. 2017. "Did the Tea Party Movement Fuel the Trump-Train? The Role of Social Media in Activist Persistence and Political Change in the 21st Century." *Social Media + Society* 3 (2). https://doi.org/10.1177/2056305117706786.

Rothstein, Bo. 2009. "Creating Political Legitimacy: Electoral Democracy versus Quality of Government." *American Behavioral Scientist* 53 (3): 311–30. https://doi.org/10.1177/0002764209338795.

Scherman, Andrés, Arturo Arriagada, and Sebastiàn Valenzuela. 2015. "Student and Environmental Protests in Chile: The Role of Social Media." *Politics* 35 (2): 151–71. https://doi.org/10.1111/1467-9256.12072.

Schumpeter, Joseph. 1967. "Two Concepts of Democracy." In *Political Philosophy*, ed. Anthony Quinton, 153–88. London: Oxford University Press.

Theocharis, Yannis, and Jan W. van Deth. 2018. "The Continuous Expansion of Citizen Participation: A New Taxonomy." *European Political Science Review* 10 (1): 139–63. https://doi.org/10.1017/S1755773916000230.

Theocharis, Yannis, Will Lowe, Jan W. van Deth, and Gema García-Albacete. 2015. "Using Twitter to Mobilize Protest Action: Online Mobilization Patterns and Action Repertoires in the Occupy Wall Street, Indignados, and Aganaktismenoi Movements." *Information, Communication, & Society* 18 (2): 202–20. https://doi.org/10.1080/1369118X.2014.948035.

Tilly, Charles, and Sidney Tarrow. 2015. *Politique(s) du conflit: De la grève à la révolution*. 2nd ed. Paris: Presses de Sciences Po.

Van Deth, Jan W. 2016. "Political Participation." *The International Encyclopedia of Political Communication*, ed. Gianpietro Mazzoleni, 1158–68. Hoboken: Wiley & Sons.

Van Laer, Jeroen, and Peter Van Aelst. 2010. "Internet and Social Movement Action Repertoires: Opportunities and Limitations." *Information, Communication, & Society* 13 (8): 1146–71. https://doi.org/10.1080/13691181003628307.

Vromen, Ariadne. 2017. "Social Media Use for Political Engagement." In *Digital Citizenship and Political Engagement: The Challenge from Online Campaigning and Advocacy Organisations*, ed. Ariadne Vromen, 51–75. London: Palgrave Macmillan.

Vromen, Ariadne, Michael A. Xenos, and Brian Loader. 2015. "Young People, Social Media and Connective Action: From Organisational Maintenance to Everyday Political Talk." *Journal of Youth Studies* 18 (1): 80–100. https://doi.org/10.1080/13676261.2014.933198.

Webster, James G., and Thomas B. Ksiazek. 2015. "The Dynamics of Audience Fragmentation: Public Attention in an Age of Digital Media." *Journal of Communication* 62 (1): 39–56. https://doi.org/10.1111/j.1460-2466.2011.01616.x.

Welzel, Christian, and Ronald Inglehart. 2008. "The Role of Ordinary People in Democratization." *Journal of Democracy* 19 (1): 126–40. https://doi.org/10.1353/jod.2008.0009.

Wood, Lesley J. 2015. "Idle No More, Facebook, and Diffusion." *Social Movement Studies* 14 (5): 615–21. https://doi.org/10.1080/14742837.2015.1037262.

Xenos, Michael, Ariadne Vromen, and Brian D. Loader. 2014. "The Great Equalizer? Patterns of Social Media Use and Youth Political Engagement in Three Advanced Democracies." *Information, Communication, & Society* 17 (2): 151–67. https://doi.org/10.1080/1369118X.2013.871318.

Zhu, Qinfeng, Marko Skoric, and Fei Shen. 2017. "I Shield Myself from Thee: Selective Avoidance on Social Media during Political Protests." *Political Communication* 34 (1): 112–31. https://doi.org/10.1080/10584609.2016.1222471.

Zittel, Thomas. 2012. "Participatory Democracy and Political Participation." In *Participatory Democracy and Political Participation: Can Participatory Engineering Bring Citizens Back In?*, ed. Thomas Zittel and Dieter Fuchs, 9–28. London: Routledge/ECPR Studies in European Political Science.

CHAPTER ELEVEN

Digital Indigenous Politics: "There's More than One Political Show in Town"

Derek Antoine

INTRODUCTION

Within Indigenous[1] communities, there are debates about whether to participate in Canadian politics or engage with settler-colonial[2] state institutions. These questions stem, in large part, from a discomfort about granting legitimacy to the state through participation in governing institutions that are decisively non-Indigenous, were (and remain) largely inaccessible, and systematically act against the best interests of Indigenous peoples (Palmater 2015; Diabo 2015; Simpson 2014). During the 2015 Canadian federal election, Assembly of First Nations national chief Perry Bellegarde called for increased Indigenous participation, releasing a list of fifty-one constituencies where Indigenous voters could

1 I use the term "Indigenous" to refer to First Nations, Inuit, and Métis people in Canada. I do this cognizant that Indigenous peoples are not a homogenous group and that those included within that term make up some of the most diverse communities in the world, with different histories, cultures, and traditions. When applicable, I make reference to specific Indigenous peoples, such as Mi'kmaq or Mohawk people.

2 Settler-colonialism is a particular form of colonialism that emphasizes dispossessing peoples from their lands to achieve domination. See Glen Coulthard's (2014) book *Red Skin, White Masks* for a broader discussion on this form of colonialism and its applicability to the Canadian context.

influence the outcome of the election. Interestingly, Bellegarde admitted that he had not voted in the previous election and was unsure about whether he would cast a ballot in 2015 (CBC 2015). For some Indigenous people, voting might mean engaging in politics and governance structures on settler-colonial terms at the expense of their own.

A similar discomfort extends to the realm of digital politics, as digital technologies have largely mimicked the problems plaguing the wider sphere of political participation: namely, that they are non-Indigenous technologies, are largely inaccessible, and often work to undermine Indigenous peoples' best interests. Indigenous peoples continue to grapple with misleading identity constructions that circulate easily through digital technologies and that underpin the logics of settler-colonialism, justify dispossession from their land and communities, and marginalize Indigenous peoples, cultures, and knowledges.

This chapter highlights the way politics and political participation are often defined on settler-colonial terms, wherein Indigenous peoples are forced to grapple with institutions, governing systems, and political norms that are not theirs.[3] This has been especially true with the rise of digital technologies and as politics has become increasingly mediated. At the same time, there are numerous examples that show how Indigenous peoples are appropriating digital technologies on their own terms to assert their sovereignty, self-determination, and self-governance practices. Digital technologies are sites of struggle for Indigenous peoples grappling with the challenges and marginalizing legacy of colonizing media technologies and practices as well as the promise of Indigenizing these technologies to reflect their worldviews and reconnect them to their communities, governance, structures, and lands. The chapter highlights examples of Indigenous communities building their own digital infrastructures to create separate but parallel infrastructures infused with Indigenous control and governance practices, of cultural activism where Indigenous media makers are using digital technologies to reconnect with their communities, learn

3 I offer this chapter as a non-Indigenous person, inspired by the ongoing work of Indigenous scholars in multiple scholarly disciplines. I am grateful to the Indigenous activists, particularly the Mi'kmaq activists in and around Elsipogtog First Nation, who have shared their perspectives on political participation and activism in Canada. Finally, I want to thank and recognize the Algonquin Nation, whose traditional and unceded territory hosts Carleton University, where this chapter was written.

languages, and practise traditions, and of media practices that straddle the line between resistance and compliance as digital technologies are used within the confines of their design but also in ways that challenge circulating misrepresentations of Indigeneity. There are also examples where digital technologies may present opportunities to experiment with non-Indigenous institutions, like voting, in ways that are culturally appropriate (see chapter 4 for a discussion of internet voting in Indigenous communities). All these examples show that there are multiple models of political participation that hold value in these communities and that can coexist with Western models.

CONTEXT

Indigenous political struggle is fundamentally about asserting and re-asserting Indigenous sovereignty, advocating self-governance and self-determination (Smith 2011; Coulthard 2014; Simpson 2014). Treaties were negotiated or agreed to between the French and British Crowns and sovereign Indigenous peoples. Yet other groups, as the Supreme Court of Canada reminded us in their 2014 decision *Tsilhqot'in Nation v. British Columbia* (2014), who do not have treaty relationships with the Crown of Canada also continue to retain their sovereignty. For instance, Mi'kmaq scholar Stephen Augustine (2016) describes the peace and friendships treaties between his people and the French and English Crowns in the sixteenth and seventeenth centuries as simple agreements that governed trade but evolved into more complex arrangements as the British Crown ventured deeper into Mi'kma'ki territory, sparking conflicts. In 1763 the British Crown unilaterally issued a Royal Proclamation formalizing its acquisition of North American territories from the French (Poliandri 2011; Conrad and Hiller 2001) and beginning a long process of dispossessing Indigenous peoples from their lands and asserting European-style colonial rule (Axelrod 2001; Reid 1995).

As Michael Asch (2014) notes, the flourishing Indigenous societies and systems of governance that pre-existed settler arrival were supplanted in this process, resulting today in politics informed by a backwards logic whereby Indigenous peoples are asked to reconcile themselves and their ways of being with the supremacy of the Canadian state. Instead, he argues, it is the Canadian state that ought to be reconciled with the aboriginality of Indigenous peoples, communities, and societies that have survived on this land since time immemorial.

What this means is that Indigenous peoples have had to grapple with the imposition of institutions that are decidedly not their own, whether political institutions of the settler Canadian state or those that have supplanted their traditional governance systems in their communities. Cherokee scholar Jeff Corntassel notes that "one of our biggest enemies is compartmentalization, as shape-shifting colonial entities attempt to sever our relationship to the natural world and define the terrain of struggle," pointing as an example to the way policymakers frame economic initiatives as "economic development," ignoring completely Indigenous notions of economics that link land, culture, and community (in Smith 2013). The same case can be made for compartmentalizing politics as voting, or some other form of democratic participation established by the settler-colonial state, in ways that can forego traditional governance systems and community-based decision-making. Mi'kmaq scholar Pam Palmater connects this struggle with Indigenous participation in settler-colonial elections, writing that, in essence, Indigenous voters are "voting for which party will be our next Minister of Indian Affairs," the party that will exercise the laws, policies, and economic structures of the state "to deny us our basic human rights, let alone our Aboriginal and treaty rights" (Palmater 2015, n.p.). Mohawk author Russ Diabo (2015) goes further, writing that "any First Nation person involved in the federal electoral process will be, wittingly or unwittingly, part of implementing the government's termination plan."

Mi'kmaq activist, politician, and leader Susan Levi-Peters makes a useful distinction between *your politics* and *our politics* when talking about her political career in Elsipogtog First Nation, where she was elected as a band councillor and Chief, as well as her candidacies in provincial and federal elections. Municipalities, provinces, and the federal government are *your politics*. These are settler-colonial institutions that serve settler-colonial interests. *Our politics*, she says, are different. These are the political institutions on reserves, in some cases band councils, that exercise many of the functions of government (Levi-Peters 2017).

Yet, there is another distinction worth mentioning. Band councils are colonial institutions imposed by the settler-state through the Indian Act, either superseding or competing with traditional forms of governance involving Elders, traditional knowledge keepers, and others

(Gabel et al. 2016). Elections, governance frameworks, and supervisorial powers remain with the federal government, evidenced by Parliament's continued passage of laws affecting Indigenous communities with little or no consultation and the appointment of co-managers or co-supervisors, of which Bill C-45 introduced in 2012 by the Stephen Harper government is a prime example, ultimately leading to what would become the Idle No More movement.[4] Indian Act Band Councils, as Levi-Peters (2017) calls them, are not how many communities governed themselves in pre-colonial times, and some communities continue to rely on parallel and separate traditional governance structures.

Restrictions to voting in Canada has meant that many Indigenous peoples have had to find alternative means of political participation in Canadian governance. The Indian Act of 1876 granted voting rights only to First Nations people possessing a university degree, who became a medical doctor, clergyman, or lawyer, or who relinquished their status while meeting certain property ownership qualifications. Very few people met these thresholds while those who did were more inclined to refuse giving up their status. While Inuit peoples acquired the right to vote in 1950, their remote geography meant they were effectively unable to participate until enough ballot boxes travelled to Inuit communities twelve years later. Ultimately, the requirement to give up Indigenous status was removed in 1960 by the Diefenbaker government. Métis people have always been able to vote.

Mohawk scholar Taiaiake Alfred (2009, 43) suggests that this ongoing colonial interference has resulted not only in the dispossession of Indigenous people from their lands and the erosion of culture but also in "political chaos[,] social discord [...] and political dependency of First Nations upon the state." Turning that around, he and others suggest, requires finding ways to break away from state institutions in favour of supporting and strengthening Indigenous ones (Alfred 2009; Coulthard 2014). Indigenous political scholarship increasingly focuses on two concepts that speak to this in the form of Indigenous resurgence and the politics of refusal, concepts that are useful in explaining digital political participation.

---

4 In 2012, the federal government introduced an omnibus bill that made sweeping changes to land, water, and environmental laws as well as changes to the Indian Act without consultations with Indigenous communities.

Indigenous resurgence is about rejecting the ongoing logics of dispossession and colonization inherent in settler-colonial institutions and, instead, adopting practices that reconnect Indigenous peoples with their cultures, histories, traditions, lands, and worldviews. Anishnaabe scholar Leanne Simpson (2011) reminds us that Indigenous peoples continue to combat tired tropes where reconnecting with these elements necessarily means clinging to an outdated past, subscribing to traditions that make Indigeneity unable to survive progress and modernity. For her, resurgence is about "recreating the cultural and political flourishment of the past to support the well-being of our contemporary citizens" and "reclaiming the fluidity around our traditions, not the rigidity of colonialism" (Simpson 2011, 51). Corntassel says that "being Indigenous today means struggling to reclaim and regenerate one's relational, place-based existence by challenging the ongoing, destructive forces of colonization" (Corntassel 2012, 88) and "taking emphasis away from state frameworks [...] back to re-localized, community centred actions premised on reconnecting with land, culture, and community" (Corntassel 2012, 92). For Corntassel, resurgence is about everyday acts of resistance that reconnect Indigenous peoples to their nationhoods and get them closer to achieving self-governance and self-determination. Mohawk scholar Audra Simpson (2014) draws on her community's history to think through the politics of refusal. The Mohawks of Kahnawa:ke rely heavily on Haudenosaunee (First Nations of the Iroquois) governance systems, with some members refusing to participate in Canadian politics and refusing to vote in band council elections, viewing band councils as foreign systems imposed on their community. Simpson writes that the Mohawks of Kahnawa:ke view the "bestowal of settler citizenship [...] with a certain 'awkwardness,'" choosing to "answer only [to Haudenosaunee] governmental authority" (Simpson 2014, 22). Indeed, the Mohawks often cite the idea of the Two Row Wampum, referring to the Two Row Wampum Treaty between their people and the Dutch Crown in 1613, to guide their contemporary relationships with other nations where two systems of government coexist side-by-side (Muller 2007; Simpson 2014). Representing the agreement is a belt where two parallel purple lines symbolize vessels travelling together down a river, continuing to coexist but never meeting (Muller 2007). In sum, as Simpson states, "there is more than one political show in town" (Simpson 2014, 11).

Both resurgence and refusal stand in contrast to the perils of the modern politics of recognition, wherein the settler-colonial state takes it upon itself to recognize Indigenous nationhood on the state's terms, reproducing the same colonizing outcomes it says it is trying to overcome rather than building relationships of reciprocity and mutual recognition (Coulthard 2014). The same is true with Indigenous peoples being forced to grapple with the logics of digital technologies that eschew Indigenous ways of life or have the potential to marginalize Indigeneity in detrimental ways, opting instead to turn away from the state and focus on their sovereignty (Coulthard 2014; Simpson 2014). When it comes to digital technologies and governance, the same idea holds true: set up parallel digital infrastructures and establish local, participatory governance structures that better align with the participating Indigenous community. Use digital technologies differently than how they are used by non-Indigenous peoples to represent Indigeneity from an Indigenous point of view. Celebrate and strengthen Indigenous nations, and be assertive, as Audra Simpson suggests, in exercising Indigenous traditions of governance over the ones that are bestowed by the settler-Canadian state. For Palmater (2015, n.p.), "the most exciting and transformative times in our recent history" did not come from participation in settler-state politics "but were linked to our very public collective actions against Canadian processes."

DIGITIZATION

Promises & Perils

Online and offline, resurgence and refusal define important ways Indigenous peoples and communities are engaging in politics to achieve self-determination and self-governance. Rather than using digital technologies to engage in *your politics,* there are countless examples where they are being used to infuse Indigenous governance and logics into digital infrastructures and media practices. Métis scholar Yvonne Poitras Pratt (2010) offers hope for digital technology use, reflecting a version of the mobilization hypothesis that digital technology use can have a positive effect on political behaviour, by arguing that it can help inform projects of decolonization when Indigenous groups assert and exercise greater control over communication technologies to define their own cultural parameters, ensuring that new media merge with old traditions. What follows are examples of the perils and promise of digital politics in this context, showing how Indigenous peoples grapple with technologies that are not their own while, at the same time, finding ways to infuse them with their cultures, governance, and politics.

Practice

Issues around representations, ownership, and governance present three challenges of digital technology for Indigenous peoples. First, as Comanche writer Paul Chaat Smith (2009) notes, various media technologies have largely embodied settler-colonial agendas since it was non-Indigenous peoples who have stood behind the cameras, financed movie scripts, and owned the broadcast networks. Lisa Parks (2005) notes the way Indigenous communities grapple with digital technologies to extend their cultural footprint yet struggle with the embedded logics of unequal power relations, historical misrepresentations, and economic disparities in technology that never completely allow them to become Indigenous media. Further, digital infrastructures tend to rely on logics that are incompatible with many Indigenous communities as they are centrally organized, rely on private capital to fund construction and maintenance, and are designed to be scaled rather than localized (McMahon 2011). Christian Sandvig adds that while digital technologies create opportunities for placelessness, that is "access to information without reference to place" as well as user equality, "the state of Indigeneity, in contrast, is a continual assertion of place and an affirmation of identity" (Sandvig 2012).

As minority users, this poses additional challenges when it comes to having a voice and standing in the digital media landscape. Historians Daniel Francis (2011) and Robert Berkhoffer Jr. (1978) have coined the terms, respectively, the Imaginary Indian and the White Man's Indian to refer to the ways that Indigenous identity and life are represented predominantly by non-Indigenous peoples in ways that marginalize and minimize their existence, often pitting notions of modernity against conjured ideas of what non-Indigenous media makers imagine Indigenous peoples to be. Familiar archetypes include the "noble savage" as the spiritual, environmentally conscious Indigenous person, personified by Italian-American actor Iron Eyes Cody from the Keep America Beautiful campaign, "angry warriors" who are savage, drunken predators determined to resist progress, or "pochahontas," symbolizing the Indigenous woman who rejects her heritage to join Western culture (Bird 2003; Bird 1996; Berkhoffer 1978; DeLoria 1995).

These challenges remain pertinent as political economic barriers often prevent Indigenous peoples from gaining access to their own representation through varying communication technologies in ways that affect digital technologies as well. The representations work to disconnect Indigenous peoples from their worldviews and governance systems (Alfred 2005; Smith 2009). Nevertheless, Kopacz and Lawton (2011) point to welcome developments, noting that Indigenous representations on viral digital websites, such as YouTube, depart from the rigid stereotypical depictions of Indigenous peoples that adorn other media formats, suggesting that high barriers of participation that deter Indigenous participation through media forms may not be applicable as digital technologies are made to be more accessible.

Nevertheless, a significant barrier to digital Indigenous political participation is state surveillance (see chapter 6). Recently released documents obtained through Access to Information and Privacy Act requests suggest that Canada's security and policing agencies rely heavily on social media to monitor Indigenous politics and surveil political actors and activists. Two documents in particular, PROJECT SITKA (2014) and Criminal Threats to Canadian Petroleum Industry (2014), detail how the Royal Canadian Mounted Police (RCMP) and the Canadian Security Intelligence Service (CSIS) consider social media an important resource to gather information on and assess Indigenous threats to the Canadian state, including opposition to resource extraction projects.

Finally, a digital divide remains as broadband internet access is 17 per cent lower in Indigenous communities than in Canada in general and available at subscription costs that are significantly higher than they are in non-Indigenous communities (Stollery 2018; CIRA 2018; Innovation, Science, and Economic Development Canada 2018). Access poses significant challenges as the bulk of political participation now occurs online. As Sandvig (2012) notes, while Indigenous communities appropriate these technologies to reflect differences, that is to reflect their different cultures, needs, and uses, the ultimate goal is appropriation toward parity. They want to have what others have – create, consume, and circulate cultural content, news, and information. They want to connect with others, find information, and build networks. None of this is possible without first having access.

Practice

Self-determination, reconnection, & disruption: Despite several significant challenges posed by digital technologies for Indigenous peoples, they do present some opportunities in the area of self-determination, reconnection, and disruption. In partnership with the First Nations Education Council, the community of Kahnawa:ke provides an important example of resurgence and refusal by building its own digital infrastructure to take control and connect digital technologies to their place, culture, and governance systems. As McMahon et al. (2015, 1) note, "digital infrastructures and information communication technologies are powerful tools that can support self-government and nation rebuilding." In the Kahnawa:ke case, they constructed a customized digital data management system to allow them more control in the storage and use of data produced in the community, a network of videoconference systems (Whiteduck and Beaton 2014), and a secure network called Tewatati connecting a series of community services, including emergency services, economic development, and schools (McMahon et al. 2015). This was part of a larger effort to rebuild education systems in Quebec in the context of settler-colonialism and find ways to ensure that authority and decision-making practices emerge from and remain in the community.

McMahon (2011) uses the term *digital self-determination* to describe what Indigenous communities are doing across Canada to take control of their digital infrastructures and infuse them with Indigenous logics. By building their own digital infrastructures, like establishing their own broadband networks, they are able to sidestep the governance structures, construction, and designs incongruent with Indigenous ways of life, worldviews, and knowledges and replace them with parallel infrastructures that are decentralized, local, follow participatory governance, and better meet the needs of their communities (McMahon 2011). Building digital infrastructure on Indigenous land further allows for a reaffirmation of place and identity along with control and the ability for modification (Sandvig 2012).

Setting up parallel digital infrastructures can be understood as a form of resurgence connecting Indigenous peoples to their communities, lands, and governance systems in ways that non-Indigenous infrastructures are unable to accomplish. It is also a refusal to rely on digital infrastructures built and governed in ways that can have detrimental effects on Indigenous communities, further applying colonizing logics on technologies that are used daily in the community. Finally, we can see increased benefits as Indigenous communities own and control the digital infrastructures that house information on their community, people, and traditions and are therefore able to determine how that information is used.

Digital technologies also create opportunities for Indigenous peoples to reconnect with language, treaties, and governance systems. Mi'kmaq activist and podcaster Annie Clair was on the frontlines of the anti-shale gas exploration protests in New Brunswick in 2013. In 2016, she partnered with the Halifax Media Co-op and the Canadian Council for the Arts to release a bilingual English and Mi'kmaq online podcast called *pjilasimikmaki*, or "Welcome to Mi'kma'ki." Clair told the Mi'kma'ki Maliseet Nations News that "I want my people to regain their language. Speaking our language is key to being able to reconnect with our culture and identity" (MMNN.ca n.d.). Her episodes tackle issues affecting her community of Elsipogtog First Nation, including the Sixties Scoop, missing and murdered Indigenous women and girls, and the reservation system. Interviewing Elders in Mi'kmaq allows her to practise her language, learn about treaty rights, and revisit Mi'kmaq cultural practices such as traditional basket weaving.

This example is important, demonstrating how accessible digital technologies have provided Clair and others a platform to interview traditional knowledge keepers and connect with the issues that are not only important in her community but those that she believes are missing from wider media landscapes. Similarly, Anishnaabe comedian and media maker Ryan McMahon launched in 2017 the Makoons Media Group, a company that "creates digital projects that makes space for Indigenous voices to disrupt, inspire, and transform the world around us" (Makoons Media 2017). Such a venture is important in a media landscape dominated by non-Indigenous voices.

Faye Ginsburg (2008) offers the term "digital cultural activism" to explain how digital technologies are enabling a form of resurgence in Indigenous communities. She views digital media as a discursive space of struggle and suggests that Indigenous youth "recognize that social change cannot simply be legislated but requires a long struggle against racism that is pervasive in the dominant culture in multiple arenas. Activists of all ages have recognized the impact of negative stereotypes and the invisibility of Aboriginal people. Many younger people are beginning to resist directly through the creation of counter-images that circulate both in home communities and in the surrounding dominant culture" (Ginsburg 2008, 301).

Imagine a young Indigenous person with a digital camera making a film about her community, interviewing her Elders about her community's history, and having to practise her language. There is creative licence in the opportunity to produce this kind of digital content while at the same time strengthening one's connection to the community, cultures, and histories that are important to self-governance and self-determination. For Ginsburg (1997, 2008), cultural activists are media makers acting in ways that underscore their sense of both political and cultural agency in creating their work. They use their platforms to mediate historical and social ruptures within their own cultures and to assert the presence and concerns of Indigenous peoples in the broader societies that encompass them, thereby bringing together old traditions in new ways.

Attawapiskat First Nation in northern Ontario gained notoriety in 2012 and 2013 as its then chief Theresa Spence called for a meeting between Indigenous leaders and Prime Minister Stephen Harper, undertaking a hunger strike until such a meeting took place. A leaked audit of the community's finances found that roughly four hundred of the band office's financial transactions lacked proper documentation, prompting government officials and many on social media to question her community's financial management (CBC 2013). In response, the hashtag #Ottawapiskat began trending on Twitter to counter many of the misleading narratives that were circulating about the community, calling attention to similar criticisms of the federal government. @Hayden_King wrote "#Ottawapiskat debt hovering around $600,000,000,000. Might be time for a third-party manager." @bigpicguy wrote "Chief Harper has been using the funds of #Ottawapiskat in very untransparent ways. He refuses to cooperate with Mr. Page, the third party mgr," referring to Stephen Harper's public disagreements with the parliamentary budget officer. @gindaanis wrote "I hear the leader of #Ottawapiskat gets free air travel while many of his people barely afford their bus passes," echoing tired criticisms often levelled on Indigenous leadership as people who live well at the expense of their communities.

These online comments through Twitter are examples of what Small (2020) and others refer to as hashtag activism, where social media users use clever keywords to draw attention to their political issues or points of view (Brewster 2014; see also chapter 12). Michelle Raheja's (2010) concept of *visual sovereignty* is also useful for understanding these tweets, describing them as forms of resistance found within media systems that are controlled by non-Indigenous peoples. Twitter, for instance, is a pervasive digital communication platform that is owned, governed, and used by a majority non-Indigenous population. As a result, many misrepresentations circulate through this medium. Visual sovereignty refers to the space between resistance and compliance where Indigenous media producers both operate within the boundaries of the platform while at the same time stretching them (Raheja 2010). This allows Indigenous media creators to use digital platforms like Twitter to deconstruct non-Indigenous generated representations of Indigenous peoples, intervene in larger discussions of Indigenous sovereignty, and advocate for Indigenous cultural and political power. Often, the audience for these acts of visual sovereignty are Indigenous peoples, not others (Raheja 2007). They play on culturally familiar references that resonate with specific Indigenous communities and remind Indigenous peoples of their voice.

Visual sovereignty helps to explain the 2017 controversy of the now infamous "appropriation prize" fund. The controversy stemmed from an article titled "Winning the Appropriation Prize" in a prominent literary journal, where its editor encouraged authors to write about things they do not know, dismissing the idea that culture could be appropriated. The article was even more problematic because it introduced a collection of articles penned by Indigenous writers who were not aware that this piece would preface their work. Canadian journalists and editors took to social media to jokingly offer funds for a real prize (Fearon 2017). Social media backlash by Indigenous voices led some of these journalists to lose their jobs or be reassigned, prompting the *Toronto Star*'s Rick Salutin to suggest that digital platforms such as Twitter change media power dynamics. He writes that "during the long winter of mass media, native writers were often confined to reacting among their peers [...] by mainstream whites" (Salutin 2017). Instead, social media provides a place where "native writers can make their voices and reactions widely heard ..." (Salutin 2017).

A final example of digital cultural activism that is worth mentioning is the Facebook Feeding My Family[5] campaign that draws attention to food subsidy policy affecting Nunavut territories. Community members post photos of food prices (and food quality) in their stores compared with those in the rest of Canada. More importantly, the community engages with commenters to counter tired tropes about food production in the North encouraging the Inuit to hunt more or move away from their communities to larger metropolitan centres. Community members are able to explain their connection to the land, the modern challenges of hunting and fishing, the effects of climate change, and dispel the notion that traditional living is incongruent with modern society.

POTENTIALS

The potentials of Indigenous digital political participation in Canada begin from an acknowledgement that diverse forms of political participation exist. Some Indigenous communities resent the supplanting of traditional models of governance, i.e., those that flourished pre-contact with European arrivals to North America, with settler-colonial ones. Others are finding ways to infuse decision-making processes like voting with their own traditions. Each Indigenous community has their own history, culture, and traditions that diverge from one another and from which unique political practices emerge. What matters is the acknowledgement, as the Two Row Wampum belt suggests, that separate models of governance and political participation can coexist side by side to the benefit of Indigenous and non-Indigenous peoples.

---

5 The campaign continues and can be found at https://www.facebook.com/groups/239422122837039/.

This chapter shows how this principle translates to the realm of digital political participation. Media is a site of political struggle where Indigenous peoples are faced with non-Indigenous technologies that exist pervasively around them, that they use, that act as prominent social forums for political participation, and that circulate information that predominantly comes from non-Indigenous producers. The concepts of resurgence and refusal are useful ways of understanding how Indigenous communities struggle with these technologies to make them their own and assert their sovereignty, self-determination, and self-governance. Indigenous peoples have survived hundreds of years of colonization and forced dispossession and the promise of Indigenous digital political participation is that they will adopt these technologies not only to survive, but to thrive in the digital era. To paraphrase Simpson (2014) once again, there can be more than one political show in town.

REFERENCES

Alfred, Taiaiake. 2005. *Wasáse: Indigenous Pathways of Action and Freedom.* Toronto: Broadview Press.

Alfred, Taiaiake. 2009. "Colonialism and State Dependency." *Journal of Aboriginal Health,* 5: 42–60.

Asch, M. 2014. *On Being Here to Stay: Treaties and Aboriginal Rights in Canada.* Toronto: Univeristy of Toronto Press.

Augustine, Stephen. 2016. *History and Treaties in Mi'kma'ki. Learning from Knowledge Keepers in Mi'kma'ki.* University of Cape Breton; Unama'ki College. http://player.communitylive.ca/Player/Player/46.

Axelrod, P. 2001. *The Promise of Schooling: Education in Canada, 1800–1914.* Toronto: University of Toronto Press.

Bargiel, Jean-Sebastien. 2012. *Federal Voter Turnout in First Nations Reserves.* Ottawa: Elections Canada. http://www.elections.ca/res/rec/part/fvt/fvt_en.pdf.

Berkhoffer, Robert. 1978. *The White Man's Indian: Images of the American Indian from Columbus to the Present.* New York: Vintage Books.

Bird, Elizabeth S. 1996. *Dressing in Feathers: The Construction of the Indian in American Popular Culture.* Boulder: Westview Press.

Bird, Elizabeth S. 2003. *The Audience in Everyday Life: Living in a Media World.* New York: Routledge.

Brewster, Shaquille. 2014. "After Ferguson: Is 'Hashtag Activism' Spurring Policy Changes?" NBC News, December 14. https://www.nbcnews.com/politics/first-read/after-ferguson-hashtag-activism-spurring-policy-changes-n267436.

Cairns, Alan C. 2003. “Aboriginal People’s Electoral Participation in the Canadian Community.” *Electoral Insight* 5 (3): 2–9.

CBC. 2013. “Attawapiskat Chief Slams Audit Leak as ‘Distraction.’” CBC News, January 7. http://www.cbc.ca/news/politics/attawapiskat-chief-slams-audit-leak-as-distraction-1.1318113.

CBC. 2015. “Perry Bellegarde, AFN Chief, Urges People to Vote, Even if He Doesn’t.” CBC News, September 2. http://www.cbc.ca/news/politics/canada-election-2015-assembly-first-nations-bellegarde-1.3212551.

CIRA. 2018. “The Gap between Us: Perspectives on Building a Better Online Canada.” https://cira.ca/sites/default/files/public/cip_report_2018_en.pdf.

Conrad, M.R., and J.K. Hiller. 2001. *Atlantic Canada: A Region in the Making*. Don Mills: Oxford University Press.

Corntassel, Jeff. 2012. “Re-Envisioning Resurgence: Indigenous Pathways to Decolonization and Sustainable Self-Determination.” *Decolonization: Indigeneity, Education & Society* 1 (1): 86–101.

Coulthard, Glen. 2014. *White Skin, Red Masks: Rejecting the Colonial Politics of Recognition*. Minneapolis: University of Minnesota Press.

DeLoria, Vine, Jr. 1995. *Red Earth, White Lies: Native Americans and the Myth of Scientific Fact*. New York: Scribner.

Diabo, Russ. 2015. “First Nations and the Federal Election: An Exercise in Self-termination.” Rocochet Media. https://ricochet.media/en/534/first-nations-and-the-federal-election-an-exercise-in-self-termination.

Elections Canada. 2015. “On-Reserve Voter Turnout – 42nd General Election.” Elections Canada. http://www.elections.ca/content.aspx?section=res&dir=rec/eval/pes2015/ovt&document=index&lang=e.

Fearon, Emily. 2017. “High Profile Canadian Journalists Pledge to Raise Money for ‘Appropriation Prize.’” *Toronto Star*, May 12. https://www.thestar.com/news/gta/2017/05/12/high-profile-canadian-journalists-pledge-to-raise-money-for-appropriation-prize.html.

Fournier, Patrick, and Peter Loewen. 2011. “Aboriginal Electoral Participation in Canada.” Elections Canada. http://www.elections.ca/res/rec/part/abel/AEP_en.pdf.

Francis, Daniel. 2011. *The Imaginary Indian: The Image of the Indian in Canadian Culture*. Vancouver: Arsenal Pulp Press.

Gabel, Chelsea, Karen Bird, Nicole Goodman, and Brian Budd. 2016a. “The Impact of Digital Technology on First Nations Participation and Governance.” *Canadian Journal of Native Studies* 36 (2): 107–27.

Gabel, Chelsea, Karen Bird, Nicole Goodman, and Brian Budd. 2016b. “Indigenous Adoption of Online Voting: A Case Study of Whitefish River First Nation.” *International Indigenous Policy Journal* 7 (3): Article 3. https://doi.org/10.18584/iipj.2016.7.3.3.

Ginsburg, Faye. 1997. “‘From Little Things, Big Things Grow’: Indigenous Media and Cultural Activism.” In *Between Resistance and Revolution*, ed. Dick Fox and Orin Starn, 118–44. New Brunswick, NJ: Rutgers University Press.

Ginsburg, Faye. 2008. "Rethinking the Digital Age." In *Global Indigenous Media*, ed. Pam Wilson and Michelle Stewart, 287–308. Durham: Duke University Press.

Innovation, Science, and Economic Development Canada. 2018. "Federal Funding to Bring High-Speed Internet to Indigenous Communities in Northern Ontario." https://www.newswire.ca/news-releases/federal-funding-to-bring-high-speed-internet-to-indigenous-community-in-northern-ontario-679283953.html.

Kopacz, Maria, and Bessie Lee Lawton. 2011. "The YouTube Indian: Portrayals of Native Americans on a Viral Video Site." *New Media & Society* 13 (2): 330–49. https://doi.org/10.1177/1461444810373532.

Ladner, Kiera L. 2003. "The Alienation of the Nation: Understanding Aboriginal Electoral Participation, 1988–2004." *Electoral Insight* 5 (3): 21–6.

Ladner, Kiera L., and Michael McCrossan. 2007. "The Electoral Participation of Aboriginal People." Working Paper Series on Electoral Participation and Outreach Practices. Ottawa: Elections Canada.

Levi-Peters, Susan. 2017. In-Person Interview with Derek Antoine.

Makoons Media. 2017. Makoons Media About. https://www.makoonsmedia.org/#about-section.

McMahon, Rob. 2011. "The Institutional Development of Indigenous Broadband Infrastructure in Canada and the United States: Two Paths to 'Digital Self-Determination.'" *Canadian Journal of Communication* 36 (1): 115–40. https://doi.org/10.22230/cjc.2011v36n1a2372.

McMahon, Rob, Tim LaHache, and Tim Whiteduck. 2015. "Digital Data Management as Indigenous Resurgence in Kahnawa:ke." *The International Indigenous Policy Journal* 6 (3): Article 6. https://doi.org/10.18584/iipj.2015.6.3.6.

MMNN. n.d. "New Bilingual Mi'kmaq/English Podcast Series Launched." Mi'kmaq Maliseet Nations News. http://www.mmnn.ca/2015/06/new-bilingual-mikmaqenglish-podcast-series-launched/.

Muller, Kathryn. 2007. "The Two 'Mystery' Belts of Grand River: A Biography of the Two Row Wampum and the Friendship Belt." *The American Indian Quarterly* 31 (1): 129–64. https://doi.org/10.1353/aiq.2007.0013.

Palmater, Pam. 2015. "The Source of Our Power Has Always Been in Our People – Not Voting in Federal Elections." *Indigenous Nationhood* (blog). http://indigenousnationhood.blogspot.ca/2015/08/the-source-of-our-power-has-never-been.html.

Parks, Lisa. 2005. *Cultures in Orbit: Satellites and the Televisual.* Durham: Duke University Press.

Poliandri, S. 2011. *First Nations, Identity, and Reserve life.* Lincoln: University of Nebraska Press.

Pratt, Yvonne Poitras. 2010. "Merging New Media with Old Traditions." *Native Studies Review* 19 (1): 1–27.

Raheja, Michelle. 2007. "Reading Nanook's Smile: Visual Sovereignty, Indigenous Revisions of Ethnography, and Atanarjuat (The Fast Runner)." *American Quarterly* 59 (4): 1159–85. https://doi.org/10.1353/aq.2007.0083.

Raheja, Michelle. 2010. *Reservation Reelism: Redfacing, Visual Sovereignty, and Representations of Native Americans in Film*. Lincoln: University of Nebraska Press.

Reid, J. 1995. *Myth, Symbol, and Colonial Encounter: British and Mi'kmaq in Acadia 1700–1867*. Ottawa: University of Ottawa Press.

Salutin, Rick. 2017. "You Mean Cultural Appropriation Isn't about Free Speech? Salutin." *Toronto Star*, May 19. https://www.thestar.com/opinion/commentary/2017/05/19/you-mean-cultural-appropriation-isnt-about-free-speech-salutin.html.

Sandvig, Christian. 2012. "Connection at Ewiiaapaayp Mountain: Indigenous Internet Infrastructure." In *Race after the Internet*, ed. Lisa Nakamura and Peter Chow-White, 168–200. New York: Routledge.

Simpson, Audra. 2014. *Mohawk Interruptus: Political Life across the Borders of Settler States*. Durham: Duke University Press.

Simpson, Leanne. 2011. *Dancing on Our Turtle's Back: Stories of Nishnaabeg Re-creation, Resurgence, and a New Emergence*. Winnipeg: Arbeiter Ring Publishing.

Small, Tamara A. Forthcoming. "The Promises and Perils of Hashtag Feminism." In *Turbulent Times, Transformational Possibilities? Gender and Politics Today and Tomorrow*, ed. Alexandra Dobrowolsky and Fiona MacDonald. Toronto: University of Toronto Press.

Smith, Christine. 2013. "Decolonization a Daily Chore." *Anishnabek News*, November 6. http://anishinabeknews.ca/2013/11/06/decolonization-a-daily-chore/.

Smith, Linda Tuhiwai. 2011. *Decolonizing Methodologies*. London: Zed Books.

Smith, Paul Chaat. 2009. *Everything You Know about Indians Is Wrong*. Minneapolis: University of Minnesota Press.

Stollery, Brad. 2018. "Canada's Digital Divide: Preserving Indigenous Communities Means Bringing Them Online." *The Star*, May 2. https://www.thestar.com/opinion/contributors/2018/05/02/canadas-digital-divide-preserving-indigenous-communities-means-bringing-them-online.html.

Whiteduck, T., and B. Beaton. 2014. "Building First Nation Owned and Managed Fibre Networks across Quebec." *Journal of Community Informatics* 10 (2). http://ci-journal.net/index.php/ciej/article/view/1107/0.

CHAPTER TWELVE

Digital Feminism: Networks of Resistance, Neoliberalism, and New Contexts for Activism in Canada

Samantha C. Thrift

INTRODUCTION

The term "digital feminism" has acquired currency in recent years as a means of succinctly referencing the online practices, networks, and discursive formations cultivated by feminists since the introduction of web-based technologies in the 1990s. While the modifier "digital" signals the importance of internet technologies to the formation of new modes of feminist praxis and community-building, the technological determinism of the phrase can obscure the ways in which the political contexts for activism have also shaped feminists' use of these tools (see introduction).

Coming into force in the 1990s, neoliberalism transformed the political and cultural contexts in which feminist activism occurred in Canada, necessitating a shift in the movement's structure, practices, and objectives. As a result, contemporary feminisms do not resemble past modes of feminist organizing, which had been dominated by institutional frameworks for claims-making against the state. In Canada, the mainstream nationalized women's movement was dominated by established brick-and-mortar organizations like the National Action Committee on the Status of Women (NAC) (1971–2001), the Canadian Advisory Council on the Status of Women (CACSW) (1973–1995) and, in Quebec, the Fédération des femmes du Québec (FFQ) (1966–present).[1] The institutionalized relationship between the national women's movement and the Canadian state had been established in the early 1970s, founded on the shared belief that systemically disadvantaged citizens had a right to engage in collective claims-making against the state which, in turn, bore responsibility to redress such inequalities (Brodie 2007). However, the creeping retraction of federal support for women's activism in Canada beginning in the mid-1980s (in conjunction with an increasingly antagonistic relationship between the nationalized movement and the state rooted in policy differences) demanded feminists innovate methods that did not rely on an institutionalized relationship. The popularization of digital technologies in the 1990s occurred at an opportune moment, as women and girls with access to these "democratized technologies" cultivated new technological, affective, and cultural infrastructures for "doing feminism in the network" (Rentschler and Thrift 2015).

By taking neoliberalism into account, this chapter examines the "digital turn" in feminism, beginning with a review of the political context for feminist organizing in Canada. Then, the chapter addresses both the promise and peril of digital technologies for feminist activism, through a brief review of cyberfeminist optimism as well as more critical perspectives that question the political effectiveness of online activisms. Third, the chapter considers how these predictions were met (or not) in digital feminist activist practice. The chapter closes with a consideration of key challenges and issues confronting Canadian feminists and what they suggest about the possibilities for feminism's digital future. Few scholarly accounts prioritize the role of digital technology when telling the story of feminism in Canada (e.g., Mitchell et al. 2001; Stewart Millar 1998), and fewer still situate that story within the political context of neoliberal entrenchment. This chapter aims to redress that gap by examining feminists' strategic response to the changing technological, political, and ideological contexts for activism in Canada.

1 For a more complete history of the women's movement(s) in Canada and Quebec during this era, refer to Backhouse and Flaherty (1992), Belleau (2007), Dua and Robertson (1999), Newman and White (2013), Rebick (2005), and Suzack et al. (2010).

CONTEXT

Neoliberal political ideology articulates a meritocratic worldview that valorizes individualism and free choice, giving rise to a "governing rationality" that presumes equally "empowered" citizens can (and should) manage their own well-being in lieu of state intervention (Brown 2015, 35). It follows, then, that neoliberal discourse "bracket[s] out the influence of structure and systemic barriers to citizen equality" as a way to rationalize the "abstention of the state" from social policy issues (Brodie 2007, 102–3). The ascendance of neoliberal rationality in the West corresponded with (and facilitated) changing ideas about feminist political struggle, emphasizing the power of individual action – and not collective resistance – to redress gender-based inequalities. The neoliberal feminist subject eschews the need for mobilized feminist response to systemic discrimination, advocating instead a politics of *self*-transformation, by "leaning in" at the workplace (Rottenberg 2014) or purchasing commodified markers of one's "girl power" (Gonick 2006; Taft 2004). The neoliberal model of feminist response "responsibilizes" girls and women to improve their own situations, which are *not* readily conceived of as symptomatic of structural inequalities stemming from their shared experiences as women under patriarchy.

Coming into force in the 1990s, this context for activism also greatly contributed to rumours of feminism's "death." The adoption of neoliberal economic policies, which favoured the withdrawal of federal support for social services and increasing privatization, certainly delivered a near-fatal blow to the Anglo-Canadian women's movement.[2] However, feminism did not perish but changed strategies and, in the process, reorganized the movement's shape, objectives, and practice.[3] Contrary to some news reporting, this did not mean that "the voices demanding change ha[d] largely fallen silent" (Galloway 2010); they were, instead,

2 Feminism in Quebec travelled a different trajectory, maintaining an active political agenda through the 1990s and 2000s and organizing, for instance, the 1995 Marche du pain et des roses. That action provided a model and inspiration for the 1996 march on Parliament, "Bread and Roses, Jobs and Justice," organized by the Canadian Labour Congress and the National Action Committee on the Status of Women.

3 Indeed, as Brenda O'Neill (2017) argues, some younger ("third wave") feminists welcomed the relative freedom that came with the dissolution of feminist institutions, signalling "a rejection of the need for hierarchical organizations to 'speak for' feminists given the risk of exclusion or silencing of voices in the movement" (448).

turning to digital technologies as more accessible and self-directed channels for feminist activism.

For Canadian feminists increasingly "disillusioned with the state as a path for gender justice" (Salime 2014, 18), continuing the work of feminism online not only made sense but became a survival strategy. During the 1990s and 2000s, as Rodgers and Knight (2011) note, feminist groups got creative as they found ways to navigate and survive the changing conditions for activism – from transforming their organizational purpose to reenergizing memberships in order to boost fundraising. Moving operations online was a vital third strategy used by organizations left without a funding source, providing a way to "equalize" the field of political participation.

Feminist websites, online discussion boards, and e-newsletters would also help repair feminism's communication infrastructure, which had been eroded by the shuttering of both feminist journals and high profile feminist "communication hubs" like NAC and CACSW.[4] In a country as territorially expansive as Canada, the internet (and eventually social media) would help overcome the "big country" distances that inhibited many from participating in face-to-face feminist organizing, much of which took place in urban centres. Because it "lower[s] the threshold for involvement in collective action" (Bakardjieva et al. 2012, 1), the internet also invites a broader range of people into feminist conversation, including minority voices that had gone unheard in offline discussions (Rosenbaum 2018, 140). In Canada, this endows digital technologies with special significance for rural women and girls, women of colour, and Indigenous feminist movements. As Tegan Zimmerman (2017, 55) notes, social media have become an "indispensable and essential tool" in contemporary feminist activism, because they "propagate meaningful and necessary critical dialogues on race, feminism, and online

4 Budget cuts in 1990 led to the bankruptcy of four feminist print publications and the closure of eighty women's resource centres, which had provided counselling and health services, legal advice, and education and training. Although other federal departments also faced shrinking budgets that year, feminists viewed these measures as particularly callous given their devastating impact on the communications infrastructure of the women's movement. Referencing the recent killing of fourteen women at Montreal's École Polytechnique, the editors of three feminist periodicals bankrupted by the new budget issued a press release with an impassioned plea: "How are we going to be able to fight the violence that women face daily if we can no longer communicate with each other across the country – if our voices have been silenced?"

representation" (also see Gilio-Whitaker 2015; Raynauld et al. 2018). Similarly, Canadian feminist websites, blogs, and online magazines – such as *Women'space* (1995–2000), *Shameless* (2004–present) and, more recently, *Herizons* (2011–present) and *GUTS* (2013–2020) – ensure that women and girls get to set the agenda of their own feminisms by identifying the issues and ideas that are important to them and talking about them in self-created digital counterpublic spheres (ideas that resonate with the mobilization hypothesis discussed elsewhere in this book). The proliferation of such feminist-created online spaces throughout the 1990s and 2000s led some to envision the internet as a veritable "clubhouse for girls" (Takayoshi et al. 1999; Harris 2008).

DIGITIZATION

Promises & Perils

In the 1990s, cyberfeminism provided a critical framework for thinking about digital technologies as important tools for women's emancipation.[5] Cyberfeminism disrupted prevailing cultural assumptions about computing technology and the internet being a male domain (Tuzcu 2016, 154; Flanagan and Booth 2002), leading some to argue that these technologies held subversive, feminist potential. This perspective was very much inspired by Donna Haraway's 1985 essay, *A Cyborg Manifesto*, wherein a vision of human/machine hybridity (the "cyborg") irrevocably undoes structuring dualisms of modern Western thinking and being, including the binary gender ideology of man/woman. In Haraway's vision, the cyborg is a "promising monster" for feminism – one that transcends the gendered, racialized, and classed identity categories that sustain patriarchal, white supremacist, and colonial domination (1991, 154). In turn, she bids feminists to not eschew digital technology as a site of patriarchal power (born of Cold War-era militarism) but to "take pleasure in the confusion of boundaries made possible by the

5 Milford (2015) makes the case that the plural form – cyberfeminism*s* – better reflects the multiple theoretical positions and praxes signalled by the term. The plurality of cyberfeminist discourses stems, in part, from the different contexts out of which cyberfeminist discourses emerge, including cyberpunk fiction, performance art, philosophical manifestos, and computing and game design (57).

new technologies" (150). Considered an "ur-text" of cyberfeminism, Haraway's manifesto provided an alternative to existing theorizations of women as the "passive victims of technological change" (Wacjman 2004, ch. 1).

Cyberfeminist writers and artists built on Haraway's ideas, arguing that new digital technologies were quintessentially suited for revolutionizing social relations. In her well-known work, *Zeroes + Ones: Digital Women and the New Technoculture* (1997), British cultural theorist Sadie Plant describes the de-hierarchized structure and networked connections characteristic of digital technoculture as "positively feminine," meaning that the eventual "digitalization of culture equals its feminization" (Paasonen 2011, 338). The art-activism of VNS Matrix (1991–7), an Australian cyberfeminist collective known for its irreverent performances, defiantly likens cyberfeminism to a computer virus with the power to infiltrate "big daddy mainframe" (VNS Matrix 1991). In the "new world order" of digital networks and connectivity, "the clitoris is a direct line to the matrix." VNS Matrix's sexualization of the "pure" data space of the virtual realm codes cyberspace as female, making a symbolic claim on digital technologies. And in her *Cyberfeminism* manifesto, Toronto-based media artist Nancy Paterson (1992) argues that "new electronic technologies" are key to creating a "political identity and unity without relying on a logic or language of exclusion" (para 7). Describing digital technologies as "patriarchy's blind spot," Paterson heralds cyberspace as the place where women can "trade-in, remodel or even leave behind the physical nature with which we are [...] burdened" (para 15). In these early works, cyberfeminism lays claim to "the digital," signalling the centrality of these technologies to the future of the feminist project.

Cyberfeminist discourses tap into the optimism surrounding the "internet revolution" of the 1990s. At the time, celebratory narratives lauded the internet as an egalitarian and democratizing technology (see introduction). Given its capacity to quickly connect people across vast distances, the internet represented the fullest articulation yet of McLuhan's "global village." In addition, the internet held "star appeal" for women and other minoritized subjects who "struggled with the straightjacket of identity" (Plant 1995, 28); pseudonymous online identity was thought to afford minority subjects freedom from the (gendered, racialized, classed, etc.) trappings of their corporeal selves. Popular narratives about technology were also shaped by science fiction and cyberpunk renderings of online worlds (or "cyberspace") as a "new frontier," where "individuals might self-actualize and be free" (Ricker Schulte 2011, 732). The significance of American frontier mythology is evident not only in the jargon of the era – with its "interface cowboys" (Gibson 1984) – but also in the idea that the internet constitutes a "digital public sphere"; that is, a place where people "could be informed, organize their own cultures, and thereby become the ultimate democratic citizens" (Ricker Schulte 2011, 732; also Rheingold 2002). While cyberfeminists' calls to "hijack the toys from technocowboys" (Evans 2014, para. 6) rejected the masculinist framing of digital frontierism, the idea that the internet could be a sovereign space for feminist self-expression, community building, and organizing took hold.

For those with access, "democratized technologies" could further empower women and girls as media creators. Influenced by the do-it-yourself ethos of the riot grrrl movement, for example, "cybergrrrls" integrated digital technology into existing feminist media-making practices, creating zines, music, compact discs, videos, and art-activism that embrace a "low-tech, amateur, hybrid" aesthetic (Kaeh Garrison 2000, 151). E-zines, among other media forms, ensured young feminists could "control how they speak, write, and inhabit discursive space" free from media gatekeeping, unencumbered by the demands of the commercial marketplace, and independent of feminist organizations' pre-existing agendas (Scott-Dixon 2001, 305). Digital technologies, then, could "enable a shift in the locus of political activism" from (decaying) institutional frameworks to networked hubs of (sub)cultural activity formed in relation to the online circulation of feminist media (Kaeh Garrison 2000, 163). Dispersed and proliferate, subcultural feminist networks held promise as a means to expand the sites of feminist political praxis during a period of neoliberal constraint.

Digital feminism also provoked cautionary, even pessimistic, responses. Writing in 1998, American artist-activist Faith Wilding cautioned against exuberant cyberfeminist visions of the internet as a "free space where gender does not matter" (9). Instead, she argued that digital technologies cannot escape the social frameworks from which they emerge, which are "embedded in economic, political, and cultural environments that are still deeply sexist and racist" (9). Digital technologies, in other words, are "master's tools" born of masculinist institutions and have "very different meanings and uses for different populations"

(9; also Chun 2006). Wilding's point was that networked technologies are neither intrinsically "feminine" nor feminist; therefore, cyberfeminists would need to *create* feminist political and cultural environments online, based on theoretically and historically informed practice, rather than presume an inherent equality of condition stemming from the internet's capacity for the free exchange of information across boundaries (see also Boler 2008). These points warn against cyberfeminist complacency about persistent issues, such as the ongoing "digital divide" (for those without access to digital technologies) and participation gap (for those without the training or skill set to use digital tools). The politics of difference are also at stake in these debates, necessitating vigilance in the creation of digital feminist communities so as not to repeat the exclusions perpetuated by hegemonic (white, middle-class, Western) feminisms.

Such critiques highlight the risk of offline power relations being reproduced in online spaces. Instead of offering "an escape from gender" (Ricker Schulte 2011, 733), digital publics evidence comparable forms of discrimination, harassment, and threat as found in the "real" world. The anonymity of much online commenting offers protection for those making sexist, misogynist, racist, and homo- and transphobic posts, thus *amplifying* the abuse already experienced by women, racialized, and queer people in offline public spaces (Braidotti 1996; Penny 2014). Others note that characterizing this kind of targeted harassment as mere "trolling" does not capture the culturally systemic and naturalized misogyny, racism, and queerphobia that informs online attacks (Banet-Weiser and Miltner 2016; Consalvo 2012; Nakamura 2002). Indeed, Laurie Penny (2014, 176) argues that online harassment is a form of "patriarchal surveillance" that is meant to police women's speech and behaviour in digital public space, where the end goal is "to shame and frighten women out of engaging online." And, as Amanda Hess (2014) points out, digital media corporations are not necessarily responsive to these issues, given the "free speech" ethos driving participatory media platforms such as Twitter.[6] Changes in digital communication platforms also tend to outpace legal frameworks, making it

6 In late 2017, Twitter announced it would censure accounts posting non-consensual nudity, "revenge porn," and hidden camera content. The regulations emerged in the wake of the #WomenBoycottTwitter campaign, which called out the company for failing to protect some users, particularly women of colour, from being victimized.

difficult to prosecute crimes of cyberstalking, nonconsensual sexting, and other forms of online predation (Citron and Franks 2014; Henry and Powell 2016). When women and other minority subjects are denied full access to and participation in this increasingly central sphere of public life for any reason, including cyberharassment, there are emotional, economic, and political ramifications. Significantly, there are also lethal consequences, as illustrated by the case of Canadian teenager Amanda Todd, who died by suicide in 2012. In a YouTube video, Todd detailed the online sexual extortion and cyberbullying she had experienced for more than a year. Her video, which accumulated more than twelve million views after her death, sparked a criminal investigation into Todd's online exploitation as well as legislative efforts to combat cyberbullying. In another case, seventeen-year-old Nova Scotia high school student Rehtaeh Parsons died from complications arising from a suicide attempt, which had followed extensive "slut shaming" in the wake of the online distribution of photos taken of her reported gang rape by four boys in 2011.

A pivotal issue for digital feminists is combating rape culture, on- and offline, as seen in feminist hashtags like #BeenRapedNeverReported and #MeToo. For feminist organizers, however, the (unpaid) labour of managing these types of campaigns can be fatiguing, leading to panic attacks or burn out (Mendes et al. 2018). The work of maintaining these campaigns involves emotionally taxing tasks like "listening to stories of abuse, harassment, misogyny, and sexism" (239). For those who choose to share their stories, participation often means recounting past traumatic experiences in social media forums, which can pose emotional and social risks. Although hidden under the guise of the "easy" activism of hashtag campaigns, digital activism often calls upon the already limited resources and labour provided by those most targeted for and affected by exploitation (see also Boler et al. 2014).

Others have also raised concerns about the political effectiveness of digital activism. In some cases, these questions stem from a perceived divide between on- and offline modes of activism. Critics fear that "slacktivism" – such as liking or sharing content on social media or signing an e-petition – risks displacing on the ground forms of political protest (Morozov 2009). Others perceive a widening gap between social media-driven activism, for example, and institutional politics (Dean 2005), positing that digital protest rarely culminates in policy change because it can be easily dismissed. The decentralized, nonhierarchical structure of online mobilizations is also critiqued for giving rise to leaderless movements that lack a clear, unifying political agenda (see chapter 10). In Canada and elsewhere, feminist activists have been navigating the vagaries of more "horizontal" modes of assembly since at least the 1970s. Rooted in a commitment to developing an "equality of condition" within feminist groups (Vickers et al. 1993, 176), this method can nonetheless create confusion around a movement's purpose or agenda in the public eye.

Further, scholarship on the political economy of digital technologies situates online activism in the context of neoliberal capitalism, arguing that online expressions of political dissent produce merely the feeling (or "fantasy") of democratic participation (Dean 2009). In this view, digital activism rarely leads to concrete social and/or political change because, in the global flow of information, online activity – including activism – becomes a commodity. Jodi Dean (2005) refers to this as "communicative capitalism," wherein digital protest is consumed as just another piece of "media chatter" that battles for visibility and relevancy alongside the commentaries of an array of other political actors – politicians, governments, television pundits, etc. – across multiple print and digital platforms (53). Therefore, governing bodies can "dismiss contrary views as 'just another opinion'" rather than being held in check or "threatened" by global information technologies (Welsh 2013, 317). Indeed, according to Darin Barney (2008), the popular logic that "if we just had more and better communication, more and better information, and more and better opportunities to participate, everything would be fine" unduly celebrates the proliferation of participatory media as a democratic good while failing to recognize that more radical forms of democracy also require motivation, judgment, and political action (91). In these formulations, "too much communication" can dilute activist practice and risk de-politicizing calls for change.

Practice

The "practice" of digital feminism is best understood in relation to the changing ideological and political context for activism in Canada, some of which has been addressed. To reiterate, by the 1990s, an ideological sea change had eroded the tenets of social liberalism that fuelled the creation of federal offices and women's organizations mandated with securing equal status for Canadian women and girls. A series of federal defunding measures led to the closure of national feminist organizations by the early 2000s. In 2006, Conservative prime minister Stephen Harper's government imposed further constraints on women's claims-making, when it closed the majority of Status of Women Canada (SWC) offices and eliminated funding for those groups doing advocacy, research, or lobbying on social justice issues. At the same time, references to "women's equality" in the SWC's mandate were replaced with "women's participation" in the life of the nation, articulating a postfeminist view of Canada as already gender equal. Former NAC president Judy Rebick condemned the Harper government's budget cuts as "the nail in the coffin" of a Canadian commitment to equality-seeking groups first established with the 1970 Royal Commission on the Status of Women (Rebick 2006).

Cumulatively, these measures effectively silence society's most marginalized by decimating the institutional infrastructure for feminist advocacy, research, and lobbying. Lacking these resources, social groups with little political power would have rare opportunity for their interests to be heard by policy makers or represented in policy making processes. Moreover, these moves delegitimized feminists' claims in the public eye. As Rodgers and Knight (2011) note, these events reflect more than neoliberalized economic policy in Canada; they also manifest an ideological interest in "reduc[ing] the prominence of feminist claimsmaking within the Canadian state" (571). This did not mean that feminism itself had "died" (despite reports to the contrary) but rather that feminists were compelled to "rethink the parameters of political agency" (Laurie and Bondi 2005, 5) in order to subvert these constraints. An institutionally led, nationalized movement premised on principles of social liberalism was no longer viable, leading feminists to revise their activist practices in order to (re)build feminism's capacity to collectively challenge the new social paradigm of neoliberal patriarchy.

Initially, a primary goal for feminists in the 1990s was to establish feminist community online via "woman friendly" websites, chat rooms, and listservs. The *Women'space* (1995–2000) website, for example, aggregated digital resources created by and for distinct feminist readerships in Canada, from "Girls WWW Resources" and "Madgrrrls" to "Francophone Women Weaving the Web" and "The Rural Womyn Zone." The site aimed to "promote accessibility to the web" and to act as a hub for "the exchange of experiences and ideas among women's groups" (readers were invited to directly communicate with the editors via email or letter). Digital feminist culture, however, provided more than a "room of one's own" for Canadian women on the web. Sites like *Women'space* helped re-build a much-needed communication infrastructure that could channel resources where they were needed, raise the visibility of local activities, and strategize feminist actions at the national and transnational level. As Scott-Dixon (2001) notes, this illustrates an important transition in feminists' political use of the internet – from "*being* online to *acting* online" (305).

In recent decades, "acting online" has taken many forms (such as feminist blogging, hashtags, memes, and apps), but common among them is the strategic use of emerging digital tools and platforms to foster activist mobilization, engagement, practice, and intervention/resistance. Feminist hashtags, memes, and blogging have been dismissed by critics as a form of "discursive activism" (Stacey 1997) that bears little real-world impact. However, the value of these modes of feminist activism lies in their capacity to intervene in mainstream narratives and shape public discourse by presenting alternative ideas about politics and culture for people to consider (Rosenbaum 2018, 140–1). For instance, the #BeenRapedNeverReported hashtag challenges victim-blaming rhetoric circulating in the wake of the 2014 arrest of CBC radio host Jian Ghomeshi on sexual assault charges. There, individuals' reluctance to report sexual violence to authorities was used to discredit their allegations. Following the initial use of the hashtag by two Canadian journalists, who related their own accounts of waiting to report, approximately forty thousand assault survivors took to Twitter to share their own reasons for not reporting – within the first forty-eight hours alone. As Keller et al. (2016, 6) observe, "[w]hile the tweets were diverse, they all carried the common theme that it remained professionally, emotionally, and even physically costly to report sexual violence to authorities, disrupting the prevalent myth that unreported assaults are illegitimate." Subsequent media coverage of the hashtag's popularity articulated a different framework for understanding that was based on survivors' experiences, providing a "new social paradigm" for interpreting and responding to sexual violence (Young 1997, 3).

Still, people's use of social media to post about experiences of racism, sexism, misogyny, harassment, or assault is viewed by some critics as a “micro-rebellion” that does little to change culture. The emphasis on individual, rather than collective, action to contest such acts of violence is an outcome of neoliberalism. Therefore, an objective of digital activism has been to circumvent the “individualization” of feminism, where personal revolutions act as stand-ins for political ones. When “collected” under a common hashtag or made visible through viral circulation, individuals’ Tweets, posts, memes, and comments testify to both the character and the pervasiveness of intersectional forms of oppression, making it apparent and undeniable. By highlighting the “interplay of the individual and the collective,” hashtag feminism disrupts neoliberal narratives that characterize discriminatory or abusive acts as anomalous or exceptional experiences, rather than structural (Baer 2016, 29; Thrift 2014).

Importantly, the outcomes of digital feminism manifest both on- and offline. Such was the case with the local activism of #SafeStampede, an instance of hashtag feminism in which (mostly) women took to social media to share personal stories of sexual harassment they experienced while attending the 2016 Calgary Stampede. The hashtag triggered an outpouring of harassment stories, pulling the curtain back on a rape culture problem at the Stampede. Based on this evidence, the local police service and municipal government implemented a nearly $50,000 fund for consent education and bystander intervention training (“Calgary Gets Consent”), to be run annually in conjunction with the Calgary Sexual Health Centre (Edwardson 2017). Certainly, not all feminist hashtags generate such responses, particularly from governments or police, however the above examples offer a counterpoint to critiques of online feminist activism being politically ineffectual.

These digital feminist practices of sharing, documenting, and naming abuses illustrate but a few ways in which feminists have expanded their capacity to collectively respond to (and intervene in) cultures of discrimination and harassment under neoliberal constraint. In application, these practices transform quotidian tools of communication, like smartphones, into “networked technologies that signify particularly mobile and ubiquitous tools of activist documentation and dissemination” (Rentschler 2014, 74). Mobile phone apps like Hollaback!, for instance, increase “feminist response-ability” (i.e., the capacity to respond, to “speak” through social media-enabled documentation) to instances of street harassment through the use of video, audio recording, and Google mapping (Rentschler 2014, 69). As Rentschler (2014, 69) notes, these practices engender a "movement culture" that is produced through the "network-ability of feminist online response," rather than feminist institutions (Rentschler 2014, 69; see also Fotopoulou 2017).

While the above examples illustrate that combating rape culture is a priority issue for digital feminists, these practices also target sexism in electoral politics in Canada. Often, scathing or irreverent humour frames these critiques, as was the case with the 2013 #askjustin hashtag – a feminist Twitter take-down of the sexist framing of a Liberal party campaign event meant to win over Canada's women voters. The "Justin Unplugged" event solicited voters to "*really* get to know the future prime minister" (emphasis in original). Styled in the pop aesthetic of a teen magazine, the invitation promised attendees three things – "Cocktails. Candid conversation. Curiosity-inducing ideas" – as well as discussion of women's "favourite virtue" and "real life heroes." Under the #askjustin hashtag, social media users from across the political spectrum mocked the sexist and condescending tone used to address women voters: "Dear Justin, Will the Keystone XL pipeline make my butt look fat?" and "#askjustin would you rather fight 100 duck-sized horses or one horse-sized duck also the ducks and horses are all ladies" (Janis 2013). The use of pointed humour in feminist hashtags and political memes, like #askjustin, "illustrates how social bonds form around memetic in-jokes, where people who get the joke come to see themselves as part of a community" (Rentschler and Thrift 2015, 343). In this example, women constituents who welcome an invitation "into" political conversation (but question terms of engagement that position them in such stereotypical fashion) constitute an online community arising from the "networked laughter" of feminist critique, demonstrating the ad hoc, "messy," and "unlikely" coalitions characteristic of online feminisms (Kaeh Garrison 2000).

POTENTIALS

In Canada, digital feminism emerged in a moment of flux, as a once-prominent nationalized women's movement lost its political standing and, along with it, the capacity to successfully lobby governments to make progressive policy changes that would improve the lives of women and girls. In 2015, however, an online coalition of Canadian women's and social justice groups (called the Alliance for Women's Rights) drew on the institutional memory of 1980s Canadian feminism to launch an election-time campaign that would compel federal leaders to address women's rights issues in their policy platforms. Called "Up for Debate," the campaign invited the five prime ministerial candidates to participate in a live televised debate on women's issues: ending violence against women and girls, ending women's economic inequality, and supporting women's leadership and organizations. The campaign aimed to reopen the conversation between feminist and political actors and to renew the Canadian state's commitment to redressing issues of gender-based inequality.

Feminism's re-entrance to the national political stage coincided with the thirtieth anniversary of the first leaders' debate on women's issues, held in 1984; the 2015 debate aimed to remediate that moment of "peak feminism" in Canada (Thrift 2018). Like much digital activism, the Alliance for Women's Rights was an ad hoc coalition, consisting of more than 175 organizations, which united temporarily in support of the Up for Debate campaign. Using social media to publicize the campaign, the Alliance circulated promotional materials that identify feminism as a national concern and highlight the agenda's relevance to a broad spectrum of Canadian women and girls, including Indigenous and other racialized minorities, immigrants and refugees, and those in poverty. This framing of feminism as a "Canadian" movement is rhetorically significant because it draws upon the rich history of national level feminist organizing here, while also asserting a wide base of support for the campaign's claim that federal political actors must confront the ongoing crisis of social inequality in Canada. And while the televised debate did not ultimately take place, in the end, four of five candidates did grant one-on-one interviews, marking the first time in decades that women's issues made it onto a federal election agenda in Canada. The Alliance for Women's Rights presented a near-seamless articulation of (past) institutional and (present) networked modes of feminist media activism, potentially signalling the emergence of a new mode of feminist mobilization based on the strategic integration of digital feminist practices with institutional frameworks for claims-making.

An ongoing challenge for feminists in Canada will be cultivating intersectional online communities and practices that use digital platforms in ways that combat racism and white supremacy, both on- and offline. As Canadian scholar and feminist activist Sunera Thobani remarked in a 2018 CBC interview, "feminism doesn't live in a space *outside* these racial politics. Young women don't grow up outside these racial politics. If anti-racist politics aren't central to how we think about feminist politics in this moment, that's a major cause of concern" (Chattopadhyay 2018). Despite being relatively "open" platforms that lower barriers to participation for many marginalized people, digital feminist spaces are in no way immune from perpetuating racial exclusions. An exemplary case of this was the controversy surrounding the release of the infamous "#FemFutures: Online Revolutions" (Martin and Valenti 2013) report in the US, which culminated in feminists of colour critiquing digital feminism as a manifestation of white feminism (Loza 2014). More recently, the centring of Western, white (and white celebrity) voices in #MeToo elided not only activist Tarana Burke's founding role but also the specificity of racialized women and men's experiences of sexual violence.[7] In Canada, Indigenous women's leadership in the Idle No More and #MMIWG (Missing and Murdered Indigenous Women and Girls) movements counters these erasures, mobilizing public and political attention on the poor environmental, economic, and security conditions experienced by First Nations peoples under settler-colonialism (see chapter 11). The #MMIWG hashtag, launched during the 2015 Canadian federal election campaign, pressured political parties to address the high rate of murdered and missing Indigenous women and girls and to convene a national inquiry into the issue, among other measures (Felt 2016). More than a hashtag, #MMIWG also takes shape online as a multi-platform campaign that continues to raise awareness through its website, digital films, and a daily tweet. Well after the 2015 election, #MMIWG activism also persisted through its inclusion in transnational feminist movements, like #MeToo and Women's March Canada, demonstrating the longevity of some digital feminist coalitions.

Mass mobilizations like the Women's Marches of 2017 and 2018 highlight the fact that digital feminism is never strictly digital and invariably

7 Also see Khoja-Moolji (2015) on the reproduction of global power relations in digital feminist activism, as illustrated by her analysis of #BringBackOurGirls.

intersects with offline activism. For instance, the raw emotion and energy that often sparks digital feminist movements can drive online protest offline, manifesting in transnational street demonstrations, such as 2011's "viral" SlutWalk and the more recent Women's Marches, as well as new feminist material cultures (i.e., "pussy hats," Nasty Woman T-shirts, and Handmaid's Tale costumes). Activists' creation and use of hashtagged slogans and feminist memes in protest signage and sartorial expression also evidences the way in which "visual cues of hashtag activism mark movements of social justice" (Geiseler 2019, 4). As Geiseler (2019) notes in her analysis of #MeToo, these cues heighten recognition of a feminist movement and stand to increase participation, both on- and offline. Alternatively, in the case of women-led movements like Idle No More that originate in on-the-ground actions, such as Attawapiskat Chief Theresa Spence's 2012 hunger strike, participants will utilize social media to support additional offline protest activity – like publicly held round dances and blockades – by disseminating information, coordinating participation, and documenting events for non-local audiences.

Indeed, some researchers argue that the transformative political potential of online activism is only realizable when "sustained by coordinated on-the-ground activism offline" (Fischer 2016, 755), like political lobbying, street demonstrations, occupations, and protest art installations. Métis artist Jaime Black's REDress project, for instance, draws public attention to the ongoing gendered and racialized violence perpetrated against Indigenous women in Canada. While the project is supported by the artist's website and propagates in online photos hashtagged with #MMIWG and #redressproject, the main intervention it poses – i.e., an unexpected encounter with a symbolic (and haunting) red dress in the outdoors – is direct, personal, highly affective and, arguably, not replicable online. Similarly, Black's 2019 Red River snow sculpture project, in which six prone figures carved from snow lay near the river bank, brings local specificity and attention to the issue of missing and murdered Indigenous women in Winnipeg – many of whom were found deceased in the vicinity of the Red River. These public works are given a digital afterlife through their online circulation in news stories and social media documentation. These examples also illustrate how digital feminist activism gets informed by the exigencies of local issues, politics, and values. As Scharff et al. (2016, 11) note, the politics of location inform the "new spaces" for activism, as material conditions of local protest shape and contribute to digital movement culture(s).

In Canada, at the same time that activists work to bridge the gap between electoral politics and digital feminist activism with campaigns like Up for Debate and #MMIWG, the virulent cyberharassment of women politicians threatens democratic processes by deterring women from running for political office, restricting their policy contributions, and inhibiting those in office from fulfilling their duties (Krook 2017, 74). Women from across the political spectrum have spoken out against the attacks, which range from sexist name-calling (e.g., "traitorous bitch," "dumb broad," "Climate Change Barbie"[8]) to rape and death threats. As women are harassed out of elected office, as was the case with two female candidates running for the Alberta Conservative party leadership in 2016, citizens are deprived of "exposure to full debate and to the contributions that women can make to solving society's problems" (Krook 2017, 75) and women are denied status as full political actors.

The misogyny targeting women in Canadian politics stands in contrast to the 2015 election of the "first feminist Prime Minister," Justin Trudeau. Trudeau became a global feminist icon (and feminist meme) following his pithy justification for creating Canada's first gender-parity cabinet: "Because it's 2015." In 2017, the government earned another "feminist first" with the unveiling of its "feminist foreign aid policy," which allocates $150 million to local women's organizations in developing countries (Wattie 2017). The Liberal government's stated commitment to advancing gender equality in Canada is also evident in its use of gender-based analysis[9] in the preparation of the 2017 and 2018 federal budgets as well as in its firm pro-choice position on women's

---

8 In late 2017, far-right media outlet *The Rebel* repeatedly invoked the sexist moniker "Climate Change Barbie" (or #ClimateBarbie) when referring to federal environment minister Catherine McKenna, whose platform pursued clean energy alternatives. The use of the sexist insult aimed to undermine McKenna's legitimacy as a political actor, by reducing her to a stereotype of "dumb blond" femininity. McKenna publicly denounced *Rebel*'s use of the term in its reporting, tweeting that "We need more women in politics. Your sexist comments won't stop us."

9 Gender-based analysis assesses the differential impact of policy, including taxation and spending measures, on women and men. These assessments can then guide policy development, so as to ameliorate the economic inequalities stemming from gender, race and ethnicity, age, and sexual orientation.

reproductive rights. This recent shift toward feminist policy making at the federal level has not engendered feminist complacency, however, as critics note the lack of political movement on Canada's persistent gender wage gap or the 2019 ousting of former attorney general Jody Wilson-Raybould and MP Jane Philpott from the Liberal caucus over the SNC-Lavalin affair – a move that sparked deep speculation and anger over the government's apparent willingness to use women and Indigenous women as political props, rather than support them as full political actors. When "feminism" is leaned on as a central pillar of federal policy making, questions arise about how Canadian feminism will be defined in coming years and whose voice(s) will be invited to participate in those conversations.

Far from achieving a sense of full-circle finality, then, feminism in Canada acquires a renewed sense of urgency and purpose – and not only because it remains unclear if gender-equality seeking governments constitute a new standard or a political fad. As Sarah Banet-Weiser (2015) observes, "when feminism is in the air the way it is in current culture, it is not surprising to find backlash from patriarchal culture" (para. 6). In recent years, this backlash has become apparent in a rising tide of right-wing populism, evidencing Canada's vulnerability to the most deplorable manifestations of reactionary politics. Digital feminism, in Canada and elsewhere, has increased feminists' capacity to collectively respond to such threats through the creation of technological, political, and cultural networks of intervention and resistance.

REFERENCES

Backhouse, Constance, and David H. Flaherty. 1992. *Challenging Times: The Women's Movement in Canada and the United States*. Montreal: McGill-Queen's University Press.

Baer, Hester. 2016. "Redoing Feminism: Digital Activism, Body Politics, and Neoliberalism." *Feminist Media Studies* 16 (1): 17–34. https://doi.org/10.1080/14680777.2015.1093070.

Bakardjieva, Maria, Jakob Svensson, and Marko Skoric. 2012. "Digital Citizenship and Activism: Questions of Power and Participation Online." *JeDEM* 4 (1): i–iv. https://doi.org/10.29379/jedem.v4i1.113.

Banet-Weiser, Sarah. 2015. "Popular Misogyny: A Zeitgeist." *Culture Digitally*, January 21. http://culturedigitally.org/2015/01/popular-misogyny-a-zeitgeist/.

Banet-Weiser, Sarah, and Kate Miltner. 2016. "#MasculinitySoFragile: Culture, Structure, and Networked Misogyny." *Feminist Media Studies* 16 (1): 171–4. https://doi.org/10.1080/14680777.2016.1120490.

Barney, Darin. 2008. "Politics and Emerging Media: The Revenge of Publicity." *Global Media Journal (Canadian Edition)* 1 (1): 89–106.

Belleau, Marie-Claire. 2007. "'L'intersectionnalité': Feminism in a Divided World; Québec-Canada." In *Feminist Politics: Identity, Difference, Agency*, ed. Dianna Taylor, Deborah Orr, Christa Rainwater, Eileen Kahl, and Kathleen Earle, 51–61. Plymouth: Rowman & Littlefield.

Boler, Meg, ed. 2008. *Digital Media and Democracy: Tactics in Hard Times.* Cambridge, MA: MIT Press.

Boler, Meg, Averie Macdonald, Christina Nitsou, and Anne Harris. 2014. "Connective Labour and Social Media: Women's Roles in the 'Leaderless' Occupy Movement." *Convergence* 20 (4): 438–60. https://doi.org/10.1177/1354856514541353.

Braidotti, Rosi. 1996. "Cyberfeminism with a Difference." *New Formations* 29 (Summer): 9–25.

Brodie, Janine. 2007. "Reforming Social Justice in Neoliberal Times." *Studies in Social Justice* 1 (2): 93–107. https://doi.org/10.26522/ssj.v1i2.972.

Brown, Wendy. 2015. *Undoing the Demos: Neoliberalism's Stealth Revolution.* Brooklyn: Zone Books.

Chattopadhyay, Piya. 2018. "What Do Longtime Feminists Think of Today's Feminism?" *Out in the Open*, CBC Radio, January 28. http://www.cbc.ca/radio/outintheopen/that-f-word-1.4494880.

Chun, Wendy Hui Kyong. 2006. *Control and Freedom: Power and Paranoia in the Age of Fibre Optics.* Cambridge, MA: MIT Press.

Citron, Danielle Keats, and Mary Anne Franks. 2014. "Criminalizing Revenge Porn." *Wake Forest Law Review* 49 (2): 345–91.

Consalvo, Mia. 2012. "Confronting Toxic Gamer Culture: A Challenge for Feminist Game Studies Scholars." *Ada: A Journal of Gender, New Media, and Technology* 1. https://doi.org/10.7264/N33X84KH.

Dean, Jodi. 2005. "Communicative Capitalism: Circulation and the Foreclosure of Politics." *Cultural Politics* 1 (1): 51–74. https://doi.org/10.2752/174321905778054845.

Dean, Jodi. 2009. *Democracy and Other Neoliberal Fantasies: Communicative Capitalism and Left Politics.* Durham: Duke University Press.

Dua, Enakshi, and Angela Robertson, eds. 1999. *Scratching the Surface: Canadian Anti-Racist Feminist Thought.* Toronto: Women's Press.

Edwardson, Lucie. 2017. "'Consent Is How We Roll' in Calgary." *Calgary StarMetro*, July 6. https://www.pressreader.com/canada/starmetro-calgary/20170706/281565175789762.

Evans, Claire. 2014. "'We Are the Future Cunt': CyberFeminism in the 90s." *Motherboard VICE*, January 20. https://motherboard.vice.com/en_us/article/4x37gb/we-are-the-future-cunt-cyberfeminism-in-the-90s.

Felt, Mylynn. 2016. "Mobilizing Affective Political Networks: The Role of Affect in Calls for a National Inquiry to Murdered and Missing Indigenous Women during the 2015 Canadian Federal Election." *Proceedings of the 7th 2016 International Conference on Social Media & Society.* London: ACM.

Fischer, Mia. 2016. "#Free_CeCe: The Material Convergence of Social Media Activism." *Feminist Media Studies* 16 (5): 755–71. https://doi.org/10.1080/14680777.2016.1140668.

Flanagan, Mary, and Austin Booth. 2002. *Reload: Rethinking Women and Cyberculture.* Cambridge, MA: MIT Press.

Fotopoulou, Aristea. 2017. *Feminist Activism and Digital Networks: Between Empowerment and Vulnerability.* London: Palgrave.

Galloway, Gloria. 2010. "'Third Wave' of Feminism Urged by Prominent Canadian Women." *Globe & Mail,* September 9. https://www.theglobeandmail.com/news/politics/third-wave-of-feminism- urged-by-prominent-canadian-women/article1379710/.

Geiseler, Carly. 2019. *The Voices of #MeToo: From Grassroots Activism to a Viral Roar.* Lanham, MD: Rowman & Littlefield.

Gibson, William. 1984. *Neuromancer.* New York: Ace Publishing.

Gilio-Whitaker, Dina. 2015. "Idle No More and Fourth World Social Movements in the New Millennium." *South Atlantic Quarterly* 114 (4): 866–77. https://doi.org/10.1215/00382876-3157391.

Gonick, Marnina. 2006. "Between 'Girl Power' and 'Reviving Ophelia': Constituting the Neoliberal Girl Subject." *NWSA Journal* 18 (2): 1–23. https://doi.org/10.2979/NWS.2006.18.2.1.

Haraway, Donna. 1991. "A Cyborg Manifesto: Science, Technology, and Socialist-Feminism in the Late Twentieth Century." In *Simians, Cyborgs, and Women: The Reinvention of Nature,* ed. Donna Haraway, 149–81. New York: Routledge.

Harris, Anita. 2008. *Next Wave Cultures: Feminism, Subcultures, Activism.* New York: Routledge.

Henry, Nicola, and Anastasia Powell. 2016. "Sexual Violence in the Digital Age: The Scope and Limits of Criminal Law." *Social and Legal Studies* 25 (4): 397–418. https://doi.org/10.1177/0964663915624273.

Hess, Amanda. 2014. "Why Women Aren't Welcome on the Internet." *Pacific Standard,* January 6. https://psmag.com/social-justice/women-arent-welcome-internet-72170.

Janis, Andrea. 2013. "Justin Trudeau's 'Ladies' Event Gets Twitter Take-Down." *CTV News,* November 7. https://www.ctvnews.ca/politics/justin-trudeau-s-ladies-event-gets-twitter-takedown-1.1532338.

Kaeh Garrison, E. 2000. "U.S. Feminism – Grrrl Style! Youth (Sub)cultures and the Technologies of the Third Wave." In *No Permanent Waves: Recasting Histories of US Feminism,* ed. Nancy Hewitt, 379–402. Piscataway, NJ: Rutgers University Press.

Keller, Jessalynn, Kaitlynn Mendes, and Jessica Ringrose. 2016. "Speaking 'Unspeakable Things': Documenting Digital Feminist Response to Rape

Culture." *Journal of Gender Studies* 27 (1): 22–36. https://doi.org/10.1080/09589236.2016.1211511.

Khoja-Moolji, Shenila. 2015. "Becoming An 'Intimate Publics': Exploring the Affective Intensities of Hashtag Feminism." *Feminist Media Studies* 15 (2): 347–50. https://doi.org/10.1080/14680777.2015.1008747.

Krook, Mona Lena. 2017. "Violence against Women in Politics." *Journal of Democracy* 28 (1): 74–88. https://doi.org/10.1353/jod.2017.0007.

Laurie, Nina, and Liz Bondi. 2005. "Introduction." In *Working the Spaces of Neoliberalism: Activism, Professionalism, and Incorporation*, ed. Nina Laurie and Liz Bondi, 1–8. Oxford: Blackwell Publishing.

Loza, Suzanne. 2014. "Hashtag Feminism, #SolidarityIsForWhiteWomen, and the Other #FemFuture." *Ada: A Journal of Gender, New Media & Cultural Studies* 5. https://doi.org/10.7264/N337770V.

Martin, Courtney, and Vanessa Valenti. 2013. "#FemFuture: Online Revolution." *New Feminist Solutions* 8: 1–34. http://bcrw.barnard.edu/wp-content/nfs/reports/NFS8-FemFuture-Online-Revolution-Report.pdf.

Mendes, Kaitlynn, Jessica Ringrose, and Jessalynn Keller. 2018. "#MeToo and the Promises and Pitfalls of Challenging Rape Culture through Digital Feminist Activism." *European Journal of Women's Studies* 25 (2): 236–46. https://doi.org/10.1177/1350506818765318.

Milford, Trevor Scott. 2015. "Revisiting Cyberfeminism: Theory as a Tool for Understanding Young Women's Experiences." In *eGirls, eCitizens*, ed. Jane Bailey and Valerie Steeves, 55–82. Ottawa: University of Ottawa Press.

Mitchell, Allyson, Lisa Bryn Rundle, and Lara Karaian, eds. 2001. *Turbo Chicks: Talking Young Feminisms*. Toronto: Sumach Press.

Morozov, Evgeny. 2009. "The Brave New World of Slacktivism." NPR, May 19.

Nakamura, Lisa. 2002. *Cybertypes: Race, Ethnicity, and Identity on the Internet*. New York: Routledge.

Newman, Jacquetta, and Linda White. 2013. "The Women's Movement in Canada." In *Gender and Women Studies in Canada: Critical Terrain*, ed. Margaret Hobbs and Carla Rice, 656–68. Toronto: Women's Press.

O'Neill, Brenda. 2017. "Continuity and Change in the Contemporary Canadian Feminist Movement." *Canadian Journal of Political Science/Revue canadienne de science politique* 50 (2): 443–59. https://doi.org/10.1017/S0008423917000087.

Paasonen, Susanna. 2011. "Revisiting Cyberfeminism." *Communications* 36 (3): 335–52. https://doi.org/10.1515/comm.2011.017.

Paterson, Nancy. 1992. "Cyberfeminism." vacuumwoman. http://www.vacuumwoman.com/CyberFeminism/cf.txt.

Penny, Laurie. 2014. *Unspeakable Things: Sex, Lies, and Revolution*. New York: Bloomsbury.

Plant, Sadie. 1995. "Babes in the Net." *New Statesman* 8 (337): 28.

Plant, Sadie. 1997. *Zeros and Ones: Digital Women and the New Technoculture*. New York: Doubleday.

Raynauld, Vincent, Emmanuelle Richez, and Katie Boudreau Morris. 2018. "Canada Is #IdleNoMore: Exploring Dynamics of Indigenous Political and Civic Protest in the Twitterverse." *Information, Communication & Society* 21 (4): 626–42. https://doi.org/10.1080/1369118X.2017.1301522.

Rebick, Judy. 2005. *Ten Thousand Roses: The Making of a Feminist Revolution.* Toronto: Penguin.

Rebick, Judy. 2006. "A Nail in the Coffin of Women's Equality?" *Rabble,* October 16. https://rabble.ca/news/nail-coffin-womens-equality.

Rentschler, Carrie. 2014. "Rape Culture and the Feminist Politics of Social Media." *Girlhood Studies* 7 (1): 65–82. https://doi.org/10.3167/ghs.2014.070106.

Rentschler, Carrie, and Samantha C. Thrift. 2015. "Doing Feminism in the Network: Networked Laughter and the 'Binders Full of Women' Meme." *Feminist Theory* 16 (3): 329–59. https://doi.org/10.1177/1464700115604136.

Rheingold, Howard. 2002. *Smart Mobs: The Next Social Revolution.* Cambridge, MA: Basic Books.

Ricker Schulte, Stephanie. 2011. "Surfing Feminism's Online Wave: The Internet and the Future of Feminism." *Feminist Studies* 37 (3): 727–44.

Rodgers, Kathleen, and Melanie Knight. 2011. "'You Just Felt the Collective Wind Being Knocked Out of Us': The Deinstitutionalization of Feminism and the Survival of Women's Organizing in Canada." *Women's Studies International Forum* 34 (6): 570–81. https://doi.org/10.1016/j.wsif.2011.08.004.

Rosenbaum, Judith E. 2018. *Constructing Digital Cultures: Tweets, Trends, Race, and Gender.* Lanham, MD: Lexington Books.

Rottenberg, Catherine. 2014. "The Rise of Neoliberal Feminism." *Cultural Studies* 28 (3): 418–37. https://doi.org/10.1080/09502386.2013.857361.

Salime, Zakia. 2014. "New Feminism as Personal Revolutions: Microrebellious Bodies." *Signs* 40 (1): 14–20. https://doi.org/10.1086/676962.

Scharff, Christina, Carrie Smith-Prei, and Maria Stehle. 2016. "Digital Feminisms: Transnational Activism in German Protest Culture." *Feminist Media Studies* 16 (1): 1–16. https://doi.org/10.1080/14680777.2015.1093069.

Scott-Dixon, Krista. 2001. "Girls Need Ezines: Young Feminists Get Online." In *Turbo Chicks: Talking Young Feminisms,* ed. Allyson Mitchell, Lisa Bryn Rundle, and Lara Karaian, 302–8. Toronto: Sumach Press.

Stewart Millar, Melanie. 1998. *Cracking the Gender Code: Who Rules the Wired World?* Toronto: Second Story Press.

Suzack, Cheryl, Shari M. Huhndorf, Jeanne Perrault, and Jean Barman. 2010. *Indigenous Women and Feminism: Politics, Activism, Culture.* Vancouver: UBC Press.

Taft, Jessica. 2004. "Girl Power Politics: Pop-Culture Barriers and Organizational Resistance." In *All about the Girl: Culture, Power, and Identity,* ed. Anita Harris, 69–78. New York: Routledge.

Takayoshi, Pamela, Emily Huot, and Meghan Huot. 1999. "No Boys Allowed: The World Wide Web as a Clubhouse for Girls." *Computers and Consumption* 16 (1): 86–106. https://doi.org/10.1016/S8755-4615(99)80007-3.

Thrift, Samantha C. 2014. "#YesAllWomen as Feminist Meme Event." *Feminist Media Studies* 14 (6): 1090–92. https://doi.org/10.1080/14680777.2014.975421.

Thrift, Samantha C. 2018. "Up for Debate: Remediating Feminist Media Activism in Canada." *Continuum: Journal of Media & Cultural Studies* 32 (1): 29–41. https://doi.org/10.1080/10304312.2018.1404673.

Tuzcu, Pinar. 2016. "'Allow Access to Location?': Digital Feminist Geographies." *Feminist Media Studies* 16 (1): 150–63. https://doi.org/10.1080/14680777.2015.1093153.

Vickers, Jill, Pauline Rankin, and Christine Appelle. 1993. *Politics as if Women Mattered: A Political Analysis of the National Action Committee on the Status of Women.* Toronto: University of Toronto Press.

VNS Matrix. 1991. "Cyberfeminist Manifesto for the 21st Century." VNS Matrix. https://vnsmatrix.net/the-cyberfeminist-manifesto-for-the-21st-century/.

Wacjman, Judy. 2004. *Technofeminism.* Cambridge: Polity. Kindle.

Wattie, Chris. 2017. "Ottawa Unveils First Feminist Foreign Aid Policy." *Globe and Mail,* June 9. https://www.theglobeandmail.com/news/politics/ottawa-unveils-new-feminism-focused-foreign-aid-policy/article35260311/.

Welsh, Lucy. 2013. "Jodi Dean: Democracy and Other Neoliberal Fantasies." *Feminist Legal Studies* 21 (3): 315–17. https://doi.org/10.1007/s10691-012-9222-9.

Wilding, Faith. 1998. "Where Is the Feminism in Cyberfeminism?" *n.paradoxa* 2: 6–13. https://www.ktpress.co.uk/pdf/vol2_npara_6_13_Wilding.pdf?.

Young, Stacey. 1997. *Changing the Wor(l)d: Discourse, Politics, and the Feminist Movement.* New York: Routledge.

Zimmerman, Tegan. 2017. "#Intersectionality: The Fourth Wave Feminist Twitter Community." *Atlantis* 38 (1): 54–70.

CONCLUSION

Optimists, Sceptics, and the Uncertain Future of Digital Politics in Canada

Harold J. Jansen and Tamara A. Small

In the preface to this book, David Taras describes the transformation of political communication in Canada as a "digital shock," a point he elaborates more fully in his masterful book *Digital Mosaic*, in which he describes the shock as a "giant storm" (2015, 4). To extend this metaphor, the contributors to this volume have been meteorologists, tackling the challenge of trying to understand the storm and predict its course, even while it is raging around them. In this final chapter, we do the same. Our objective in editing *Digital Politics in Canada* was to reflect on the use of digital technologies by both political actors and Canadians over the last twenty years in order to understand what digital politics looks like in Canada. We begin by taking a holistic view of the contributions in this book: taken together, what do these chapters exploring a wide range of political activity tell us about the nature of digital politics in this country? *Digital Politics in Canada* closes a considerable research gap by providing a comprehensive, multidisciplinary, historical, and focused analysis of Canadian digital politics. And yet, it is incomplete. As we write, new forms of digital politics are developing. Indeed, much of the discussion of digital politics in the 2019 federal election was about the possibility of misinformation in the campaign (Jackson 2019; Small 2020). Those of us who work in this academic field know all too well that much of the digital politics becomes history as soon as it is published. We conclude this chapter by considering the future of digital politics from both a practitioner and academic perspective.

OPTIMISTS, PESSIMISTS, OR SCEPTICS: WHO'S RIGHT?

The introduction to this volume began by reflecting on a number of academic perspectives and hypotheses that have developed to help understand digital politics. In the early days, Bridgmon and Milewicz (2004) put it this way: "While most agree on the importance of information and communication in democracy, there is no consensus on the impact that new communication technologies will have. Will the Internet, for instance, greatly improve the quality of democracy, diminish the quality, or have no effect at all?" A key finding of the chapters in this book has been that, although the storm has not necessarily completely revolutionized the way in which Canadians interact politically, either as individuals or institutions, there has been considerable adaptation and incorporation of digital technology into the political process. These technologies have become an integral part of the workflow in the offices of Members of Parliament (as Marland and Power demonstrate in chapter 1), the campaign activities of political parties and candidates in Canadian elections (Small and Giasson, chapter 6), and in the writing and dissemination activities of journalists (Waddell, chapter 7). Even in domains where the impact of digital politics might be significantly less than hoped for or expected – such as e-government (Roy, chapter 2) and "open government" (Longo, chapter 3) – we see considerable incorporation of digital technology. Citizens expect to be able to file their taxes and access other government services online and expect government information and proposals to be available in digital formats with the ability to provide feedback. And, as Goodman and Gabel demonstrate (chapter 4), although Canadian governments have been hesitant to embrace online voting, digital technology is integral to the administration of the vote at the level of the polling station and even to services such as allowing voters to check whether they are registered to vote and where they need to vote. Finally, although many people might assess the desirability of this differently, digital technology has allowed an expansion of the scope and scale of surveillance activities (Parsons, chapter 5) and these are now a routine and regular part of security and law enforcement practices.

These changes to institutions are consistent with what we described in the introduction as the normalization hypothesis. Political institutions have their own logics, relations of powers, and histories that make them quite resilient. Digital technology has provided an additional set of tools to these institutions that can be incorporated selectively to achieve certain outcomes. For example, as Longo points out in chapter 3, open government practices designed to elicit feedback on government policy do so through closed feedback channels that are not truly deliberative or empowering. Much of the incorporation of digital technology has been done in a way that maintains the power and processes of established political actors.

Even in the realm of the media, where digital technology has arguably been most disruptive (see Wadell's chapter 7 in this volume), journalists continue to play an important and central role. In the 2019 Canadian federal election, for example, two of the biggest campaign stories – Conservative leader Andrew Scheer's American citizenship and the revelation that Prime Minister Justin Trudeau had worn "brownface" makeup to a party – were broken and reported by journalists (CBC News 2019). Those revelations were spread, debated, and discussed online, but journalists from traditional media outlets were still central players in this case. Andrew Chadwick (2013) has described this blending of traditional and digital media as the "hybrid media system," and this seems an apt description of the incorporation of digital practices within the existing institutional context of media in Canada.

When we turn our attention to citizen behaviour in the Canadian context, the contributors to this book find that citizens have adopted and incorporated digital technologies into their lives but that this technology works in conjunction with, and in support of, more traditional political activities. In chapter 8, Jansen, Koop, Small, Bastien, and Giasson found little evidence of a resurgence of political engagement and participation as a result of the rise of digital technology; however, they did find that these activities are being transformed to incorporate more digital elements, particularly among youth and among those most engaged with and interested in the political process. Harell, Stolle, Duguay, and Mahéo also highlighted in chapter 9 the importance of psychological engagement with politics as a key consideration in explaining the extent to which young Canadians are using digital technology to be politically active. Among individuals, digital technology has not obliviated the democratic divide.

On the other hand, Lalancette and Raynauld argue in chapter 10 that social media has provided a new set of tools that has expanded the range of political actors able to generate and mobilize around their claims and that it has generated different forms of leadership and engagement. In chapter 11, Antoine identifies many significant challenges that digital politics poses for Indigenous communities in Canada but points to several examples of resistance, resurgence, and cultural self-determination enabled by engagement with digital technology. Similarly, Thrift notes the many challenges that digital politics poses for feminisms but highlights in chapter 12 the ways that digital technology has increased the ability of feminists to respond to the threats posed by backlashes against feminism and the rise of right-wing populism.

It would seem, then, that the most profound impact of digital politics on Canadian politics has been in the arenas of protest and social movements, where the decentralized nature of social media, with its emphasis on distributed content creation and network building, is a natural analogue. When it comes to individuals engaging in more conventional forms of political participation and engagement, however, the evidence is more consistent with the reinforcement hypothesis we discussed in the introduction. Largely, the evidence seems to suggest that digital technology has provided additional tools to those people already engaged in the political process. Digital technology might be transforming how people engage in politics – in addition to or instead of consuming news from the television, they might be getting information from online sources, for example – but it does not appear to be mobilizing the previously disengaged into the political process.

Taken together, the finding that political institutions have incorporated digital technology into their daily operations and the conclusion that these technologies have largely reinforced existing patterns of inequality of political engagement suggest that the cyber-pessimist perspective is a more accurate picture of the impact of digital technology on the Canadian political process. Many of the dreams of those early optimists, who hoped for a democratic renaissance ushered in by digital technology's ability to connect citizens with more information, with their political leaders, and with each other in new and exciting ways, have not come to fruition. This does not mean that digital technology has not changed Canadian politics, because it clearly has, as documented throughout this book. But the transformations have been more modest than the early optimists expected or hoped for.

What this reveals is that, perhaps, the distinction between cyber-optimism and cyber-pessimism in the early literature was too blunt. A more measured take on the impact of digital technology would suggest that some aspects of the political process have been changed more significantly than others and that it would be a mistake to expect wholesale change of the political landscape. Furthermore, despite the early optimists' expectation of generally salutary effects on the political process, it is clear that the digital technological revolution has produced both positive and negative effects. In the words of our chapters, digital technology contains both promises *and* perils.

For example, the very ubiquity of digital technology, especially with the rapid adoption of mobile smartphone technology, has meant that more people are able to be connected and mobilized more quickly and cheaply than at any previous point in human history. However, this also means that more people are potentially subject to surveillance, either by governments or by corporations. More people are also available to be manipulated for political purposes, as demonstrated dramatically by the scandal that revealed the improper use of Facebook user data by the firm Cambridge Analytica in order to target political ads (see introduction).

Social media most clearly exemplifies the tendency of digital technology to both enhance and detract from the health of democracy. Twitter allows for networks and decentralized leadership of the type that facilitated the Idle No More movement or the Black Lives Matter protests. At the same time, Twitter also provides networks and connections for racism and misogyny. Twitter allows for easy, cheap, and nearly instantaneous access to political information, but it also allows for bots and other agents to spread false and misleading information (Woolley and Howard 2018). Facebook permits people to form connections with other citizens to engage in serious discussion of the political issues of the day and allows access to news in a centralized way that is quick and easy. But Facebook also allows people to select the citizens and sources with whom they interact and whom they choose to ignore, a feature exacerbated by the use of algorithms in people's news feeds to give them more of what they like to read. This combination contributes to the development of "echo chamber" politics that heighten political divisions and inhibit understanding of differing perspectives. Moreover, Facebook is also at the centre of the misinformation crisis that started in the 2016 American presidential election and spread to election campaigns in Europe (Communications Security Establishment 2019).

The experiences of the United States and European countries are a reminder of the global impact of digital technology. Canada is not alone in seeing digital technology alter how politics unfolds. The fact that Canada has not seen the same level of misinformation campaigns suggests (The Canadian Press 2019), though, that the context of digital politics matters. Although some scholars have pointed to social media as a cause of democratic deconsolidation in established democracies (e.g., Mounk 2018, chapter 4), the Canadian case might suggest that it is the context of a more polarized political environment that might affect how social media affects political debate. Although Canada has largely escaped the polarization seen, for example, in its neighbour to the south (Adams 2017), there is evidence that the country is moving in that direction (Kevins and Soroka 2018). As the political context changes in Canada, so too might its digital politics. This is why a volume such as this is needed. As noted in the introduction, American politics dominates the digital politics literature. And while there is much to be gleaned from such important, and often innovative, literature, it is crucial to reflect on the ways Canada's unique politics will shape the use of digital technologies by political actors and individuals.

DIGITAL POLITICS: A MOVING TARGET

It is not just the changing context of politics that makes the future of digital politics difficult to determine but also the very nature of digital technology. This is demonstrated by American political scientist Richard Davis's excellent 2005 book titled *Politics Online: Blogs, Chatrooms, and Discussion Groups in American Democracy*. The book provides a detailed analysis of the electronic discussion community in the United States. In the early 2000s, blogs were *the* technology for political action. This was epitomized in *Blog for America,* the blog of the Howard Dean campaign for the 2004 Democratic presidential nomination. At the time, Dean's campaign was seen as an "important shift in the American political landscape" (Hindman 2005, 127). However, by the time Davis's book was published, the social media revolution had begun with the arrival of MySpace and Facebook, and blogs took a backseat. For some of the readers of this collection, it might be hard to imagine how important blogs were at one point in time. The reality is that when it comes to politics, digital technologies are a "moving target" (Taras 2008). As has been seen in the chapters in this collection, the technology du jour changes from year to year. In the early days of the internet, digital politics was all about websites and email. Today digital politics, rightly or wrongly, is synonymous with social media.

Digital technologies as a moving target matters for both practical politics and the academic study thereof. For political actors, from government to political parties to journalists, all have had to confront the changing nature of digital technologies in their attempts to inform, communicate, and engage with their respective publics. For instance, Jeffery Roy's chapter (chapter 2) traces the Canadian government's movement from website to social media. Today, the numerous websites that make up the Government of Canada's digital presence exist alongside Facebook pages, Twitter feeds, and YouTube channels. Indeed, the government is reported to have spent more than $14,000 on Snapchat filters in 2016 in order to "enhance Canada's visibility, recognition, and branding" (Duggan 2017). This means that public servants across the government are responsible for the development of content and maintenance for all these applications. And as seen with the Snapchat example, the use of these applications is not cost neutral. Canadian political parties also make use of the variety of digital technologies during and between elections (Small 2016). Political actors feel they must make use of the full scope of digital tools available, since each has different user bases.

Blumler and Kavanagh (1999, 213) suggest the current era of political communication is marked by a "hydra-headed beast" with "many mouths ... which are continually clamouring to be fed." Consider the previous broadcast era: certainly, television of the 1960s is not the same as television today. Grainy black and white television changed to high-definition colour and a few channels multiplied to a far more fragmented universe of choices. Those changes, however, are far less dramatic and constant than those experienced in the digital era. Political actors are constantly trying to feed the beast that is digital technologies. While websites and email may not be considered the sexy parts of digital politics, they remain stalwarts. Most government agencies, political parties, media organizations, and interest groups operate a website, seeing it as their digital hub. Other applications have come and gone. For instance, around the 2008 federal election, political parties and interest groups were using MySpace as part of the campaign. Will Snapchat filters be a long-term part of political communication like email or go by the wayside like electronic discussion boards? Time will tell. Moreover, new applications and technologies will come in the future, and political actors will need to react. They will need to learn how to effectively marry their own political goals with the affordances of the new technology. For political actors, the moving target of digital technologies is complicated, time consuming, expensive, and ongoing. Often commentators and scholars criticize or lament that political actors are not using digital technologies the right way; this is especially true of their interactive capabilities. As our discussion of the normalization hypothesis shows, sometimes political actors may choose to do this. At the same time, however, it is also possible that political actors do not ever really get the time to figure out how to use digital technologies the right way before a new application or platform comes along.

These changes have significant implications for the study of digital politics in Canada and elsewhere. Digital technologies create challenges in terms of the object of study and the techniques and skill needed to analyze them. What drives academic study may not be the importance of the platform but rather factors such as novelty or ease of study.[1] As Small and Giasson note in chapter 6, Twitter dominates academic analyses of digital campaigning not because it is the most important social media (Facebook is) but because it is often easier to study. Until recently, it was far easier to obtain large amounts of Twitter data compared to Facebook data. However, in April 2018, Facebook, along with Social Science One, launched a project on the effects of social media on democracy and elections that would allow scholars greater access to Facebook data (Social Science One 2018). Twitter is also over-studied because it is public. Digital technologies that are less public are more difficult to study. For example, despite being one of the oldest digital technologies for politics, email also remains understudied. To the best of our knowledge, there are only two published analyses of email use

1 It is worth noting that this was also the case during the broadcast era, where media studies of newspapers outpaced television studies.

by Canadian political parties (see Marland and Matthews 2017; Thomas and Sabin 2019). This is despite the fact that Canadian parties have likely sent thousands and thousands of emails to subscribers over the last two decades. What do those emails say? How has email changed over time? This information is basically unknown to us now. But analyzing emails is complicated by the inability to ever be certain that one has a complete dataset, as political actors might send certain political messages to one group and other messages to another. SMS or text message suffer from a similar problem – how does the researcher get access to the digital content being sent? Another example is political memes – we might never know how many were made, who made them, or how many people saw them (Lalancette and Small 2020). Related to all this is the "ephemeral" nature of digital content, which presents a considerable research challenge (Karpf 2012). Tweets and Facebook posts may get deleted. How does one study something like Snapchat where the content is set to automatically delete? David Karpf (2012) points out that many types of publicly available digital content go unsaved and disappear. The scholarship of digital politics has missed a lot. This may be especially problematic for Canadian digital politics, because, as discussed, the Canadian case is less comprehensively represented in the literature than the United States and the United Kingdom.

Snapchat and political memes also raise another important issue regarding the study of digital politics: the growing importance of visuals online, especially on social media. Snapchat, Instagram, and other visual social media are growing in terms of users. Images and video also dominate on more text-based social media like Twitter and Facebook. In contrast, in the early days of the internet, literacy was a key skill for engaging in digital politics. Andrew Mattan (2018) highlights the importance of images and visuals to political communication while also noting that few scholars have empirically analyzed how political actors are using visual content to engage, inform, and communicate with citizens on social media. Lalancette and Raynauld (2019) explain this trend by noting that traditional theoretical framework and methodological approaches are better equipped for the study of text: "Scholars are still trying to figure out the best ways to collect and analyze visual data. The constant changing nature of digital media platforms often makes it hard to develop approaches that can be used over a long period of time" (11).

The previous comment is also relevant when thinking about the sheer amount of digital content that exists now. In the broadcast era, the objects of research were more finite. It was possible to know how many political ads were produced by a political party in a given election or find all of the newspapers articles that mentioned a particular protest movement. Things are not so simple in the digital age. In 2010, the American Library of Congress began to collect every public tweet ever sent on Twitter, going back to 2006. The Library of Congress stopped seven years later, citing the overwhelming volume of content. By 2013, the archive included some 170 billion tweets and it was increasing at a rate of half a billion tweets a day (Wamsley 2017). In addition to billions of political tweets, there are posts on Facebook, Reddit, and Instagram. We are now in the era of big data. This is certainly a methodological challenge for those who study digital social movement politics, such as the Maple Spring, Idle No More, and digital feminism (chapters 10 to 12) or those who want to study a political event such as an election. Scholars have noted a computational shift in social sciences (Lewis, Zamith, and Hermida 2013). According to Shah, Cappella, and Neuman (2015, 7), working with big data in the social sciences "remains challenging, not least because of the issues of generalizability, ethics, and theory ... but also because of the acquisition, archiving, and analysis of these types of data, which are not easily processed using conventional database applications." The nature of digital technologies as a moving target affects political science as much as it does political actors. Big data means that political scientists not only need to be trained in new methodological and data analyzing skills but also need to be aware of the limitations inherent in such data.

The changes discussed above are not unique to Canada. At the same time, one crucial lesson of *Digital Politics in Canada* is that the nature and direction of those changes will be affected by Canada's political institutions and political culture. Digital technologies will continue to evolve in ways we cannot completely predict or foresee, but Canadians will adapt them and adapt to them in their own distinct way.

REFERENCES

Adams, Michael. 2017. *Could It Happen Here? Canada in the Age of Trump and Brexit.* Toronto: Simon & Schuster Canada.

Blumler, Jay G., and Dennis Kavanagh. 1999. "The Third Age of Political Communication: Influences and Features." *Political Communication* 16 (3): 209–30. https://doi.org/10.1080/105846099198596.

Bridgmon, Phillip, and Mark Milewicz. 2004. *E-Politics: Technology in American Government*. Dubuque, IA: Kendall Hunt Publishing Co.

The Canadian Press. 2019. "Canada's Election Has Been 'Largely Clean' of Misinformation, Research Shows." Global News, October 10. https://globalnews.ca/news/6017741/canada-election-misinformation-research/.

CBC News. 2019. "What We Know about Justin Trudeau's Blackface Photos – and What Happens Next." CBC, September 20. https://www.cbc.ca/news/politics/canada-votes-2019-trudeau-blackface-brownface-cbc-explains-1.5290664.

Chadwick, Andrew. 2013. *The Hybrid Media System: Politics and Power*. Oxford: Oxford University Press.

Communications Security Establishment. 2019. "2019 Update: Cyber Threats to Canada's Democratic Process." Ottawa: Communications Security Establishment. https://cyber.gc.ca/sites/default/files/publications/tdp-2019-report_e.pdf.

Duggan, Kyle. 2017. "Federal Government Spent $14K on Snapchat Filters Last Year." *iPolitics*, May 9. https://ipolitics.ca/2017/05/09/federal-government-spent-14k-on-snapchat-filters-last-year/.

Jackson, Hannah. 2019. "Experts Warn of Disinformation during Election but Say Political Attack Ads within Legal Limit." Global News, September 22. https://globalnews.ca/news/5907430/canada-election-combating-disinformation/.

Karpf, David. 2012. "Social Science Research Methods in Internet Time." *Information, Communication, & Society* 15 (5): 639–61. https://doi.org/10.1080/1369118X.2012.665468.

Kevins, Anthony, and Stuart N. Soroka. 2018. "Growing Apart? Partisan Sorting in Canada, 1992–2015." *Canadian Journal of Political Science/Revue canadienne de science politique* 51 (1): 103–33. https://doi.org/10.1017/S0008423917000713.

Lalancette, Mireille, and Vincent Raynauld. 2019. "More than Meets the Eye: Insights on and Opportunities in the Study of Visuals and Digital Politics." Paper presented at the Canadian Political Science Association at the University of British Columbia conference, Vancouver, BC, June 4 to 6.

Lalancette, Mireille, and Tamara A. Small. 2020. "Not a Leader! Theresa May's Leadership through the Lens of Internet Memes." In *Power Shift? Political Leadership and Social Media*, ed. Richard Davis and David Taras, 202–19. New York: Routledge.

Lewis, Seth C., Rodrigo Zamith, and Alfred Hermida. 2013. "Content Analysis in an Era of Big Data: A Hybrid Approach to Computational and Manual Methods." *Journal of Broadcasting & Electronic Media* 57 (1): 34–52. https://doi.org/10.1080/08838151.2012.761702.

Marland, Alex, and Maria Matthews. 2017. "'Friend, Can You Chip in $3?' Canadian Political Parties' Email Communication and Fundraising Emails." In *Permanent Campaigning in Canada*, ed. Alex Marland, Thierry Giasson, and Anna Lennox Esselment, 87–108. Vancouver: UBC Press.

Mattan, Andrew. 2018. *Tweeting Pass the Media: An Analysis of Visual Image Management on Twitter during the 2018 Ontario Provincial Election.* Guelph, ON: Department of Political Science, University of Guelph.

Mounk, Yascha. 2018. *The People vs. Democracy: Why Our Freedom Is in Danger and How to Save It.* Cambridge, MA: Harvard University Press.

Shah, Dhavan V., Joseph N. Cappella, and W. Russell Neuman. 2015. "Big Data, Digital Media, and Computational Social Science: Possibilities and Perils." *The Annals of the American Academy of Political and Social Science* 659 (1): 6–13. https://doi.org/10.1177/0002716215572084.

Small, Tamara A. 2016. "Two Decades of Digital Party Politics in Canada: An Assessment." In *Canadian Parties in Transition*, 4th ed., ed. A. Brian Tanguay and Alain-G. Gagnon. Toronto: University of Toronto Press.

Small, Tamara A. 2020. "Regulating Social Media: Digital Campaigning in the Era of Misinformation." In *The Canadian Federal Election of 2019*, ed. Jon H. Pammett and Christopher Dornan. Montreal: McGill-Queen's University Press.

Social Science One. 2018. "Social Science One." https://socialscience.one/home.

Taras, David. 2008. "Preface." In *Making a Difference: A Comparative View of the Role of the Internet in Election Politics*, ed. Stephen Ward, Diana Owen, Richard Davis, and David Taras, ix–xii. Lanham, MD: Lexington Books.

Taras, David. 2015. *Digital Mosaic: Media, Power, and Identity in Canada.* Toronto: University of Toronto Press.

Thomas, Paul E. J., and Jerald Sabin. 2019. "Candidate Messaging on Religious Issues in the 2016–17 Conservative Party of Canada Leadership Race." *Canadian Journal of Political Science/Revue canadienne de science politique* 52 (4): 801–23. https://doi.org/10.1017/S0008423919000346.

Wamsley, Laurel. 2017. "Library of Congress Will No Longer Archive Every Tweet." NPR, December 26. https://www.npr.org/sections/thetwo-way/2017/12/26/573609499/library-of-congress-will-no-longer-archive-every-tweet.

Woolley, Samuel C., and Philip N. Howard, eds. 2018. *Computational Propaganda: Political Parties, Politicians, and Political Manipulation on Social Media.* New York: Oxford University Press.

Contributors

Editors

Tamara A. Small is an associate professor of political science at the University of Guelph. Her research focus is digital politics, specifically the use of digital technologies by Canadian political actors as well as the former's impact on the latter. She is the co-author of *Fighting for Votes: Parties, the Media, and Voters in an Ontario Election* (UBC Press) and the co-editor of *Political Communication in Canada: Meet the Press, Tweet the Rest* (UBC Press) and *Mind the Gaps: Canadian Perspectives on Gender and Politics* (Fernwood Press). In 2018, she held the Fulbright Visiting Research Chair at Vanderbilt University.

Harold J. Jansen is a professor of political science at the University of Lethbridge. His research interests include electoral system reform and experimentation in Canadian provinces, political party and election financing in Canada, and the impact of digital technology on the Canadian political process.

Contributors

Derek Antoine is an instructor in the School of Journalism and Communication at Carleton University, where he recently earned a PhD. His research looks at discourses of Indigenous activism, primarily on

Mi'kma'ki territory. His teaching focuses on media and activism, political communication, persuasion, and propaganda.

Frédérick Bastien is an associate professor in the Department of Political Science at the Université de Montréal. He is a member of the Centre for the Study of Democratic Citizenship and the Groupe de recherche en communication politique. His research interests focus on mediatization, online technologies, journalism, and research methods. He is the author of *Breaking News: Politics, Journalism, and Infotainment on Quebec Television* (UBC Press, 2018), several book chapters, and journal articles, appearing in *Journalism, Canadian Journal of Political Science, Canadian Journal of Communication, Communication,* and *Hermès.*

Philippe A. Duguay obtained his PhD in political science from the Université du Québec à Montréal. His dissertation was on the influence of online socialization on political behaviour and attitudes. His research interests and collaborations centre on political communication, digital heuristics, and political behaviour online, with a focus on attitudes toward immigration and radicalization leading to violence.

Chelsea Gabel is an associate professor in the Department of Health, Aging, and Society and the Indigenous Studies Program at McMaster University and holds a Canada Research Chair in Indigenous Well-Being, Community-Engagement, and Innovation. She has published widely on Indigenous experiences with digital technology, including online voting. She leads the First Nations Digital Democracy Project, a project that has brought together a unique collaboration of academic, community, government, and industry partners to address a number of substantial gaps in our knowledge of Indigenous civic and electoral engagement, local governance, online voting, and the impact of digital technology on these areas.

Thierry Giasson is the chair of the Department of Political Science at Université Laval, in Québec City. Dr. Giasson is the director of the Groupe de recherche en communication politique (GRCP) and a member of the Centre for the Study of Democratic Citizenship. His research focuses on political journalism, civic and partisan uses of online technologies, as well as on the effects of political communication and marketing practices on electoral campaigns, political participation, and civic engagement in Québec and Canada. He is the co-editor of the series *Communication, Strategy, and Politics* at UBC Press, where he most recently published *Political Elites in Canada* (2018).

Nicole Goodman is an associate professor of political science at Brock University where she holds the Chancellor's Chair for Research Excellence (2019–2022). Her research examines the impact of technology on civic participation and democracy. She is recognized internationally as a leading expert on electoral modernization and has published extensively on the topic of electronic voting. She currently represents Canada on the International Institute for Democracy and Electoral Assistance Board of Advisers.

Allison Harell is a full professor in the Department of Political Science at the Université du Québec à Montréal and holds the UQAM Research Chair in the Political Psychology of Social Solidarity. She co-directs the Consortium on Electoral Democracy and is associate director of the Centre for the Study of Democratic Citizenship. Her research focuses on political behaviour and public opinion formation in Canada and other advanced industrialized democracies.

Royce Koop is an associate professor of political studies at the University of Manitoba. His research interests include representation, political parties, and local politics. He is the author of *Grassroots Liberals: Organizing for Local Politics* (UBC Press), co-author of *Representation in Action: Canadian MPs in the Constituencies* (UBC Press), and co-editor of *Parties, Elections, and the Future of Canadian Politics* (UBC Press).

Mireille Lalancette is a full professor of political communication at the Université du Québec à Trois-Rivières. She has published about the construction of the mediatized image of politicians, gender, and representation, and has studied the use and impact of social media by citizens, grassroots organizations, and Canadian political actors. A researcher for the Groupe de recherche en communication politique (GRCP), she is the co-author of *ABC de l'argumentation pour les professionnels de la santé ou toute autre personne qui souhaite convaincre* (PUQ). She is also the co-editor of *What's #Trending in Canadian Politics? Understanding Transformations in Power, Media, and the Public Sphere* (UBC Press).

Justin Longo is an associate professor in the Johnson Shoyama Graduate School of Public Policy at the University of Regina, where he holds a Research Chair in Digital Governance. He is also an associate member of the MacArthur Foundation Research Network on Opening Governance. His research interests span the governance issues that arise from the intersection of advanced technology with social and political life. His recent publications include "The Limits of Policy Analytics: Early Examples and the Emerging Boundary of Possibilities" in the journal *Politics and Governance* and "The Evolution of Citizen and Stakeholder Engagement in Canada, from Spicer to #Hashtags" in *Canadian Public Administration.*

Valérie-Anne Mahéo is a guest researcher at Université de Montréal and postdoctoral fellow at McGill University. Her research interests include youth's political participation, social inequalities, education programs, and the use of new technologies for information campaigns. She has published her research on voting aid applications in *Political Communication* and *Policy & Internet.*

Alex Marland is a professor of political science at Memorial University of Newfoundland. His book *Brand Command: Canadian Politics and Democracy in the Age of Message Control* (UBC Press, 2016) won the Donner Prize for best public policy book by a Canadian. The follow-up, *Whipped: Party Discipline in Canada* (UBC Press, 2020), looks at the hidden ways that Canadian parliamentary parties coordinate message discipline.

Christopher Parsons is a senior research associate at the Citizen Lab, in the Munk School of Global Affairs & Public Policy with the University of Toronto. His research focuses on the privacy, security, and political implications of third-party access to telecommunications data. Among his recent publications are "Shining a Light on the Encryption Debate: A Canadian Field Guide" (with Lex Gill and Tamir Israel) and "Government Surveillance Accountability: The Failures of Contemporary Canadian Interception Reports" (with Adam Molnar).

Stephen Power completed a master's thesis in political science at Memorial University of Newfoundland examining the PMO's use of social media to circulate digital photographs of Justin Trudeau. He published about the Newfoundland and Labrador access to information systems in *The Democracy Cookbook* (ISER Books, 2017).

Vincent Raynauld is an associate professor in the Department of Communication Studies at Emerson College and affiliate professor in the Département de Lettres et Communication Sociale at Université du Québec à Trois-Rivières. He is also serving as a research associate in the Groupe de recherche en communication politique (GRCP) (Canada). His areas of research interest and publication include political communication, social media, research methods, e-politics, and political marketing.

Jeffrey Roy is a professor in the School of Public Administration, Faculty of Management, at Dalhousie University, where he specializes in democratic governance, business and government relations, and digital government reforms. In addition to teaching and research, he has consulted to governments at all levels, the private sector, as well as the United Nations and the OECD. He is a member of the Editorial Board of *Canadian Public Administration*, a featured columnist in *Canadian Government Executive*, and author of several books (the most recent, *From Machinery to Mobility: Government and Democracy in a Participative Age*, published by Springer in 2013). His research has been supported by several funding bodies including the Social Sciences and Humanities Research Council of Canada and The IBM Center for the Business of Government. Professor Roy is also a member of the Transparency Advisory Group (TAG) for Public Safety Canada.

Dietlind Stolle is James McGill Professor in Political Science at McGill University and the director of the Inter-University Centre for the Study of Democratic Citizenship (CSDC). She conducts research and has published on voluntary associations, trust, social capital, ethnic diversity, the political effects of pregnancy, and new forms of political participation. Her book *Political Consumerism: Global Responsibility in Action* (Cambridge University Press, 2013, with Michele Micheletti) won the Comparative Politics Prize of the Canadian Political Science Association.

David Taras holds the Ralph Klein Chair in Media Studies at Mount Royal University. He is the co-author most recently of *The End of the CBC?* with Christopher Waddell and an editor of *Power Shift? Political Leadership and Social Media.*

Samantha C. Thrift is an instructor in the Department of Communication, Media, and Film at the University of Calgary. Her research examines feminist media activism in electoral politics, media constructions of feminist identity, and activism and memory. Her work on hashtag feminism, political memes, and Canadian feminist media activism appears in *Feminist Media Studies, Continuum,* and *Feminist Theory.*

Christopher Waddell is a professor emeritus in the School of Journalism and Communication at Carleton University. He is also a former political journalist serving as a reporter, Ottawa Bureau chief associate, and national editor at the *Globe and Mail* (1984–91) and parliamentary bureau chief for CBC Television News (1993–2001). With David Taras of Mount Royal University in Calgary, he is the editor of and a contributor to *How Canadians Communicate IV: Media and Politics* (published in May 2012) and *How Canadians Communicate V: Sports in 2016,* both published by Athabasca University Press. Their latest book, *The End of the CBC?,* was published by University of Toronto Press in the spring of 2020.

Index

The letter *t* following a page number denotes a table.